Lexical Strata in English

In *Lexical Strata in English*, Heinz Giegerich investigates the way in which alternations in the sound patterns of words interact with the morphological processes of the language. Drawing on examples from English and German, he uncovers and spells out in detail the principles of 'lexical morphology and phonology', a theory that has in recent years become increasingly influential in linguistics. Giegerich questions many of the assumptions made in that theory, overturning some and putting others on a principled footing. What emerges is a new, formally coherent and highly constrained theory of the lexicon – the theory of 'base-driven stratification' – which predicts the number of lexical strata from the number of base-category distinctions recognised in the morphology of the language and which, on the phonological side, automatically accounts for the 'Strict Cyclicity Effect'.

Finally, he offers new accounts of some central phenomena in the phonology of English (including vowel 'reduction', [r]-sandhi and syllabification), which both support and are uniquely facilitated by the theory of 'base-driven stratification'.

HEINZ GIEGERICH is Professor of English Linguistics in the Department of English Language at the University of Edinburgh. His books include *Metrical Phonology and Phonological Structure* (1985) and *English Phonology* (1992). He has published numerous articles on phonological theory in relation to English and German in journals such as *Lingua, Journal of Linguistics, Linguistische Berichte* and *English Language and Linguistics*. In addition, Professor Giegerich has written several short monographs and contributions to edited volumes and encyclopaedias.

CAMBRIDGE STUDIES IN LINGUISTICS

General Editors: S. R. ANDERSON, J. BRESNAN, B. COMRIE,
W. DRESSLER, C. EWEN, R. HUDDLESTON, R. LASS,
D. LIGHTFOOT, J. LYONS, P. H. MATTHEWS, R. POSNER,
S. ROMAINE, N. V. SMITH, N. VINCENT

Supplementary volumes

Earlier issues not listed are also available

LEXICAL STRATA IN ENGLISH

Morphological causes, phonological effects

HEINZ J GIEGERICH

University of Edinburgh

CAMBRIDGE
UNIVERSITY PRESS

PUBLISHED BY THE PRESS SYNDICATE OF THE UNIVERSITY OF CAMBRIDGE
The Pitt Building, Trumpington Street, Cambridge CB2 1RP, United Kingdom

CAMBRIDGE UNIVERSITY PRESS
The Edinburgh Building, Cambridge CB2 2RU, United Kingdom
http://www.cup.cam.ac.uk
40 West 20th Street, New York, NY 10011-4211, USA
http://www.cup.org
10 Stamford Road, Oakleigh, Melbourne 3166, Australia

First published 1999

Printed in the United Kingdom at the University Press, Cambridge

Typeset in 10/13 Times   [SE]

A catalogue record for this book is available from the British Library

Library of Congress cataloguing in publication data

Giegerich, Heinz J.
Lexical strata in English: morphological causes, phonological
effects / Heinz Giegerich.
    p.   cm. – (Cambridge studies in linguistics; 89)
Includes bibliographical references and index.
ISBN 0 521 55412 8 hardback
1. English language – Lexicology.   2. English language – Morphology.
3. English language – Phonology.   I. Title.   II. Series.
E1571.G54   1999
423′.028 – dc21   98–48367   CIP

ISBN 0 521 55412 8 hardback

Contents

Acknowledgements

This book has benefited in many ways from the help provided by my colleagues. Some have read and commented on individual chapters or more, others have supplied useful information, others still have simply argued with me or just listened. Foremost among these are John Anderson, Linda van Bergen, Derek Britton, Phil Carr, Victoria Cumming, Bryan Gick, Edmund Gussmann, Bettina Isensee, Roger Lass, Chris McCully, Steve McGill, April McMahon, Scott Montgomery, Ingo Plag, Paul Salmon †, Claire Sigsworth, Graeme Trousdale, Jolyon Warr, John Wells and Richard Wiese, as well as three meticulous and extremely helpful anonymous reviewers for the Press. I do not expect any of these colleagues to agree with my analyses, or to endorse the theoretical framework adopted and developed here; but I very much hope not to have inadvertently misrepresented their various contributions. All errors in this book are, of course, my responsibility alone.

Audiences at a number of conferences and visiting lectures, in Britain and elsewhere, have listened to and commented on expositions of various parts of the material presented here. I have learnt much on those occasions in terms of both substance and presentation, to the benefit of this book.

But no audience could have been more sceptical, demanding, challenging, encouraging and appreciative than my captive one, comprising the Senior Honours students in English Language at Edinburgh University. No one else has had such power, and indeed such success, in making me re-think my arguments time and again, and clarify points that otherwise would be clear only to myself (at best!), and now almost certainly obscure to the reader. Let us not forget the value of teaching-led research when we extol the virtues of research-led teaching.

Charles Jones, colleague and Head of Department, has supported this endeavour in a number of ways and relieved me of departmental duties at a difficult time. Judith Ayling and her successor at the Press, Andrew Winnard, have been most efficient, patient and encouraging in guiding this project through the various stages of its evolution.

I thank all these people very much.

1 A requiem for Lexical Phonology?

Shortly after the appearance of the first main-stream book on Lexical Phonology (Mohanan 1986), Gussmann published an incisive and detailed review (1988), which – as is strangely more apparent now than it was then – captured the mood of the time. In it, he attacked not just the book under review but the entire programme of Lexical Phonology, meticulously dismantling Mohanan (1986) chapter by chapter and concluding: 'If the critical assessment of lexicalism presented here and elsewhere were to be accepted, then Mohanan's book would very likely come to stand as a requiem for Lexical Phonology' (Gussmann 1988: 239). As at that time phonologists were beginning to abandon in droves not only derivationalist theories but also English – one of Mohanan's main concerns – Gussmann's review could not have come at a better time for some, and at a worse time for others. Such was the mood of the time.

The title of Mohanan (1986), *The theory of lexical phonology*, misleadingly suggested that the book reported, and indeed was, the state-of-the-art. It wasn't anything like that; but the misled reviewer can be forgiven for responding in kind. Mohanan (1986) was an easy target not only for a reviewer hostile to the programme but, perhaps even more so, for the theory-internal and therefore constructively minded critic. To Gussmann's credit, most of his comments could have come from either quarter: those who had been doing independent and, at least in part, rather differently focused work on this framework, shared Gussmann's disagreement with many of the points made by Mohanan; see, for example, the contributions to Hargus and Kaisse (1993) and Wiese (1994). I return to those points below. But anyone who interprets Mohanan (1986) as the requiem for Lexical Phonology envisaged by Gussmann may as well regard Chomsky and Halle (1968, henceforth 'SPE') as the swan-song of phonology in the generative enterprise, which it clearly was not although its deep flaws became apparent as quickly as did Mohanan's after its publication. And anyone who does either or both will have a problem assessing the progress made in phonological theory since.

Of course we know now that neither Gussmann nor Mohanan did finish off the theory of Lexical Phonology. But Gussmann's critique inflicted such damage, to the work's standing if not to the programme's, because it highlighted major structural weaknesses rather than just bad analyses. Here is an example.

> The failure of the Lexical Phonology seems in no small measure to have been due to the superficial or impoverished view of morphology that it resorted to. . . . There is the whole area of conditions on rules and rule interactions within morphology, of blocking, of the semantics of derivatives, of . . . morpheme vs. word-based models, etc. (Gussmann 1988: 238)

It would have been useful there to draw a distinction between the programme itself and its practitioner. Progress had been made particularly in this area by Kiparsky (1982) and others; but there is indeed little trace of it in Mohanan (1986), who – admittedly, like many others – tends to treat the short name of the programme, Lexical Phonology, in its literal sense.

'Lexical Phonology' is of course a misnomer in that it refers only to half of the story. The programme's central hypothesis is that '[m]orphology and phonology apply in tandem' (Booij 1994: 3). This tandem application is subject to the sub-theory of 'level-ordering' or 'lexical stratification', whereby morphology and phonology interact in a series of ordered 'levels' or 'strata'.[1] But there were, and still are, the questions of just how many strata are needed, what they contain, whether they are universal and – most importantly – why. Here are the morphological sides of two competing models of the 1980s:

(1)		Kiparsky (1982)	Halle and Mohanan (1985) Mohanan (1986)
	Stratum 1	'+'-affixation: *-ity, -ic,* irregular inflexion: *cacti, oxen*	'+'-affixation: *-ity, -ic,* irregular inflexion: *cacti, oxen*
	Stratum 2	'#'-affixation: *-ness, -less,* compounding	'#'-affixation: *-ness, -less*
	Stratum 3	regular inflexion	compounding
	Stratum 4	—	regular inflexion

The stratal split between '#'-affixation and compounding is in Mohanan's model motivated by a single phonological rule of rather dubious status;[2] on the morphological side it gives rise to the now-infamous 'loop': given that '#'-affixation and compounding freely interact (*rule-*

governedness, to re-aircondition etc.; Kiparsky 1982), Mohanan is forced to allow the morphology recourse to the previous stratum while maintaining the split for the phonology. This loop – 'a noose for Lexical Phonology' (Gussmann 1988: 237) – weakens the theory beyond recognition: effectively, the theory's central hypothesis of morphology–phonology interaction is abandoned. As Kiparsky's (1982) three-strata model similarly needed a loop to account for regular inflexion occurring inside compounds (*systems analyst, drinks dispenser* etc.; Sproat 1985), two-strata models are now standard in the literature on English (Kiparsky 1985; Booij and Rubach 1987; McMahon 1990; Borowsky 1993), albeit in rather different versions. But the question of why this should be so remains unanswered.

The two models of stratification given in (1) above are 'affix-driven': the morphology of a given stratum is defined by the sum of affixes that are diacritically marked for attaching on it. (The morpheme and word boundary symbols '+' and '#' (respectively), introduced by SPE but replaced by brackets in Lexical Phonology, serve here merely to express this diacritic marking.) The problem with such models is that a number of (English) affixes display morphological and phonological behaviour that is consistent with both strata. And the 'Affix Ordering Generalisation' (Selkirk 1982b), whereby crucially no '#'-affix can occur inside a '+'-affixed form, appears in many cases not to hold. But in the literature

> ... counter-examples of affix ordering (Aronoff 1976) tended to be dismissed or explained away. However, the number of such counter-examples has turned out to be too large to be dismissed (Aronoff and Sridhar 1983). The ordering of levels (strata) as a replacement for the SPE boundaries came to be seen as not very desirable, 'in large part because of the lack of control over the number of levels' (Aronoff and Sridhar 1983: 10). (Gussmann 1988: 237)

Some ten years on, the literature on lexical stratification records no progress on this issue, damaging to the theory though it is.

This is not the place (and no longer the time) to launch another review of Mohanan (1986) or to re-launch Gussmann's. My point is that it was as premature then as it is now to talk of nooses and requiems: Mohanan (1986) is a mere example of an unfinished agenda. But before I outline how the present contribution to Lexical Phonology is intended to advance the agenda (if not to finish it), let us briefly consider the phonological side of the theory.

I am not so much concerned here with individual phonological rules as I am with constraints on rules and the long-standing attempt at limiting the abstractness of phonological derivations. This is another area in which Lexical Phonology had promised, and indeed made, progress well before Mohanan (1986). Once again it is progress ignored by Mohanan; and curiously it is a major weakness of that work that is missed in Gussmann's critique. This progress largely concerned the status of the Strict Cycle Condition (Kean 1974; Mascaró 1976), which confines structure-changing cyclic rules to derived environments, with regard to lexical stratification (Kiparsky 1982). But rather than devising a phonology in such a way as to make it comply with that condition, Mohanan (1986) and most other researchers in the field (notably Halle and Mohanan 1985) devised points in the derivation at which rules would be exempt from the condition. Their Stratum 2 is non-cyclic by stipulation, for the single purpose of providing a safe haven for unconstrained rules of Vowel Shift, Vowel Reduction and others. A large part of SPE's rule apparatus, with all its abstractness problems – free rides, indeterminate underliers, never-surfacing feature combinations, etc. – simply re-appeared in Lexical Phonology as if the abstractness debate in Generative Phonology had never happened. And curiously, little further progress has been made since, except that the notion of structure-changing rules itself has increasingly been abandoned in derivationalist theories (Archangeli 1988; Kiparsky 1993), driven in part by what may well be viewed as misplaced pessimism regarding the constrainability of structure-changing devices (McMahon 1992).

I intend to show in this study that the hypothesis of affix-driven stratification cannot be sustained: this hypothesis fails on a larger scale than has been recognised even by its fiercest critics (for example Szpyra 1989). In its place I formulate a theory of 'base-driven' stratification (first sketched in Giegerich 1994a), which defines strata by reference not to affixes but to affixation bases (where affixes are in principle free to attach on more than one stratum). I show that English, which recognises the morphological categories 'root' and 'word' (Selkirk 1982b), has two lexical strata while German has three (Wiese 1996): root, stem and word-based respectively. Base-driven stratification exercises full control over the number of strata in a given language, but it makes rather fewer predictions than did its predecessor model regarding the stratum or strata on which a given base form can attract a given affix. The Affix Ordering Generalisation, with all its problems, loses its crucial diagnostic status in determining the stratal affiliation of affixes. For stratum 1, I abandon the notion of affixation 'rules' and propose a framework in which affixed forms are listed, thus accommodating the semantic idiosyncrasy, lack of productivity and morphological blocking that characterise stratum-1 formations (Kiparsky 1982, S. Anderson 1992). I show that this framework is an automatic consequence of base-driven stratification.

Turning to the phonological side of the theory, I show that base-driven stratification predicts the Strict Cyclicity Effect on all non-final lexical strata (Giegerich 1988): only on the last lexical stratum can structure-changing phonological rules affect underived environments. There, however, the Alternation Condition exerts diachronic pressure on structure-changing rules to move onto earlier strata and commonly to undergo rule inversion (Vennemann 1972b). A relevant example of (partial) inversion is the synchronic rule of Vowel Shift (McMahon 1990); the present study formulates the principles governing this phenomenon, and looks at further examples.

One striking case is the alternation of full and central vowels found in pairs such as *atom – atomic, totem – totemic*; *occur – occurrence, deter – deterrent* (in Received Pronunciation, 'RP'). In the present framework, such alternations cannot be due to the operation of a synchronic rule of Vowel Reduction: their underlying representations cannot contain full vowels. It follows that such alternations can only be driven by orthographic information (if they are predictable at all): in an adequately constrained derivational framework, such cases breach the limit of what can be predicted on phonological grounds alone. It follows, as I argued also in Giegerich (1992c, 1994b), that there must be rather more to orthographic representations than linguistic theory (notably SPE) has hitherto recognised. In more general terms, the theory makes point-blank predictions as to which alternations are of a phonological (and hence automatic) nature, and which are not.

The theme of rule inversion re-emerges in my treatment of [r]-sandhi. There I argue that the 'standard' generative account, which assumed synchronic breaking and /r/-deletion in cases such as *hear*, is inadequate on both empirical and formal grounds. But the inverse [r]-insertion account is also unsatisfactory. I propose instead an analysis that treats [r] and schwa, in non-rhotic varieties of English, as 'allophones' of the same underlying segment: [r]-sandhi is the result of a (partial) autosegmental re-alignment of the schwa melody. This implies that the low vowels, [ɑː] and [ɔː], must be underlying centring diphthongs in modern RP as they were, even in surface terms, at the turn of the century (Sweet 1908). What we witness there is 'rule inversion in progress': I shall argue, in more detail than in Giegerich (1997), that London English now has monophthongal underliers for the long low vowels while the (mainstream) RP inventory has not (yet?) been so re-structured. And again we shall see that relevant vowel alternations (such as those of the type (RP) *abhor – abhorrent – abhorring, deter – deterrent – deterring*) are predicted by base-driven stratification.

The book concludes with a study of syllabification in base-driven stratification. I argue there against re-syllabification rules of the form proposed – 'slip-shod at best': Gussmann (1988: 234) – by Mohanan (1986) and much of the later literature. Syllabification is structure-building throughout the lexical derivation; and syllabicity alternations such as *rhythm – rhythmic, metre – metric – metering* are once again the automatic effect of base-driven stratification. In fact, cases like that and their German equivalents provide independent support for the stratification theory that constitutes the main theme of this work.

Indeed, this work is concerned with the single issue of base-driven stratification and the analyses facilitated by that theory. Other issues – the format of phonological 'rules' and even the validity of such devices in phonological theory – play no part: that would have been a different agenda. I also do not attempt a complete account of the segmental phonology of English: on this – with more critique of, and reference to, Halle and Mohanan (1985) and Mohanan (1986) – see McMahon (forthcoming).

At least in 1986 the requiem seems to have been some way off.

2 *Affix-driven stratification: the grand illusion*

2.1 The origins

Let us assume that the English lexicon is divided into two strata. This is not only the position that appears to have met with broad consensus in recent research; it will also be extensively argued for in later chapters. Moreover, it happens to be the position most closely associated with Siegel's (1974) original observations and claims, which were to prove seminal to the framework while in turn harking back at least to SPE. Such origins are worth investigating, especially when – as we shall see – they are also the origins of a major flaw in most current stratification models.

At the root of the two-strata model lies the familiar generalisation, dating back to SPE and beyond (for example Bloomfield 1933), and related to the more general 'close-juncture' vs. 'open-juncture' distinction found in the American structuralist tradition (for example Trager and Smith 1951), that the derivational morphology of English has two types of affixation processes, distinguished from each other empirically by a syndrome of differences in terms of morphological and phonological behaviour that will be discussed in some detail below. The well-known 'stress-shifting' vs. 'stress-neutral' effect on the affixation base is one such difference in behaviour. In formal terms, SPE expresses the distinction by associating affixes with different boundary symbols, '#' and '+', where the former 'word boundary' serves, among other things, to block the cyclic application of stress rules – #-affixes therefore lie outwith the domain of the stress rules, their presence having no effect on the stress pattern of the base – while the latter 'morpheme boundary' does not block the cyclic (re-)application of stress rules. Witness the stress shifts caused by the addition of +-affixes in *átom – atóm+ic – àtom+íc+ity*, and the absence of such shifts in *átom – átom#less – átom#less#ness*.

Siegel (1974) contributes the following claims/generalisations to the analysis of the behaviour of the two types of affixation. First, she claims

7

that (with few exceptions) every affix is firmly associated with one (and only one) of the two boundaries. SPE, although implying the same but of course essentially unconcerned with issues morphological, had been less strongly committed to this claim. But SPE does say that '[#-affixes] . . . are assigned to a word by a grammatical transformation, whereas the affixes that determine stress placement are . . . *internal to the lexicon*' (SPE: 86; my emphasis).

While this distinction has been superseded by the Lexicalist Hypothesis (N. Chomsky 1970b) and its aftermath, in which the transformational approach to word formation has been abandoned, its motivation is, nevertheless, worth bearing in mind. We shall in fact see in this chapter and the next that behind this distinction lies an important insight regarding systematic differences in the format of affixation processes, and one that has been lost in the early versions of the theory of Lexical Phonology and Morphology, where all affixes were held to be assigned to their bases, in the lexicon, by rule.

Second, Siegel argues that the two classes of affixes thus emerging (+-affixes are 'Class I' and #-affixes 'Class II') are attached under extrinsic ordering such that all Class I affixes are attached before, and all Class II affixes after the operation of the stress rules. This accounts for the two affix classes' different attitudes towards the stress patterns of their bases, as well as rendering the boundary distinction redundant (Strauss 1979, 1982).[1] And from this ordering follows, third, the morphological prediction that no Class II affix can occur inside a Class-I formation: while $atom\text{-}less_{II}\text{-}ness_{II}$ and $atom\text{-}ic_I\text{-}ity_I$ are well formed, $*atom\text{-}less_{II}\text{-}ity_I$ is not. Since Selkirk (1982b) this prediction has been known as the Affix Ordering Generalisation (henceforth 'AOG'). But the question of whether this is a significant generalisation about English, or merely a less-than-fully substantiated claim, has never been settled although ample doubt has been cast (Aronoff and Sridhar 1983; Szpyra 1989; Wójcicki 1995). Nor has it been entirely clear whether the ill-formedness of items like *atomlessity* is really due to the stratification-induced AOG or to other constraints within the morphological system. I shall discuss this issue further in Section 2.2.1, and the more general voices of dissent later in this chapter.

In the evolution of the theory of morphology–phonology interaction, the step from Siegel's original claims to a stratified lexicon was only a minor one. The mechanical foundations had been laid by Siegel; the recognition that the lexicon was the site of such interaction, in the wake of N. Chomsky's (1970b) Lexicalist Hypothesis, was all that was needed to establish the lexicon as a stratified module of the grammar. Stratum 1 comprises the morphology defined by Siegel as Class I (+-level affixation) as well as cyclic phonological rules, among the latter the rules of stress, Trisyllabic Shortening (*nation – national*), etc. On stratum 2 are located the morphology involving (among other things) Siegel's Class-II (#-level) affixes as well as the remainder of the lexical phonological rules. Boundary symbols are replaced by morphological brackets. To prevent bracket-sensitive phonological rules of stratum 2 from being triggered by brackets introduced on stratum 1, the Bracket Erasure Convention stipulates the deletion of all but the outermost brackets at the end of each stratum (Mohanan 1986: 29 ff.). Hence the stratum-2 rule of *mn*-Simplification (to be discussed further in Section 4.3.3), which deletes the pre-bracket [n] in the stratum-2 formation *damn*]*ing* (as well as in the morphologically simple form *damn*]), is prevented from affecting the stratum-1 form *damnation*: the internal bracket following the *mn*-sequence is no longer present at the point of the rule's operation. Bracket Erasure moreover serves to prevent the postlexical phonology from having access to word-internal (morphological) structure.

SPE's boundary symbolism had actually been more sophisticated than that. In addition to the '+'/'#' distinction among affixed constructions, that model had posited '##' within compounds (hence *atom#less* vs. *atom##bomb*).[2] In a lexical phonology/morphology, this distinction can be expressed in terms of brackets. Kiparsky (1982) proposes the following bracketing conventions: roots and words are represented as '[X]', prefixes as '[Y' and suffixes as 'Z]'. If this proposal is adopted (as it has been, widely, in the literature) then [[*atom*]*less*]] is structurally distinct from [[*atom*][*bomb*]]. Phonological differences between suffixations and compounds (e.g. syllabification differences: compare *popping* and *pop art*) are taken care of by the presence or absence of an initial bracket '['; and, given that on the morphological side compounding and stratum-2 suffixation freely interact (as in *brightness measure* vs. *rule-governedness*) (Kiparsky 1982), SPE's '##' boundary need not be encoded in terms of an additional stratum in a stratified lexicon. The separate stratum for compounding, proposed by Halle and Mohanan (1985) and Mohanan (1986), can be abandoned, and with it the infamous 'loop' back into the previous stratum that that model had required recourse to. What had necessitated the third stratum in those authors' model had been the assumption that all morphemes – roots, words and affixes alike – are identically bracketed as [X] (Mohanan 1986: 127ff., 143 f.). Under such a bracketing convention, compounds are nondistinct from prefix- and suffix-derivations; a stratal distinction between affixation and compounding was hence needed in that model in order to express (for example) syllabification differences such as the one noted above. Further arguments have been put forward against Kiparsky's (1982) split between Class-II affixation/compounding (his stratum 2) and regular inflection (his stratum 3) (Sproat 1985; Booij and Rubach 1987), which brings the number of recognised strata in English down to two.

The current view on the stratification of the English lexicon, then, not only has its intellectual roots in the '+' vs. '#(#)' boundary distinction of SPE and Siegel (1974); it also continues to rely crucially on the original assumptions behind that particular distinction. It does so in two respects. First: the only stratal split in the English lexicon that has stood up to closer scrutiny has been the one that corresponds to the original '+/#' distinction. There are two strata, ordering SPE/Siegel's +-level affixation (and associated phonological rules) before the unstructured rest of the morphology (and associated phonology). Second, and more problematically, that stratal split is a direct descendant of Siegel's claim that there are +-affixes and #-affixes – that, in other words, the information regarding the stratal siting of a given morphological process is exclusively and comprehensively encoded in the affix involved, and not for example in the base of the process. This encoding is essentially diacritic: just as the distribution of boundaries among affixes was essentially *ad hoc* – dictated by individual behaviour rather than derived from more general principles – in the SPE framework, so is the association of affixes with strata in the lexical framework. The morphological side of a given stratum (and, thereby, the stratum itself) is crucially defined by the range of affixes that attach on it. Only in that way can the continued reliance on Siegel's AOG in arguments about lexical stratification be explained. (See for example, Kiparsky (1982, 1985); Halle and Mohanan (1985); Mohanan (1986); as well as textbook accounts such as Spencer (1991); Carstairs-McCarthy (1992); Katamba (1993).) Again, then, the definition of strata relies on the diacritic information lodged with each affix. If the assumption that every affix is diacritically marked for either stratum 1 (= '+') or stratum 2 (= '#') turns out to be false then such an affix-driven stratification model faces trouble whose seriousness increases with the number of affixes that are found to violate the AOG and/or to operate on both strata. I return to this issue below, noting here merely that it would be hardly surprising if such comprehensive and unambiguous (but entirely arbitrary) diacritic marking of affixes were found to be unstable in a natural language, both in diachronic and in synchronic terms.

Siegel (1974) does identify a generalisation regarding the nature of the bases found in her Class-I and Class-II affixation processes. Distinguishing the morphological categories 'Stem' and 'Word' (along with Prefix and Suffix), where a stem (e.g. *loc-* in *loc + ate*) is a bound form that belongs to no syntactic category (Siegel 1974: 104f.), she notes that ' Class II affixes, with the exception of . . . [*gruesome, feckless*, etc.; HG], do not attach to stems. In the overwhelming number of cases, Class II affixes attach to words. Class I affixes attach to both stems and words' (Siegel 1974: 151). But this category distinction among affixation bases is of little consequence to her model; and her generalisation has had little impact on subsequent researchers' understanding of the formal properties of lexical strata, except perhaps that stratum 2 is occasionally (and informally) referred to as the 'word level' – a term, however, that has a separate (phonologically moti-vated) origin in SPE. The only notable development of the stratification model that makes explicit reference to base-category distinctions has been Selkirk (1982b), whose contribution will be discussed in Chapter 3 below. Disregarding that development for the moment, we are left with a partial redundancy in the definition of lexical stratification: strata are defined not only by the diacritic marking of affixes but also by (albeit partially overlap-ping) base categories in that stratum 1 appears to have bound roots (Siegel's 'stems') and words as bases, while all stratum-2 bases are words.

2.2 Some diagnostics for stratal association

I discuss in this section some of the morphological and phonological prop-erties that have been identified in the literature as distinguishing the outputs of stratum-1 affixation processes from those of stratum 2. A similar list of such properties is found in Szpyra (1989: Section 2.2), to which the present discussion is indebted. These will serve later (as they have done in the litera-ture) as diagnostics for the stratal membership of individual affixes. Some such diagnostics follow from what was said in Section 2.1; others have not been touched upon and require more detailed exposition. And all of them will be discussed further in the chapters that follow.

2.2.1 *The Affix Ordering Generalisation*

As was noted before, one of the strongest predictions made by the affix-driven stratification model concerns the stacking of affixes: while multiple stratum-1 affixation, multiple stratum-2 affixation as well as the occurrence of stratum-1 affixes 'inside' the products of stratum-2 affixation are possible, no stratum-2 affix can occur 'inside' the product of a stratum-1 affixation. Typical examples, cited in the literature (and in the classroom), involve *-ic*, *-ity* as stratum-1 and *-less*, *-ness* as stratum-2 affixes: *homelessness, tonicity* and *tonicness* are well formed (with the apparent failure of the Blocking Effect – Section 2.2.3 below – in the last two forms left to be explained), while **homelessity* is not. But there are two kinds of problem with this seemingly clear-cut generalisation. The first is that, as Fabb (1988) has shown, a number of (stratum-1) suffixes fail to stack for idiosyncratic reasons even if such stacking would conform with the AOG. For example, the suffixes *-(u)ous* and *-ize* fail to stack (**sens-uous-ize*), although both of them are apparently stratum 1. The AOG here clearly has to be amended by further, idiosyncratic constraints on stacking. Such an additional constraint would seem to be at work in the case of **mongol-ism-ian* – cited by Katamba (1993: 114) – where *-ism* is claimed to be stratum 2 and *-ian* stratum 1, and the form's failure to occur held to be predicted by the theory. But *-ism* has been identified by Goldsmith (1990: 261) as a case of possible dual (stratum-1 and stratum-2) membership; and in the present case, this suffix meets Goldsmith's criteria for stratum-1 status. The ill-formedness of the example must, therefore, be subject to an explanation along the lines of Fabb's observation of idiosyncratic stacking failure among certain affixes; it does not actually involve the AOG.

Perhaps more seriously, even the ill-formedness of **homelessity* is arguably subject to an alternative explanation: *-ity* is not only ruled out after (native) stratum-2 suffixes but more generally after native bases. The derivational morphology of English relies heavily (if not without exceptions: *oddity*) on the generalisation that non-Germanic affixes cannot attach to Germanic bases *(*shortity, *bookic)* while, conversely, Germanic affixes are quite free to attach to non-Germanic bases *(tonicness, solemnly, container)*. Various researchers have employed the feature [± Latinate] to express this constraint (Saciuk 1969; Aronoff 1976; Booij 1977; Plank 1981); indeed, the term 'lexical stratification' was used by Saciuk and Plank, referring to the [± Latinate] constraint, before it acquired its formal sense in the theory of Lexical Phonology and Morphology. [+ Latinate] affixes tend to require [+ Latinate] bases whereas [– Latinate] affixes are not subject to any such constraint. The [± Latinate] dichotomy seems to correspond to some degree to the stratal division of the English lexicon at least inasmuch as stratum-1 affixes tend to be Latinate; affixes typically associated with stratum 2 seem to display a greater etymological mix than do affixes attaching on stratum 1. But the stratal split and the etymological one are certainly not congruent. As we shall see, *-ism* and other Latinate suffixes may well be stratum 2; Germanic noun-forming *-th* is stratum 1 (see Section 2.2.2), for example. Where the stacking of Latinate onto native suffixes is concerned, then, any AOG enforced by lexical stratification is in reality part of a larger generalisation that rules out the attachment of non-native suffixes to native bases in general, not just to native suffixes. The stacking of non-native affixes is, as we have seen, subject to individual constraints (Fabb 1988) which may have little to do with the AOG; and the stacking of native affixes seldom happens across the stratal divide for the simple reason that few (if any) such affixes beyond noun-forming *-th* are unambiguously sited on stratum 1. The significance of any observed effects of the AOG in English is therefore limited – a somewhat disappointing result, given the high profile that this generalisation has enjoyed in the literature since Siegel (1974).

2.2.2 Categorial status of the base

As we saw earlier, stratum-1 affixes are free to attach to either words or what Siegel (1974) calls stems – bound morphemes that have no obvious membership of the syntactic categories Noun, Verb, Adjective or Adverb. (Bringing the terminology into line with tradition in morphological theory as well as with the subsequent literature – for example Selkirk 1982b – I shall henceforth refer to such morphemes as '(bound) roots'.) Stratum-2 affixes attach to words only, provided cases such as *gormless, gruesome, fulsome, feckless, wistful, grateful* etc. are treated as exceptions (if they are regarded as morphologically complex at all). Note that these bound roots found with 'stratum-2' suffixes (if their Class-II analysis, as proposed by Siegel, is to be upheld) are also probably the only non-Latinate bound roots in the language. Under the assumption, then, that any given affix is assigned to one and only one stratum (and ignoring the *gormless* cases), its occurrence with a bound root is evidence of its stratum-1 status. An affix's non-occurrence with bound roots does not, however, prove its stratum-2 status (although it makes such status appear likely): stratum-1 affixes do not *require* bound roots as bases. To give some examples, adjective-forming *-al* is held to be a stratum-1 suffix given that it attaches to bound roots (1a) as well as words (1b). Noun-forming *-al*, not attested with bound roots (1c), may be a stratum-2 suffix under the base-category diagnostic.

(1)   a. social   b. cantonal   c. denial
          final   baptismal   trial
          lethal   tonal   approval
          phenomenal   hormonal   survival

2.2.3   Productivity and semantic uniformity

Affixation on stratum 1 is held to be less productive than that on stratum 2 (Kiparsky 1982), as well as tending to be semantically irregular (in the sense of non-compositional). The former is said to be due to the well-known Blocking Effect among competing morphological processes, whereby the operation of a relatively unproductive morphological rule pre-empts the operation of its productive competitor in cases where the result of that competitor rule would have a semantically identical output (Paul 1887; Aronoff 1976; Plank 1981; Kiparsky 1982; Scalise 1984; Van Marle 1986; Rainer 1988). For example, the highly unproductive suffix *-th*, forming abstract de-adjectival nouns (*width, length, warmth* etc.) blocks the application of its competitor *-ness*, although the latter is otherwise fully productive and, like *-th*, attaches to native bases: *wideness, longness, warmness* are possible only if they differ semantically from *width, length, warmth* (Giegerich 1994a). Similarly, *-ity* (largely restricted to Latinate bases), blocks *-ness* although the latter is not in principle restricted to native bases: *distinctness, acuteness, sedateness*. Forms such as *chasteness* are possible only if they differ semantically from *chastity*. (For further discussion, see Aronoff 1976: Section 3.2.) This Blocking Effect is achieved automatically in a stratified lexicon if, of two competing morphological processes, the less productive one is ordered on an earlier stratum: the Elsewhere Condition, motivated elsewhere in the grammar and likely to be a universal principle of grammatical structure (Kiparsky 1982), will ensure the non-application of the more general rule in every case where the more special rule has applied. Assuming, first, that Blocking is an empirically verifiable fact, and second, that the Elsewhere Condition is a principle of Universal Grammar, the model predicts that unproductive morphological processes must be sited on stratum 1 provided the language has at its disposal, as is likely, productive competitor processes (which will then be on stratum 2).

This is not to say, however, that all stratum-1 processes are unproductive: a productive process that has no (less productive) competitor may well be sited on that stratum. Nor does the model predict that stratum 2 cannot contain less-than-fully productive processes if those have no fully productive competitors. I shall discuss this issue more fully in Chapter 3, where the synchronic status of the diacritic feature [± Latinate] will be addressed again. In this connection we note here merely that the productivity of Latinate affixes is considerably impaired by their tendency only to attach to Latinate bases, while native (Germanic) affixes do not suffer from such a systematic restriction on their productivity. The fact that bound roots in English are, with few exceptions, of Latinate origin has already been noted in Section 2.2.2.

As regards the semantic (ir-)regularity of morphological rules, Aronoff (1976: Section 3.2) has argued that unproductive morphological processes are more likely to display such irregularity than fully productive processes are, and that probably productivity and semantic regularity (compositionality) are linked. Thus, while both *-ity* and *-ness* produce abstract nouns, formations involving the former are known frequently to have non-abstract meanings (*curiosity, oddity, fatality, variety, opportunity*; Marchand 1969). Possibly the only non-abstract *-ness* formation is *(Royal) Highness*. (Note that this form is not blocked by stratum-1 *height*!) If we accept Aronoff's stipulated link between productivity and semantic compositionality then we can use the semantic non-compositionality of a morphologically complex form as a diagnostic of stratum-1 status.

We see, then, that in the current stratification model the Blocking Effect results in a tendency for less-than-fully productive affixes to congregate on stratum 1 – a tendency that is perhaps reinforced by the predominantly Latinate nature of stratum-1 formations (Section 2.2.1 above). Non-compositional semantics tends to cluster on stratum 1 for the same reason. But the model does not rule on principled grounds that the stratum-1 morphology is less productive and/or less semantically transparent than the stratum-2 morphology is: as long as the mechanisms that carry out morphological operations are held to be the same on both strata (Kiparsky 1982), such distinctions cannot be drawn in principled terms.

2.2.4   *Stress behaviour*

Stratum-2 affixes are, as we have seen, assumed to be stress-neutral while those of stratum 1 are stress-'shifting'. The latter may mean two things: they may either effect a shift of stress within their base (2a), or they may, as in (2b), themselves carry the main stress of the word (thereby 'shifting' the main stress from the base to the affix).

(2)   a. sólemn – solémnity   b. páy – pàyée
          Méndel – Mendélian   Túrner – Tùrnerésque
          tótem – totémic   Fároe – Fàroése

Under the well-founded assumption that the main stress rules of English are sited on stratum 1, the stress shifts in (2a) clearly suggest that the words listed there are put together on stratum 1: note that *solemnity* and *Mendelian* conform with the stress pattern found in underived nouns (*America*); *-ic* has its own (pre-stressing) regularities.

The stress evidence for stratum-1 status provided by the cases in (2b) is not so convincing. The suffixes exemplified there invariably carry the main word stress; and at least in the case of nouns (*payee*) final primary stress is exceptional by all recent accounts of the stress system of English (Selkirk 1980; Hayes 1982; Halle and Vergnaud 1987; Giegerich 1992a: Chapter 7). These suffixes may then be lexically marked for attracting the main stress, which would in turn not in principle stop them from attaching on stratum 2, i.e. after stress assignment by rule has happened, especially when they, as they do in (2b), leave the stress pattern of the base intact. This is not always the case, however. Consider (3):

(3)   escápe – èscapée
       Japán – Jàpanésque
       Vietnám – Vìetnamése

On the one hand, these examples clearly display stress shifts within the base, suggesting that they are handled on stratum 1. On the other hand, what happens in these cases is precisely what is also attested in the postlexical phonology, namely 'Iambic Reversal' (*thìrtéen – thírtèen (mén)*, *Hèathrów – Héathròw (áirport)*, etc.). So the stress shift found in (3) may either be postlexical (which seems unlikely), or it might happen on stratum 2 (and note that the word status of the bases in these cases makes them possible candidates for stratum-2 formation). Given that this rule has also been posited for the equivalent of our stratum 1 (Kiparsky 1979), it would be odd not to find it operating on stratum 2; in fact, under the 'Continuity of Strata Hypothesis' for phonological rules (Mohanan 1986: 47), this rule *cannot* be missing from a stratum if it is present on both neighbouring strata. The stress evidence for the stratum-1 formation of the cases cited in (2b) and (3) is, therefore, at best weak.[3]

Consider, further, the well-known cases where the selectional restrictions on an affix make reference to foot-structure information: noun-forming *-al*, for example, is known only to attach to verbal bases that are end-stressed (*denial*, *trial* etc.; see (1c) above) with the sole exception of *burial*, i.e. after the assignment of stress to such bases. For that reason, Siegel (1974) and subsequent investigators treat it as Class II/stratum 2. This analysis is consistent with, although (as we have seen) not forced by, the fact that *-al* only attaches to words. But the stress evidence alone is again not decisive: if there is a phonological cycle before the morphology then stress information is available to a stratum-1 suffix at the point of attachment. I shall argue in Chapter 4 on independent grounds that stratum-1 phonological rules cannot be allowed to apply before the first morphological operation – there can be no pre-morphology cycle. Here I note merely that an affix's sensitivity to the stress pattern of the base can be used as a diagnostic for its stratum-2 attachment only if there is no pre-morphology cycle.

There is, finally, a more general point. The generalisation that one stress-shifting instance, or one stress-neutral instance, suffices to class a given affix as stratum-1 or stratum-2 respectively is only as strong as is the 'one-affix-one-stratum' hypothesis of the affix-driven stratification model itself. *Obésity*, not displaying a stress shift, is formed on stratum 1 on the evidence of the stress shift in *solémnity* only if *-ity* is assumed to attach on a single stratum. Conversely, *-ness* in *slowness* is a stratum 2 formation on the grounds of stress-neutrality alone only if the stress-neutrality evidence provided by *driverlessness* is assumed valid for all *-ness* formations. If the claim that *-ness* is invariably a stratum-2 suffix is false, then the stress behaviour of *slowness* provides no evidence for the stratum-2 origin of that particular form: like *bonus*, it conforms with the stress rules for nouns.

2.2.5   Syllabification behaviour

In English, the syllabification mechanisms of stratum 1 (to be dealt with in Chapter 8) appear to have few characteristics that set them apart from those of stratum 2. Here is one of them: base-final sonorants that are syllabic when the base is a free word, or when it figures in a stratum-2 suffixation, are non-syllabic before a stratum-1 vowel-initial suffix.[4] Some examples of such bases, with stratum-1 and stratum-2 suffixes respectively, are given in (4a–4c):

(4)	a. cylinder	b. cylindric	c. cylinderish
	metre	metric, -ician, -ist	metering
	hinder	hindrance	hindering
	Lancaster	Lancastrian	Lancasteresque
	enter	entry, -ance	entering
	baptism	baptismal	——

The formal mechanisms accounting for such alternations (which were already observed for +-suffixes in SPE) need not concern us yet (see Section 8.5.2 below); the consensus is that final sonorant consonants cannot be syllable nuclei on stratum 1 (Hayes 1982), while of course they can be (parts of) onsets in forms such as those in (4b). On stratum 2 they can become nuclei (or trigger schwa epenthesis).

The view that the /r/ in *cylinder* is not syllabified prior to the attachment of *-ic* is at least consistent with (if not explanatory of) the stress behaviour of such words: if the /r/ were syllabified before stress assignment then the regular stress pattern for this noun would be **cylínder* (as well as **caléndar* and a few other cases; Hayes 1982): nouns regularly stress the penultimate syllable if it is heavy. If the /r/ is unsyllabified then the heavy syllable is 'final' (at the point of stress assignment) and, hence, not regularly subject to stress in nouns.

However, this failure to syllabify prior to stress assignment cannot be the case for all instances of final (surface-)syllabic sonorants. Consider the following set of examples, arranged like those in (4) above:

(5)   a. motor   b. motóric, motorist   c. motoring
          Anderson   Andersónian   Andersonish
          totem   totémic   totemy

Here, a vowel is clearly underlyingly present before the final sonorant, evidenced in these cases by the alternation of the schwa or syllabic sonorant with a full vowel, under the stress shift induced by the stratum-1 morphology. There is nothing wrong, phonotactically or otherwise, with **mótric* except that it does not exist. In Chapter 5 below I return to the question of what exactly this underlying vowel is – whether it is the full vowel that shows up, under stress, in the derivative or an empty vowel slot. Suffice it to say here that the underlying representations of the items in (5a) must end in /Vr/, /Vn/ and /Vm/ respectively, whatever vowel the 'V' stands for, while those in (4a) end in /dr/, /tr/, /zm/ etc. Let us assume here that the underlying contrast /CVr/ – /Cr/, neutralised as it is on the surface (*motor – metre*), is always evidenced by the availability (or, at least, possibility) of alternations between schwa and a full vowel in the former case, and their absence in the latter. The hypothetical derivatives from *Peter* are a case in point: if the *-ian* derivative is *Petrian* then the underlying representation ends in /tr/; if it is *Petérian* (as it probably is) then the underlying form is / . . . tVr/.

We see, then, that stratum-1 formations may give rise to syllabicity alternations of the *metre – metrist/metric* kind while stratum-2 formations do not do so. But, as we have seen, stratum-1 formations may not do so either (*motorist*). The evidence suggests that syllabicity alternations are a sufficient condition (but not a necessary one) for stratum-1 membership.

The issue is further complicated by the existence of pairs like trisyllabic *twinkling*$_A$ vs. disyllabic *twinkling*$_N$, as in *he is twinkling* vs. *in a twinkling* 'short while' (SPE: 86), as well as *crackling*$_A$ vs. *crackling*$_N$ ('roast-pork fat') (Kiparsky 1985: 135). Such cases are also discussed by Mohanan (1985), who – like SPE – holds the lexical-category difference in each such pair responsible for the syllabicity difference: *-ing*-nouns (which are gerunds) are said to be formed on stratum 1 (they contain the +-boundary in the sense of SPE) while the corresponding adjectives (which are participles) are stratum 2 (containing SPE's '#'). But it is not at all clear that the syntactic-category correspondence of the syllabicity alternation, observed in isolated pairs such as these, should give rise to a valid generalisation. If it did then the sonorants in gerunds such as *the babbling of brooks, my relatives' meddling* and *No Loitering!* cannot be syllabic. This is highly doubtful; a more promising generalisation involves the semantics of the *-ing* formations that contain nonsyllabic sonorants: *twinkling* and *crackling* are not only gerunds but, clearly and more importantly, semantically non-compositional ones. Similarly, *lightening* transparently refers to 'making or becoming brighter' while *lightning* is, specifically, the electric flash preceding thunder. As long as the loss of sonorant syllabicity is restricted to individual lexical items it cannot be a postlexical phenomenon. Within the lexicon, its criteria are probably semantic (and perhaps pragmatic) rather than morphological or syntactic, as SPE and Mohanan (1985) have suggested: if there are an +*ing* and an #*ing* (or, in our terms, a stratum-1 and a stratum-2 -*ing*) of different syllabification behaviours, then it is the semantic (non-)compositionality of such formations (Section 2.2.3 above) that decides their stratal association. While such purported generalisations seem to be too weak to decide over issues as crucial to the model as the single-stratum hypothesis for affixes (Siegel 1974), they do suggest that stratum-2 suffixes may have unproductive and semantically non-compositional stratum-1 counterparts. I return to this question below, for the moment merely noting that 'syllabicity loss' among sonorants in individual lexical items is a diagnostic of the stratum-1 status of those items – as is shown by the reliable cases in (4) – bearing in mind that stratum-1 derivatives do not *have to* display such syllabicity loss – (5) above – and that this diagnostic may well endanger the 'one-stratum-per-affix' hypothesis in cases like -*ing*. As we shall see below, there are more suffixes that behave just like -*ing*.

2.2.6   *Phonotactic behaviour*

The boundary symbols '+' and '#', corresponding as we saw above to the American structuralist notions of 'close juncture and 'open juncture', impose different phonotactic restrictions. A string containing '+' must satisfy the phonotactic constraints that hold in a string containing no boundary, while a string containing '#' is not subject to such constraints. A given segment sequence may be well formed if it contains '#' but ill formed if it contains '+' or no boundary (as well as being subject to different syllabification mechanisms; see Section 2.2.5 above). This difference has received little systematic attention in the literature on lexical stratification; but it is clear that (given the way lexical stratification merely re-encodes the original +/#-distinction) the same difference in terms of phonotactic constraints should be found between stratum-1 and stratum-2 formations. Goldsmith (1990: Chapter 5) contains a full discussion of this diagnostic of lexical stratification whose results are in line with those the present discussion is developing towards. In (6) below are listed some complex forms, all containing #- (stratum-2) suffixes, that violate the phonotactics of the morphologically simple word:

(6)   keenness
        wheelless
        wholly
        bullying
        Toryish

Needless to say, not all stratum-2 formations must display such violations of the single-word phonotactics: the fact that *slowness, telling, bullish* and a multitude of others happen to conform with the phonotactics constitutes no argument against their possible stratum-2 attachment. But what makes this possible feature of stratum-2 affixation interesting for our purposes is that it is the first diagnostic in the present study *against* stratum-1 status: in the previous sections, we have identified the possibilities of bound-root attachment, stress-shifting and loss of sonorant syllabicity as diagnostics *for* stratum-1 status while the respective opposites are not diagnostics against stratum-1 status. Given that we are at this point only concerned with fairly standard diagnostics for (or against) particular stratal associations of given affixes, the diagnostic displayed in (6) – involving geminates in all cases – will suffice. I return to this issue in Chapter 8, as part of a more specific discussion of syllable structure in the vicinity of morphological boundaries. More differences between stratum-1 and stratum-2 syllabification will come to light at that point.

2.2.7 Cyclic phonological rules and allomorphy

Stratum-1 processes are known to display 'root modifications' – or, more generally 'base modifications' of various sorts. Those connected with stress shifts were discussed in Section 2.2.4 above; but there are also numerous kinds of modification caused by cyclic phonological rules, as well as cases of allomorphy. Among the former is Trisyllabic Shortening: inapplicable in stratum-2 formations (cf. *mightily*), cyclic (cf. *nationality*, where the shortening environment is only met in the intermediate form *national*) and subject to the Strict Cycle Condition (cf. the rule's non-application in *Oberon*), this is clearly a stratum-1 rule whose application in a given form may then serve as a diagnostic for the stratum-1 status of that form. A problem with this particular rule is that it has a substantial number of exceptions: *obscenity* has shortening while *obesity* does not; *ominous* does but *numerous* does not (Goldsmith 1990: 351); *comparative* does but *denotative* does not (Szpyra 1989: 71ff.). While this is a problem for the rule itself rather than for its stratal siting, it means that the absence of shortening in a context that would predict it to happen is not a diagnostic for the stratum-2 status of the form in question. But we may take the occurrence of shortening to indicate a stratum-1 formation.

As regards allomorphy, cases such as *amplify – amplification*, widespread with a number of derivational affixes, serve as diagnostics of stratum 1. Some such regularities may be stated in terms of 'phonological' rules of similar status to that of Trisyllabic Shortening, such as the 'Spirantisation' found in *permit – permissible*; but this is of no relevance here. What is relevant is that all such base modifications (including, as we saw above, those involving stress) are taken to be associated with stratum 1, and hence serve as stratum-1 diagnostics. However, once again, the absence of such modification in a given form is not necessarily a stratum-2 diagnostic; nor has, to my knowledge, the association of such phenomena with stratum 1 and their absence from stratum 2 been explained on principled grounds.

2.3 Dual membership: a problem for affix-driven stratification

Counterexamples to the hypothesis that every affix is firmly associated with a single stratum – or, in Siegel's (1974) terms, with one of the two available boundaries – began to emerge in the literature as soon as Siegel formulated the hypothesis. (She herself noted that some prefixes, not here discussed, have dual membership; Siegel 1974: 105.) Aronoff (1976) explicitly argues that there are two suffixes of the form *-able*, associated with '+' and '#'

respectively, and implies a similar analysis for -*ment* (Aronoff 1976: 54). Aronoff and Sridhar (1983) name -*ation* and a few more; Selkirk (1982b: 80f.) tables the stratal associations of a number of English affixes, without giving the reasons that have led her to each individual decision but discussing (on pp. 100ff.) the 'dual class' association of -*ize*, -*ment*, -*able*/-*ible* and -*ist* in some detail. But she reiterates Siegel's claim that 'the vast majority of English affixes belong either to Class I or Class II . . .' (Selkirk 1982b: 100) – a claim that is actually surplus to the requirements of Selkirk's (non-affix-driven) stratification model. I return to the details of Selkirk's approach to lexical stratification in Chapter 3 below.

The suffixes identified by these authors will be individually reviewed in Section 2.4. As I noted earlier, the existence of dual-membership affixes poses a serious problem for an affix-driven stratification model: if a substantial number of affixes are found to attach on both strata then the definition of a given stratum by means of the affixes that attach on it disappears. An affix-driven stratification model is only as reliable as are the diacritic stratum-associations that come with the affixes of the language. To take an extreme case (not very dissimilar from the one that will be made below): if all affixes are found to attach on both strata then the definition of a given stratum *qua* the sum of affixes that attach on it becomes impossible. But while the notion of *affix-driven* stratification will become vacuous in such a case, the notion of *stratification* as such is not necessarily under threat. As we saw earlier, the AOG, heavily relied on by most authors in establishing stratal associations despite its problems (Section 2.2.1 above), is but one of a substantial number of criteria that decide the stratal membership of affixes. The basic insight that English has two lexical strata – implied, after all, by the statement that a given affix occurs on both – may still stand in the light of stratification criteria more reliable than the AOG.

The question at this point is whether an affix that attaches on both strata should be treated as one dual-membership affix or as two single-membership affixes. Aronoff (1976) claims the latter option in the case of -*able*, for example; but Kiparsky (1982: 86) does not commit himself as to whether stratum-1 and stratum-2 -*ment* are different suffixes or the same. This is not a trivial question. If an affix attaches on two strata then this is, in the affix-driven framework, counter to the basic hypothesis; it will, therefore, inflict damage to the model unless the behaviour of that affix is extremely exceptional. If, instead, we are dealing with two homophonous affixes, then there is no problem for the framework, provided they both display the behaviour associated with the respective strata that they attach on, and provided we have independent reasons for calling them two separate affixes. Differences in phonological behaviour alone are clearly not good enough reasons for any two-separate-affixes analysis, for it is on precisely those grounds that the two separate affixes have been posited in the first place. In the case of $-y_N$ vs. $-y_A$ (*harmony* vs. *faulty*) we have good independent reasons for positing two separate affixes in the face of homophony; in the case of *-able* there are no strong reasons, given that 'both affixes' produce adjectives with by and large similar meanings, taking into account the semantic non-compositionality that we expect on stratum 1 in any case. I discuss *-able* in some detail in Section 2.4.1 below.

Leaving aside for the moment the damage suffered by the affix-driven model if a substantial body of affixes is found to occur on both strata, let us look at some such affixes in more detail. As Szpyra (1989) notes:

> a given affix can be said to possess 'dual membership' if, when attached to one item, it displays morphological and phonological features of Class I and if, when appended to a different form, it behaves as a member of Class II. In other words, duality is both morphological and phonological since in a model whose major assumption is that (Kiparsky 1982: 33) 'phonological rules operate in tandem with morphology in the lexicon', there cannot be cases of systematic disparity between the morphological, phonological and semantic structure of words. (Szpyra 1989: 46)

Szpyra then attempts to show, for the two dual-class affixes *-ize* and *-ant/ -ent*, that their dual-class membership in terms of some diagnostics fails to correlate with other aspects of diagnostic behaviour, that *-ize*, for example, is on phonological grounds both Class I and Class II but on morphological grounds uniformly Class I. Such a result, if correct, would not only damage the stratification-by-affix hypothesis but destroy it (a result not altogether unwelcome to Szpyra): as she rightly points out, the model does not permit any disparity between an affix's stratal siting in morphological and in phonological terms. There is, however, no reason to believe that *-ize* really is as uniformly Class I in morphological terms as Szpyra claims. Let us review her arguments briefly.

1. 'All verbs in *-ize* are . . . subject to nominalization by means of [the] stress-changing Class I suffix *-ation*, for example *alcoholization*, *legalization* . . .' (Szpyra 1989: 49). This is only a problem if, in turn, Szpyra's analysis of *-ation* as a uniformly Class-I suffix is correct. However, there are good reasons to treat *-ation*, too, as a suffix of dual membership; Aronoff and Sridhar (1983) had already suspected this. The suffix *-ation* attaches to *-ize* verbs (and others) with full productivity and, as we saw in Section 2.2.4, its

stress behaviour in such cases does not force it onto stratum 1: while bearing the main word stress, it leaves the stress contour of its base intact (*alcoholization*, etc.) apart from subordinating it to the main stress on the suffix (which would in such an analysis, as in the case of other suffixes, have to be lexically marked). If it is the case that *-ation* has dual membership, then *-ize* in turn is free to have the same behaviour.

2. '*-ize* always attaches outside Class I, but never outside Class II suffixes, for example *centr-al$_I$-ize*, **grate-ful$_{II}$-ize* . . .' (Szpyra 1989: 50). This is clearly true for the examples she cites (although the case of *grateful*, containing a bound root, will below be treated as a stratum-1 formation), but the reason for this behaviour may well be the constraint on *-ize*, Latinate as it is itself, only to attach to Latinate bases, and not the stratification-induced AOG. As we saw in Section 2.2.1 (and shall discuss in more detail in Section 3.1), the [± Latinate] constraint on English word formation is independent from the stratification-induced AOG and makes the latter redundant in many individual cases. *Winterise* and *tenderise* are exceptions to that constraint (and note the syllabicity of the [r], which, as Szpyra herself notes for the former, suggests its stratum-2 status in that form). To eliminate the interference of the [± Latinate] constraint with the putative stacking generalisation claimed by Szpyra, one would have to see whether *-ize* ever stacks onto Latinate stratum-2 suffixes. And, indeed, in the case of stratum-2 *-al$_N$* Szpyra's claim may well lose its force. If, for example, ?*proposalize* (meaning 'propose') is ungrammatical then this is equally well explained by the Blocking Effect exerted by *propose*, rather than by the AOG.[5]

Szpyra gives three further arguments intended to support the suffix's non-stratum-2 status, all involving attachment to bound roots and 'truncations' (which are nondistinct from bound-root-attachment if, as it is in the present framework, truncation as a formal device is rejected; Kiparsky 1982). Of course these are strong arguments in favour of stratum-1 attachment in the relevant instances, but they are not really arguments against the possibility that *-ize* may have dual membership. We see, then, that (contrary to Szpyra's claims) *-ize* is both stratum 1 and stratum 2 in phonological and morphological terms, which in any case Selkirk (1982b: 105) had already recognised. And if that is the case then Szpyra's discussion provides no evidence to suggest that the distinction between stratum-1 and stratum-2 *-ize* in terms of phonological diagnostics fails to correlate with those on the morphological side.

For *-ent/-ant*, Szpyra (1989: 51ff.) makes the same claim: in her view this, too, is a suffix that has dual membership in phonological terms but only stratum-1 membership on morphological grounds. Again I subscribe to her phonological analysis but reject the morphological side of the argument. On the phonological side she shows that this suffix can be stress-shifting as well as stress-neutral (*presíde – président* vs. *defý – defíant*), noting also the existence of stress doublets like *precédent/précedent*. Next, she notes that the suffix triggers a laxing rule in the stress-shifting cases, failing to see, however, that the stress shift is in each case clearly caused by the laxing rule: *president* has antepenultimate stress given that (after laxing) the penult is light. Assuming that the laxing takes place on stratum 1 (but that such rules need not be exceptionless; Section 2.2.7 above), these cases are no less regular than is the laxing rule itself. The non-laxing stress-neutral cases such as *defiant, reliant* etc., to which she (correctly) ascribes stratum-2 phonological behaviour, are then also perfectly regular.

On the morphological side, Szpyra argues that nouns in *-ent/-ant* 'are often subject to adjectivization . . . by means of Class-I *-ial*' (Szpyra 1989: 52). Actually, it would appear that *-ial* suffixation is quite regular for the (laxing and stress-shifting) *-ent/-ant* that we have identified as a stratum-1 suffix while it never happens in the (non-laxing and stress-neutral stratum-2) *defiant* cases. And the further stress shift induced by the addition of *-ial* (*precéde – précedent – precedéntial*) is not only regular in all cases (heavy penult) but also expected of a stratum-1 formation.

Next, she argues that *-ent/-ant* adjectives usually take the negative prefix *in-*. As this prefix is Latinate, this is only to be expected; there is no reason to believe that *in-* is restricted to stratum 1, as she claims it is, given that it is subject to the overriding [± Latinate] constraint and, given further, that *-ent/-ant* formations in turn are subject to the same constraint.

Szpyra's final argument for the solely-stratum-1 status of this suffix is that it 'attaches only to underived verbs and never to Class-II derivatives' (Szpyra 1989: 53): *attendant* vs. **housant, *sharpenant, *de-lousant*. Again this is clearly a true generalisation (albeit with the exception of *coolant*, if conversion into verbs takes place on stratum 2; Kiparsky 1982). But again this stacking failure is readily explained by the overriding [± Latinate] constraint, which, as far as I can see, *-ant/-ent* breaches only in the cases of *coolant, claimant*. It would appear, then, that *-ent/-ant* is another instance where Szpyra fails to take the [± Latinate] constraint into account: this constraint, operative on both strata and, in principle, independent of stratification, imposes restrictions on (stratum-2) stacking that she wrongly identifies with the AOG. *-ent/-ant* has dual membership in both phonological and morphological terms, and there is no more cause for doubting the correlation of the stratum-specific morphological and phonological features of this suffix than there is for those of -*ize*.

Szpyra (1989) is clearly right, then, in claiming that -*ize* and -*ant*/-*ent* have dual membership – I shall return to both suffixes in Section 2.4 below – but wrong in claiming that their phonological and morphological behaviours fail to match. As I noted earlier, such findings damage the stratification-by-affix hypothesis; but they are capable of destroying it only by stealth rather than in a single blow. This, too, will be shown to be the case: in the following section I shall argue that dual membership (with correlating phonological and morphological diagnostics) is far more common among English derivational suffixes than has been recognised in the literature (including Szpyra 1989). The abundance of unnoticed dual membership among English affixes is rather surprising, given that analysts such as Szpyra (1989) have been clearly interested in identifying as many such cases as possible: as we noted earlier, every instance of dual membership seriously undermines the stratification-by-affix hypothesis. We shall in fact see that dual membership should be considered normal for derivational suffixes. It will become clear that lexical stratification cannot be affix-driven in the light of such facts; but the findings of Szpyra (1989) damage the *affix-driven* stratification model only, and not the idea of lexical stratification as such. Given that affix-driven stratification crucially relies on the diacritic stratum-marking of affixes, the failure (for example, the loss over time) of such diacritics should be unsurprising. In Chapter 3, a stratification model will be developed that predicts dual membership for affixes unless they specifically carry a single-stratum diacritic. This stratification model will be base-driven rather than affix-driven. In the remainder of this chapter I hope to show that dual membership is a normal fact of English morphology.

2.4   Dual membership among English derivational suffixes

As we have seen, there cannot be – and, indeed, there never has been in the evolution of the model – any dispute of the fact that some English affixes occur on both strata. But the claim, made by both Siegel (1974) and Selkirk (1982b), that 'the vast majority' of affixes can be pinned down to a single stratum persists in the beliefs of lexical phonologists. The published enumerations of dual-membership affixes are indeed small (frequently occupying footnotes; e.g. Kiparsky 1982: 86), although notably no two such lists are ever quite the same. Szpyra (1989: Section 2.2.3), for example, gives -*ize*,

-ant/-ent, *-ive*, *-able/-ible*; Selkirk (1982b: 104f.) had explicitly discussed *-ize*, *-able/-ible* and *-ment* as members of both strata, moreover identifying *-ist* for dual membership in her table (on p. 80), while not marking *-ism* for such behaviour although it occurs in both the Class-I and the Class-II section of that table. Given that neither these authors nor others list the stratal associations of English derivational affixes in comprehensive form, the published lists of dual-membership affixes must similarly be treated as lists of examples rather than exhaustive accounts – which has probably contributed to the widely held but erroneous belief that dual membership is the exception rather than the rule.

In what follows I shall enumerate, with brief discussion in each case, the derivational suffixes of English that can be plausibly regarded as being sited on both strata. This list will be substantial (if, again, probably incomplete); but it should be noted that the way in which the diagnostics (discussed in Section 2.2 above) are applied here is somewhat more permissive of dual membership than has been the practice in the literature. To give one example, Selkirk (1982b: 80) lists the diminutive suffix *-ette* (*sermonette*) for Class I, presumably on the strength of its stress behaviour, which, in contrast, I regard as consistent with (although of course not enforcing) stratum-2 attachment: *-ette* bears the main stress but does not affect the stress pattern of the base apart from subordinating it (recall Section 2.2.4). In more general terms, the comparative length of my list is explained not so much by the implication that other authors have overlooked crucial facts (although this does seem occasionally to be the case) but by a difference in terms of the underlying hypothesis. While previous authors on the subject have endeavoured to confine as many affixes as possible to single strata, occasionally at the cost of having to resort to the exception-marking of counterexamples, the present effort is not driven by such an objective: as I noted above, the hypothesis pursued here is that it is normal for affixes to occur on both strata.

An obvious example of this difference in attitude towards individual affixes' stratal association, driven by a difference in the underlying hypothesis, is my treatment of *-less*. As was noted in Section 2.2.2, all authors since Siegel (1974) have treated this suffix as stratum 2 only, despite its possible occurrence with bound roots (*gormless, feckless, reckless, ruthless, hapless*). While it is true that most of these bound roots are non-recurrent 'cranberry morphs', *hap-* (*hapless*) is arguably not, if Strauss's (1979; 1982: 28) analysis is adopted whereby all adjectives ending in *-y* (e.g. *happy*) are morphologically complex. Furthermore, note that the occurrence of non-recurrent bound roots has in other instances not prevented scholars from treating such items as morphologically complex: Selkirk (1982b: 81), for example, exemplifies Class-I *-ible* with *legible*, calling *leg-* a verb root, and similarly treats *mollify* as complex (Silkirk 1982b: 98), making no distinction between recurrent and non-recurrent bound roots. It is in fact a contentious issue whether or not items such as *gormless* should be treated as morphologically complex at all: speaker's intuitions on such matters are variable. The model of stratum 1 that will be developed in Chapter 3 will accommodate such variation in that it will allow for (and indeed predict) speaker-specific differences in the amount of structure imposed on lexical items. I shall, therefore, include *-less* among the cases of dual membership: the bound roots noted above receive their suffix on stratum 1. It follows that *-ness* (*business*), *-some* (*gruesome*) and *-ful* (*wistful*) are subject to a similar analysis.

The picture that will emerge will be one where perhaps 'the vast majority of suffixes', to use the familiar phrase, *may plausibly be* assigned on both strata. Such an analysis may not in all cases be unavoidable (unlike in the cases discussed by Aronoff (1976), Selkirk (1982b), Szpyra (1989)) such are, as we have seen, the indeterminacies in the available diagnostics. What I hope to show is that anyone claiming that dual membership is a normal fact of the morphology of English has rather less explaining to do than anyone claiming that it is not.

2.4.1   -able/-ible

Probably as a result of Aronoff's (1976: Section 6.2) detailed discussion, which identified the different behaviour of #*able* and +*able* beyond dispute, *-able* has been a showpiece of dual membership in the literature (Selkirk 1982b: 104f.; Szpyra 1989: 57ff.; S. Anderson 1992: Section 7.2.1). I briefly summarise Aronoff's argument, to which subsequent analysts have added little, and adapt it to the present framework.

First, *-able* attaches to bound roots (7a–7b) and words (7c):

(7)	a. affable	b. navigable	c. debatable
	arable	appreciable	dependable
	capable	demonstrable	noticeable
	formidable	tolerable	perishable
	probable	mutable	manageable

This distribution does not in itself argue for dual membership: while the forms in (7a–7b) must originate on stratum 1, attachment to free bases as in

(7c) does not enforce stratum-2 status. But, second, the existence of doublets involving (7b)/(8) shows that *-able* does engage in two distinct kinds of morphological processes:

(8)   navigatable
        appreciatable
        demonstratable
        toleratable
        mutatable

In Aronoff's framework of word-based morphology, the *+able* forms in (7b) are subject to the truncation of the suffix *-ate* while *#able* does not trigger truncation. (See S. Anderson (1992: Section 10.2.3) for discussion.) In a stratified lexicon, truncation rules are not only unnecessary but also extremely 'costly' in terms of the devices they involve (Kiparsky 1982); forms such as those in (7b) then contain bound roots that attract *-able* and *-ate* alternatively. And in (8), *-able* attaches to complex bases (*navig+ate*, etc.). But, given that *navigate* could still be a stratum-1 base, the existence of such doublets still would not indicate dual membership if it were not accompanied by a recurrent semantic difference that is indeed diagnostic of such dual association: forms such as those in (7b) are semantically non-compositional while those in (8) are transparent. For example, *tolerable* is 'moderately good', *toleratable* 'able to be tolerated', *appreciable* is 'substantial', *appreciatable* 'able to be appreciated', and so forth.

Third, phonological differences, again giving rise to doublets, support an analysis involving dual membership:

(9)   cómparable – compárable
        réparable – repáirable
        réfutable – refútable

The first member of each pair displays stress-shifting behaviour (a diagnostic of stratum 1), correlating with the semantic criterion of non-compositionality. *Cómparable* means 'roughly the same', *compárable* is, again transparently, 'able to be compared'.[6]

I add to Aronoff's discussion, which clearly suggests that, in the present model, *-able* should figure on both lexical strata, the following point. Although Latinate in origin (and being restricted to Latinate bases in all cases where stratum-1 attachment has been identified above), *-able* attaches with full productivity and semantic transparency not only to Latinate transitive verbs (for example those on *-ate*) but also to native transitive verbs: *singable, drinkable, loveable, likeable, changeable* etc. If this suffix is subject to the [± Latinate] constraint then this constraint is clearly suspended on stratum 2.

Aronoff treats -*ible* as an allomorph of +*able* (in our terms of stratum-1 -*able*). Apart from the criteria noted above (semantic non-compositionality, stress-shifting), -*ible* formations are subject to extensive root allomorphy (again a criterion for stratum-1 membership), as in *perceptible, derisible*. Note the non-compositional semantics of both examples, 'large enough to be relevant' and 'ridiculous' respectively. -*ible* is, moreover, clearly subject to the [± Latinate] constraint: there are no Germanic bases that would attract this suffix rather than its allomorph, -*able*. A final argument in favour of -*ible* being a stratum-1 (only) competitor of -*able* is the unpredictability of their distribution: there is no synchronic rule that would predict, for example, that the bound root *ed*- takes -*ible* while *prob*- takes -*able*. I return to such unpredictability in Section 3.2 below, noting here merely that irregularity of this sort is clearly incompatible with productivity (on the part of the two suffixes involved). This I regard as supporting the stratum-1 status of -*ible*. Whether -*ible* is an allomorph of -*able*, or simply a competitor suffix, is not a question on whose answer much depends, although it will become clear in Chapter 3 that the notion of 'allomorph', applied in this context, is rather meaningless.

2.4.2   -ant/-ent

The dual membership of this suffix was already noted in Section 2.3 above, in connection with Szpyra's (1989) discussion. Its occurrence on stratum 1 is confirmed by the fact that it attaches to bound and free bases: see (10) and (11) below.

(10)   celebrant
        irritant
        lubricant
        applicant
        stimulant
        tenant

The (non-shifting) stress pattern displayed by the forms in (11) below is consistent with either stratum. Arguments supporting -*ant* attachment on stratum 2 are based on the productivity of this suffix: at least in specialised commercial jargon (in many cases spilling over into everyday core lexis), where the suffix denotes chemo-technical/medicinal substances, it appears to be fully productive and even to develop the freedom to violate the [±

Latinate] constraint. Some examples are given in (11a); (11b) lists examples of *-ant* producing agent nouns in legal/corporate jargon, which similarly appear to have considerable productivity.

(11) a. depressant   b. contestant
        digestant   disputant
        repellant   accountant
        pollutant   consultant
        propellant   informant
        disinfectant   complainant
        inhalant   defendant
        coolant   claimant

Within their respective jargons, such formations are semantically trans-parent as well as probably fully productive, breaching the [± Latinate] con-straint in some attested forms: *claimant, coolant*. Their relatively small incidence (if compared, for example, with *-less* formations) may well be explained through the fact that the rule attaching *-ant* is productive in highly specialised jargons, where the number of bases that are candidates for this suffix is probably small.

-ent may again be treated as a competitor of stratum-1 *-ant*. Arguments in favour of this analysis (apart from the unpredictability of the distribution of *-ent* vs. *-ant*, as also observed in the case of *-ible*) are as follows. First, *-ent* formations are subject to a (suffix-specific) laxing rule, which gives rise to vowel as well as stress alternations:

(12)   preside – president
        confide – confident
        prevail – prevalent
        reside – resident
        coincide – coincident

Second, *-ent* formations are subject to further (stress-shifting) affixation through *-ial* (*president – presidential*). And, given that *-ent* fails to figure in the jargon-specific cases of productivity discussed above, the conclusion that it is a stratum-1 suffix is probably safe. (See also Szpyra (1989: 51ff.), who, however, treats *-ent* and *-ant* as interchangeable throughout their dis-tribution.)[7]

2.4.3   -ee

This suffix again attaches to both bound and free bases, with the latter not subject to the [± Latinate] constraint, as shown in (13a) and (13b) respec-tively:

(13)   a. evacuee   b. trustee
           nominee   payee
           vaccinee   transferee
           lessee   appointee
           donee   escapee

   -ee always bears the main stress of the word; moreover, disyllabic bases such as *escápe* display Iambic Reversal (*éscapée*). Such stress modifications would appear to suggest stratum-1 attachment of forms such as those in (13b), and therefore possibly of all *-ee* formations. But, as I noted in Section 2.2.4 above, such stress behaviour does not provide conclusive evidence for stratum-1 attachment in that it does not constitute stress 'shifts' in the sense associated with stratum 1, as for example in *sólemn – solémnity*. First, stress invariably placed on the suffix may well form part of the suffix's underlying representation – in the present case such an assumption of underlying stress is supported by the fact that final stress is in any case exceptional among English nouns (Hayes 1982; Giegerich 1992a: Section 7.2). The change of the stress in the base is one of automatic subordination rather than shift. Second, the Iambic Reversal found in *escapee*, etc. is triggered by a rule that is attested postlexically as well as on stratum 1 (Kiparsky 1979); it must therefore, under the 'Continuity of Strata Hypothesis' (Mohanan 1986) be expected also to be operative on stratum 2. We conclude, then, that the forms in (13b) are consistent with both lexical strata (while those in (13a) must be stratum 1).

   The argument for dual membership comes once again from the productivity of the suffix in certain jargons. Marchand (1969: Section 4.24.1) notes that the *-ee* formation transparently denoting direct passives 'has recently come into favour especially with words of official military jargon'; examples in (14a) below. Moreover, Bauer (1983: Section 8.2.1), drawing examples from Marchand (1969), Lehnert (1971) and Barnhart *et al.* (1973), argues that *-ee* has a recently developed productive use with playful or whimsical connotations, again transparently forming semantically passive nouns from verbal bases; see (14b).

(14)   a. draftee   b. flirtee
           enlistee   kissee
           rejectee   kickee
           selectee   huggee[8]
           trainee   shavee

   Given that such formations conform with the behaviour associated with stratum 2, they may be regarded as produced on that stratum by fully productive (albeit jargon-specific) affixation rules; the comparatively small number of attested forms, especially in the military jargon (14a), may again be explained by the small number of available bases.

2.4.4 -er *and its variants*

On the grounds of its full productivity, -er is usually assumed to be a uniformly stratum-2 suffix (Kiparsky 1982). Indeed, the large number of semantically transparent forms – exemplified in (15) below – clearly confirms that the suffix is well-established on stratum 2. Note that attachment to native and Latinate bases is possible.

(15) | singer | producer |
|---|---|
| writer | transcriber |
| fighter | informer |
| driver | seducer |
| rider | commander |
| eater | examiner |

However, such a single-stratum analysis poses a number of problems, all of which disappear when a dual-membership analysis is adopted. Such dual membership is in any case necessitated by the occasional attachment of the suffix to bound roots (Marchand 1969: Section 4.30.13):

(16) astronomer
      astrologer
      adulterer
      philosopher
      presbyter
      bio-/lexico-/stenographer etc.

The first problem arises with forms such as *pedlar*, *burglar* and *butler*, which in historical terms do not derive from verbs plus -er, and which synchronically – although interpreted as complex by many speakers – do not necessarily have free bases. While *peddle* is part of the standard language, *burgle* is not current in all varieties of the language, and *buttle* does not appear to occur outside Bertie Wooster's lexicon. Such forms are historical back-formations, perhaps with facetious origin. A stratum-1 analysis of *burglar* etc. expresses such facts easily: the root can then be treated as bound in those varieties of the language that do not have the verb *burgle*. The back-formation of the verb regularises the form and may therefore be expected to occur.

The second problem is also exemplified by *pedlar*, *burglar* and *butler*, although it is by no means confined to those somewhat unusual forms (nor in fact to this particular suffix, as we shall see). It concerns the non-syllabic-ity of the base-final sonorant in the suffixed form, a diagnostic of stratum-1 formations. *Entry, hindrance, baptismal* etc. exemplify the syllabification behaviour of relevant stratum-1 forms; *entering, hindering, summery* etc. examplify that of stratum-2 forms (see Section 2.2.5 above). The variation found among *-er* formation is exemplified below. Cases where (in RP, fol-lowing D. Jones 1991) non-syllabic sonorants are preferred are listed in (17a); those cases where syllabic sonorants are preferred are listed in (17b):

(17)   a. wrestler   b. meddler
           bungler   bottler
           fiddler   wriggler
           smuggler   rattler
           settler   haggler
           sprinkler   waddler

If syllabification behaviour is to be explained through lexical stratification (see Section 2.2.5 above) then the forms listed in (17a) must be produced on stratum 1. Such an analysis is supported by the semantics, which is in all cases somewhat specialised (if not entirely inconsistent with that normally associated with *-er* formations: all forms denote agents). A *wrestler* is not just somebody who wrestles but somebody who takes part in the associated spectator sport; a *fiddler* is somebody who plays the fiddle in a folk band, a *settler* is a colonist. Being a *bungler* is a personality trait; and a *sprinkler* is a fire fighting device in buildings.[9] In all cases, alternative forms with syllabic [l] are possible, with transparent semantics; for example: *fiddler* – 'someone who fiddles/fidgets', *settler* – 'this baby settles easily at night, is a good *settler*', etc.

The forms in (17b) are of a more 'one-off' nature; they are spontaneous formations that have fully transparent agent meanings. One might suspect that *bottler* ('someone who bottles, e.g. wine') is disyllabic for the members of that trade, who will be familiar with the term. Recall from Section 2.2.3 above that semantic non-compositionality is not a necessary condition for stratum-1 status: a form may establish itself on stratum 1 purely through the phonological structure simplification caused by frequent use. This may be the case in *smuggler*, which shows no signs of non-compositionality but is clearly so well-established that it is listed (unlike *waddler*, for example, which is trisyllabic) even in pocket-size dictionaries. If there is a semantic difference between *smuggler* and its hypothetical trisyllabic variant then the latter may denote somebody who smuggles on the specific occasion to which the term refers, rather than habitually.

It is probably safe to assume that instances of this suffix with deviant spelling (*-ar, -or*) are stratum-1 formations (as suggested by Kiparsky 1982: 86):

(18)   a. professor b. burglar
          tutor   beggar
          author   pedlar
          editor   bursar

This assumption is supported by the fact that such formations are particularly free to attach to bound roots (as discussed above regarding *-ar*). While there seems to be no reason not to treat the cases in (18b) simply as deviant spellings of *-er* (which, as we have seen, can occur on both strata), *-or* (18a) appears to constitute a genuinely different suffix in that, unlike *-er* formations, it attracts the further, stress-shifting (stratum-1) suffix *-ial*: *professorial, tutorial*, etc. Note also that *-or* is subject to the [± Latinate] constraint, unlike *-er*. Alternations between schwa and [ɔ], as exemplified by *proféssor – professórial*, suggest that *-or* probably has the phonological representation /Vr/ (to be discussed in Chapter 5 below) while *-er* is represented as /r/, whose syllabicity is a matter of stratum-specific syllabification.[10] The discussion of *-er* will be continued in the context of *-ess* (Section 2.4.9 below).

2.4.5   -(e)ry

This suffix, forming nouns (either abstract or denoting places) from nominal bases, has two prosodically conditioned allomorphs: *-ry* and *-ery*. Examples denoting places are given in (19a) and (19b) respectively:

(19)   a. chickenry b. rookery   monkery
          camelry   hennery   nunnery
          heronry   gullery   rockery
          pheasantry froggery   rosery
          gannetry   cattery   grapery
          rabbitry   piggery   nursery
          ravenry (?)   sealery   winery

The forms listed above have bases which are free forms unrestricted by the [± Latinate] constraint. While this is, as we have seen, not of itself a compelling reason to treat them as stratum-2 formations, there are two arguments in favour of such an analysis.

The first argument is that the suffix is fully productive, especially when it denotes 'a place where numbers of animals/birds live/roost'. There is no limit to the productivity of this suffix as long as the following restrictions are taken into account (which are compatible with full productivity). First, the formation of *doggery* is (in that sense) blocked by *kennel*, and that of *battery* ('bat roost') and **ternery* ('tern colony') by the existence of homophonous morphologically-simple or stratum-1 forms (see Section 3.5.1 below). Second, there is clearly a prosodic restriction on this suffix whereby its base must constitute a single (mono- or disyllabic) foot: **jack-dawery/jackdawry* is ill-formed although jackdaws are extremely gregarious.[11]

The second argument for the stratum-2 origin of forms like those in (19) is again the fact that the allomorphs of -*(e)ry* are prosodically conditioned: -*ry* attaches to disyllabic feet, -*ery* to monosyllabic feet. This points to stratum-2 attachment, given that foot structure (assigned on stratum 1) must be available to the rule attaching the suffix. Such prosodic conditioning of affixes is not unusual: the allomorphs of -*(e)teria* as well as the restrictions on -*al*$_\text{N}$ (*refusal*, etc.) are subject to similar prosodic conditioning. I show in Section 4.2.1 below that such restrictions are indeed firmly indicative of stratum-2 attachment.

Nevertheless, there are instances of this suffix that equally firmly indicate its stratum-1 attachment. Consider the examples listed in (20):

(20)   monastery
          surgery
          laundry
          foundry
          vestry
          vintry
          pantry

In each case, -*(e)ry* denotes a place. In each case, moreover, the base is either a bound root (*monast-*, etc.), or it is not a noun. In *laundry*, the base is arguably the verb *launder*; but in this case the non-syllabicity of the [r] indicates stratum-1 attachment (as does in any case the irregularity of the lexical category of the base). Note also the fact that the prosodic conditioning mentioned above is inoperative in these stratum-1 formations: if such conditioning were in operation we would expect **pantery*, **vintery*, **vestery*.

We conclude, then, that -*(e)ry* attaches on both strata: productively and subject to prosodic conditioning on stratum 2, and unproductively (as well as not affected by prosodic restrictions on its allomorphs) on stratum 1.

2.4.6   -esque

This adjective-forming suffix behaves similarly to *-(e)ry* in that it attaches freely (unconstrained by [± Latinate]) to a clearly defined range of bases (nouns, often proper names), displaying several of the diagnostics for stratum-2 attachment in addition to its productivity, which appears to be unlimited when the suffix attaches to proper names, as in (21a). Non-name examples – given in (21b), from Lehnert (1971) – are sporadic.

(21)   a. Andersonesque   b. picturesque
           Hemingwayesque   humoresque
           Garboesque   lionesque
           Turneresque   statuesque
           Rembrandtesque   sculpturesque
           Handelesque   arabesque
           Lendlesque

Note also that the meanings of the examples in (21b) are not immediately obvious (*humoresque*, for example, is a noun denoting 'a musical caprice') while the formations in (21a) are semantically transparent. On the grounds of productivity and semantic transparency alone, we have reason to suspect that only forms such as those in (21a) reflect the productive (stratum-2) pattern: the feature 'proper name' probably figures in the subcategorisation frame of the productive rule attaching adjective-forming *-esque* to nouns.[12]

Further indicators suggesting that (21a) contains stratum-2 forms relate to phonotactics and to syllabification. On the phonotactic side, such forms may contain vowel-hiatus sequences (*Garboesque, Hemingwayesque*) not found in morphologically simple forms and are therefore ruled out among stratum-1 formations. In terms of syllabification, base-final syllabic sonorants are retained in the complex forms: *Turneresque, Handelesque, Lendlesque* – this is again, as we have seen before, a diagnostic of stratum 2.

The forms in (21b), on the other hand, appear to form a group with *-esque* formations attaching to bound roots, exemplified in (22):

(22)   burlesque
           picaresque
           gigantesque
           grotesque
           chivalresque

Such forms display the semantic unpredictability also found in the examples of (21b): a *burlesque*, for example, is a play. But unlike those, they are indisputably stratum-1 formations on formal morphological grounds – their attachment to bound roots – alone. And as I indicated earlier, the question of whether an item like *burlesque* is analysed as morphologically complex by all speakers (which it probably is not) is of very little relevance within the model of stratum 1 that will be developed in Chapter 3 below.

We note, then, that *-esque* is another suffix that attaches on both strata. Such an analysis is not only required by the facts: the bound-root bases in (22) and the phonotactic peculiarities of (21a) allow no alternative account; it also allows us to identify the particular context in which the suffix operates with full productivity. By consigning cases like those in (21b) to stratum 1 (as is suggested by their semantic behaviour), we are able to say that *-esque* is fully productive, yielding transparent outputs, in the rather narrow context of proper names and only there. It would appear that such a two-strata analysis is rather more insightful than one that involves no spread across the stratal divide.

2.4.7   -ess

This suffix appears to pose no problems for the derivational morphology of English: fully productive earlier this century (if somewhat archaic and perhaps shunned now for its implications of sexism) and unaffected by the [± Latinate] constraint, it adds the feature of femininity to animate nouns (including agent nouns on *-er/-or*), as exemplified by *lioness, peeress, manageress, authoress* and many others. But the stratal assignment of this suffix, in morphological and especially phonological terms, is nonetheless not straightforward. On the morphological side, the occurrence of *-ess* with a few bound roots (*Negress, abbess*) gives rise to at least sporadic stratum-1 attachment. Stratum 1 will also accommodate formations which have, in diachronic terms, lost the preceding noun-forming *-er/-or* (probably for euphonic reasons; Marchand 1969: 287), resulting synchronically in the irregular attachment of the suffix to bound roots or, apparently, verbs:

(23)   adulteress   (*adultereress, etc.)
        murderess
        sorceress
        adventuress
        empress

On the phonological side we encounter the same problems regarding the syllabicity of base-final sonorants as also occur with *-er/-or*; see (17) above.

The morphologically simple base *tiger* has non-syllabic [r] in *tigress*; but *pantheress* has syllabic [r] (or schwa). Complex bases containing agent-forming *-er* vary similarly (examples from Lehnert (1971)):

(24)   a. waitress   b. teacheress
            paintress   speakeress
            temptress   farmeress
            huntress   preacheress
            interpretress   porteress
            philosophress   weaveress
            wardress   danceress

Unlike the cases in (17) above, the present ones do not lend themselves to a semantic explanation. To some degree the occurrence of schwa in the forms listed in (24b) is predictable on phonotactic grounds: *[tʃr], *[mr], etc. (in *teacheress, farmeress*) are impossible syllable onsets (Section 8.2.1 below). But *speakeress, porteress* are not amenable to such an explanation; non-syllabic [r] is in fact especially common after [t]. We are left with a situation, then, where the syllabicity of [r] is unpredictable before *-ess*, in simple roots as well as in cases where the [r] represents the agent-forming suffix *-er*. This must mean that *-ess* attaches relatively freely on both stratum 1 and stratum 2; and the stratum-1 origin of forms such as those in (24a) may not have any positive reasons (beyond simply being possible within the model). These forms may be older, or the segment sequences involved may be especially liable to simplify; but such tendencies clearly do not amount to synchronic generalisations.

Note that the stratum-1 analysis of the forms in (24a) implies that the *-er* suffix itself must be attached on stratum 1 in those forms. Again, this is independently motivated only in some cases (in *waiter* on semantic and in *philosopher* on morphological grounds); in most cases, it again seems to represent random variation.

The suffix *-or*, identified in Section 2.4.2 as stratum-1, displays similar variation before *-ess*; but in this case individual forms vary freely. Lehnert (1971) lists the following doublets:

(25)   janitoress – janitress
        traitoress – traitress
        tutoress – tutress
        rectoress – rectress

Other forms (*authoress, tailoress; editress, dictatress*) do not display such variation; note again the frequency of [t] before non-syllabic [r], resulting in the recurrent final string *-tress*. While the stratal assignment of such formations presents no problem once we accept the occurrence of *-or* on stratum 1 and that of *-ess* on both strata, the possibility for *-or* to be non-syllabic does: as I noted in Section 2.4.2, the assumption that *-or* is underlyingly /Vr/ is well-motivated (through alternations like *tutor – tutorial*) and makes a non-syllabic variant of this suffix impossible. We have to assume that bound roots such as *tut-* are free to take (on stratum 1) both *-er* (possibly followed by *-ess*, and in that case surfacing as non-syllabic [r]) and *-or* (possibly followed by *-ial*, and in that case surfacing with stressed [oː]). In word-final position the phonological distinction between the two suffixes is in any case neutralised. Such an analysis, although less than elegant and somewhat non-explanatory, at least accounts for *tutress – tutorial* (which will be highly problematic in any model). It is, moreover, supported by orthographic doublets such as *convener – convenor*, as well as more indirectly by occasional forms such as *managerial*. Clearly, the distinction between the two suffixes is somewhat confused in the language. But what is interesting is that a stratified lexicon offers various independent arguments which confine the confusion to stratum 1.[13]

2.4.8   -ette

The case for dual membership presented by this suffix is perhaps weaker than that of other suffixes. It is not strong enough to provide the crucial proof that dual membership is possible among suffixes (if such proof were still needed); but given that precedents have already been established, what can be shown for *-ette* is that it may well be present on both strata.

One of the problems posed by this suffix is that it occurs in a number of hardly assimilated French loans:

(26)   noisette   brunette
        marionette   cassette
        briquette   pirouette
        silhouette   baguette
        serviette   epaulette

In the somewhat unlikely case that such items are treated by English speakers as morphologically complex at all (an issue to which I return in more general terms in Section 3.3.3 below), they must be stratum-1 formations, with the suffix attaching to bound roots. Other such cases are perhaps more likely to be interpreted as complex: *couchette* has a clear diminutive sense, and *vinegarette/vinaigrette* has a synchronic link with *vinegar*. (Note the non-syllabic [r] in *vinaigrette*, indicating the stratum-1 origin of the form.)

The suffix is productive in certain semantic areas, relating to literary/journalistic genres (27a) and 'the language of trade' (Marchand 1969: 290) – in particular in jargons such as those of rail transport, real-estate and catering (27b) – as well as denoting female office bearers of various kinds (27c):

(27)   a. novelette   b. kitchenette   c. majorette
          storyette   roomette   sailorette
          essayette   partitionette   officerette
          lecturette   wagonette   censorette
          featurette   dinnerette   conductorette
          leaderette   luncheonette   usherette
          sermonette

The period of productivity enjoyed by the suffix, in its various usages, may well be (or have been) short-lived in some cases: some of the items in (27c) now appear dated (while they clearly did not appear so to Marchand (1969: 290)). *-ette* formations provide interesting data for the study of productivity in word formation. Without launching into a discussion of this notion at this point, we may conclude that the rule attaching *-ette* to nominal bases has, or has had, a more limited life-span than others; it is highly jargon specific; and given that one of the jargons in question is that of marketing (27b), the suffix may not appear productive to speakers of English who are not paid to find names for commercial commodities. Particular speakers of the language have productive rules of the derivational morphology suiting their particular requirements.

On the grounds of productivity, formations such as those in (27) may, then, be tentatively attributed to stratum 2. Other diagnostics bear this out. *Storyette, essayette* show hiatus vowels that are impossible in morphologically simple or stratum-1 forms. The non-syllabic [r] in *usherette, officerette* similarly suggests stratum 2 (recall Sections 2.4.4 and 2.4.8 above). All items under discussion contain free forms as bases; there are no stress shifts; and the primary stress on the suffix itself is, as we have seen, not a diagnostic of stratum-1 attachment (especially not in nouns, where final primary stress is exceptional). Note, moreover, that *-ette* is not subject to the [± Latinate] constraint in (27) while in (26) it (obviously) is. I conclude tentatively that *-ette* attaches on both strata. (Interestingly, if such a conclusion were to be avoided then the case for either stratum would hardly be simpler than that for both.)

2.4.9   -ise

This suffix is a particularly straightforward case of dual membership: it attaches to a substantial number of bound roots while in other forms displaying indisputable open-juncture (stratum-1) behaviour. Bound roots are exemplified in (28):

(28)   baptise
        fraternise
        evangelise
        exorcise
        acclimatise
        theorise
        utilise

Such examples, as well as the non-syllabicity of the base-final [m] in *rhythmise* and stress shifts in forms such as *canalise*, *immunise*, clearly demonstrate that stratum-1 attachment is possible.

On the other hand, forms such as the following can be regarded as products of stratum 2: those in (29a) display hiatus vowels, impossible in stratum-1 forms; and those in (29b) have syllabic base-final sonorants:

(29)   a. Bermudaise b. winterise
        Judaise   summerise
        Hinduise   tenderise
        Toryise   weatherise

I discuss the retention of sonorant syllabicity further in Section 2.4.12 below, noting here merely that this is not a decisive criterion for the stratum-2 status of forms such as those in (29b).But the argument in favour of stratum 2 is supported by the following facts. The suffix is highly productive, unaffected by the [± Latinate] constraint and subject only to the phonological limitation whereby it does not attach to words with final stress (*bookise*, *springise*, *reviewise*). Goldsmith (1990: 270), argues 'that there is a prohibition in English against adjacent stresses across open juncture when the material on the right is suffixal.' And the open-juncture (stratum-2) status of such forms is consistent with the '*mn*-simplification' likely in (hypothetical) *autumnise* – in contrast with the (stress-shifting and *mn*-retaining) form *solémnise*.

2.4.10   -ism *and* -ist

I discuss these two suffixes together because their behaviour is similar in a number of ways. For example, they share a substantial number of bound roots, as in (30a.b):

(30)   a. fascist   b. fascism
        plagiarist   plagiarism

a. sophist　b. sophism
　 populist　　 populism
　 anarchist　　anarchism
　 sadist　　　 sadism
　 masochist　　masochism

But this correspondence is not exceptionless: either suffix may occur without its counterpart:

(31)　a. linguist　b. albinism
　　　 pianist　　 myopism
　　　 theorist　　amorphism
　　　 physicist　 mongolism

The reason for the existence of pairs such as those in (30) and their failure in (31) is semantic: in (30), the suffixes denote an attitude/doctrine and its practitioner/adherent respectively, while in (31), -*ist* forms simply denote agents and -*ism* forms (medical) conditions.

The semantic patterns in (30) as well as those in (31a) are also found with forms containing free bases. *Flutist*, containing *flute* (and competing with *flautist*), fits with (31a); but overall this pattern appears unproductive, and such meanings are idiosyncratic. A *pianist* might be someone in favour of quietness (in which case there would be a form *pianism*). But the forms in (30), with both -*ist* and *ism*, are extremely productive with free bases:

(32)　a. sexist　　b. sexism
　　　 rightist　　 rightism
　　　 racist　　　 racism
　　　 extremist　　extremism
　　　 escapist　　 escapism
　　　 conformist　 conformism
　　　 Jensenist　　Jensenism
　　　 Marxist　　　Marxism
　　　 Unionist　　 Unionism

And many more. The productivity of such forms, as well as the absence of stress shifts in *capitalist*/-*ism* and also *protestantism* (where **protestantist* is blocked by *protestant* itself unless it denotes a student of reform churches) suggest that this pattern occurs on stratum 2 (as well as on stratum 1: see (30) above). *Catholicism* (with stress shift and [k]~[s] allomorphy) is then stratum 1. I suggest tentatively that the pattern (31a) is entirely stratum 1, on account of its semantic idiosyncrasy, even where it contains free bases (*cartoonist, rapist, humorist*). But little depends on this particular decision.

A further productive pattern, occurring with -*ism* alone, denotes (speech) mannerisms (Goldsmith 1990: 261f.):

(33)   Indianaism   Germanism
        Toryism   Woosterism
        Yankeeism   Bertieism
        Turkism   New-Yorkism

These are usually nonce formations, fully productive in that, as far as I can see, any personal or place name can be so suffixed denoting 'a (speech) habit typical of –'. These cases are interesting in that they, too, straddle both strata. *Anglicism* must be stratum 1; and at least some of those in (33) must be stratum 2 due to their phonotactics: the heterosyllabic (hiatus) sequence [i.ɪ] is not found in morphologically simple forms and cannot therefore arise in stratum-1 formations. *Cátholi*[k]*ism* would be a habit characterising catholics, formed on stratum 2 (Goldsmith 1990: 261).

We conclude, then, that -*ist* and -*ism*, cannot be pinned down to a single stratum except perhaps in their more specialised meanings.

I turn finally to the possible attachment of -*ic* to -*ist* forms. This is relevant to the discussion in that -*ic* must be regarded as a stratum-1-only suffix: it invariably moves the stress to the base-final syllable (*totémic*, *sadistic*), triggers no '*mn*-simplification' (*hymnic*) but sporadically an affix-specific laxing rule (*tone/tonic*). If our previous observations regarding -*ist* are correct then it follows that, under appropriate semantic conditions, any stratum-1 -*ist* should be able to take -*ic*, while stratum-2 -*ist* should be unable to be followed by -*ic*. This clearly seems to be the case. In particular, the forms with bound roots listed in (30a) above can take -*ic* while most of those with free bases cannot: *fascistic* vs. **sexistic* (32a). A problem arises with the forms in (34a) below, which have free bases but can take -*ic* while those in (34b) cannot:

(34)   a. legalistic   b. *cartoonistic
           humanistic   *defeatistic
           socialistic   *alarmistic
           hedonistic   *careeristic

Goldsmith (1990: 268ff.), drawing on Strauss (1983), argues that this distribution is not a matter of stratification at all but that it follows from the prohibition of stress clashes in open juncture, noted in Section 2.4.9 above. Forms such as those in (34b), he states, are ruled out because they contain such a clash, while those in (30a) and (34a) do not contain a clash. (Bound roots have no stress.) He concludes (without argument) that -*ist* is a uniformly stratum-2 suffix, and that the -*istic* cases are accounted for on prosodic grounds alone while constituting '. . . an argument against the Affix Ordering Generalization, and thus against a stratal approach to English morphology and to lexical phonology' (Goldsmith 1990: 271ff.).

I regard Goldsmith's prohibition against stress clash to be roughly correct but his conclusions to be false. First, as we have seen, -*ist* cannot be a stratum-2-only suffix: attachment to bound roots is impossible on stratum 2. Second, attachment to free roots is possible on either stratum. Forms such as those in (32a) can be produced on stratum 2 (and the productivity of the suffix suggests that stratum 2 contains the relevant rule) but they may be stratum-1 formations. Their stress patterns fit either stratum. Third, if prosodic conditioning were alone responsible for the distribution of -*istic* then (*ceteris*, especially semantics, *paribus*) -*istic* forms should be possible whenever their prosodic conditions are met. (35a) below lists some cases where they are probably not possible while being prosodically acceptable; (35b) lists recorded examples (from Lehnert 1971) that violate the prosodic condition in that they have a (weak) stress before -*istic*:

(35)   a. *Unionistic   b. parallelistic
             *Leninistic   Rousseauistic
             *Methodistic   monarchistic
             *Orangeistic   cubistic

I suggest that unpredictable stratal assignment of -*ist* forms containing free roots is the only way of accounting for what seems to be a largely unpredictable distribution of -*istic* forms. The existence of *Zionistic* vs. **Unionistic* alone suggests that this is not a prosodic matter but one of semantics (-*istic* forms often seem to have pejorative connotations), or of chance. The latter form will exist as soon as somebody coins it (as will, perhaps less likely, *cartoonistic*). As long as -*ist* forms containing free bases are in principle free to be formed on either stratum, we may as well conclude that any -*istic* form originates on stratum 1, to account for the stress shift, in line with the assumption that -*ic* is always stratum 1, but perhaps for no other reason. But even on that stratum, -*ic* attachment will only happen if there is a semantic demand for such a form. Looking again at the examples in (31) above, we find that *linguistic* is possible (making no direct semantic reference to *linguist*) while **theoristic* is not. No case against the stratal approach to English morphology and to lexical phonology can be construed on the basis of such facts.

2.4.11   -ous

There are strong arguments in favour of treating *-ous* as a stratum-1 suffix; but, as we shall see, forms exist that suggest that the suffix is also present on stratum 2. The arguments for stratum 1 range over several of the available diagnostics. Bound-root attachment and stress-shifting are exemplified in (36a) and (36b) respectively:

(36)   a. ambitious   b. moméntous
           garrulous   courágeous
           raucous   advantágeous
           sonorous   rebéllious
           querulous   harmónious
           blasphemous   victórious

Stress shifts are especially common among formations on *-eous/-ious*, which also show an especially high incidence of bound roots (*rumbustious, cautious, beauteous, courteous* etc.). I regard *-eous/-ious* as synchronically unpredictable variants of *-ous* on stratum 1.

-ous is common with free bases, as in (37) below. (37a) gives examples of the general pattern; (37b) demonstrates the retention of base-final syllabic sonorants and (37c) the absence of such syllabicity:

(37)   a. riotous   b. murderous   c. disastrous
           adventurous   feverous   monstrous
           poisonous   slaughterous   leprous
           hazardous   blusterous   fibrous

Note that the cases in (37b) contain Germanic bases. Lehnert (1971), moreover, lists doublets involving sonorant (non-)syllabicity, including the following:

(38)   thunderous – thundrous
        wonderous – wondrous
        slumberous – slumbrous

Such variability of sonorant syllabicity strongly suggests once more that the suffix is capable of attachment on both strata, an analysis that is borne out by the productivity of the suffix in its basic sense 'full of –, of the nature, character or appearance of –' (Marchand 1969: 339).

It is of course possible to account for syllabicity variation, such as that within (38) and between (37b) and (37c) in purely phonological terms. All such forms could be produced on stratum 1 if any bases retaining its sonorant syllabicity were analysed as ending in /V/, and any one losing its syllabicity as ending in /r/. Recall from Section 2.4.4 that we have committed ourselves to the 'V'-less representation /r/ only in the case of the agent-forming suffix *-er*, which interestingly figures in none of the *-ous* forms cited in (37 and 38). (This stacking failure is probably accounted for by the semantics of *-ous* forms.) Note, however, that such an underlying /V/ would not be supported by alternations of the *janitor–janitorial* kind (discussed in Section 2.4.4 above): bases such as those in (37b) are Germanic and do not undergo the stress-shifting suffixation that gives rise to such alternations. This solution would therefore be entirely diacritic. The alternative solution offered here, while not being more explanatory in all cases, has the advantage of arising automatically from the morphological and phonological basics of the model. A model that allows suffixes to attach, in principle, freely on both strata will automatically produce such syllabicity differences – as we have seen before in connection with other suffixes – if forms such as those in (37b) are assumed to be stratum-2 products, those in (37c) stratum-1 products, and those in (38) of (speaker-specifically) variable origin. The argument provided by the behaviour of *-ous* is not that this suffix *must* attach on both strata, but that such an analysis is advantageous given that it is generally possible – indeed common – for suffixes to do so. One positive argument in favour of dual membership (here especially of stratum-2 membership) is, of course, the productivity of the suffix.

2.4.12   -ment

This suffix, discussed in detail by Aronoff (1976: 53ff.), represents one of the better-known cases of dual membership. The facts are as follows: *-ment* attaches to bound roots as well as to Latinate verbs; (39a) and (39b) respectively:

(39)   a. ornament   b. employment
            increment   discernment
            regiment   containment
            fragment   derangement
            sentiment   government
            tenement   development
            experiment   judgement

On the grounds of such a distribution, *-ment* might be a stratum-1-only suffix: such suffixes are, as we have seen, able to attach to bound and free bases while stratum-2-only suffixes can only attach to free bases. But, similar to the *-ist(ic)* cases discussed in Section 2.4.10 above, *-ment* fails to attract a further suffix in some but not all instances: -*al*, itself a stratum-1-only suffix as evidenced by its ability to attach to bound roots as well as its uniformly pre-stressing behaviour (*flóral, cantónal, ornaméntal*). Aronoff observes that the instances where -*ment* fails to attract -*al* follow a pattern. -*al* attaches all to -*ment* forms containing bound roots but fails to go with forms containing free bases, with three exceptions:

(40) a. ornamental   b. *employmental
          incremental   *discernmental
          regimental   *containmental
          fragmental   *derangemental
          sentimental   governmental
          tenemental   developmental
          experimental   judgemental

Given that forms such as those in (39a) must be, and forms such as those in (39b) may be stratum 1, we can account for the distribution of -*al* in (40b) by allocating the -*ment* forms taking that suffix to stratum 1, and those that do not to stratum 2. This is not only consistent with the structure of the stratification model but also supported by the fact that two of the three -*mental* forms in (40b) have somewhat idiosyncratic meanings. While -*ment* forms with verb bases (39b) denote abstract nouns, *governmental* can only occur in the sense referring to the (concrete) institution of the government; the theory of government (in syntax or political science) is not a *governmental* theory. And the meaning of *judgemental* contains a subjective element not predicted by the components of the form. Such observations support the decision to derive those two forms on stratum 1, where semantic non-compositionality is commonly (if not, as we have seen, necessarily) found. I return to this suffix in Section 3.1.1 below.

2.4.13 -y

Adjective-forming -*y* is a highly productive suffix attaching to a large number of nominal bases, as exemplified in (41a); it is also highly productive in compounds as exemplified in (41b), from Marchand (1971: 353):

(41) a. sunny   rocky   b. headachy
          bushy   filthy   open-airy
          rosy   dirty   goosefleshy
          hilly   frothy   other-worldy
          beaky   salty
          leaky   scary

While there can be little doubt that such forms originate on stratum 2, the suffix also attaches to bound roots (Strauss 1979; 1982: 28), as well as occasionally giving rise to allomorphic voicing alternations in its bases – (42a) and (42b) respectively:

(42)   a. empty   b. worth – worthy
            dizzy   louse – lousy
            holy   scurf – scurvy (?)
            grisly
            haughty
            paltry
            flimsy

These are clear indicators to suggest that -*y* at least occasionally attaches on stratum 1 (although the morphological complexity is in many such cases doubtful). Further evidence comes once again from variation in the retention of base-final sonorant syllabicity. (43a) lists forms retaining syllabicity, (43b) forms not retaining it and (43c) forms in which it varies speaker-specifically:

(43)   a. summery   b. angry   c. wintery/wintry
            buttery   hungry   crumbly
            leathery   wriggly
            jittery   squiggly
            ambery   purply
            slippery   bubbly
            spidery

A survey through Marchand (1969) and Lehnert (1971) shows immediately that these forms, too, show a preponderance of stratum-2 attachment, in line with (41) above. But the two in (43b) – as well as the disyllabic form *wintry* – must be stratum 1, an argument supported by the fact that the suffix in any case attaches to some bound roots. As regards the cases in (43c) involving [l], there is the possibility that syllabicity loss in this particular phonological context may be a postlexical phenomenon.[14] However, if the observation is correct whereby some speakers have the disyllabic form *bubbly* ('champagne') contrasting with the trisyllabic (transparent) adjective then a purely postlexical account of such variation is impossible.

2.4.14   -less, -ness, -ful *and* -some

These suffixes have been discussed, on various occasions, earlier in this chapter; I repeat the main points for the sake of completeness.

All four suffixes can be regarded as fully productive, attaching on stratum 2. With one exception, all other diagnostics point towards the same conclusion: they have transparent semantics, never give rise to stress shifts, display no allomorphy and trigger no stratum-1 phonological rules. (Syllabicity alternations also do not arise; but these are in any case impossible in cases where the suffix has an initial consonant.)

The one diagnostic that occasionally fails is that which requires of stratum-2 formations free (noun) bases. Here are again some of the examples where this criterion is not met:

(44)   a. gormless   b. vengeful   c. fulsome   d. business
           feckless   wistful   winsome
           hapless   grateful   gruesome
           reckless   bashful
           ruthless

All these examples contain bound roots, a firm diagnostic of stratum-1 forms. Despite the fact that at least some such forms violate the phonotactics of morphologically simple and stratum-1 forms, the model to be developed in the following chapter allows no alternative to treating them as stratum-1 formations (contrary to Siegel (1974), as we have seen). Given that most of the bases in question are not only bound but also one-off ('cranberry') roots, they cannot possibly constitute inputs to fully productive morphological rules. If *gorm-* were an input to a productive rule attaching *-less* then it should also be an input to the equally productive rule attaching *-ful*. Moreover, a morphological rule could not assign a semantic interpretation to such forms unless formatives like *gorm-* were stored with an independent meaning (which clearly cannot be done in a non-arbitrary way).

As I noted above, an alternative analysis might be to treat such forms as morphologically simple, rather than as stratum-1 formations. I shall argue in Section 3.3.3 that this may well be the case, not only in forms such as these but, indeed, in all stratum-1 formations involving single affixes. The model to be developed predicts that speakers will be able to manipulate stratum-1 formations freely without necessarily recognising their morphological complexity. But note that such an analysis still leaves the deviant phonotactics unaccounted for. I discuss this particular phonotactic problem in Section 8.5.4 below. Here I conclude that an analysis whereby these items are stratum-1 formations avoids major exceptions in morphologically productive rules without incurring extra cost in a model which treats dual membership as unmarked. As we have seen in this section, some twenty English suffixes argue rather strongly for such a model.

2.5   Summary

We have seen in this chapter that the morphology of English has a substantial number of suffixes that, under the standard diagnostics of stratal membership, cannot be pinned down to a single stratum. Even those discussed in Section 2.4 are unlikely to constitute the full list of such suffixes. As yet another example, not discussed above, consider the suffix *-ite*, which similar to *-esque* productively (although blocked by *-ian*) attaches to names, denoting 'adherent of –, person from –' (*Ishmaelite, Israelite, Pre-Raphaelite*). Appearing clearly to be a stratum-2 suffix, it occurs in one form that establishes its presence on stratum 1: *Jacobite* must be a stratum-1 form given (as we shall see in Chapter 3) its semantic non-compositionality ('follower of King James II of Scotland') and shortening of its first vowel (compare *Jacob*). In principle, one such deviant form is enough to make a suffix a member of both strata. Previous critics of the (affix-driven) stratification model (Aronoff and Sridhar 1983; Szpyra 1989) have rightly made much of such sporadic counterexamples to the hypothesis that the vast majority of affixes attach on a single stratum. It is unfortunate for this hypothesis that counterexamples inflict severe damage on it – and there have now been enough counterexamples to discredit the hypothesis comprehensively. This clearly means that an attempt to define lexical strata in terms of the affixes that attach on them must be fundamentally misguided; and recall that such an attempt would in any case be as diacritic in nature as is the marking of individual affixes for their stratal association itself. This issue, which is of considerable importance for a model that seeks to maintain a stratified lexicon in the presence of widespread dual membership, will be explored further in Chapter 3. But before we do so, let us briefly isolate some of the patterns that emerge from our observations of dual membership.

First, even suffixes that predominantly attach on stratum 2 are likely occasionally to be found with bound roots. *-(e)ry*, *-er* (and, as we just saw, *-ite*), among others, exemplify this pattern.

Second, suffixes that predominantly attach on stratum 1 may be (in diachronic terms: may become) productive on stratum 2, often with a semantic interpretation that specialises on one particular aspect of the range of meanings available to the suffix in question on stratum 1: recall, for example, *-ise*, *-ism* and others.

Third, such stratum-2 productivity of Latinate suffixes may occasionally (and seems therefore able in principle to) breach the [± Latinate] constraint, as we saw in cases such as *drinkable, coolant, payee, winterise, murderous* and others: these suffixes are confined to Latinate bases on stratum 1 but breach the constraint occasionally on stratum 2 (as in the examples given above). Similarly, Latinate stratum-2-only suffixes such as *-al*$_N$ occasionally take Germanic bases: *withdrawal, upheaval.* This constraint is, then, a mere tendency on stratum 2.

Fourth, a number of suffixes have 'allomorphs', which may be distinct only in orthographic terms (unless occurring before a stress-shifting suffix): *-able/-ible, -ant/-ent, -er/-or* and others. Such 'allomorphy', whose selection is unpredictable in synchronic terms, is invariably confined to stratum 1.

Fifth, forms that may be expected of stratum 2 may instead be produced on stratum 1, as exemplified above with cases of the non-syllabicity of base-final sonorants: *smuggler, wintry, twinkling* and many others. This may be (but does not have to be) connected with semantic non-compositionality.

In general terms, the picture that emerges is this: each stratum is charac-terised by a number of semantic, morphological and phonological proper-ties, which partially overlap. On stratum 1, suffixes may attach to bound or free bases while stratum-2 suffixes have free bases. On stratum 2, base-final syllabic sonorants are preserved in complex forms while on stratum 1 they may or may not be. Stratum-1 suffixation is in principle stress-shifting, but stress shifts do not show up in every stratum-1 form. Nor do stratum-1-specific phonological rules or the application of stratum-1-specific phono-tactic constraints. And so forth. Such partial indeterminacies may well have constituted the diachronic cause for what is something of a synchronic mess. An adequate model of the lexicon will at the very least be able to accommodate such facts in a descriptively adequate synchronic account. I hope to show in the following chapters that such a model, for English, must contain two strata.

3 *Principles of base-driven stratification*

3.1   Further failings of affix-driven stratification

The single major point made in the preceding chapter was that, in the face of the dual stratum-affiliation displayed by a substantial number of English affixes, the hypothesis of affix-driven lexical stratification cannot be sustained. But while the failure of a large number of affixes to serve unambiguously in the definition of lexical strata suffices alone to discredit the affix-driven model, that model has a number of further, apparently unrelated, weaknesses on the morphological side that are worth noting – especially given that the replacement model to be proposed in this chapter must of course seek to avoid all the weaknesses of the current model. I hope to show in this section that those further weaknesses of the affix-driven model all amount to a systematic failure to explain certain stratification-related facts; further below I shall demonstrate that these facts are amenable to a unified explanation that follows automatically from a stratification model whose morphological diagnostics arise from characteristics of the affixation base (along the lines sketched in Section 2.2.2 above) rather than from the diacritic marking of affixes. I shall refer to the replacement model that will be presented in this chapter as one of 'base-driven stratification'.

3.1.1   *Stratification, stacking restrictions and etymology*

One of the outcomes of Chapter 2 has been the recognition that any significance attached to the perceived effects of the AOG (Siegel 1974; Selkirk 1982b) is less straightforward regarding lexical stratification than has been assumed in the literature. Given that affixes in principle can, and in practice are likely to, occur on both strata, the ungrammaticality of forms such as *employmental, *discernmental etc. (Aronoff 1976) can neither follow from nor give rise to the generalisation that -al is 'a stratum-1 suffix', and -ment 'a stratum-2 suffix', in absolute terms (which would be the straightforward interpretation of this kind of ill-formedness in terms of the AOG); all that is really demonstrated by such forms is that *-al* cannot follow *-ment* if (and perhaps only if) the latter is attached to bases such as *employ*, *discern*. There is more than one possible reason for such stacking failures among suffixes in individually observed forms. One possibility is that there might be an etymologically motivated constraint that rules out the attachment of *-al* to *-ment*. This possibility can be eliminated in this case, given that, first, the only such etymological constraint known in English is the one, not here violated, that forbids the attachment of Latinate suffixes to Germanic bases (Section 2.2.1 above). More subtle etymological and donor-language differences, such as may be found among the components of other examples, are of no attested synchronic relevance in English. I return to the [± Latinate] constraint presently. Second, no such constraint can be in operation here since *incremental, ornamental* etc., also involving the attachment of *-al* to *-ment*, are well formed.

Another possible explanation for ruling out **employmental* etc. is that a stacking restriction might be at work here that is not brought about either by a stratal split in the lexical morphology of the language or by an etymological mismatch of the two affixes. Perhaps the most notable such restriction is the one accounting for the exceptionless generalisation whereby regular English inflection cannot occur inside the products of derivational suffixation (**legsless, *eventsful, *brothershood*). This observation had prompted earlier researchers to posit a final lexical stratum containing regular inflection either as the sole set of morphological processes (Halle and Mohanan 1985; Mohanan 1986) or together with compounding (Kiparsky 1982); but, as we already noted in Section 2.1, this stratum has been abandoned in more recent work (Sproat 1985; Booij and Rubach 1987; McMahon 1990) despite the striking robustness of the ordering generalisation involving derivational and inflectional suffixes. Such stacking restrictions not corresponding to stratal splits may not be as general as the one just noted; they may even be idiosyncratic to individual affixes (and therefore unlikely to correspond to stratal splits even in a hypothetical model that proliferates the number of stratal splits beyond Mohanan's (1986) four). Fabb (1988), holding the view that all stacking restrictions among suffixes are idiosyncratic rather than stratification-induced (a view with which I take issue in Section 3.2), gives **sensibleize, *sensuousist* as examples; and indeed the apparent ill-formedness of such cases cannot be explained in terms of any stratification-induced constraint: all four suffixes involved are not only in principle able to occur on stratum 1 (if not exclusively on stratum 1: recall Section 2.4); they also meet the actual conditions for stratum-1 attachment in the two cases at issue.

While the possibility of accounting for the ill-formedness of *employmental* etc. along Fabb's lines can again be eliminated in the face of the well-formedness of *incremental, ornamental*, it is important to note that both this possibility and that of an etymological explanation compete with the AOG and are in principle independent of it. They therefore must be eliminated in every observed case of stacking failure before that case can be invoked as an example of the AOG.

As indeed they have been here: if the failure of *employmental, *discernmental* to occur is at all systematic, rather than being due to an accidental gap, then its explanation must derive from the stratification model itself. While it is reasonably clear that $-al_A$ is a uniformly stress-shifting (and therefore stratum-1) suffix, *-ment* must, in the absence of any alternative explanation, be attached on stratum 2 in *employment, discernment* while it must be attached on stratum 1 in those cases where *-ment* and *-al* can stack (*incremental, ornamental*). A result like this shows once again that the status of the AOG is considerably less significant than has been assumed in the literature. Given the freedom of many affixes to occur on both strata, stratification-induced stacking failure is in principle only informative regarding the specific forms in which it is observed, and not in general terms regarding the affixes involved. But the present case also gives an indication as to where the true source of the generalisation may be found: it lies in the base rather than in the affix. Consider again the examples in (1) below, from Aronoff (1976: 53ff.):

(1) a. ornament   *orna$_V$ ornamental
       increment   *incre$_V$ incremental
       regiment   *regi$_V$ regimental
       fragment   *frag$_V$ fragmental

     b. employment   employ$_V$ *employmental
       discernment   discern$_V$ *discernmental
       containment   contain$_V$ *containmental
       derangement   derange$_V$ *derangemental

In (1), it is only the *-ment* attaching to bound roots that allows further suffixation with *-al*; the *-ment* attaching to words is unavailable for such stacking. And, as we noted in Section 2.2.2, this distribution is in turn consistent with (indeed, independently supportive of) the analysis required by the *-al* distribution whereby *-ment* is stratum 1 in (1a) and stratum 2 in (1b). The fact that *-ment* plus *-al* attaches only to bound roots provides a principled explanation for the otherwise entirely *ad-hoc* analysis of *-ment* being attached on both strata.[1] In more general terms, such a finding indicates that a stratal split, with an attendant AOG, based on individual forms rather than entire affixation rules is *ad hoc* without crucial reference to the nature of the base. This reduces the status of the AOG even further than I argued earlier; in fact, it makes it redundant while at the same time according a crucial role to the morphological category of the base in stratification-based generalisations in English morphology.

Let us return to the [± Latinate] constraint, briefly discussed in Section 2.2.1 above. I noted there that it is ultimately this constraint, and not the AOG, that is responsible for the ungrammaticality of some apparent 'text-book' examples of the AOG, such as **homelessity*. While we came across some breaches of the [± Latinate] constraint on stratum 2 (Section 2.5 above), the constraint is exceptionless in the case of *-ity* (and generally on stratum 1, for those suffixes that are subject to it). The relationship between the AOG and the [± Latinate] constraint needs clarification, especially given that the ill-formedness of **homelessity* seems also to be predicted by what is left, after the discussion in the preceding paragraphs, of the AOG: *-ity* is probably a stratum-1-only suffix and, as I shall show in more detail below, only such instances of *-less* are handled on stratum 1 as attach to bound roots (*gormless, hapless* etc.). *Homeless* is then clearly a stratum-2 formation, unavailable for *-ity* attachment.

The reason why the relationship between the two constraints is not altogether unambiguous is that, at least within the confines of an affix-driven stratification model, they both make very similar stacking predictions in the cases of a substantial number of suffixes. The [± Latinate] constraint allows Germanic suffixes to stack onto Latinate suffixes (*atomicness*) but bars Latinate suffixes from stacking onto Germanic ones (**homelessity*). And on the stratification side, there is a strong tendency for suffixes attached on stratum-1 to be Latinate while the suffixes most typically associated with stratum 2 tend to be Germanic. Exceptions are Germanic stratum-1 *-th*$_N$ (*warmth*) and Latinate stratum-2 *-al*$_N$ (*refusal*), among others. This tendency is of course watered down by the fact that many suffixes, including Germanic ones such as *-less*, have dual membership; nevertheless it is evident that (exceptions to this tendency apart) the stacking effects of the [± Latinate] constraint are largely expressed by lexical stratification. The presence of *-ness* etc. on stratum 1 is, after all, sporadic. It appears, therefore, as if the [± Latinate] constraint, amounting to synchronic recourse to etymological information, is largely, if perhaps not completely, redundant in a stratified lexicon. Given that the independent stipulation of the [± Latinate] constraint presumably makes it necessary for every affix of the language to be diacritically marked with regard to that feature (in the absence of firm native speakers' intuitions about etymology as well as of reliable phonotactic diagnostics of (non-)Latinateness on the part of affixes), this would be a welcome result for English morphology and, specifically, for an affix-driven stratification model. Recall that that model already requires affixes to be diacritically marked for their stratal associations; having to appeal to two overlapping but in principle independent diacritics in every process of affixation would probably over-stretch the ability of the native speaker of English to master the derivational morphology of the language.

Unfortunately, reference to such an etymologically motivated diacritic is by no means redundant under affix-driven stratification. The need to maintain it merely fails to show up fully in such a model, for reasons that will become clear presently. There are two types of instance where the [± Latinate] constraint has to be maintained. First, as was noted above, the dual membership of a number of affixes heavily dilutes the tendency of the [± Latinate] distinction to correlate with strata 1 and 2 respectively. Stratum-1 *-ity*, for example, not only fails to attach to stratum-2 *-less* formations (recall *homelessity*) but also to stratum-1 forms involving that suffix: *gormlessity* is no less ill formed than *homelessity* is, but the AOG fails to account for stacking failures that occur within a single stratum. This is, of course, not an isolated case (consider *wistfullity*, *businessic*, as well as *gratefulize*, noted in Section 2.3 above); it would therefore be clearly misguided in such instances to forego the [± Latinate] constraint, putting these stacking failures down to idiosyncratic restrictions on individual affixes in the sense of Fabb (1988). Given, then, that dual membership among affixes is more widespread than had been assumed by analysts such as Siegel (1974), Selkirk (1982b) and others, the diacritic feature [± Latinate] is in turn rather less redundant in affix stacking than could have been assumed.

Second, imagine a hypothetical (say, historical) variety of English that displays an extremely tidy version of lexical stratification, such that all and only stratum-1 affixes are Latinate, and all and only stratum-2 affixes Germanic. Such a variety of English (in which no affix could have dual membership) does not exist, of course; but (disregarding a possible change in the number of lexical strata) the lexicon may perhaps have looked something like this (if not quite as 'perfect') in late Middle English, when

Latinate formations first entered the language on a large scale, innovating stress-shifting suffixation in English (Halle and Keyser 1971). Even in such a situation the morphology would need crucial recourse to the feature [± Latinate] – its necessity in Present-day English is not just caused by the irregularities left behind by linguistic change, for example by the diachronic widening of the domains of affixes from (originally) one to both strata. The problem is that the [± Latinate] constraint does not merely hold among affixes.

It is not only the case that Latinate affixes fail to stack onto Germanic affixes while Germanic affixes are free to stack onto Latinate ones (*homelessity* vs. *atomicness*); Latinate affixes also fail to attach to Germanic roots while Germanic affixes are free to attach to Latinate roots: *shortity*, *bookic* vs. *solemnly, disdainful* etc. It is in fact this latter generalisation (to whose exceptions I turn below) that has given rise to the [± Latinate] constraint in the literature on English, as well as Dutch and German, morphology (Bloomfield 1933; Saciuk 1969; Aronoff 1976; Booij 1977; Lieber 1981; Plank 1981). The full effect of the [± Latinate] constraint is, then, that Latinate affixes fail to attach to non-Latinate bases regardless of whether or not those are themselves morphologically complex. Clearly, then, this constraint is a generalisation about the morphology of English that is independent from and superordinate to the AOG, of which by now very little is left in any case. Given that *shortity* is impossible, the non-existence of *homelessity* tells us nothing at all about the way affix-driven stratification is organised in English.

As we have seen, then, the [± Latinate] diacritic would be fully redundant in an affix-driven stratification model of English only (1) if the [± Latinate] split corresponded one-to-one to the stratal split, (2) if affixes had no dual membership and (3) if the constraint did not affect roots (that is, if items such as *shortity, *bookic* were well formed). That English fails to meet these condition has long been known at least as regards the latter (see Bloomfield (1933) and others); nevertheless, the literature on stratification in the lexical framework has paid scant attention to the [± Latinate] constraint, and especially to cases like *shortity* etc. It is obvious that an affix-driven stratification model cannot even attempt to handle such cases without invoking the [± Latinate] diacritic, with all the problems that that would involve. The feature would have to be written into all affixation rules, incurring as we have seen massive redundancies against the (equally diacritic) stratal-assignment feature for affixes.

Affix-driven stratification, then, requires independent diacritics for stratal assignment and for [± Latinate]. At the very least, bases as well as affixes have to be marked for [± Latinate], and affixes for their stratal assignment. It is not immediately obvious why a base-driven stratification model should perform any better especially in regard of the [± Latinate] diacritic. At face value, such a model would have to make a similarly diacritic stratal-association distinction between bases that are subject to affixation on stratum 1 (and, subsequently, stratum 2) and bases that are available on stratum 2 only. Assuming that it is normal for affixes to have both strata as their attachment domains, such affixes as attach on a single stratum would have to be diacritically marked. The [± Latinate] diacritic would, apparently, again have a distribution among bases as well as affixes that is in principle independent from the distribution of the stratal diacritic.

But base-driven stratification offers additional arguments that promise a simplification of diacritic marking and therefore argue in favour of such a model. The first such argument is that, as we noted in Section 2.2.2, the distinction between stratum-1 and stratum-2 affixation bases is not arbitrary but at least in part motivated by a morphological-category distinction: stratum-1 bases may be bound roots while stratum-2 bases must be words. No corresponding distinction can be identified, in an affix-driven model, among affixes: there are no affixes that attach to bound roots only. This empirical correlate of stratal base distinctions not only eliminates the need for stratal-association diacritics at least in part; it also has some bearing on the need for the [± Latinate] diacritic in a base-driven model. As was demonstrated in Section 2.3 above, bound roots in English are extremely common in the Latinate section of the derivational morphology: *matern-(-ity/-al)*, *bapt-(-ise/-ism)*, *(re-/con-)-fer* etc.; but in the Germanic section they amount to a mere handful and, with the possible exceptions of *hapless* and *business*, those are non-recurrent 'cranberry morphs': *gormless*, *wistful* etc. The second argument is that (as will be shown below), exceptions to the [± Latinate] constraint such as *withdrawal, winterise* etc. at least cast some doubt on the status of that constraint on stratum 2 beyond a mere tendency – for it is on stratum 2 that such sporadic attachment of Latinate affixes to Germanic bases generally takes place. The third argument is the most important one. As I shall argue in Section 3.2, the outputs of the stratum-1 morphology in any case have to be individually listed for semantic and other reasons (as is shown beyond doubt especially in the *gormless* cases). Such listing, whose format is provided by a base-driven affixation model (and unavailable to its affix-driven competitor), will obviate in its entirety any diacritic marking on the part of stratum-1 affixes.

It would appear, then, that base-driven stratification offers insights into the relationship between the stratal split and the [± Latinate] constraint, as well as simplifying this relationship, that systematically evade the affix-driven model.

3.1.2   Non-productivity and non-compositionality on stratum 1

> First, productivity goes hand in hand with semantic coherence. However, we have no real evidence as to which of these is primary, or even as to whether they are really distinct matters. The second point concerns the relationship between lexical listing and productivity. Here a simple causality emerges. The listing of the output of a WFR [= word formation rule. HG.] in the lexicon leads to a loss in productivity. (Aronoff 1976: 45)

I deal in this section with Aronoff's first point – the stipulated link between the non-productivity of a morphological process and the semantic non-coherence (non-compositionality) of its outputs, showing how both are associated with characteristics of stratum 1. Aronoff's second point – the link between lexical listing and non-productivity – will here be touched upon briefly and receive a fuller discussion in Section 3.2 below.

The reason why the productivity-compositionality link is of relevance to the present discussion is, of course, that both non-productivity and semantic non-compositionality have been observed to be common properties of the stratum-1 morphology; they are, in fact, held to be characteristics of the morphology of that stratum. But in the same way that non-productivity and non-compositionality have been linked only by (albeit clearly well-founded) stipulation they have not, to my knowledge, been linked in formal terms), the association of those two properties with stratum 1 has also only been observed. This association is stipulated as a characteristic of that stratum, but is not in any way integrated with the formal properties of the stratal split, except as the cumulative result of the Blocking Effect (Kiparsky 1982), to which I return presently. The formal mechanisms of the affix-driven stratification model are apparently (if, as I shall argue below, only apparently) able to accommodate such a difference between the two strata. However, they fail to provide a principled explanation for it: in an affix-driven stratification model, the Blocking Effect predicted by stratification (Section 2.2.3 above) does not fully amount to such a principled explanation, as we shall see.

We are faced, then, with a stipulated three-way link between non-productivity, non-compositionality of output and stratum 1. Let us first establish the role of blocking in this link. Blocking, '. . . the non-occurrence of one form due to the simple existence of another' (Aronoff 1976: 43), is a widely observed phenomenon in English morphology, within pairs of competing morphological rules, especially where one rule is located on stratum 1 and the other on stratum 2. In such cases, the attachment of a stratum-1 affix to a given base blocks the alternative attachment of the competing stratum-2 affix to that base. Stratum-2 *longness*, for example, is blocked by the highly unproductive stratum-1 suffix *-th*$_N$ (*length*) as long as the two forms are synonymous.[2] In the inflectional morphology, the attachment of the irregular plural suffix *-en* to the base *ox*, assumed to happen on stratum 1, prevents the formation of the regular plural **oxes* on stratum 2. To account for the blocking failures that are frequently found in similar cases of the inflectional morphology, resulting in doublets such as *cacti/cactuses*, *referenda/referendums*, *spelt/spelled*, we may provisionally follow Kiparsky's (1982: 7) explanation, involving the optionality of the irregular inflection in such cases; but this subject will be addressed again below.

The Blocking Effect is produced by the Elsewhere Condition (henceforth 'EC'; Kiparsky 1982: 8), which enforces disjunctive ordering among competing rules that have different degrees of generality:

(2)   *Elsewhere Condition*
       Rules A, B apply disjunctively to a form ϕ iff:
        (i) SD$_A$ is a proper subset of SD$_B$; and
        (ii) SC$_A$ is distinct from SC$_B$.
       In that case rule A, applying first, blocks rule B.

EC automatically orders the less productive one of two competing morphological rules before the more productive one, either within one stratum or across the stratal divide. Both ordering and blocking are predicted from the productivity differential of the two rules involved, the latter by virtue of the disjunction. Importantly, the definition of blocking is more specific here than the definition given by Aronoff, cited above, was (although Aronoff clearly implied the version given here): the more specific rule is assumed here to block the more general one; blocking cannot happen in the opposite direction. *Length* blocks *longness* under identical semantics; but the ill-formedness of **coolth* cannot be explained through blocking by *coolness*. The reason for this more specific understanding of blocking is conceptually straightforward: in this way, the generality of the empirically more general rule can be given formal status. Formations in *-ness* can then be described as fully productive except where it is blocked, while the opposite possibility would give rise to the counter-intuitive statement that *-th* is fully productive except where it is blocked.

Formations in *-ness* are, moreover, affected by blocking through *-ity*. The rule attaching *-ness* is the more general one of the two in that *-ness* can take Latinate as well as non-Latinate bases while *-ity* only takes Latinate bases. The structural description of the *-ity* rule is therefore a proper subset of that of the *-ness* rule. Given that the structural changes of the two rules are distinct, *-ity* is disjunctively ordered before *-ness*. The fact that *-ity* formations, but not *-ness* formations, are subject to stratum-1 phonological rules (Trisyllabic Shortening: *sincere – sincerity*; stress: *solemn – solemnity* etc.) is consistent with this ordering prediction and in addition puts the two rules on different strata, rather than merely ordering them disjunctively on the same stratum.

Conversely, if there is independent evidence for the ordering of competing rules – if, for example, one of the two rules is for independent reasons sited on stratum 1 and the other on stratum 2 – then EC predicts lesser productivity on the part of the former. In the case just discussed, EC would predict lesser productivity for the *-ity* rule even in the absence of the [± Latinate] constraint. Similarly, given that *-th*$_N$ formations must be sited on stratum 1 for the independent reason that they involve base allomorphy (*long – length, deep – depth*), EC predicts that this rule is less productive than its competitor *-ness*. Again this is correct: although not distributionally distinct from *-ness* in terms of [± Latinate], *-th* is restricted to a mere handful of bases.

Note that the disjunctive order imposed by EC does not need to straddle the stratal divide: two competing processes may be sited on the same stratum, as are, for example *-th* and *-ity*. (But note that these do not fall under the jurisdiction of EC given that the non-Latinate input to the former is not a proper subset of the (Latinate) input to the latter.) In such a case, blocking would be achieved under disjunctive ordering but there would be no independent evidence for such disjunctive ordering, given the absence of stratum-specific differences between the outputs of the two processes. This means that of two competing processes, EC neither forces the unproductive one onto stratum 1 nor the productive one onto stratum 2; both strata can contain both kinds of processes. EC predicts merely that where two competing processes are assigned to different strata for independent reasons, the stratum-1 process will be less productive (Kiparsky 1982: 7), as is exemplified by *-th* vs. *-ness*. Such independent reasons are, as we have seen, typically provided by the [± Latinate] split in the morphology: many of the stratum-1 diagnostics (bound roots, stress shifting etc.) are associated primarily or even solely with Latinate formations. For competing pairs of affixes differing in terms of [± Latinate], then, EC makes the prediction within the two-strata model that the Latinate affix must be disjunctively ordered before the non-Latinate one, blocking the latter, but that this ordering will straddle the stratal split only in the presence of independent reasons for doing so.

There is a further scenario under which a stratum-1 process may be fully productive under EC: that where that process has no unproductive competitor with which it could enter into disjunctive ordering. An example of this may be *-ian*, deriving adjectives from proper nouns denoting persons (*Andersonian, Jonesian* etc.): fully productive and without precisely synonymous competitors, this suffix displays stress-shifting behaviour whenever the base meets the relevant conditions and must hence be assumed to be attached on stratum 1. But this seems to be an isolated case, unusual perhaps for the absence of a (Germanic) competitor suffix. (Hence perhaps the suspension of the [± Latinate] constraint: *-ian* attaches to any proper name despite its Latinate etymology.)[3]

We see, then, that EC makes rather complex predictions regarding the productivity of the morphologies of strata 1 and 2: certainly it is not the case that all and only stratum-2 processes are predicted to be productive. While the morphology of English seems to bear out the predictions made by EC, there is one further point to note – namely that the substantial number of bound roots, mainly Latinate and all handled on stratum 1, plays a major part in making virtually all of the stratum-1 morphology sporadic and, if the term is appropriate in this context, unproductive in nature. Consider the following:

(3) a. spir-   -ant   *-ent
     conson-   -ant   *-ent
     sibil-   -ant   *-ent
     sonor-   -ant   *-ent
     obstru-   *-ant   -ent
   b. matern-   *-ar   -al   -ity   *-ise
     patern-   *-ar   -al   -ity   *-ise
     fratern- *-ar   -al   -ity   -ise
     avuncul- -ar   *-al   *-ity   *-ise

These are just two of the many groups of semantically related bound roots found in English. Under full productivity, the affixation patterns within such a group should be identical; but they are clearly not. In (3a),

obstru- is the only root that, for no synchronic reason, takes *-ent* rather than
-ant. Moreover, and again for no synchronic reason, only *consonant* is
attested to take the further suffix *-al* (*consonantal* vs. *spirantal, *sibilantal
etc.). In (3b), *avuncul-* is odd in that it takes the adjective-forming suffix *-ar*
and not *-al*. Among the ones that take *-al*, two take alternative noun-
forming *-ity* and one takes verb-forming *-ise* – again, there is no discernible
synchronic reason for the gaps. Moreover, *maternity, fraternity* and *fraternize* are semantically non-compositional: the meaning of the complex form
is not derivable by the rule that attaches the suffixes in question. I return to
such 'rules' in the next section, focusing here on the gaps in the affixation
patterns of bound roots. Bound roots have no lexical categories (Selkirk
1982b), as is shown here, for example, by *matern-* and *fratern-*: *-al* attaches
to nouns (*formal, baptismal* etc.) and *-ity* to adjectives (*sincerity, obscenity*).
But both attach to *matern-* and *fratern-*, which must therefore either bear
both lexical categories or none at all. I shall argue below, with Selkirk
(1982b), that bound roots (and indeed roots in general) have no lexical category. But if that is the case then bound roots constitute a formally homogeneous class (whose only internal structure may be semantic, irrelevant as
the examples in (3) show) and, under full productivity, any bound root
should take any affix that can in principle attach to bound roots. *Obstruity
and *fraternant should then exist. Before we pursue the bound-root issue
further (and also address the question of what it means for a word to
'exist'), let us conclude that the productivity of any affix that can attach to
bound roots is severely restricted for the simple reason that such an affix
only attaches to an unpredictable, and possibly very small, subset of the
bound roots of the language. Bound-root attachment is a diagnostic of the
stratum-1 morphology: most stratum-1 affixes, as we have seen, are attested
with bound roots. Seen in this light, then, non-productivity is indeed itself a
diagnostic of stratum 1.

   But it is hard to see how all stratum-1 non-productivity (especially that
associated with bound roots) can be accounted for by the morphological
effects of EC. Given that bound roots figure only in stratum-1 derivations
but never on stratum 2, no bound root constitutes (an element of) a proper
subset of the inputs to a stratum-2 morphological rule (in the sense of EC,
given in (2) above). EC therefore fails to order processes involving bound
roots disjunctively before processes involving words. An objection here
might be that few morphological processes in English (probably none)
involve only bound roots and that the ordering of such a process against a

purely word-based process is imposed, by EC, with reference to the free bases involved in the former process. Under such an argument, *ferocity* is stratum 1 because it is produced by the same process as *solemnity* is; and the latter is ordered before (and blocking) the competing stratum-2 *-ness* form by EC (as well as, of course, showing independent diagnostics of stratum-1 formation). But *ferocity* would automatically comply with the stratal assignment of *solemnity* only if every affix were restricted to a single stratum. And while *-ity* indeed seems to be restricted to stratum 1 for different reasons, the relative ordering of *ferocity* against *-ness* formations, let alone its stratal association, is not determined by EC. The occurrence of bound roots in stratum-1, but not stratum-2, morphological rules must therefore be predicted by a principle other than EC. While we have been treating the occurrence of bound roots within complex forms as diagnostics of the stratum-1 origin of those forms (see also Siegel (1974) and Chapter 2 above), it is worth noting at this point that, once again, a base-driven model will be needed to account for the occurrence of bound roots exclusively on stratum 1.

Let us turn now to semantic non-compositionality, linked through Aronoff's (1976) stipulation with non-productivity and also typically associated with the stratum-1 morphology. We came across some cases of non-compositionality in (3b) above; but the phenomenon is not restricted to formations out of bound roots (although these will be especially relevant to the discussion below). The competition between *-ity* and *-ness* again provides examples in general terms. Both suffixes form abstract nouns out of adjectives (4a) and (4b); but the former produces the occasional count noun which may or may not have an alternative abstract interpretation (4c):

(4)   a. sincerity   b. goodness   c. variety
         solemnity   shyness   calamity
         opacity   keenness   fatality
         intensity   brightness   opportunity

Aronoff (1976: 43) employs the term 'semantic drift' for the characterisation of such forms, a term that has clear diachronic connotations: it makes sense to assume that the examples in (4c) once had compositional semantics, denoting abstract nouns. No such 'semantic drift' happens in the case of (stratum-2) *-ness*; but an affix-driven stratification model provides no explanation for the occurrence of 'drift' (or, incidentally, of non-compositional semantics not caused by diachronic 'drift'), among stratum-1 formations. Nor are these *-ity* formations isolated cases. Semantic behaviour (compositionality vs. its absence) in many cases provides a correlate for differences in morphological and phonological behaviour that give rise to dual stratal membership.

We came across numerous isolated cases of the link between semantic non-compositionality and stratum-1 association in our survey in Chapter 2. Rather than reviewing all those cases again, let us return to Aronoff's (1976: 53ff.) discussion of *-ment*. This suffix, too, has dual membership: stratum-1 *-ment* takes *-al* as a further suffix (*incremental*) while stratum-2 *-ment* does not (**discernment*); the dual membership is supported by the fact that stratum-2 *-ment* attaches to words while stratum-1 *-ment* does not; recall (1) above. Aronoff gives three counterexamples to this generalisation: *governmental, departmental* and *developmental*. In these, *government* denotes an agency (rather than being an abstract noun); and *department* is synchronically unrelated to the verb *depart*. Aronoff rightly concludes that neither of the two can therefore derive from verbs; both must derive from non-verb roots. *Developmental* may be left unexplained here; the model that will be proposed below permits such sporadic stratum-1 assignments of what might be (except, in this case, for their stress-shifting behaviour) stratum-2 formations as well.

It might of course be suggested that an appeal to the semantics of such formations is merely an attempt (which is successful in only two out of the three counterexamples) at rescuing a generalisation that is desirable but flawed. However, such a correlation of the semantics of certain affixations with their stratal associations is by no means an isolated phenomenon. Aronoff himself (1976: 121ff.) has made the same point in his discussion of *-able*, which (like *-ment*) carries either the '+' or the '#' boundary. (In our terms, the suffix occurs on both strata.) Stratum-1 (= '+') *-able* (see (5a) below), identified by stress-shifting behaviour, by attachment to bound roots (in Aronoff's terms, subject to truncation) or by base allomorphy, may display semantic drift. However, stratum-2 (= '#') *-able* formations (5b) may not – they always denote 'able to be X-ed':

(5)   a. cómparable   ('equivalent')
          tolerable   ('moderately good')
          appreciable   ('substantial')
          perceptible   ('large enough to matter')

       b. compárable
          toleratable
          appreciatable
          perceivable
          loveable, likeable, drinkable, . . .

Further still, recall the 'gerunds' that, according to SPE (p. 86) have non-syllabic sonorants unlike their 'participle' counterparts, for example *crack-ling*, where the (trisyllabic) participle has compositional meaning while the gerund, which has a nonsyllabic [l], denotes 'roast pork fat'. I suggested in Section 2.2.5 that the syllabicity difference is due to the non-compositional semantics rather than the lexical category 'noun'; here are a few more examples:

(6)   twinkling   ('short while')
       coupling   ('mechanical device connecting railway carriages')
       kindling   ('chopped wood used to start a fire')
       sprinkling   ('small amount in cooking')
       lightning   ('electric flash')

While all these are nouns diachronically related to verbs (*twinkle, couple, kindle, sprinkle, lighten*), they do not denote activities (as semantically compositional gerunds do) but concrete (count or mass) nouns. If the lexical category 'noun' were responsible for the non-syllabicity of the [l] then, first, all gerunds of comparable phonological composition would have to have nonsyllabic [l], which they do not (*the babbling of brooks, no loitering* etc.); and second, participles would have to have syllabic [l] without exception. Again, this is not the case: *some piddling little problem* contains a participle whose [l] is probably nonsyllabic. And *piddling* here means 'insignificant' rather than being derivable from the verb *piddle*. We see, then, that once again semantic non-compositionality gives rise to behaviour consistent with stratum-1 in other respects. This has nothing at all to do with the gerund-participle distinction invoked by SPE and Mohanan (1986); the semantics alone decides whether a given *-ing* form is produced on stratum 1 or on stratum 2.

The most striking cases of semantic non-compositionality, however, are not those of (diachronic) drift but those where the affixation base has no discernible independent meaning in the first place. Once again, the *gormless* cases may serve to exemplify the problem: as long as the facetious back-formation of the noun *gorm* (as in *person without gorm*) fails to establish itself in the language, the base *gorm* has the 'cranberry' property of failing to recur in other formations, and therefore has no meaning that can be identified in a non-circular way. As we saw earlier, such cases are infrequent in the Germanic section of the English vocabulary (but notably, most of the few Germanic bound roots are such 'cranberry morphs'). But they abound in the Latinate vocabulary, with just about every attested affix that occurs on stratum 1:

(7)   affable   levity
        mercenary   frustrate
        tangible   regiment
        fallacy   modify
        frugal   vestry
        organise   picaresque
        urban   celibate
        nuisance   imperative
        tenant

To name but a few. Of course, one might take issue with the alleged 'cranberry' status of some of these bases either by denying their morphological complexity altogether or by invoking a link between, for example, *tenant* and *tenable*, or between *organise* and the free form *organ*. But such links would clearly be synchronically inactive for most speakers, requiring as they do (in the absence of a semantic link) a degree of etymological knowledge that is by no means a prerequisite for the use of such vocabulary.

In any case, the question of whether a Latinate bound root is recurrent or not is of little significance concerning the semantic interpretation of Latinate complex forms. Semantic drift makes a compositional interpretation impossible in many cases (*fraternise, opportunity*); in other cases (especially with prefixes), bound roots tend to make no contribution to the meaning even where they are recurrent:

(8)   receive   reduce
        deceive   produce
        conceive   conduce
        perceive   adduce

Here we have roots that are 'true morphemes with no meaning' (Aronoff 1976: 102). Given that the prefixes make no reliable semantic contribution to the complex form either, there is no way a semantic interpretation of such words can even make reference to the fact that they are morphologically complex, let alone derive anything from it.

We see, then, that semantic non-compositionality is rife among stratum-1 formations due to drift, cranberry morphs or the more general impossibility of deriving a form's meaning from its parts even where those may be perfectly recurrent. Such non-compositional meanings have to be listed, instead of being derived by the rules that are responsible for the formal side of the morphological structure. The lack of productivity, discussed in the first half of this section, points in the same direction: if lack of productivity is the non-occurrence of forms that are predicted by the structural description of a given morphological rule, then most stratum-1 morphological rules are non-productive (especially if, as we saw earlier, bound roots are taken into account). In order to account for the set of outputs of a less-than-fully productive process listing is again necessary, although the precise form of such listing has yet to be established. This is the link between non-productivity and non-compositionality suggested by Aronoff and quoted at the beginning of this section. I shall in the next section explore this idea further and show, moreover, that the standard format of affixation rules is not viable on stratum 1 for reasons that are in part independent from and in part related to the foregoing argument.

3.1.3 The format of affixation processes

It is at least consistent with an affix-driven approach to lexical stratification that the lexicon should contain a repository of basic lexical items to which affixes are attached by rule, and that affixation rules should themselves be affix-driven in the sense that a given affix should attach to a range of bases whose properties are amenable to generalisation (expressed in a subcategorisation frame). Hence it has been assumed that all affixation rules have the form (9) below, regardless of their stratal association and of their productivity (Lieber 1981; Kiparsky 1982).

(9)   Insert A in the environment $[Y \_\_\_ Z]_L$

Here, L is the lexical category specification of the base, and '$[Y \_\_\_ Z]$' is short for any further details of the subcategorisation frame that restrict the attachment of the affix A. Such details may include features such as [± transitive], which is required, for example, in the case of the 'patient-forming' suffix *-ee*, which attaches to transitive verbs (*employee*). Moreover, they will include the diacritic feature [± Latinate] where appropriate, separating *abusive*, *preventive* from **findive*, **lovive* (Lieber 1981: 35f.), as well as the further diacritic feature specifying the stratal association of the affix. Recall from Section 3.1.1 that these two diacritics are in principle independent of each other and that in an affix-driven model every subcategorisation frame has to be specified for both (again, at least in principle). Such prolific diacritic marking alone casts some doubt on the appropriacy of (9) as the general affixation format, as we observed in Section 3.1.1; but there are further problems, all connected with the model's failure to deal in a principled fashion with incomplete productivity and semantic non-compositionality.

First, it lies in the very nature of non-productivity (or incomplete productivity) that productivity-related restrictions on a given affix cannot be stated in a generaliseable form. If by 'non-productivity' we mean the failure of a form to occur although its occurrence is predicted by the relevant rule, then any restriction that can be encoded in the rule's subcategorisation frame by means of a generalisation is not a restriction on productivity. If, for example, the subcategorisation frame for -al_N is fully specified as 'a usually Latinate, disyllabic end-stressed prefixed transitive verb base', and if blocking through -*ment* and other suffixes is taken into account, then -al_N is quite possibly fully productive despite the fact that its actual incidence is comparatively small: *refusal, dismissal* etc. For the expression of genuine non-productivity, a format like (9) needs recourse to further diacritic marking; and such diacritics have to be allocated to bases as well as to the subcategorisation frame of the affix in question. There are two ways of doing this. In the case of -th_N, for example, either all (adjectival) bases not available for -*th* must carry the diacritic [− -*th*], or all bases that are candidates for -*th* must be marked [+ -*th*]. For reasons of both economy and intuition, the latter alternative is preferable; but note that such diacritic marking of all candidates for -*th* is equivalent to the simple listing of such candidates. Given this, the restriction whereby all bases carrying [+ -*th*] must be adjectives may as well be expressed in terms of a simple redundancy relationship – I return to this issue below: such listing of bases, necessitated by the non-productivity of a morphological process, obviates the subcategorisation frame in the statement of that process. As we saw in Section 3.1.1, non-productivity is typically associated with the stratum-1 morphology. A further argument in favour of individual listing is, in the case of -*th*, the extensive base allomorphy (*hale – health, wide – width, long – length* etc.), whose regularity, in terms of phonological rules such as Pre-Cluster-Shortening and Vowel Shift, is at best partial.[4]

Second, a general affixation format such as (9) fails to account for the semantics of the outputs of affixation rules. If Lieber's (1981: 64ff.) proposal is adopted whereby lexical semantics is as a matter of principle independent of morphology, then this failure is both comprehensive and programmatic; but this solution is inappropriate in the cases of those stratum-2 derivations whose outputs are semantically compositional without exception. There is no reason for not including the semantics of the output in the statement of the rule that attaches -*less* to nominal bases on stratum 2. But if the view is taken that morphological rules do handle the semantics (Aronoff 1976; Kiparsky 1982), then non-compositional outputs will again have to be individually listed even when the non-semantic mechanics of the rule are regular. This listing again obviates the rule itself; and again it will be typically associated with the stratum-1 morphology, as we saw in Section 3.2. This observation is only mildly at variance with those made by Kiparsky, who states:

> Derivational processes at later levels are semantically more uniform than those at earlier levels, where various specialized uses are prone to develop. . . . The greater semantic coherence of the general word-formation processes which are ordered at later levels is a consequence of their productivity (as suggested by Aronoff (1976, 45)). The fact that they do not require word-by-word specification but apply across the board to a whole category (subject to blocking as discussed) means that there is no foothold for imposing word-specific semantic conditions on them either. In other words, imposing an additional word-particular semantic restriction adds a relatively small increment of complexity to an early (level 1) process because the words it applies to must be listed anyway, but it adds a large increment of complexity to a late process because its context can otherwise be given categorially. (Kiparsky 1982: 8)

What is missing in Kiparsky's argument is the final step, namely the recognition that in the face of both non-productivity and semantic non-compositionality on stratum 1, affixation rules of the format (9) have no motivation whatever on that stratum. If stratum-1 affixes can be systematically restricted by subcategorisation frames at all, then those have the status of well-formedness conditions rather than rules. Such subcategorisation frames may contain semantic information (such as 'personal name' in the case of *-ian*: *Andersonian* etc.); but, as will become clear presently, they certainly cannot have the form given in (9) above.

As we saw in Section 3.1.2, attachment to bound roots is empirically connected with the non-productivity of affixation processes as well as with the typical non-compositionality of their outputs. We have already confirmed the empirical link of the latter two properties of stratum 1 with the need for listing, following Aronoff (1976); but we have not established that the alternative to listing, namely rules of the format (9), is not only undesirable but downright impossible on stratum 1. The following, third, point is decisive in this sense: stratum-1 affixes are typically able to attach to bound roots, and no bound roots figure on stratum 2. Bound roots, as we noted before, have no lexical category specification (Selkirk 1982b) – recall, for example, that both *-ity* and *-al* attach to *matern-* although at face value the former attaches to adjectival and the latter to nominal bases (as in *sincerity* and *consonantal* respectively). I shall discuss the properties of roots at length in

Section 3.2.1 below and repeat here merely the fairly moderate claim that the stratum-1 morphology is characterised by its ability to operate on bases that bear no lexical categories, that is, by its ability to evade the crucial ingredient of any subcategorisation frame, namely its lexical-category specification, given as 'L' in (9). If this claim is accepted, and if the format (9) is to be maintained, then it follows at the very least that the subcategorisation frames of probably all stratum-1 affixation rules have to be amended by lists of bound roots to account for forms such as *matern + ity*, *matern + al, deterg + ent, magn + ify* and many more. Given that, in the absence of lexical-category specifications, bound roots constitute a homogeneous morphological class within which no formal distinctions are possible, any such listed subset of bound roots is formally random and incapable of generalisation.

In Section 3.2.1 below, the claim whereby bound roots bear no lexical category specifications will be generalised into one whereby *no* members of the morphological category Root, bound or free, bear such specifications. This will mean that a putative stratum-1 affixation rule of the format in (9) cannot contain the lexical-category specification 'L' in its subcategorisation frame. Evidently, a subcategorisation frame without 'L' is not viable; the affixation format (9) is therefore inapplicable on stratum 1. Affixation on stratum 1 is not governed by 'rules' as we know them.

Taking bound roots into account, and anticipating further arguments, we have to conclude that any attempt at generalising – along the lines of (9) – the range of bases to which a given stratum-1 affix attaches is doomed in that it fails to capture the facts. We see, then, that on stratum 1 the case for listing can be made on various counts while at the same time the possibility of affixation rules, of the form (9) above, has to be rejected on formal grounds.

3.2   Base-driven affixation on stratum 1

3.2.1   *The nature of the category 'Root'*

As I noted earlier (Sections 2.1 and 2.2.2), as early as in Siegel's (1974) precursor to affix-driven lexical stratification, the observation was made that Class-1 affixes attach to both 'stems' and words while Class-2 affixes attach to words only, where 'stems' (in our terminology, 'bound roots') are defined as bound non-affixes that bear no lexical-category specifications. While we noted also at that point that, in the face of diacritic marking of affixes in regard of their stratal affiliation, this categorial distinction among affixation bases is redundant in an affix-driven model, the ability of stratum-1 affixes to attach to bound roots has been a recurrent theme in the preceding sections, and one that has become increasingly important while at the same time the affix-driven stratification model has been progressively discredited. There is a redundancy relationship between the diacritic stratal affiliation of affixes and the categorial characterisation of bases; but it works the other way around: the morphological category of the base plays the primary part in lexical stratification; any diacritic marking of affixes for exclusive occurrence on a specific stratum is a secondary feature of English morphology. As we saw in Chapter 2, it is quite normal for English affixes not to bear such diacritics.

This view, which has evolved in the preceding chapters and which will constitute the central assumption behind the model proposed here, was first adopted by Selkirk (1982b), who argued that the distinction between strata 1 and 2 is the consequence of a category distinction among affixation bases. In particular, her claims are . . .

> (i) that there are two (recursive) category levels or types that play a role in English word structure – Word, along with a 'lower' category type, Root – and (ii) that Class I affixes attach to . . . categories of type Root (and with them form roots), while Class II affixes attach to categories of type Word (and with them form words). (Selkirk 1982b: 77f.)

Under this model, the inputs to all stratum-1 affixation are members of the category Root. Given that multiple stratum-1 affixation is possible (e.g. *nationality*), the outputs of stratum-1 affixation must again be members of the category Root. Root must therefore be a recursive category: unlike in the traditional understanding of the term (see, for example, Matthews 1991: 64ff.; Katamba 1992: 45), roots may be morphologically complex as long as such complexity is the result of the stratum-1 morphology. Similarly (and uncontentiously), both the inputs and the outputs of the stratum-2 morphology are members of the recursive category Word.

Two issues arise from this basic model. First, given that the two strata are conjunctively ordered in that a given form can undergo stratum-1 and stratum-2 affixation successively, there must be a point in the derivation at which roots are converted into words in order to become candidates for stratum-2 affixation (or in any case in order to be able to exit from the lexicon as free forms, in the sense of the syntax). As we shall see, this root-to-word conversion is not only unavoidable in this model; it also plays an important role in the phonology and elsewhere (indeed, Elsewhere). I shall return to it.

Second, while it is uncontroversial that the category Word should be recursive, the proposed recursiveness of Root is less obvious – if only because it runs counter to the traditional understanding of the term. It is clear that the inputs as well as the outputs of stratum-2 processes are words: *home*, *homeless* and *homelessness* are free forms, available for exit from the lexicon and entry into the syntax. But it is less clear why *sensation*, *sensational* and *sensationality* (all outputs of the stratum-1 morphology) should be roots rather than words. That this must be so is an effect of the architecture of stratum 1, rather than following from the characteristics of these particular forms. And it is an interesting effect in that it puts the categories Root and Word on comparable distributional and derivational footings.

It is clearly (and hardly controversially: see again Matthews 1991; Katamba 1992) a characteristic of the category Root that its members do not have to be free forms; indeed, the 'bound root' is usually taken to be the prototypical manifestation of that morphological category in the classroom situation. However, if that were the only possible manifestation of Root then the fact that virtually all stratum-1 affixation processes involve bound and free forms interchangeably could not be accounted for. Conversely, if the 'free root' were taken to be the prototype and bound roots such as *matern-* treated as exceptions of some sort, then of course the principled distinction between the categories Root and Word would vanish, and with it the explanation of the perhaps strongest morphological diagnostic of stratal association: that stratum-1 affixes can attach to bound roots. The view taken here (as in Selkirk 1982b: 98) is that it is simply immaterial for roots whether they are bound or free, in surface terms. But that leaves us still unable to draw a principled distinction between Root and Word in terms of their local characteristics.

The crucial difference between roots and words is, I suggest, that the former bear no lexical category specifications. For bound roots this is again uncontroversial – at least it ought to be. As we saw earlier, the assignment of the category label 'noun' to the bound root *gorm-* is motivated only by the fact that *-less* attaches to it. Given that **gorm* never figures as a noun elsewhere in the grammar, such an argument is circular. The same must be said for *moll-* in *mollify*, which Selkirk (1982b: 98f.) calls an 'adjective root'. Recall here my earlier observation whereby *matern-* must be an adjectival as well as nominal root (*maternity*, *maternal* respectively) if bound roots are to be bearers of lexical categories.

The extension of this analysis to free roots (as found in *accidental*, *divinity* etc.) is more problematical. On the one hand, given the freedom of stratum-1 affixes to attach to bound roots, it is clearly not essential for the bases of -*al*$_A$, -*ity* etc. to be nouns, adjectives or whatever – recall Section 3.1.3. On the other hand, a mechanism has to be found which associates such forms with lexical categories not only for the purposes of the syntax but also for the expression of generalisations on the very next stratum of the lexicon, where for example regular plural suffixes are attached to nouns (only) – e.g. *accidents* – and adverb-forming -*ly* to adjectives (only): *divinely*. I shall argue below that the assignment of lexical categories to roots is part of the root-to-word conversion, mentioned above.

The next extension of the analysis is the inclusion of stratum-1 complex forms in the definition of Root as a morphological category that is not specified for syntactic categories. Selkirk's (1982) arguments in favour of the recursiveness of this category can be regarded as conclusive: if Word is a recursive category, uncontroversially on the strength of the possibility of multiple affixation on stratum 2 (recall *home, homeless, homelessness*), then Root should also be a recursive category given that multiple affixation is also possible on stratum 1: *sensation, sensational, sensationality* etc. Such an inclusion of (stratum-1) complex items in the definition of Root is at variance with the standard definition of that category as '. . . that part of a form of a word which remains when all derivational and inflectional affixes have been removed . . .' (Lyons 1970a: 325); but in the present framework the conclusion that Root is a recursive category is inescapable: stratum-1 complex forms are distributionally nondistinct from neither simplex forms nor, notably, from bound roots. -*ity*, to take just one example, attaches to complex forms (*sensationality*), free roots (*obesity*) and bound roots alike (*maternity*). The fact that -*ity* formations, among others, are not subject to further stratum-1 suffixation (see Fabb 1988) does not form part of the systematic characteristics of the stratum-1 morphology as a whole (although it needs to be accounted for, as it will be below).

Our understanding of the category Root as recursive on stratum 1 and unspecified for lexical categories follows, then, from the recognition that in suffixation processes all members of that category – complex or simple – are freely interchangeable with a subclass of that category, namely that of the bound roots, and that, therefore, the essential properties of that subclass must be shared by all members of the category. Note that we have already rejected the only alternative way of expressing this natural-class behaviour of stratum-1 bases: that of treating all roots – bound or free – as fully specified for lexical categories. Rather than arbitrarily calling *moll-* an adjective root and *gorm-* a noun root, we adopt the opposite analysis and treat *sensation, sensational* and, indeed, *sensationality* as roots that crucially bear no lexical categories. Apart from avoiding the unwarranted lexical-category labelling of bound roots, this analysis also furnishes us with a clear formal distinction between (English) roots and words: roots are not members of lexical categories, but words are. (The additional difference whereby words are of necessity free forms does not necessarily follow from the fact that words have lexical categories. As we shall see in Section 3.3 below, German recognises the intermediate category Stem: bound forms specified for lexical categories.)

This leaves the question of how to account for the fact that *sensation* is a noun of English, and that (this) *-al* is an adjective-forming and *-ity* a noun-forming suffix. More generally, if we assume (with Selkirk 1982b) that Root and Word are linked by a one-way derivational path (corresponding to strata 1 and 2 respectively), such that all morphologically simple words arise derivationally out of roots, then even items like *lamp, laugh, nice* etc. must (rather counter-intuitively) enter into the lexical derivation (and, hence, be stored) without lexical-category specification. As I indicated above, such forms acquire lexical-category membership in the process of becoming words, i.e. in the transition from stratum 1 to stratum 2. I turn now to this process of transition, hoping to restore the intuitive appeal of the analysis.

3.2.2   Root-to-word

The picture of the morphology of lexical stratification that has emerged so far has been one where the inputs and outputs of stratum-1 morphological processes must be roots, and those of stratum-2 processes must be words. While this is certainly the case for 'genuine' morphological operations – affixations and, as we shall see, compounding – it is also clear that there must be one class of morphological operation whose inputs are roots and whose outputs are words. In the absence of such a process, no lexical item could transit from stratum 1 to stratum 2. Let that process have the following form:

(10)   *Root-to-Word Conversion*
$$[\ ]_r \rightarrow [[\ ]_r]_L \qquad (L = N, V, A)$$

Rule (10) is short for three separate rules, converting roots into words of the categories Noun, Verb and Adjective respectively. It is not predictable for a given root whether or not it is subject to (10): bound roots, such as *gorm-* and *matern-*, are not. Nor is the specific subrule that a given root will undergo (if any) predictable from other (e.g. morphological or phonological) properties of that root, except by its semantics.[5] In principle, each root will therefore be diacritically marked as to its behaviour in regard of (10): whether it can become a word in the course of the derivation and, if so, what category label it will bear.[6] If the inputs to the lexical derivation are of the form in which they are stored in the mental lexicon, then the morphology within the lexical derivation is the appropriate site for such category assignment.

There may be objections to the proposed diacritic marking of roots as to whether they acquire noun, verb or adjective status in the derivation, and it may be suggested that they might as well carry such lexical-category labels in the first place. But this, apparently simpler, alternative is unavailable for several reasons connected with the architecture of the model, as we have seen. First, roots cannot be members of lexical categories. Second, they must undergo something like rule (10) in order to become candidates for the stratum-2 morphology. And third, while the synchronic distinction in the behaviour of what are traditionally called free and bound roots is fully expressed by candidacy (or not) for rule (10), English has no way of distinguishing between free and bound roots in structural (e.g. phonotactic) terms: the fact that *modern* is free and *matern-* bound is entirely arbitrary, subject only to diacritic marking. I return to this matter briefly in Section 4.2.1. Chapter 4 will moreover demonstrate a further, entirely independent, motivation for having (10) in the synchronic derivation.

Essentially, the same analysis applies to derivational suffixes. Every suffix is assumed to be diacritically marked for the subrule of (10) that a construction formed with that suffix will undergo (e.g. *-ity* formations become nouns through (10)); this diacritic becomes the property of the complex form through percolation from its head (the suffix). And again we may assume that such diacritic marking may be driven by the semantic entry for the suffix in question, although here the possibility of semantic non-compositionality among affixed forms has to be taken into account. It would appear, however, that such semantic non-compositionality does not affect the lexical category of the item: *-ity* formations may deviate from the 'abstract noun' prototype (as in *opportunity*), but their non-compositionality never alters the fact that they figure as nouns in the grammar. (I return to this matter, and in general to an analysis whereby the outputs of the stratum-1 morphology are 'listed', in Section 3.2.3.)

I noted before that, with the exception of rule (10), the inputs and outputs of all stratum-1 rules are roots and the inputs and outputs of all stratum-2 rules are words. Rule (10) alone has roots as inputs and words as outputs; therefore the question of the stratal siting of that rule arises. It might be located on stratum 2. Its root-input specification would then automatically make it the first morphological rule that is applicable on that stratum, given that in that case all forms entering stratum 2 would have root status. (This is the position held, broadly, by Borowsky (1993).) It might, alternatively, be located on stratum 1; and all its outputs would automatically be barred from further stratum-1 morphological operations by virtue of being words.

This decision appears somewhat arbitrary at this point, but one reason for locating (10) on stratum 1 is the essentially stratum-1 nature of the rule's applicability: there is, as we saw earlier, no way of predicting on formal grounds that *divine* is subject to this rule while *matern-* is not. Such unpredictability is consistent with the nature of stratum 1 but not with that of stratum 2. Further reasons for siting rule (10) on stratum 1 will materialise once the further morphological and phonological implications of that rule have been clarified. The assumption (to be elaborated in Section 3.2.3 below) is, then, that all items whose categorial status is that of Root are listed together with the morphological processes they undergo on stratum 1: rule (10) is among those processes. All products of the stratum-1 morphology are candidates for rule (10) unless they are diacritically marked as bound roots; all outputs of (10) are ineligible for further stratum-1 derivation and are automatically propelled into stratum 2. Given that, as all analysts agree, stratum 1 has cyclic rule application (Kiparsky 1982; Halle and Mohanan 1985; Mohanan 1986; Booij and Rubach 1987), the integration of (10) into the morphology of that stratum may look like this:

(11)   *Cycle 1*   *Cycle 2*

$$
[\text{matern}]_r \left\{ \begin{array}{l}
\rightarrow [[\text{matern}]_r\, \text{al}]_r \left\{ \begin{array}{l} \rightarrow \dots (?) \\ \rightarrow [[[\text{matern}]_r\, \text{al}]_r\,]_A \rightarrow (\textit{to stratum 2}) \end{array} \right. \\[2em]
\rightarrow [[\text{matern}]_r\, \text{ity}]_r \left\{ \begin{array}{l} \rightarrow \dots (?) \\ \rightarrow [[[\text{matern}]_r\, \text{ity}]_r\,]_N \rightarrow (\textit{to stratum 2}) \end{array} \right. \\[2em]
\rightarrow {}^*[[\text{matern}]_r\,]_L\ (\text{n/a})
\end{array} \right.
$$

Example (11) above gives, as an example, the derivation of forms involving the bound root *matern-*. On the first cycle, the complex roots *maternal* and *maternity* are formed; given that *matern-* is not marked for undergoing rule (10), the conversion of that root into a lexical-category-bearing word is impossible. On the second cycle, *maternal* and *maternity* are subject to rule (10), becoming adjective and noun respectively, and exit from the stratum. While no further suffixes appear to be applicable in this case, further derivation is possible in principle, without affecting the argument.[7]

3.2.3   The format of root affixation

We saw in Section 3.1.3 that the affixation format given in (9) above ('Insert A in the environment $[Y \_\_\_ Z]_L$') is inappropriate for the statement of stratum-1 affixation on a number of counts. The main points were these. First, productivity restrictions, which are extremely common on stratum 1, are by their very nature not amenable to the type of generalisation expressed in a subcategorisation frame. Second, non-compositional semantics, again a common feature of stratum-1 formations, necessitates the listing of outputs in many cases, which makes morphological derivation by means of rules of the form (9) redundant to a significant degree. And third, the fact that bound roots regularly figure in stratum-1 affixation led us in Section 3.2.1 to the generalisation that no stratum-1 affixation base (here referred to as the recursive category Root) carries a lexical-category specification. This means that stratum-1 affixation rules formulated along the lines of (9) would have to lack a crucial ingredient of their subcategorisation frames, namely 'L'. Any attempt at maintaining (9) and at accommodating such facts (or at avoiding the conclusions we have drawn from them) – for example, the use of diacritics to handle lack of productivity, the partial listing of semantic irregularities or the additional listing of bound roots with the subcategorisation frame for a given affix – leaves a central question unanswered: why is it that stratum 1 displays this syndrome of properties while stratum 2 so conspicuously lacks it?

I have been arguing that lexical strata are defined by the categories of their affixation bases – stratum 1 is root-based, stratum 2 word-based – and not by the categories of their affixes: affix-driven stratification, which in any case relies entirely on the diacritic marking of affixes with regard to their stratal assignment, is not viable given that a substantial number of affixes fail to display the unambiguous stratal association that such a model crucially depends on. Lexical stratification, then, is base-driven rather than affix-driven. I propose now that base-drivenness is the defining characteristic not only of stratification as such but also of the morphology of at least one of the strata, namely stratum 1.

Consider first the alternative. In the light of the failure of (9) on stratum 1, we might decide to replace the subcategorisation frame by a list of roots available to a given affix. This would still necessitate a list of outputs (to account for non-compositional semantics), disguising the fact that adding the affix A to one root and adding it to another do not necessarily have generaliseable results. If semantic generalisations are to be had at all in the cases of non-compositional outputs then these typically rest with bases rather than affixes: *opportunity* has more to do with *opportune* than it does with *-ity* (which means *abstract* noun, under compositional semantics). Similarly, the noun *kindling* is semantically related to the verb *kindle* but it does not share the semantics usually associated with gerunds. Further arguments against affix-driven affixation to listed bases will emerge later in this section.

I propose that all lexical items (morphologically simple roots as well as affixes) are listed in the lexicon, and that moreover each such lexical entry, in the case of roots similar to a dictionary entry, contains a list of all stratum-1 morphological operations that the particular item is potentially subject to. This list – which is, as we shall see, the linguist's and not necessarily the speaker's – contains all available affixes as well as, where appropriate, rule (10) with the lexical category that it specifies for the form in question. Some examples are given in (12) below:

(12)   a.

$$\text{matern} \begin{cases} \rightarrow \text{-al} \\ \rightarrow \text{-ity} \end{cases}$$

moll $\rightarrow$ -ify

gorm $\rightarrow$ -less

b.

$$\text{serene} \begin{cases} \rightarrow \text{-ity} \\ \rightarrow \text{-ade} \\ \rightarrow \text{Adj (10)} \end{cases}$$

$$\text{nation} \begin{cases} \rightarrow \text{-al} \\ \rightarrow \text{N(10)} \end{cases}$$

An entry such as that for *nation* (12b) is short for the following. *Nation* is a root of the language, formally represented as [*nation*]. The operations available are, first, 'Attach *al* to [*nation*]', where 'attach' is taken to mean the placement of a pair of brackets round the concatenated form: [[*nation*]*al*]], and second, 'Input [*nation*] to rule (10) and assign the lexical category 'Noun'. The semantics of both the simple root and the affixed form are assumed to be listed with the entry except where the affixed form has compositional semantics. In that case the semantics of the root and that of the affix (on whose entry see below) are amalgamated by default.

Example (12a) contains a sample of bound roots, all of which have been discussed before. While the analysis of *matern-*, attracting *-al* and *-ity*, is unproblematic, *moll-* and *gorm-*, taking only one suffix in each case, raise the question of whether such items are to be regarded as morphologically complex at all. I return to this question below.

The forms in (12b) are free roots, identified as such by their ability to undergo rule (10). But both analyses illustrate a problem, as well as two different ways of dealing with it. First, is *serenade* synchronically related to *serene/serenity*, or is the analysis in (12b), where they are treated as related, unrealistic in synchronic terms? Similarly *organ* and *organize*, *tenable* and *tenant* (in (7) above) are hardly to be regarded as synchronically related. The possibility of non-compositional semantics opens up in principle the possibility of synchronic relatedness in the absence of strong semantic support. Second, is *nation* morphologically simple, or should it have been analysed as the bound root *-nate-* suffixed by *-ion*? Note that *-nate-* also takes *-ive*, as well as the prefix *in-*. The approach to the stratum-1 morphology whereby morphologically simple and complex forms are listed, along the lines of (12), does not require us to construe an answer to such a question that holds true for all speakers alike. While it is difficult to imagine how, under a rule-driven approach, different speakers' morphological analyses can diverge in any significant way, the approach involving listing does not imply that all speakers share the same list. In the cases at hand, a speaker may well store *serenade* (as well as *gormless* and *mollify*) as separate, unanalysed roots; alternatively, he or she may derive *nation* from *-nate-*, where the latter would then be listed for *-ion*, *-ive* as well as *in-*.[8] The suffix *-ion* is in any case listed as potentially subject to *-al* attachment (*sensational*, *implicational*, *fractional*). Note that such differences in the depth of the analysis of individual forms make no difference to the speaker's potential command of this section of the vocabulary: not only morphologists and etymologists master the vocabulary of English that is generated on stratum 1.

'The stratum-1 lexicon of English' is, then, the maximal expansion of a list along the lines of (12), representing the sum-total of the maximally structured vocabularies of all speakers. It is unlikely that a single speaker exists who is in command of all of it, just as probably no speaker has full command of all items listed in the Oxford English Dictionary. A speaker may add -*ize* to his or her entry of *matern*-; and if *maternize* is unknown to all other speakers of the language (as it probably is), then such an innovation may give rise to linguistic change although -*ize* itself is already present in the list.

I turn now to the listing of suffixes, whose format I assume to be that in (13):

$$
\begin{array}{l}
(13) \quad \text{-al} \left\{ \begin{array}{l} \rightarrow \text{-ize} \\ \rightarrow \text{-ity} \\ \rightarrow \text{Adj (rule (10))} \end{array} \right. \\[2em]
\text{-ade} \rightarrow \text{N (rule (10))} \\[1em]
\text{-ity} \rightarrow \text{N (rule (10))} \\[1em]
\text{-ify} \left\{ \begin{array}{l} \rightarrow \text{-ation (= -ification)} \\ \rightarrow \text{V (rule (10))} \end{array} \right. \\[2em]
\text{-ize} \left\{ \begin{array}{l} \rightarrow \text{-ation} \\ \rightarrow \text{V (rule (10))} \end{array} \right.
\end{array}
$$

As (13) shows, I assume that suffixes are listed, in the same way as roots are, with the information regarding follow-on morphological processes; on the formal and semantic interpretation of such entries see (12) above. This implies that the first ('innermost') suffix attached to a given root is subject to idiosyncratic restrictions associated with that root (as shown in (12) above), but that any further suffix is only subject to the restrictions imposed by the preceding suffix, and not to any restrictions associated with the basic root. *Maternality* is then a form that is available in the language; but as long as it is taken to mean the same as *maternity*, it will be blocked by that form. In the light of what was said above regarding the concept of 'the stratum-1 lexicon of English', the empirical claim made here is that genuine 'coinages' – lexical innovations – will always involve basic roots, either in the form of neologisms or in the form of novel combinations of existing roots and affixes. Once *maternize* is coined, the further derivative *maternization* is automatically available rather than being a further innovation. This claim was also made in Kiparsky's (1982) account, with which the present one has much in common (as has been noted on earlier occasions):

> idiosyncratic marking for susceptibility to morphological processes or lexical phonological processes . . . [is] concentrated in *basic* lexical entries. [. . .] In English morphology, at any rate, the overriding generalization is surely that affixation is unpredictable for basic lexical entries (especially of

course at level 1) but that for derived lexical items it can be defined generally for a given head, even at level 1. (Kiparsky 1982: 27)

The most striking fact about (13) is that every suffix is listed for undergoing
rule (10). This too seems to be a general property of the morphology of
English. If it is the case, as Kiparsky (1982: 23) claims, that the morphology
of English does not have bound derived lexical items, then this claim is here
expressed by a redundancy rule to the effect that all suffixes must be listed
for rule (10). The present model clearly does not need to posit such bound
derived forms on internal grounds: it does not 'overgenerate' in the way
Allen's (1978) model does. But it is also worth noting that the model does
not rule out that possibility *a priori*. A hypothetical language may have
essentially the same stratum-1 structure as English does; but it may have
bound derived forms.

The statement of rule (10) with every suffix expresses familiar statements
such as '-*ize* is a verb-forming suffix'. In the present framework such a statement would run: '-*ize* forms roots that can become verbs'. Generalisations
such as that whereby all bound roots that attract -*able* can also take -*ate*
(*navigable – navigate, demonstrable – demonstrate*) can in the present framework be expressed as redundancy relations between the affixes that attach
to a given kind of base, obviating the truncation that Aronoff (1976) proposes for such cases. In fact, the present model obviates truncation altogether (as does any model that recognises bound-root bases; e.g. Kiparsky
1982). Note that this particular redundancy is not reversible – not all -*ate*
forms take alternative -*able* (*frustrate* – **frustrable, motivate* – **motivable*) –
until, of course, somebody coins such forms.

Note, further, that this model does not facilitate generalisations of the
form 'suffix A attaches to members of the lexical category X (only)'.
(Translated into our terms, such a generalisation would run, 'all roots
taking A can also become members of X through rule (10)'.) While this is
occasionally the case (-*ian* appears to attach to proper nouns only), it is not
a general property of English stratum-1 suffixes but a matter of individual
redundancy relations. Most stratum-1 suffixes have the option of, as we
have seen, highly idiosyncratic bound-root inputs; moreover -*ize*, for
example, attaches to bound roots (*baptize*) and to roots that can surface as
nouns (*terrorize, victimize*) as well as, predominantly, adjectives (*publicize,
nationalize, velarize*). It is clearly appropriate that the present model should
not facilitate such generalisations. To find out the lexical-category membership (to be precise: the lexical-category *potential*) of the bases available to a
given affix, or the range of such bases in more general terms, one would

have to check the entire lexicon. To give another illustration, speakers confronted with *warm* will know that this form can be turned into a noun through the attachment of *-th* (and that *-th* generally gives rise to nouns), but they will be unable to produce a list of all the items (adjectives?) that *-th* can attach to without conducting a search through a dictionary. This is precisely why reverse dictionaries (such as Lehnert 1971) and, of course, handbooks of word-formation, whose authors have done the search, are useful. Such observations regarding speakers' 'knowledge' of morphology constitute perhaps the strongest argument against the alternative approach to listing, briefly discussed above: the statement of affixation rules in the format of (9), where the subcategorisation frame is replaced by a list of bases, simply fails to reflect the way in which morphological knowledge is structured. We witness, then, the accumulation of strong arguments in favour of base-driven affixation on stratum 1. Such a model meets the need for listing that was established on various counts in earlier sections (as well as obviating all diacritic marking, [± Latinate] and otherwise). And, interestingly, it does not forego any of the valid predictions made by its affix-driven predecessor model (Kiparsky 1982).

3.2.4   *Illustration: stratum 1 in German*

I give at this point a brief demonstration of some stratum-1 affixation in German. This demonstration will add nothing new to the argument; but it will serve to emphasise the two central points made above in relation to English. First, unlike in English, the overwhelming majority of Latinate simple roots in German are bound. The conclusion that roots have no lexical category specifications is therefore inescapable. Second, the selection of affixes is strongly idiosyncratic to individual roots; and the semantics of the resulting forms is highly non-compositional. The conclusion that the affixes available to a given root are listed with that root is therefore equally inescapable; it is inescapable on two counts. In particular we shall see that the choice between competing affixes, while perhaps subject to diachronic explanation, cannot be predicted in synchronic terms. To demonstrate these points, I shall look at various Latinate agent-forming suffixes in some detail.

A selection of agent-forming suffixes is given and exemplified in (14) below, followed by observations that serve to back the points just made. (For details regarding the individual suffixes, see Fleischer 1974: 194ff.)

(14) *-eur*   *-or*

Kommandeur	('commander')	Inspektor	('inspector')
Ingenieur	('engineer')	Professor	('professor')
Souffleur	('prompter')	Direktor	('director')
Jongleur	('juggler')	Revisor	('auditor')
Gouverneur	('governor')	Lektor	('publisher's reader')
Friseur	('hairdresser')	Juror	('jury member')
Masseur	('masseur')	Aggressor	('aggressor')
Regisseur	('(film) director')	Assessor	('teacher on probation')
Inspekteur	('chief of staff')	Doktor	('doctor')
Charmeur	('charmer')	Kommentator	('commentator')

-ent   *-ant*

Student	('student')	Kommandant	('commandant')
Präsident	('president')	Intendant	('(theatre) manager')
Patient	('patient')	Garant	('guarantor')
Assistent	('assistant')	Applikant	('applicant')
Dozent	('lecturer')	Duellant	('duellist')
Referent	('spokesperson')	Simulant	('malingerer')
Dezernent	('head of department')	Gratulant	('well-wisher')
Produzent	('producer')	Passant	('passer-by')
Interessent	('interested person')	Ministrant	('server at mass')
Inserent	('advertiser')	Debütant	('debutant')

Anticipating a proposal made in Section 3.3 below whereby, in German, rule (10) converts roots into stems (rather than words) on stratum 1, note that only four of the roots contained in these examples are 'free' to exit from the stratum without further affixation – that is: they are subject to rule (10): *Charme, Duell, Debüt, Interess-*. Notably, all are nouns rather than, as expected of the bases of agent-forming suffixes, verbs. The rest are bound roots, not subject to rule (10) prior to further suffixation.

There are no consistent semantic differences between the suffixes; historical differences whereby *-or* may have denoted a 'professional agent' and *-ant/-ent* an 'incidental agent' are not synchronically relevant beyond slight tendencies, which are obscured by semantic non-compositionality (see in particular *Intendant, Dezernent, Dozent* (vs. *Doktor*), *Assessor* etc.).

The distribution of the suffixes is not governed by synchronic rules; nor are the suffixes interchangeable. **Frisant, *Professent, *Ministrent, *Gratuleur, *Duellor* etc. are nonexistent. Where they appear to be interchangeable (*Kommandant/Kommandeur, Dozent/Doktor, Inspekteur/ Inspektor*), their products differ in meaning (if, as in the first doublet, only in the specialised military jargon in which they originate).

Feminine agent nouns can be formed productively with the further suffix *-in* (probably attached on stratum 2): *Kommandeurin, Kommandantin, Inspektorin, Studentin* etc.; but this is blocked by *-euse* (*Souffleuse* etc.), a feminine alternative to *-eur* (but not to any of the others). **Kommandeuse, *Inspekteuse, *Charmeuse* and others are, however, idiosyncratically non-existent.[9]

In many cases, the suffix *-ier* is available to form inputs to rule (10) producing verb stems, as in *kommandier-, frisier-, soufflier-, studier-* etc.; but again a number of the roots contained in (14) are idiosyncratically unavailable for *-ier* attachment (**jurier-, *mentier-, *garier-* etc., with the last example (but not the others) stacking *-ier* onto *-ant*: *garantier-*). Even this fairly widespread derivation of roots is thus subject to idiosyncratic gaps.

Finally, alternative suffixations producing nouns in the field 'action/institution/abstract' are possible in a number of cases, involving suffixes such as *-ur* (*Frisur* 'hair-cut'), *-age* (*Massage* 'massage'), *-ion* (*Inspektion* 'inspection'), *-at* (*Inserat* 'advertisement') etc. But, again, such options are haphazard; moreover, in many cases such suffixes are stacked onto the forms in (14) rather than replacing the agent suffix (*Dozentur* 'lectureship' and others). Such cases provide a rich seam of material for the study of the morphological blocking effect (*Inspektorat* 'inspectorship' is also possible); and there are certainly redundancy relationships such that, for example, *-euse* is possible only with roots also taking *-eur*; and *-ion* tends to go with roots that also take *-or*; but as we have seen, such relationships are complex and far from exceptionless.

Based on this case study, which, although limited, I regard as representative of the Latinate morphology of the language, I conclude that stratum 1 in German is structured along the same lines as that in English. Riddled with unpredictable affix distributions, unexpected gaps and semantic non-compositionality, this is a morphology that can only be appropriately stated in listed form. I give some sample lexical entries in (15).

15)

$$
\text{fris-} \begin{cases} \rightarrow \text{-eur} \\ \rightarrow \text{-euse} \\ \rightarrow \text{-ur} \\ \rightarrow \text{-ier-} \end{cases}
$$

$$
\text{mass-} \begin{cases} \rightarrow \text{-eur} \\ \rightarrow \text{-euse} \\ \rightarrow \text{-age} \\ \rightarrow \text{-ier-} \end{cases}
$$

$$\text{duell} \begin{cases} \rightarrow -\text{ant} \\ \rightarrow -\text{ier-} \\ \rightarrow -\text{N (rule (10))} \end{cases}$$

3.3 Base categories and the number of strata: stem in German

I turn in this section to the predictions made by the base-driven stratification model regarding the number of lexical strata in universal terms. English has, as we have seen, two lexical strata of which the first is root-based and the second word-based. Moreover, the root stratum is characterised by the individual listing of morphological operations (and the absence of affixation rules of the format given in (9) above), while the morphology of the word stratum does have such rules: that morphology may be regarded as fully transparent and productive.

Such an organisation of the lexicon is of course not necessarily universal; nor is its universality predicted by the present model. The listing of root-based morphological processes, also found in German (Section 3.2.4 above; Giegerich 1994a: Section 3.2) and probably Dutch (Booij 1977), is possibly a characteristic of languages that have – as do Germanic languages – a substantial portion of morphologically unassimilated loan material. However, languages lacking such material may well have a productive, regular and hence rule-governed morphology throughout the lexicon. What the model does predict is that if a language has any listed morphological processes at all then it will accommodate those on stratum 1: this is necessitated through the morphological blocking effect, produced by the Elsewhere Condition (EC), that such irregular items will exert on the regular morphology (see Section 3.1.2 above and particularly Section 3.4.1 below).

If we assume that the inputs to lexical derivations universally warrant the term 'Root' (Strauss 1985) and that the outputs are words, then languages universally have a root stratum. However, that stratum may contain rule (10) – the Root-to-Word Conversion – as its sole morphological operation. This will be the case in a language whose entire morphology is word-based (Giegerich 1988). As we shall see in Chapter 4, the phonology of the root stratum in such a language will be severely constrained in that it will only allow structure-building phonological rules to operate on that stratum. (Structure-changing rules will be blocked by the Strict Cyclicity Effect.)

Consider now a hypothetical language whose entire morphology is root-based. Given that Root-to-Word Conversion takes place on stratum 1, that language need not have a word stratum in order to produce the word outputs of the lexicon: these are produced as early as on stratum 1. Such a language will have a second (final) stratum containing phonological rules only – the 'postcyclic' rules as envisaged by Booij and Rubach (1987) and Booij (1994). In the unlikely case that that language has no such rules (see Section 4.3.2 below for discussion), the language will have one stratum (the root stratum) only. The present model does not predict, then, that the minimal number of lexical strata must be two: it is possible for a language to have a root stratum only.

Nor does the model predict that the universally maximal number of lexical strata is two: this is the case only in languages in which – as in English – Root and Word are the only base categories. If we define Root as a morphological category that has no lexical-category specification and that is bound in the sense that it needs to undergo *at least* rule (10) (as well as, in the cases of 'bound roots' in the traditional sense such as *matern-*, further affixation) before it is able to emerge from the lexicon, and Word is defined as a morphological category that is free as well as fully specified for lexical categories (Section 3.2.1 above), then there is room for at least one further, intermediate category. Languages may display, for example, morphological processes defined on bases that carry (fully or partially specified) lexical categories but that cannot figure as free syntactic forms. Such bases are not words; but they may be termed stems if the category Stem is defined as specified for lexical categories but subject to further (for example, inflectional) affixation (Bauer 1983: 20; Szymanek 1989: 21; Matthews 1991: 64ff.).

As is well known, the distinction between Stem and Word as morphological categories (of which the former is primarily relevant to the inflectional morphology) has collapsed in the history of English as part of the decline of the inflectional system (Kastovsky 1992; 1996; Dalton-Puffer 1996; more generally Wurzel 1984): the regular inflection of Present-day English is entirely word-based while the bases of irregular inflection (*cactus*/*cacti* etc.) are adequately analysed as roots (Section 3.4.1 below). But in German the situation has remained different. Not only are there very clear indications that the German lexicon warrants a division into three strata on the phonological side (Giegerich 1987; Wiese 1996: Chapter 5); there is also strong evidence to suggest that on the morphological side these three strata are respectively root-based, stem-based and word-based. Wiese (1996) presents a number of morphological arguments in favour of such a stratal organisation, primarily (but not exclusively) on the grounds of inflectional regularities, re-assessing in terms of strata earlier proposals by Wurzel (1970; 1984) and Lieber (1981) whereby some inflectional morphemes are 'stem-forming'. The examples discussed below, drawn from the derivational morphology, are consistent with the principles of Wiese's analysis (if not agreeing with it in every detail), while also demonstrating the need for the intermediate category Stem as defined above.

There are a number of derivational suffixes in German that form, for example, nouns and adjectives on verbal bases. As these are fully productive, and not attested for (productively) attaching to bases other than verbs, they are clearly not handled on stratum 1: as we saw in the previous section, stratum 1 in German is strikingly similar to its English counterpart. But they are not word-level processes either since their bases are not words (that is, free forms in the sense of the syntax). In (16a) I give examples of adjective-forming -*bar* ('-able'), attaching to transitive verbs, and in (16b) examples of noun-forming -*ung* (roughly '-ing'), attaching to transitive and intransitive verbs. (For details, see Fleischer 1974: 251ff., 164ff.)

(16)	a.	trinkbar	'drinkable'	b.	Schöpfung	'creation'
		eßbar	'edible'		Zündung	'ignition'
		brauchbar	'useful'		Lesung	'reading (N)'
		lesbar	'legible'		Trennung	'separation'
		analysierbar	'analyseable'		Filtrierung	'filtration'
		operierbar	'operable'		Finanzierung	'funding (N)'

The bases of both -*bar* and -*ung* are clearly stems, in the familiar definition (Matthews 1991: 64 ff.): they are members of the lexical category Verb but lack the inflection that would enable them to enter the syntax as free forms.[10]

The same range of stems occurs in the first elements of verb-plus-noun compounds. Examples are given in (17), hyphenated for transparency:

(17)	Trink-Wasser	'drinking water'
	Trenn-Wand	'dividing wall'
	Senk-Fuß	'flat foot'
	Lauf-Bahn	'career'
	Fahr-Schule	'driving school'
	Filtrier-Werk	'filter station'

Such derivational phenomena strongly suggest, then, that German morphology has a stem-based component warranting therefore a separate stratum, which must be the second of three. The stem stratum follows the root stratum, on which forms such as *filtrier-*, *finanzier-*, *analysier-* originate. The suffix -*ier* is a root-based (stratum-1) derivational suffix (Section 3.2.4 above) whose products enter the stem stratum as verbs by virtue of rule (10), which in German conducts a Root-to-Stem Conversion. And the stem stratum precedes the word stratum, on which some of the inflection as well as, for example, word compounding takes place. Compounds such as

Frauenverein 'women's club', *Leibesfülle* 'obesity') have first elements that are either inflected or carry juncture suffixes (*Fugenelemente*) that are homophonous with stratum-3 (the word stratum) inflectional morphemes.[11] Such compounds must therefore themselves be formed on stratum 3. (But see Wiese 1996: Chapter 5.)

For the transition from stratum 2 to stratum 3 (the word stratum), German again requires a rule of the form (10) to facilitate Stem-to-Word Conversion. Such a rule is needed at least for monomorphemic items that are able to surface, as words, in their uninflected forms: *Haus* 'house', *Segel* 'sail', *gut* 'good' and many others. If Stem is, like Root, a recursive category, as is shown by the possibility of multiple stem-level affixation (e.g. *Lesbarmachung* 'making something legible (N)'; recall (16) above), then morphological processes on German's stratum 2 cannot automatically produce words but must, like their stratum-1 counterparts, leave that conversion to the stratum's version of rule (10) in all cases. The situation is then parallel to that found on stratum 1 (in German and English) except that, in the present cases, inflectional classes give rise to redundancy statements as to whether a given stem can become a word (recall *Haus*, *Segel*, *gut* etc.).

In general terms, the picture that emerges here is one in which there is no principled upper limit to the number of lexical strata. The two strata of English and the three of German may have intuitive plausibility given that the categories on which they are based – root, stem and word – are well known and happen to owe their labels to traditional grammar. But the model of base-driven stratification does not rule out analyses positing more than three strata for certain languages, as long as these strata are defined in terms of generalisations concerning the properties of affixation bases. As we saw in Chapter 2, the four-strata analysis of English presented by Halle and Mohanan (1985) and Mohanan (1986) is not among those that are possible within the present model (see Section 4.3 below for further discussion). But this does not mean that the four-strata analysis of Turkish, proposed by Inkelas and Orgun (1994) is equally ruled out.

3.4   Interactions between the strata

3.4.1   Blocking in word formation

We saw in Section 3.2 that roots and suffixes (as well as prefixes, not here discussed in detail) are listed as lexical entries, roots as '[X]', suffixes as 'Y]' and prefixes as '[Z' (Kiparsky 1982; McMahon 1989: Section 1; Section 2.1

above). The listing of roots includes information as to which suffixes they attract on stratum 1, and whether they are able to undergo rule (10). The same sort of information is lodged with suffixes (although, as we saw, any English suffix occurring on stratum 1 is also subject to rule (10)). Stratum 1, then, contains a multitude of morphological operations but, beyond rule (10), no morphological *rules* in the sense of statements of generalisations: any morphological process on that stratum is specific to the two lexical entries that it concatenates. Recall too that rule (10) is driven by root-specific idiosyncrasies in that it is only applicable to an arbitrary subset of roots and in that it assigns lexical categories in a fashion that is similarly arbitrary as long as no formal link with the semantics of the root is established.

On stratum 2, in contrast, we assume the presence of affixation rules of the format (9). Affixation on that stratum can be assumed to be productive, semantically compositional as well as amenable to generalisations of the sort expressed in the subcategorisation frame of (9). In particular, that subcategorisation frame will include the lexical category specification of the base, given as 'L' in (9).

The productivity of stratum-2 processes is, of course, affected by the Blocking Effect, which was discussed in some detail, albeit within the affix-driven stratification framework, in Section 3.1.2 above. We saw there that the observed productivity differences between morphological processes on the two strata can be only partially explained through Blocking and the Elsewhere Condition (see (2) above) in an affix-driven model. Meanwhile, the model has been considerably modified, and a renewed discussion of morphological blocking and related phenomena is in order.

The first point to note here is that the notion of 'unproductive morphological rule', entertained in Section 3.1, has been abandoned and replaced by listing. Stratum 1 has no affixation rules – EC therefore appears to be inapplicable given that that condition makes reference to 'rules' A and B. But this is only apparently the case. Statements such as '-*th* blocks -*ness*' are only short for the blocking effects observed in individual formations: what happens is that the formation of *warmth* blocks that of **warmness* with identical semantics. In the present model such blocking is performed by rule (10), in turn triggered by the listed formation of *warmth* from *warm*: the formation of the noun *warmth*, through rule (10), on stratum 1 blocks the formation of a noun with identical meaning through a general morphological process – in this case **warmness*, produced by the productive affixation rule for -*ness* on stratum 2.

The crucial involvement of listing and rule (10) in the blocking effect sheds light on further aspects of blocking that could not be accounted for in the affix-driven framework: blocking on semantic and on phonotactic grounds, as well as on blocking failures. I shall deal with each in turn.

First, given that rule (10) also processes morphologically simple roots, it is now possible to account for the fact that morphologically simple forms block the formation of complex forms with the same meaning: the lexical item responsible for blocking is not necessarily the product of an affixation process competing with that whose output is blocked. Thus, *hotness* is blocked by *heat* (under identical semantics), *dogess* by *bitch*, *parentess* by *mother* and *stealer* by *thief* (Plank 1981: 174). *Burglarize* is blocked by *burgle* in those varieties of English in which that back-formation has developed. In each such case, the conversion of the morphologically simple form into a word, on stratum 1, renders the semantically competing word-formation through affixation ungrammatical. Let us consider the mechanics of such blocking, through the Elsewhere Condition (2), in some more detail. The input to rule (10) converting the root *bitch* ('specifically female dog') into the noun *bitch* is, in semantic terms, a proper subset of the input to the putative derivation of *dogess* from *dog*: *bitch* is already female at the input stage but *dog*, while denoting the same species, is unmarked for sex (standing for 'male dog' only by default). The outputs of the two derivations, *bitch* and *dogess*, are distinct lexical items (of which the latter forms part of the general set of items containing the suffix *-ess* and denoting feminine animate entities). Hence rule (10) producing *bitch* blocks the production of *dogess*. In contrast, the form *lioness* is not blocked given that the input to rule (10) – *lion* – is not a proper subset of the input to the formation of *lioness* (also *lion*).

Second, and more tentatively, we may also suggest that through rule (10), the existence of a given morphologically simple form will block the formation of a morphologically complex form not of the same meaning but of the same phonological shape. Consider the string /lɪvr/, occurring in English as a lexical item (*liver*). This string is a proper subset of all the strings containing /lɪv/ (*live, liver, living,* ...). The output of rule (10) is distinct from that of the rule which produces *liver* by attaching agent-forming *-er* to *live* in that the latter is morphologically complex. Given that rule (10) is the more specific one of the two rules able to produce *liver*, it will prevent the morphologically complex form *liver* ('someone who lives') from occurring. Similarly, someone who prays is not a *prayer* but a *worshipper*: the semantically irregular stratum-1 formation *prayer* blocks the regular (stratum-2) agent-formation. The attachment of the diminutive suffix -*let* to *toy* is blocked; and a place where bats roost is a *bat roost* rather than a *battery*: again, the morphologically simple forms *toilet, battery* block the production of those strings through otherwise productive and transparent processes. (See Jespersen (1942: 231); Plank (1981: 166f.) for some more examples.) If this tentative reasoning is correct then EC makes the prediction that the language may contain pairs of homophonous lexical items only if neither member of the pair is morphologically complex. Unlike *liver/*liv + er*, pairs such as *seal/see, leak/leek, bank/bank* etc. are then permissible: neither member of such a pair can block the other given that both become words through rule (10) on stratum 1.

Third, the assumption that all stratum-1 outputs are listed accounts for the commonly observed failures of blocking (see again Plank 1981: Section 3.2). As was noted in Section 3.2.3, it lies in the nature of such listing of stratum-1 outputs that the range of stratum-1 formations available to a given speaker is highly specific to that speaker, and possibly even to certain registers of that speaker. A speaker who is unfamiliar with *warmth*, or who at least does not have that form in his or her active vocabulary, will freely produce *warmness*. More likely perhaps, a speaker who is unfamiliar with the formations given in (18a) below (i.e. -*ity* and others) will resort to the competing, and attested (although allegedly ungrammatical) -*ness* forms in (18b). (For discussion see Williams (1965: 285), who observes that, in particular, 'the -*ness* suffix seems to be thriving at the expense of the -*ity* suffix'.)

(18)   a. ability   b. ableness
         cruelty   cruelness
         brevity   briefness
         ferocity   ferociousness
         passivity   passiveness
         malice   maliciousness
         naiveté   naiveness
         humility   humbleness

Some of these cases have interesting sociolinguistic implications, which are borne out by the present model of stratum 1: items such as those in (18a) form part of the Latinate vocabulary, a substantial portion of which is considered sophisticated and learnèd. By using forms like those in (18b), the speaker reveals gaps in his or her stratum-1 list (which may for example consist in a failure to list rule (10) with certain roots – e.g. *malice*, where the speaker only has *malicious* without having acquired the conversion of the root *malice* into a noun), or in the failure to have -*(i)ty* listed with certain roots (*cruel, passive*). Such speaker-specific blocking failures can only be explained through the assumption that the items expected to perform the blocking are themselves speaker-specific and therefore, as we have seen, not only in many cases learnèd but also, in all cases, individually learnt.

I return finally to the blocking effect in the inflectional morphology, and its occasional failure. Cases such as *oxen* are straightforward given that *ox* is listed with the irregular plural morpheme *-en* on stratum 1. The need for listing is a particularly obvious one in this case: *-en* occurs only with two other, highly irregular, nouns in the standard language (*children, brethren*). And if we assume that any morphological operation that is listed is sited on stratum 1 for that reason, then we achieve the blocking of **oxes* automatically for all those standard speakers that list *-en* with *ox*. But a learner who first acquires the singular form *ox* is predicted by the model to produce *oxes* until he or she acquires (that is, lists) the irregular plural. Similarly, speakers will have *spelled* as the regular past-tense form of *spell* until they acquire the stratum-1 listed irregular form *spelt*. This may never happen: forms such as *spelt, dreamt, leapt, leant* are not invariable standard forms in all standard varieties of English, unlike the plural form of *ox* and the irregular past tense form of *keep*. But the model does predict that any speaker who has acquired the form *spelt* will not use *spelled* (except as a slip of the tongue) as long as the listed form is there to be drawn on. The 'optionality' of such formations is a notion that may apply to the stratum 1 of certain variants of the standard language, a theoretical construct in any case (as I argued in Section 3.2.3); but it does not apply to the stratum 1 of the actual individual speaker.

Doublets such as *cacti/cactuses, referendums/referenda* etc. are subject to a similar explanation; but they also exemplify the speaker-specificness in the recognition of morphological complexity that was noted in Section 3.2.3 above. A speaker has three options of handling *cactus* and its plural:

(19)
    a. [cact]$\begin{cases} \rightarrow \text{us]} \\ \rightarrow \text{i]} \end{cases}$

        -us] $\rightarrow$ N$_{[-\text{Plural}]}$

        -i] $\rightarrow$ N$_{[+\text{Plural}]}$

    b. [cact] $\rightarrow$ us]

        -us] $\rightarrow$ N

    c. [cactus] $\rightarrow$ N

If the speaker's morphological analysis of such a form is true to the donor language, he or she will analyse *cactus* as in (19a), consisting of the bound root [*cact-*], subject to listed suffixation through either -*us*] or -*i*], where both suffixes are recurrent in the language and listed separately. Both suffixed forms (but not the root) are subject to rule (10), forming nouns that are in addition specified for singular/plural. The speaker who uses the form *cactuses*, on the other hand, has two options regarding his or her stratum-1 entry, which reflect degrees of morphological and etymological expertise but not competence in producing the form itself. (We came across other instances of the possible irrelevance of speaker-specific morphological analysis to the speaker's stratum-1 competence in Section 3.2.3.) The speaker may either isolate the suffix -*us*, on the strength of its recurrence (*crocus*, *bonus*) and simply convert the suffixed form [[*cact*]*us*]], through rule (10), into a noun that is not specified for number. This is the option (19b), which is available for regular plural formation on stratum 2. Such an analysis is paralleled by *bonus*, *chorus* and others, for which the root-based plural forms **boni*, **chori* are unavailable. Alternatively, he or she may include the unanalysed root [*cactus*] (19c) in the stratum-1 list, failing to isolate the suffix -*us*. The regular plural can then again be formed on stratum 2. Etymologists will approve of such an analysis in the case of *walrus*; and the native speaker cannot necessarily be expected to draw etymological (and attendant morphological) distinctions such as that between *cactus* and *walrus*. It is surely a welcome and realistic outcome of our analysis that the native speaker's competence is not dependent on his or her mastery of such distinctions. Either way, we see that a less-than-fully acquired stratum-1 morphology gives rise to regular morphology (similar to the -*ity* vs. -*ness* cases discussed above), in this case under the additional systemic pressure exerted by the (essentially word-based) inflectional system of English.

3.4.2   The stratal affiliation of affixes

We saw in Chapter 2 that English has stratum-1 affixes, stratum-2 affixes as well as a substantial number of affixes that occur on both strata. Having abandoned the affix-driven stratification model, we now have to address the question of how such stratal affiliations can be expressed and what predictions the base-driven model makes for them. Let us return briefly to the way affixation works on the two strata.

In Section 3.2 we saw that basic roots as well as affixes constitute lexical entries, and that each such entry is listed with the affixes that can attach to it. (Recall the samples given in (12) and (13) above.) Such statements of 'concatenation options' (to avoid the misleading term 'rules', which suggests generalisation) are idiosyncratic to each lexical entry. The implementation of such options, as they are specified with lexical entries, constitutes what we mean by 'the morphology of stratum 1'. Stratum 1 has root affixation (as well as root compounding (*sad-o-masoch-*, *morph-o-syntact-* etc., with *-o-* as the recurrent juncture element) but it has no rules for such processes, merely implementing what is underlyingly specified with each lexical entry. The morphology of stratum 2, in contrast, is driven by affixation rules of the format (9) above (as well as containing word compounding).

This means, first of all, that no morphological rule in English needs to bear a diacritic marker specifying the stratum on which it applies. In general terms, the subcategorisation frame of an affixation rule specifies the morphological category of the base – Word, Stem or whatever – along with its lexical category (Noun, Verb etc.) where applicable. In English-specific terms, the situation is simplified through redundancies: if stratum 1 only has listed morphology but no affixation rules, all affixation rules automatically apply on stratum 2. And given that that stratum is the only one on which affixation bases bear lexical-category labels (unlike in German, where both the stem-stratum and the word-stratum affixation bases bear such labels), the statement of a lexical category in the subcategorisation frame automatically ensures the rule's restriction to stratum 2. While it is in principle possible for an affixation *rule*, in the proper sense, to have roots as inputs, English does not appear to utilise this option. But even if English could be shown to have such stratum-1 affixation *rules* – if, that is, stratum 1 in English could be shown to contain fully productive morphological processes[12] – then their subcategorisation frames (specifying root inputs) would obviate their diacritic stratal specification.

An English affix listed as a lexical entry may or may not figure in the affixation options listed (for stratum 1) with the roots of the language; and it may or may not figure in an affixation rule proper. If both are the case then the affix can be said to 'occur' on both strata. If only the former is the case then the affix attaches on stratum 1 only. And if only the latter is the case then the affix attaches on stratum 2 only. None of these possibilities requires diacritic marking. And interestingly, none of them seems *a priori* more likely than any of the others. The facts investigated in Chapter 2 bear this out. In diachronic terms, an affix that is listed with some frequency for stratum-1 attachment may well give rise to a rule and become productive.

The suffix *-ism* appears to be such a case (see Section 2.4.10 above). An affix that is associated with a rule may attach sporadically to bases not permitted by the rule (for example to bound roots), thus finding entry into the stratum-1 list. Such cases are, as we have seen, fairly common among Germanic suffixes such as *-less*, *-ness* etc. (Section 2.4.14). Perhaps the state of equilibrium is one where all affixes occur on both strata: this was already suggested, on the basis of the affixation evidence in English, in Chapter 2.

The identification of the synchronic stratal association of a given affix is, then, a question that is of comparatively little importance to the study of English morphology. What is more interesting, given the availability of both strata to just about any given affix, is the identification of the criteria that will lead to a given affix's (diachronic) spread from one stratum into the other. Essentially, what makes a stratum-2 affix enter the list for stratum-1 affixation? And what makes a stratum-1 affix develop a rule, enabling it to be attached on stratum 2? Such questions require detailed diachronic study, which I do not conduct here. But the synchronic snapshot provided by the morphology of Present-day English at least allows some speculation.

As we saw in Chapter 2 (and also in this chapter), the two strata of English are distinguished by a syndrome of interrelated properties. Phonological properties of stratum-1 suffixation include stress alternations (*átom – atómic*), syllabicity alternations (*rhythm – rhythmic*) and the application of stratally restricted phonological rules such as Trisyllabic Shortening (*serene – serenity*). Stratum-2 forms are characterised by the absence of those phonological features. The semantic diagnostic of stratum-1 processes is the non-compositionality of their products; the morphological diagnostic is the non-productivity of the processes involved. (Both are expressed through the listing of all stratum-1 formations, as we have seen.) In general terms, stratum-1 formations 'behave like' morphologically simple forms (in phonological, morphological and semantic terms) while stratum-2 formations have (phonologically, morphologically, semantically) transparent complexity.

A given stratum-2 form may move onto stratum 1 for any one of those three possible reasons. A word-formation process of the language may 'freeze' diachronically, as did the formation of abstract nouns through *-th* (*warmth*). An individual form may lose its phonological transparency over time and/or it may lose its semantic compositionality: either process may cause the other, although semantic drift is usually held responsible for the loss of phonological transparency (Faiss 1978; Allen 1980; Anshen and Aronoff 1981). The syllabicity loss in noun forms like *twinkling, coupling,* *lightning* is possibly subject to such an explanation, appealing to semantic drift as the cause for such forms' move to stratum 1. Similarly, the form *sprinkler* ('fire fighting device in buildings') has nonsyllabic [l] while the trisyllabic (stratum-2) form transparently denotes 'someone who sprinkles'. But note that such syllabicity loss is also possible as a structural simplification caused merely by frequent use: a frequent user of the participle (rather than the gerund) *coupling* may pronounce the form consistently without *l*-syllabicity while maintaining its semantic transparency. As long as this does not happen across the board in all comparable phonological contexts but only in individual words, the syllabicity loss cannot be due to a postlexical phonological rule but must be explained through the production of the form on stratum 1. Semantic non-compositionality is, then, not a necessary condition for stratum-1 formations.

The present model facilitates such re-analysis of individual affixation processes through the way in which the morphological base-categories of successive strata relate to each other. In terms of base categories, an affix attaching to a morphologically simple word (on stratum 2) may also attach on stratum 1: every simple word is also a root (while not every root is also a word: *matern-*, *gorm-* etc. are not). An affix attaching to a free form has the freedom to do so on either stratum; but one attaching to a bound form (a bound root) must do so on stratum 1. The only way for such a formation to move to stratum 2 is the development of the bound root into a word (for example through back formation, as has happened, in some varieties of English, in *burgle* (< *burglar*) and may happen facetiously in *gorm* (< *gormless*). In German, every word is a stem but not every stem is a word. Affixes attaching to bound stems must be stratum 2 while affixes attaching to free forms may be stratum 3 or 2 (or, indeed, stratum 1).

In formal terms, it follows that any two contiguous strata in English as well as German are partially overlapping domains by virtue of the fact that their morphological base categories constitute a natural class (Wiese 1996: Chapter 5). In German, Root and Stem share the feature (not shared by Word) that they may be bound; Stem and Word share the feature (not shared by Root) that they carry lexical-category specifications. Languages may therefore be expected to collapse two adjacent strata. This has happened in English, where the category Stem has been lost through the decline of the inflectional system (Kastovsky 1992; 1996). In synchronic terms, such an analysis makes the prediction that a given morphological process may be found on two (or more) contiguous strata but not on non-contiguous strata (for example strata 1 and 3 in German). We witness, then, the extension of the 'Continuity of Strata Hypothesis', formulated (through stipulation) by Mohanan (1986: 46) for phonological rules, so as to cover morphological processes. Mohanan does in fact include morphological processes in the hypothesis; but in his affix-driven model multiple-strata attachment can be no more than an embarrassing exception. As we saw in Chapter 2, models such as his depend crucially on the assumption that morphological processes are confined to single strata – a false assumption, as we saw. The present model predicts, rather than stipulates, that the 'Continuity of Strata Hypothesis' must be true on both the phonological and the morphological side.

4 Deriving the Strict Cyclicity Effect

4.1 Strict Cyclicity and the Elsewhere Condition

4.1.1 Identity rules

There is general agreement in the literature that the phonological side of lexical derivations should be subject to a constraint to the effect of (1) below:

(1) *Strict Cyclicity Effect (SCE)*
Structure-changing cyclic rules apply in derived environments only
(where a 'derived environment' is an environment created by either a
morphological rule or a phonological rule on the same cycle)

SCE expresses a simultaneous link between the confinement of a given phonological rule to derived environments and two of its properties: with its cyclicity and with its structure-changing nature. These two properties are not themselves linked: rules may be cyclic and structure-building rather than structure-changing; or they may be non-cyclic and structure-changing. This dual link is borne out by the facts of lexical organisation following standard assumptions. The link between cyclicity and SCE is manifested in the probably well-founded assumptions that, first, stratum 1 is cyclic as well as displaying SCE, and that, second, the final stratum (stratum 2 for English, in the present model) is assumed to be non-cyclic as well as not displaying SCE. In the earlier models comprising more than two lexical strata, this link was similarly present in intermediate strata: in Kiparsky's (1982) model, comprising three strata, stratum 2 was assumed to be cyclic and subject to SCE like stratum 1. And in Halle and Mohanan's (1985) four-strata model, strata 1 and 3 were assumed to be cyclic and constrained by SCE while strata 2 and 4 were non-cyclic and not SCE-bound. I shall argue below that that particular analysis is unacceptable on formal grounds; recall also from Chapter 3 that the three-strata model of Kiparsky (1982) is unwarranted for English, if not for German. Anticipating the rejection of an intermediate stratum that is neither cyclic nor subject to SCE, we may note here that on the grounds of the cumulative evidence provided by existing models (except Halle and Mohanan's), one might postulate, in the place of (1), that structure-changing rules on non-final strata apply in derived environments only. I return to this issue below; let us ignore this possible alternative for the moment and assume that (1) is the appropriate statement of the constraint in question.

The link between the structure-changing nature of certain rules and their restriction to derived environments is more straightforward. Structure-building rules are obviously not so restricted even when they apply on stratum 1: syllabification and stress assignment, for example, must be permitted to apply in underived forms. This, too, is an issue to which I return below; again, let us assume that (1) states the facts correctly.

At the risk of re-stating the obvious, I summarise by way of illustration the probably most persuasive case for SCE presented in the literature: Kiparsky's (1982) analysis of Trisyllabic Shortening (TSS) in English. Szpyra (1989: 71ff.) has subsequently argued that Kiparsky's account has an unacceptable number of exceptions. (The case of *obesity* (vs. *obscenity* etc.) had of course been known before, and was commonly used to illustrate the well-established assumption that lexical rules may have exceptions.) And the formulation of Kiparsky's original rule has since been modified by Myers (1987), largely accounting for the problems identified by Szpyra. But given that Myers' revision of the rule affects neither its stratal siting nor its interaction with existing constraints (see also Booij 1994), I use Kiparsky's essentially SPE-based and, in terms of its formal background, less demanding version for exposition (actually simplifying it even further).

TSS shortens the stressed vowel in a trisyllabic foot. First, it is a stratum-1 rule in that syllables added by the morphology of stratum 2 fail to give rise to shortening: the stressed vowels in forms such as *fatherless, weariness, coherently, metering* etc. remain long without exception. Second, TSS is a cyclic rule (in line with the assumption that stratum 1 is cyclic). The shortness of the first syllable in *nationality* (compare *nation*) must be produced by the application of TSS to the intermediate form *national*, given that no rule is available to shorten the first vowel in *nationality* itself: the first vowel in, for example, *hypochondria* (which has comparable suprasegmental structure) is long while that in *hypocrisy/hypocrite* is shortened, and that in *hypothesis* in turn remains long in the absence of an intermediate form that satisfies the TSS context. The fact that stress assignment bleeds TSS on the same stratum clearly demonstrates the cyclicity of TSS.

Third, and most importantly for present purposes, TSS is subject to SCE.

This constraint accounts for the fact that underived trisyllabic forms such as *Oberon, nightingale* fail to shorten, as well as ruling out abstract analyses positing underlyingly long vowels in *camera, pedestal*. Given that neither these forms nor *Oberon, nightingale* etc. engage in long–short alternations, no analysis involving shortening is warranted in either class. (For further details of this analysis see Kiparsky 1982: 35 ff.)

While SCE has enjoyed universal acceptance in Lexical Phonology, the status of that constraint in the grammar has remained somewhat unclear. Stipulated in a similar form as the Strict Cycle Condition ('SCC') by Mascaró (1976) (see also Kean 1974), (1) represented a clear improvement over its predecessor in the literature, the Alternation Condition ('AC'; Kiparsky 1973) which, in various formulations, basically forbade the application of structure-changing rules to all instances of a given morpheme. AC's main problem was that it could not be imposed as a formal condition on the grammar. Given that it is impossible to ascertain in advance whether or not a given rule will apply to all instances of a particular morpheme, the only way of ensuring a given rule's AC-compliance was a check through its entire output after the grammar had produced it. (See Kiparsky (1982: 39ff., 1993: 277ff.) for discussion.) I discuss AC in some detail in Section 4.3.3 below. SCC, in contrast, does not have that particular problem: rather than stigmatising existing objectionable derivations *a posteriori*, it blocks such derivations *a priori*, preventing them from being produced in the first place. This was an important advance in the development of an urgently needed constraint on the abstractness of phonological derivations; but SCC nevertheless retained a number of further problems, all connected with its essentially stipulative nature. Formulated as a free-standing condition on phonological derivations, SCC is not only unconnected with other principles of the grammar; it also posits, as we have seen, mutually unrelated and seemingly arbitrary links between structure-changing power, cyclic rule application and derived environments. Moreover, the notion of 'derived environment' is in itself heterogeneous in that it refers to the products of both morphological and phonological derivation. Clearly, the persuasiveness of SCE (and with it that of Lexical Phonology as an adequately constrained derivational framework) would be much enhanced if such multiple arbitrariness could be avoided by deriving the whole of SCE from a single independently motivated principle of the grammar.

Kiparsky (1982) proposed to do just that, arguing that SCE is the equivalent on the phonological side of lexical derivations to the Blocking Effect on the morphological side of lexical derivations, like the latter automatically produced by EC, here repeated from Section 3.2:

(2)   *Elsewhere Condition (EC)*
        Rules A, B apply disjunctively to a form ϕ iff:
        (i) SD_A is a proper subset of SD_B; and
        (ii) SC_A is distinct from SC_B.
        In that case Rule A, applying first, blocks rule B.

Crucial to Kiparsky's proposal is the assumption '. . . that every lexical entry constitutes an identity rule whose structural description is the same as its structural change' (Kiparsky 1982: 46). In (3) I demonstrate the blocking of TSS through EC in the underived form *nightingale*:

(3)   a. /niːtVngaːl/ → /niːtVngaːl/
        b. $C_oVC_oVC_oVC_o$ → $C_oVC_oVC_oVC_o$

Vowel Shift, turning the /iː/ and /aː/ of (3a) into [aɪ] and [eɪ] respectively, is for the moment assumed to be a stratum-2 rule and hence unavailable to the derivation at this stage (but see Section 4.3.2 below). (3a), then, gives the lexical entry of *nightingale* as it is produced on stratum 1. The application of the identity rule (3a) constitutes 'rule A' in EC. Its structural description is a proper subset of the structural description of TSS (simplified in (3b)). The structural change of the identity rule is distinct from the structural change of TSS in that the former retains a long vowel. TSS is 'rule B' in the sense of EC; the identity rule blocks TSS.

The reason why TSS is not blocked in the same fashion in derived forms is that only the output-forms of the stratum (more precisely: of any given cycle) constitute 'lexical entries', and hence identity rules. In *nightingale*, as we have seen, the identity rule is ordered disjunctively before TSS; in *sanity*, on the other hand, there is no identity rule of the form [[saːn]ɪtɪ] as this form is not a lexical entry as long as it contains a long vowel. Hence there is no 'rule A' whose input could be a proper subset of that of TSS, and consequently no blocking. But given that the fully derived form [[san]ɪtɪ] is again a lexical entry (an identity rule), the same blocking effect is achieved on the next cycle: counterfeeding of lexical rules on the next cycle is prevented.

Finally, Kiparsky's proposal accounts for the restriction of SCE to structure-changing rules in that structure-building rules do not produce outputs that are 'distinct', in the technical sense, from their inputs or from the output of an identity rule. Structure-building rules do not produce 'distinctness' (*viz.* 'contrast') in the way structure-changing rules do. If we replace TSS in (3b) by (any part of) the mechanism of syllabification, for example, then the output of the identity rule *nightingale* will not be distinct from the output of the syllabification process in the sense in which the result of a structure-changing operation will be 'distinct'.

Kiparsky's proposal succeeds, then, in predicting from EC that structure-changing rules apply in derived environments only. But it effectively severs the link, also expressed in SCE, between blocking and cyclic rule application. While EC-induced blocking is not inconsistent with cyclic rule application, it will also work under non-cyclic application. As was noted before, this link may well have been accidental in the first place (I return to this issue in Section 4.2.2 below); what is more serious is that the possible alternative restriction of SCE to non-final strata, tentatively noted above, remains equally unaccounted for in Kiparsky's proposal. There is no explanation for the exemption of the second (final), presumably non-cyclic stratum in English – the word level – from SCE. Kaisse and Shaw's (1985: 23) observation, relating to Kiparsky's account of SCE, whereby '. . . the relaxation of Strict Cyclicity may be seen as the percolation of a post-lexical characteristic only to the immediately preceding lexical stratum' follows from that account of SCE only if either EC or identity rules fail to operate on the final stratum; and given that there is no reason to assume the suspension of EC on that stratum, its failure to display SCE must be due to the absence of identity rules.

What, then, is the status of identity rules in lexical derivations? It is reasonably clear that if the grammar contains a set of identity rules comprising, as Kiparsky argues, not only underived but also derived lexical items, then all those items ('lexical entries' in Kiparsky's terms) must be listed. The set of identity rules produced on a given stratum (in the TSS case, on stratum 1) is that of the completely (including phonologically) derived items on that stratum. The identity rules express (and rewrite as themselves) what the speaker 'knows' to be produced on the stratum. In the case of *nightingale*, the speaker lists the form given in (3a) above (i.e. the output of the lexical derivation minus Vowel Shift, which is assumed not to take place on that stratum); and this listed form enters into a relationship of disjunctive ordering (through EC) with the processes that *might* happen on the stratum, thus ensuring that they don't happen. As regards structure-building rules (e.g. syllabification and stress assignment), the identity rule *nightingale* contains syllable and foot structure; it cannot therefore block the assignment of those properties. What this means – and Kiparsky is less than explicit about the technical details – is that the entire output of a given stratum, morphological and phonological, must be listed.

We saw in Sections 3.3 and 3.4 that in English, stratum 1 (but not stratum

2) is indeed characterised by the listing of lexical entries (i.e. of morphologically simple and complex forms) rather than by the operation of affixation rules; so there is, in English at least, a correlation between listing and SCE. This point is made by Borowsky (1993: 220), but not by Kiparsky himself. As was discussed in Section 3.3, Kiparsky notes the necessity for listing on stratum 1 but does not address this issue in principled terms. As we have also seen, an affix-driven model like his, employing affixation rules throughout the strata, cannot account for this fundamental difference between the two strata of English. Such a model cannot, therefore, bar identity rules from stratum 2: if stratum 1 has them then there is no principled reason for their absence from stratum 2.

In any case, as Mohanan and Mohanan (1982) noted, even under the assumption of listing the assertion that 'every lexical entry *constitutes* an identity rule' is too weak to carry conviction as long as those rules do not, as rules do (and identity rules by definition do not), derive something from something else. Items and processes have different ontologies. An identity rule is a notational device which (thanks to EC) serves to ensure that listed information overrides rule-governed information. It serves no other purpose in the grammar; nor is it a necessary conceptual consequence of the notion of 'listing'. If we are to uphold the essence of Kiparsky's proposal, namely the prediction of SCE through EC on cyclic and/or non-final strata, then his identity rules have to be replaced by rules that are restricted to cyclic and/or non-final strata on principled grounds, as well as performing an actual derivational task in the grammar.

4.1.2   *Morphological default rules*

In the model of lexical stratification proposed in Chapter 3 we need not look far to find the rule that performs the blocking function that serves to derive SCE from EC. We shall see in this section that rule (10) of Chapter 3 (the 'Root-to-Word' conversion, in the two-strata model for English) performs just that function. Let us briefly review the relevant features of this model and the morphological motivation of that rule.

First, morphological operations are defined in terms of a hierarchy of morphological categories such as Root and Word (with the possibility of intermediate categories such as Stem). Roots are bound or free, and not carriers of lexical-category information. Stems, in languages recognising that category, are bound or free forms specified for lexical categories. Words are free forms fully specified for lexical categories. German has all three categories whereas English only has Root and Word. These categories are hierarchical such that every English word contains a form of the category Root; every German word contains a stem, which in turn contains a root. The categories are, moreover, recursive in that the output of every morphological process is a member of the same morphological category as is its input.

Second, lexical strata are defined in terms of this hierarchy of recursive morphological domains rather than in terms of the range of affixes that attach on a given stratum. The domain of stratum 1 is the morphological category Root: the inputs and outputs of all morphological processes of that stratum are roots. The domain of the final lexical stratum is the morphological category Word: the inputs and outputs of all morphological processes of that stratum are words. English, then, has a root stratum and a word stratum while German has, in addition, an intermediate stem stratum. The basics of this stratification model, which I have been referring to as 'base-driven stratification', were developed by Selkirk (1982b).

Third, it follows from the absence of syntactic-category specifications in roots that the root stratum cannot have affixation rules of the format, proposed by Lieber (1981) – 'Attach A in the environment [Y ____ Z]$_L$' – for the simple reason that the lexical-category specification 'L' is a crucial ingredient of such subcategorisation frames. Indeed, we saw in Section 3.1 that the morphology of stratum 1 requires, for a number of independent reasons, the listing of all forms derived from a given basic root with the root itself. Section 3.3.3 outlined the formal framework for this particular version of listing. Identity rules of the kind suggested by Kiparsky (1982) and discussed in Section 4.1.1 above have no place in that framework. Conceptually suspect as they are, they served in Kiparsky's model merely to express the 'listed' nature of the products of the stratum-1 morphology while that morphology itself was conducted by rules that were nondistinct from those of stratum 2.

Fourth, it follows from the recursive nature of the morphological categories Root, Stem and Word as well as from the definition of strata in terms of these morphological base categories that any item handled by the morphology of a given stratum will be unable to transit to the next stratum unless the grammar contains a device that specifically facilitates this transition. This device is rule (10) of Chapter 3, here re-stated and generalised.

(4)   *Morphological Default*

$$[\ ]_{x,\,(L)} \rightarrow [[\ ]_x\,]_{x+1,\,L}$$

(where 'x' is the morphological category of stratum X (root, stem, . . .)
and L (= N, V, A) is absent from the structural description on stratum 1)

Any non-final lexical stratum must contain a rule of the form (4), whose function it is to convert members of the morphological category characterising that stratum into members of the next-lower morphological category. This 'conversion' is here formally expressed through the addition of a set of brackets to any given form. As we saw in Section 3.3.2, the additional introduction of lexical-category information is specific to the stratum-1 version of the rule ('Root-to-Word' in English, 'Root-to-Stem' in German), under the assumption that German stems carry full lexical-category specifications.

The rule in (4) is that of 'Morphological Default' in that it is automatically the last morphological operation that any item produced on a given stratum can undergo on that stratum: having obtained membership of the lexical category 'x + 1' (e.g. 'Stem') on stratum X (e.g. the root stratum), no form can undergo any further morphological operations on stratum X given that all such operations are 'x-based'.

The interaction of rule (4) with the rest of the morphology on a cyclic stratum (stratum 1 in English) is demonstrated in (5). *Nation* is, for the sake of simplicity, assumed to be morphologically simple (see Section 3.3 for discussion); outputs of rule (4) are in italics.

(5)   *Cycle 1*   *Cycle 2*   *Cycle 3*

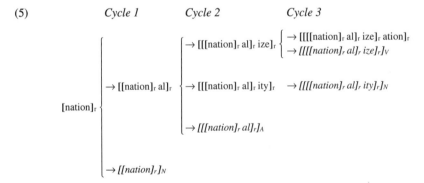

On the first cycle, the root *nation* can undergo two morphological processes: it can either attract the suffix -al, producing the root *national*, or it can undergo rule (4) producing the word *nation*$_N$. The latter is unavailable for further stratum-1 derivation and exits to stratum 2. The root *national* is available for the attachment of -ize and -ity on the second cycle, again producing roots, as well as undergoing rule (4) to produce the word *national*$_A$ on that cycle (which again exits from the stratum). On the third cycle, the root *nationalize* turns into the root *nationalization*, as well as into the word *nationalize*$_V$ through rule (4); the root *nationality* has only rule (4) available to it (*-ity* attracts no further stratum-1 suffixes). On the fourth cycle (not pictured in (5), the derivation of *nationalization* will continue in that the word *nationalization*$_N$ will be formed, possibly along with the further root ?*nationalizational*. And so forth.

The morphological motivation for having rule (4) in the grammar was amply discussed in Section 3.3.2; indeed, we saw there that rule (4) is a matter of necessity in the present model (see also Selkirk 1982b), and that the rule must operate prior to a given item's exit from the stratum, rather than immediately after the item's entry into the next stratum. The root-to-word conversion in English must happen on stratum 1 rather than on stratum 2, as Borowsky (1993) suggests.[1] The reason for this is twofold. First, it is a defining characteristic of the morphological processes on stratum 1 that their inputs are roots, and one of the morphological processes of stratum 2 that their inputs are words. The inputs of rule (4) are roots. Second, the morphological processes that any given root can undergo (on stratum 1) are listed with that root; the morphological processes available to a given word are not listed but subject to the subcategorisation frames of affixation rules. The availability of rule (4) for any given root is subject to listing: bound roots such as *matern-* do not undergo rule (4). The availability of stratum-1 morphological processes to this bound root is shown in (6). We see that rule (4) is unavailable on the first cycle, while on the second cycle both *maternal* and *maternity* undergo the root-to-word conversion.

(6)   *Cycle 1*   *Cycle 2*

$$[matern]_r \begin{cases} \rightarrow [[matern]_r \, al]_r & \begin{cases} \rightarrow \dots (?) \\ \rightarrow [[[matern]_r \, al]_r]_A \end{cases} \\ \rightarrow [[matern]_r \, ity]_r & \rightarrow [[[[matern]_r \, ity]_r]_N \\ \rightarrow *[[matern]_r \,]_L \, (n/a) \end{cases}$$

To complete the demonstration, consider a form that is unavailable for stratum-1 affixation altogether. The case of *nightingale* will prove instructive: trivially, the only morphological operation available is rule (4), which turns the root into the word *nightingale*$_N$, for exit from stratum 1.

(7)   *Cycle 1*

$$[nightingale]_r \qquad \rightarrow [[nightingale]_r]_N$$

As regards the phonological side of the derivation, (7) serves to make the basic point. The derivation of the word *nightingale*$_N$ from *nightingale*$_r$ acts as 'Rule A' in EC ((2) above), blocking the application of TSS to that form. EC ensures, as shown in (3) above, the disjunctive ordering of rule (4) before TSS.

In the derivations starting off with *nation*$_r$, sketched in (5) above, the Root-to-Word conversion prevents structure-changing rules from applying to the morphologically simple form on the first cycle: again, EC orders rule (4) disjunctively before any structure-changing rule whose structural description is met by *nation*. Structure-building rules such as syllabification and stress assignment, on the other hand, are free to apply to *nation*. The treatment of structure-building rules by EC was discussed in Section 4.4.1; but the precise location (whether this happens in *nation*$_r$ or in *nation*$_N$) of such structure-building processes in the present derivation remains to be determined. I return to this issue in Section 4.2.1. The form *national*$_r$, also derived on the first cycle, is eligible for structure-building as well as structure-changing rules: in this particular case, TSS will apply (Kiparsky 1982; Myers 1987). The shortened (as well as syllabified and stressed) form *national*$_r$ enters the second cycle, for further morphological processing. *Nationality, nationalize* are formed (and the input stress pattern modified in these forms where appropriate), and rule (4) converts *national*$_r$ into *national*$_A$.

If my previous arguments are correct whereby (4) is a genuine morphological operation and stratum-1 affixes attach to roots (rather than words), then the conversion of any root into a word, through rule (4), must be ordered alongside the affixations that that root is subject to, rather than on the cycle preceding them. For example, the application of (4) to *nation* must happen on the same cycle on which *national* is formed. Throughout the derivation, the conversion of a given root into a word takes place on the cycle following that on which that root is formed. This means, appropriately, that in the derivation (5), the only instance of SCE caused by rule (4) is that whereby the fricative [ʃ] in *nation* cannot derive from a /tɪ/ sequence as long as that form is treated as morphologically simple. If *nation* were analysed as morphologically complex (cf. *native, innate*), an analysis that is possible but not, as we saw in Section 3.3, necessary for every speaker, then the [ʃ] could of course be derived by rule. This is a welcome result; but some of its details again remain to be discussed. There are, again appropriately, no further instances of SCE in (5). The conversion of *national*$_r$ into *national*$_A$, and further root-to-word conversions on the third cycle, merely prevent the application of further structure-changing rules to such forms on subsequent cycles. In more general terms (although not relevant to the present example), the siting of rule (4) as described here prevents next-cycle counterfeeding (Kiparsky 1982; Giegerich 1988, 1994a).

Rule (4), then, is not only indispensable on the morphological side of the present, base-driven stratification model, but it also facilitates SCE under EC, replacing in the latter function the identity rules proposed by Kiparsky (1982). The present account therefore reduces further the arbitrariness inherent in Kiparsky's account; but it retains the advantages which that account held over previous studies where SCE was stipulated as a free-standing condition on lexical derivations ('SCC'). In particular, the following drawbacks of the account involving identity rules are absent from the present one. First, unlike identity rules, rule (4) is strongly motivated in the grammar; as we saw in Section 4.1.1, the conceptual status of identity rules is highly disputable and their motivation in morphological terms poor. And second, the present model makes the prediction – again one that identity rules cannot handle in a principled way – that in any stratified lexicon (comprising for example two strata for English or three for German), the final stratum cannot display SCE. All and only non-final strata have rule (4). This result supports the suggestion, tentatively made in Section 4.1.1, that the blocking of structure-changing rules in underived environments may be restricted to *non-final* rather than *cyclic* strata. I return to this issue in Section 4.2.2 below.

4.2   Implications

4.2.1   *There is no pre-morphology cycle*

It was widely assumed in the earlier literature dealing with cyclic rule-application in Lexical Phonology (Kiparsky 1982; Mohanan 1986) that on a cyclic stratum:

> [t]he phonological rule system is scanned for applicability of rules every time there is a new form at a given stratum (i.e. phonological rules are scanned for applicability *to the forms entering the stratum*, as well as to the forms created by a morphological operation at the stratum). (Mohanan 1986: 49; my emphasis)

This means that phonological rules not only apply after each morphological operation but also before the first morphological operation, that is, to morphologically simple roots. The general view of cyclic rule application whereby every morphological operation triggers a check through the phonological rules is upheld, in such a model, by the assumption that the entry of an underived form into the stratum constitutes in itself some sort of morphological operation (Inkelas 1993: 89). But it is by no means obvious that that should be the case, for two reasons. First, items entering stratum 1 undergo no structural change in doing so: the case for calling such entry a 'morphological operation' (tantamount to 'morphological rule') is at least as weak as is the case for identity rules. Second, the spatial metaphor connected with the notion 'entry into a stratum' makes sense only if, prior to its 'entry', the form in question is in some other formally defined component of the grammar. And there is neither a 'stratum 0' nor any other entity of formal status containing such forms. The idea that there is a repository of underived items, although widely held and probably correct, is both informal and not crucially dependent on the assumption that such a repository does not form part of stratum 1 itself.

Mohanan's claim that there is a phonological cycle prior to the first morphological rule is, then, stipulative: it does not automatically follow from the general architecture of the stratum. That claim is not thereby automatically a false one; but it is known to result in overgeneration: it falsely predicts all roots to be subject to phonological rules. But bound roots apparently universally fail to constitute phonological rule domains in that they are not subject to stress assignment and in some cases (though apparently not in English) fail to conform to morpheme structure constraints (Brame 1974; Kiparsky 1982; Harris 1983; Inkelas 1993). Given that it is impossible, at least in English, to distinguish between bound roots and free roots in structural (e.g. phonotactic) terms, both in the present model and in its predecessors, any model that recognises a pre-morphology phonological cycle faces the problem of having to exclude bound roots from that cycle in a structurally arbitrary way.

In the present model, the distinction between bound roots and free roots is expressed in such a way that free roots undergo rule (4) while bound roots do not. Recall that this distinction is subject to listing (roots are listed as to whether they undergo (4) or not). It is not a distinction that follows in English from structural properties of roots: the fact that *matern-* is a bound root in Present-day English while *modern* is free is entirely arbitrary in terms of the structures of those morphemes. Morphologically simple free roots, then, re-write themselves and turn into words on the first cycle. If it is true that free roots are subject to phonological rules while bound roots are not then it is at least conceivable that such phonological rules operate on the first cycle (affecting the output forms of first-cycle (4)), rather than necessitating a pre-morphology cycle.[2] Under the present model a formal distinction between free and bound roots cannot in fact be drawn without reference to their possible candidacy for rule (4).

Indeed, in the present model a pre-morphology phonological cycle cannot exist. To achieve the blocking effect through rule (4), which is as we have seen a morphological rule, we must ensure that no phonological rules apply prior to the application of that (or any other) morphological rule. In *nightingale* (7), a structure-changing rule such as TSS would fail to be blocked if it were available before the first (and, in this case, only) morphological rule, namely the root-to-word conversion (4). Similarly in (5), the palatalisation /tɪ/→[ʃ] in the morphologically simple form *nation* would be free to go ahead if phonological rules were allowed to apply before (4) does. This means that for SCE to be achieved on the first cycle, the model requires the assumption (contrary to what Mohanan (1986: 49) stipulates and what others assume) that, in cyclic rule application, no phonological rules apply prior to the application of the first morphological rule. The model has no facilities to restrict the range of such phonological rules, applying in this case before (4), to those of the structure-building kind (e.g. syllabification, stress assignment), whose application before (4) would probably be unharmful and possibly even desirable. We have to stipulate therefore that only morphological rules can trigger phonological rules in any given cycle. As we saw above, this stipulation follows no less (and perhaps intuitively more) from the general notion of cyclic rule application than Mohanan's did; certainly, it is more restrictive and therefore in principle welcome.

I noted earlier that the present model, while having to stipulate the absence of a pre-morphology cycle, facilitates not only the distinction between bound and free roots in derivational (if not structural) terms but also the application of phonological rules to underived free roots. It does so on the first cycle, triggered by the morphology, in an appropriately constrained way: in *nation* (5) as well as in *nightingale* (7), structure-building rules are free to apply to the output forms of rule (4), $nation_N$ and $nightingale_N$ respectively, while structure-changing rules are blocked by EC as discussed. In contrast, no phonological rules of any sort can apply to bound roots in isolation, for the simple reason that forms such as *matern-* do not undergo rule (4) and therefore fail to re-materialise on the first cycle ((6) above).

Consider now the availability of phonological structure, built by rule, to the further stages of the derivation. Here the model makes the rather interesting prediction that no such structure forms part of the input to further stratum-1 morphological derivation if it has been built on the first cycle, i.e. in morphologically simple (free) roots. Returning once again to *nation* (5), we note that the output *nation*$_N$ of rule (4) makes a straight exit from the stratum rather than being input to the formation of *national*. This means that morphologically simple free roots have no syllable structure and no stress at the point of input to morphological derivation on the first cycle. Syllable structure and stress in *national* are assigned from scratch. No first-cycle affixation can be restricted with regard to the syllabic or stress pattern of its base. This is in line with the central point made in Chapter 3 whereby the morphology of stratum 1 is listed, rather than subject to generalisations in the form of subcategorisation frames. But the model makes the further and more specific prediction that syllabic or stress patterns cannot even figure in additional (for example redundancy) statements regarding stratum-1 affixation, perhaps of the form that 'stratum-1 affix A may be listed only with roots bearing final stress'.

This further restriction predicted by the model removes one particular indeterminacy from Lexical Phonology. It predicts unequivocally that any first-cycle affixation process that is restricted by the syllable structure or stress pattern of the base must be sited on stratum 2. In previous, less constrained models allowing a pre-morphology phonological cycle, such phonological information was available to a stratum-1 affix at the point of attachment; such affixes could therefore be either stratum 1 or stratum 2. Two such cases deserve discussion.

First, the well-known case of -*al*$_N$, exemplified in (8) below and discussed extensively by Ross (1972), Siegel (1974) and Odden (1993), among others. Consider the examples given below:

(8) a. arrival   acquittal   b. withdrawal
        survival   approval   betrothal
        appraisal perusal   upheaval
        retiral   reversal   bestowal
        referral   disposal   trial
        dismissal rehearsal   rental
                                  burial

This suffix is treated as stratum 2 by Siegel (1974: 164ff.) and Selkirk (1982b: 80) on the grounds of its sensitivity to the stress pattern of the base: with the sole exception of *burial*, its bases have final stress. Moreover, bases often (but not always) consist of prefixed bound roots; they are always free forms (verbs), which are usually transitive. Further phonotactic restrictions, involving the base-final sequence (but not relevant here) have been suggested by Ross (1972).

In a model that permits a pre-morphology cycle, *-al* may be attached on either stratum 1 or stratum 2: on stratum 1, stress could be assigned to the base prior to the attachment of the suffix, on the pre-morphology cycle in the cases of (at least) *trial* and *rental* (8b). Siegel's and Selkirk's decision to affiliate the suffix with stratum 2, while undoubtedly correct, is arbitrary in such a model. In the present model, on the other hand, *-al* must indeed be a stratum-2 suffix given that stratum 1 has no pre-morphology cycle on which stress could be assigned prior to the attachment of the suffix.

I believe this analysis to make correct empirical predictions on all counts. First, we expect stratum-2 suffixes to attach to free forms (words) only. The suffix *-al* indeed fails to attach to bound bases. Second, we expect stratum-2 suffixes to be productive. Despite the comparatively small number of examples quoted in the literature (but see Lehnert (1971) for more), *-al* may probably be treated as productive given the extremely tight restrictions on its base and given also the fact that it competes with a number of other noun-forming suffixes (*-ment*, *-ion* etc.): *-al* is therefore heavily subject to blocking. And third, *-al* does attach to Germanic bases ((8b) above), a fact categorically denied by Odden (1993: 137), with whom most of those examples actually originate. Such breaches of the [± Latinate] constraint are, as we saw in Chapter 2, common among stratum-2 suffixes.

A second and more complex case is presented by the German suffix *-(er)ei*, deriving pejorative *nomina actionis* from verbs (Fleischer 1974: 134ff.; Giegerich 1987; Hargus 1993). This suffix bears the main stress of the word, as well as selecting its long and short allomorphs on eurhythmic grounds:

(9)   a. Sing-erei   'singing'   b. Segel-ei   'sailing'
          Trompet-erei   'blowing the trumpet'   Bügel-ei   'ironing'
          Lackier-erei   'varnishing'   Meuter-ei   'mutiny'
          Arbeit-erei   'working'

Contrary to the analysis presented in Giegerich (1987: 455), our present model again predicts that *-(er)ei* must be attached on stratum 2, a revision that is strongly supported by the unrestricted productivity of this suffix. But this again means that the final stress on such forms cannot be due to the stress rules, which are assumed to be sited on stratum 1 in German as they are in English. Given that final stress in German is in any case synchronically exceptional (Hayes 1986, *contra* Giegerich 1985), this is not a worrying result. There is nothing to prevent affixes, if they are treated as lexical items as they are in the present account, from bearing stress in their underlying representations. But what makes this case complex is the syllable-count in the base that determines the selection of allomorphs. While *sing*- counts as a monosyllabic foot (9a) and *segel, meuter-* (ending in syllabic liquids) as disyllabic feet (9b), bases ending in syllabic nasals count as monosyllabic at the point of the attachment of the suffix:

(10)   Atm-erei   *Atem-ei   'breathing'
        Widm-erei   *Widem-ei   'dedicating'
        Ordn-erei   *Orden-ei   'ordering'

I return to this issue in Section 8.5.2, presenting an analysis whereby on stratum 1 only vowels and liquids (but not nasals) can constitute syllabic nuclei in German. For the purposes of the present argument this means that in the outputs of rule (4), forms such as [zeːgl] constitute two syllables, while final (post-obstruent) nasals (as in [aːtm]) remain unsyllabified at that stage. This is then the phonological structure with which such forms enter into stratum 2, ready to undergo the morphology of that stratum.

But let us return to the more general issue of the availability of rule-governed phonological structure at the later stages of morphological derivation. On the first cycle, as we have seen, no such structure forms part of the input to affixation because there is no phonological cycle preceding such affixation. Morphologically simple free roots are subject to structure-building phonological rules, but separately: the outputs of rule (4), subject to such rules, exit from the stratum rather than being input to further affixation on the stratum. Interestingly, the model makes a different prediction for the morphologies of the second and subsequent cycles. The results of both structure-changing and structure-building rules obtained on the first cycle do form inputs to second-cycle affixation. In (5) above, syllable structure and stress are assigned to the root *national* on the first cycle. Moreover, TSS applies on the first cycle to that form, which then forms the input to second-cycle *nationalize* and *nationality* (as well as undergoing rule (4)). This prediction is clearly correct, as evidenced by the fact that the first syllables in both forms contain short vowels which must be the result of first-cycle shortening (Kiparsky 1982; recall Section 4.1.1). This difference between the inputs to morphological operations on the first and subsequent cycles is of course due to the fact that, unlike that of later cycles, the first-cycle morphology is not preceded by any phonological cycle in the present model. As a result, first-cycle derivations are subject to constraints that are stronger than those found on later cycles. First-cycle derivatives must be syllabified and stressed from scratch, without input from the base, while later-cycle derivatives have syllable-structure and stress inputs provided by their morphologically complex bases. In turn this means that on the first cycle, stress or syllable structures are erected in an entirely structure-building fashion. The stress pattern of a complex form derived on that cycle cannot contain any reflexes of the stress pattern of the base obtained through structure-changing rules. Such a prediction will not be uncontroversial (see, for example, Kiparsky 1979); whether it is correct remains to be seen. But it does relate, in a rather interesting way, to the prediction made by the morphological side of the present model whereby the first (innermost) suffix attached to a given root is governed by root-specific idiosyncrasies in morphological and, notably, semantic terms, whereas further suffixes attached are merely subject to the more general constraints imposed by the preceding suffix (Section 3.3.3 above). Unpredictably, *fratern-* takes *-ize*, *-al* and *-ity*, giving rise to idiosyncratic meanings, while *fraternize* takes *-ation* like all *-ize* forms do, with the meaning associated with all forms containing *-ization*.

> [I]diosyncratic marking for susceptibility to morphological processes *or lexical phonological processes* . . . [is] concentrated in *basic* lexical entries. . . . In English morphology, at any rate, the overriding generalization is surely that affixation is unpredictable for basic lexical entries (especially of course at level 1) but that for derived lexical items it can be defined generally for a given head, even at level 1. (Kiparsky 1982: 27; my emphases)

If it is the case (as is predicted by the absence of a phonological cycle prior to the first morphological rule) that phonological structure assigned by rule to the morphologically simple root does not constitute an input to forms derived on the first cycle but that, rather, such first-cycle forms undergo phonological processing from scratch, then first-cycle derivatives must behave like morphologically simple items in phonological terms as they may do in semantic terms. There is on the first cycle, then, a parallelism of semantic and phonological non-compositionality that is not expected among later-cycle derivatives.

4.2.2   SCE and (non-)cyclicity

We noted as early as in Section 4.1.1 above the possibility that instead of being linked with *cyclicity*, the blocking of structure-changing rules in underived environments may be confined to *non-final* strata: given that in a two-strata lexicon the first stratum is assumed to be cyclic as well as subject to SCE, and the second non-cyclic as well as not SCE-bound, either restriction imposed on the constraint would yield the same result. Indeed, in Section 4.1.2 we saw that by virtue of the fact that only non-final strata contain rule (4), SCE itself can be present on non-final strata only. I turn in this section to the relationship between SCE and cyclic rule application, in particular to the predictions made by the present model regarding SCE for a putative lexical stratum that is non-cyclic.

A number of proposals endorsing non-cyclic lexical strata are on record. Kiparsky (1982) had assumed that all lexical strata are cyclic, thus encountering the problem that the absence of SCE on the final stratum was explicable neither through non-cyclicity nor, as we saw in Section 4.1.1, through the principled absence of identity rules on that stratum. But subsequently, Kiparsky (1985) argued that the final stratum (the 'word level') of a two-strata lexicon is non-cyclic. Booij and Rubach's (1987) 'post-cyclic rules', corresponding to the phonological side of Kiparsky's 'word level', have the same characteristic of non-cyclicity. Halle and Mohanan (1985) and Mohanan (1986: Section 2.5.7) in addition stipulate that stratum 2, of their four-strata lexicon of English, is non-cyclic. 'What this means is that it is necessary to specify, for each stratum, whether it is cyclic or non-cyclic' (Mohanan 1986: 50). Such arbitrary stipulation of cyclicity is of course highly unsatisfactory, especially when the decision as to whether a given stratum is cyclic or not is driven by but one criterion, namely the desirability of having SCE on that stratum.

As long as SCE is produced by an independent condition on the grammar ('SCC': Section 4.1.1 above), as it was in (Halle and) Mohanan's model as well as (implicitly) in Kiparsky (1985), the non-cyclicity of a given stratum exempts that stratum from SCE. This was clearly the primary motivation for the various non-cyclicity proposals mentioned above: strata designated as non-cyclic provide homes for structure-changing phonological rules that, contrary to SCE, apply in underived environments. The standard version of Vowel Shift, for example, raises the stressed tense vowel in the underived form *serene*, deriving it from underlying /eː/ (compare *serenity*, affected by TSS); that of Vowel Reduction turns the /ɒ/ in *atom* into schwa (compare *atomic*). The stipulated non-cyclicity of the 'word-level' in Kiparsky (1985), of the 'post-cyclic rules' in Booij and Rubach (1987), and of the second of four strata in Halle and Mohanan (1985), Mohanan (1986) serve no other apparent purpose than to ensure SCE-exemption for phonological rules that do not seem to yield to that constraint. Alternative, SCE-compliant analyses of the relevant phenomena have, however, been proposed (McMahon 1990; Giegerich 1992c, 1994a). If those proposals (to be discussed in detail in Section 4.3 and Chapter 5) are adopted, then any justification for the provision of non-cyclic strata in order to defeat SCE at certain points of the derivation simply vanishes. Note that only non-cyclic *intermediate* strata are still of relevance to this discussion; as we saw above, final strata are in any case systematically exempt from SCE in the present model for reasons unrelated to (non-)cyclicity.

The primary criterion for any decision as to whether a given stratum is cyclic or not is, of course, not SCE but the observed interaction of morphological and phonological rules. On a non-cyclic stratum, the entirety of morphological rules precedes the entirety of phonological rules. Evidence in favour of the cyclicity of certain strata (for example, stratum 1) is well-documented and has been discussed above: the first vowel in *nationality* is short because *national* on the previous cycle, but not *nationality* itself, is subject to TSS (Kiparsky 1982). But positive evidence in favour of the *non-cyclicity* of a given stratum is much harder to come by. Indeed, Mohanan (1986: Section 2.5.7) cites none when arguing for the non-cyclicity of his stratum 2; the stratum's failure to comply with SCE characteristically constitutes the only argument. Researchers have tended to find no conclusive evidence for the cyclicity of certain rules or strata but no evidence for their non-cyclicity either; but the fact that Halle and Mohanan's (1985) version of Vowel Shift, essentially that of SPE, does not require cyclic rule application makes it non-cyclic only under the assumption that non-cyclicity is the unmarked option for a given stratum.

As we have seen, the final stratum of however many is under the present model exempt from SCE due to the systematic absence of rule (4) on that stratum. The possible non-cyclicity of that stratum is an independent empirical issue, to be decided solely on the grounds of observed morphology–phonology interactions. This raises the question of whether it is possible under this model for intermediate strata to be non-cyclic and/or exempt from SCE. The model of Halle and Mohanan (1985) and Mohanan (1986) constitutes, as we discussed, a case in point: while that model has to be rejected for its insupportable proliferation of strata (see, for example, Gussmann 1988), the idea that intermediate strata in the present model might behave like their second, non-cyclic stratum cannot be dismissed without scrutiny. Let us hypothesise, for the purpose of this question, that stratum 2 (the stem stratum) in the German three-strata lexicon is non-cyclic. Assume also, for argument's sake, that the following German suffixes are stem-based and therefore attach on stratum 2.

First, *-bar* ('-able'), forming adjectives out of transitive verb stems, as in (11):

(11) lesbar   'readable'
      eßbar   'edible'
      brauchbar   'useable, adequate'
      analysierbar   'analyseable'

Second, *-keit* (roughly '-ness'/'-ity'), forming abstract nouns out of adjective stems, as in (12):

(12) Eitelkeit   'vanity'
      Heiserkeit   'hoarseness'
      Ähnlichkeit   'similarity'
      Lesbarkeit   'readability'

Given that Stem in German is a morphological category intermediate between Root and Word, that stratum has rule (4) to facilitate stem-to-word conversion. The stratum is therefore predicted to be subject to SCE – but to what extent? Consider the following sample derivation, with simplified bracketing and italicised stem-to-word conversions.

(13)

$$[\text{les}] \begin{cases} \rightarrow [[\text{les}]\text{bar}]] \begin{cases} \rightarrow [[\text{Les}]\text{bar}]\text{keit}]] \rightarrow [[[Les]bar]keit]]]_N \\ \rightarrow [[les]bar]]_{Adj} \end{cases} \\ \rightarrow *[[les]]_V \text{ (n/a)} \end{cases}$$

Given that both *lesbar* and *Lesbarkeit* (but not the unaffixed stem *les-*) are convertible into words – they are potentially free forms – the stem-to-word-conversion rule (4) must apply as indicated in (13). Under cyclic application of phonological rules, structure-changing rules would be free to apply to *lesbar*, produced on what would be the first cycle, and to *Lesbarkeit* produced on what would be the second cycle (compare (5) above). Structure-changing rules can apply to a given form on the cycle prior to that on which the form undergoes rule (4). Under non-cyclic application, however, there will be no such phonological rules interspersed with the morphology; all phonological rules apply after the completion of all the morphology (which includes all stem-to-word conversions). Phonology begins where the derivation (13) ends. In that case, the stem-to-word conversion of *lesbar* will block structure-changing rules from applying to that form; and similarly the stem-to-word conversion of *Lesbarkeit* will block structure-changing rules from that, further derived, form. In other words, for a non-cyclic stratum our model makes the prediction that *all* structure-changing rules are blocked by EC provided that stratum contains rule (4) – provided, that is, the stratum is non-final. This is an important result. In the present model, analyses such as Halle and Mohanan's (1985), whereby non-final strata are designated as non-cyclic in order to legitimise SCC-defeating structure-changing rules (such as Vowel Shift and Vowel Reduction), are impossible. If such strata exist at all then they cannot contain the very rules which they are intended to accommodate. This means, first, that if a non-final stratum contains structure-changing rules then it must be cyclic, and second, that no devices are available to exempt a non-final stratum from SCE.

It follows from these observations that in the present model, SCE is not crucially linked with cyclic rule application. As we have seen, non-cyclic non-final strata display SCE in even stronger terms than cyclic non-final strata do; and final strata have no SCE regardless of whether or not they are cyclic. This means that the term 'SCE' is a misnomer (which we retain despite its non-compositional semantics to honour tradition).

4.3   The abstractness of the final stratum

4.3.1   The final stratum and the free-ride problem

The lexicon has a final stratum, then, on which SCE does not hold. This prediction made by the base-driven stratification model conforms with an assumption to the same effect concerning the properties of that stratum (the 'postcyclic' or 'word' level) in most alternative models (e.g. Kiparsky 1985; Booij and Rubach 1987; Borowsky 1993). The reasoning behind this assumption has been the apparent need for the grammar to have structure-changing rules that crucially apply in underived environments – the same reason as that for which Halle and Mohanan (1985) stipulate non-cyclicity for their stratum 2. We saw above that Halle and Mohanan's analysis, facilitated by a model that is now notorious for its lack of constraints, is appropriately ruled out in the present model: the predictions made here are such that no intermediate stratum, cyclic or not, can bypass SCE. But this raises the question of what we are to make of a model which, as does the present one, offers on the final stratum the same kind of refuge for apparently unconstrainable phonological rules that we found unacceptable in Halle and Mohanan's intermediate stratum.

One such rule is Vowel Shift. Central to SPE's highly abstract account of the English vowel system, focal point of the psycholinguistic critique (and rejection) of that account (cf. Jaeger (1986), Wang and Derwing (1986) and the literature cited there), this rule has persisted in the post-SPE literature. The minor modifications and refinements that have been proposed (e.g. Halle 1977; Halle and Mohanan 1985) have left untouched its most worrying characteristic: that it affects tense/long vowels, thereby operating in many cases in the underived member of a pair of morphologically related forms that show the relevant alternation. It was not until McMahon (1990) that a radical re-formulation of the rule was published; I discuss this version in Section 4.3.2 below, concentrating in the remainder of the present section on the problems inherent in the 'standard' (SPE) version that McMahon later tackled.

As is well known, Vowel Shift raises non-high (and diphthongises high) tense/long vowels in much the same way as the fifteenth-to-seventeenth century sound change did that was to give rise to this synchronic rule of Present-day English. A simplified version is given below, omitting irrelevant details such as the rule's dependence on stress, as well as the question of how tenseness and length relate to each other, in Vowel Shift and otherwise.

(14)   *Tense Vowel Shift*

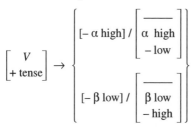

The examples of the shift from /eː/ to [iː] given in (15) below illustrate the integration of the 'standard' version of Vowel Shift into a two-strata model. (Irrelevant representational details such as SPE's off-glide notation for long vowels are omitted in favour of IPA symbols.)

(15)   a. Mendel – Mendelian

/ɛ/	/ɛ/	Underlying Vowel	
(n/a)	[eː]	*CiV-Tensing*	(Stratum 1)
(n/a)	[iː]	Vowel Shift	(Stratum 2)
[ə]	*(n/a)*	Vowel Reduction	(Stratum 2)

b. serene – serenity

/eː/	/eː/	Underlying Vowel
(n/a)	[ɛ]	Trisyllabic Shortening (Stratum 1)
[iː]	*(n/a)*	Vowel Shift (Stratum 2)

In both cases, Vowel Shift affects tense/long vowels – in (15a) the result of Pre-*CiV* Lengthening triggered by the attachment -*ian* on stratum 1, in (15b) the vowel of the underlying representation. Note that both the lengthening rule operating in (15a) and TSS, which makes the vowel in *serenity* ineligible for Vowel Shift, can be assumed to be sited on stratum 1 (Halle and Mohanan 1985; McMahon 1990). Both operate in derived environments. Vowel Shift, however, is not so restricted. While the [eː] in (15a) would qualify for derived-environment status in the sense of SCE (it is the result of a structure-changing phonological rule which, under cyclic rule application, would have operated on the same cycle), that in (15b) is underlying /eː/. The structure of a large number of alternating pairs whose vowels are differentiated by Vowel Shift is like that found in (15b): the tense vowel in the morphologically simple form undergoes Vowel Shift while that in the morphologically complex form is shortened instead of shifting. *Divine – divinity, metre – metrical, declare – declarative, profound – profundity*, all frequently cited examples, follow the same pattern, which appears to point to the inevitable conclusion that Vowel Shift is a rule which cannot be restricted to derived environments, and which therefore must be sited on the final stratum in order to escape SCE.

But the problem is that such analyses give rise to precisely the kind of unwarranted abstractness that SCE seeks to ban from the grammar. The absence of SCE on the final stratum predicts Vowel Shift not only in members of alternating pairs like those in (15a) and (15b) but also in non-alternating forms such as *ride, free, name, pool* etc. If the rule is permitted to apply in the underived member of an alternating pair then it is also permitted to apply in non-alternating forms. SCE, in anybody's formulation, is unable to distinguish between these two kinds of potential input, however desirable the former and objectionable the latter may be. Any structure-changing phonological rule that is located on the final stratum faces the problem of such 'free-ride' derivations (Zwicky 1970). To give two further examples: if there is a rule of *mn*-Simplification (Mohanan 1986: 22), deleting pre-bracket /n/ in *hymn, autumn*, and if that rule is sited on stratum 2 – as not only its operation in underived environments but also its failure to operate before stratum-1 suffixes suggest (*hymnic, autumnal*) – then the grammar has no formal means of preventing free-ride derivations such as *sum* from */sʌmn/. And if Vowel Reduction, turning unstressed lax vowels into [ə], is similarly a stratum-2 rule, then it will not only appropriately reduce the second vowel in *atom* (compare stratum-1 *atomic*) but also inappropriately permit the derivation of any non-alternating schwa (*camera, about, common, a* etc.) from an underlyingly full (lax) vowel whose quality cannot be determined.

I return to the issue of '*mn*-Simplification' in Section 4.3.3 below and to that of Vowel 'Reduction' in Chapter 5, proposing radically different analyses of the facts. For the moment we have to conclude that an SCE-free stratum in lexical phonology is effectively as unconstrained, in derivational terms, as SPE's 'standard' generative phonology was.

4.3.2   McMahon's Vowel Shift analysis

Central to McMahon's (1990) argument is the observation that the excessive abstractness inherent in the SPE-type account of vowel-shift alternations is ultimately due to the desire to derive both kinds of alternations found in (15a) and (15b) by means of the same mechanisms. It is precisely these mechanisms, necessitating abstract underliers and involving, as we have seen, an unconstrainable rule of Vowel Shift, that cause the free-ride problem. But SPE had regarded such a unified analysis of all vowel-shift alternations as imperative under Occam's Razor. According to SPE, the only possible alternative analysis which, positing surface-true underliers, derives [iː] from /ɛ/ (*Mendelian*, (15a)) as well as [ɛ] from /iː/ (*serenity*, (15b)) must be 'surely in error' (SPE: 180), involving as it does the mirror-image duplication of height-changing 'Vowel Shift' (and other) rules needed to arrive at the appropriate surface forms.

McMahon, in contrast, does just that. Assuming that SCE is the only derivational constraint available in the grammar for the avoidance of spurious free-ride derivations (a point to which I return in Section 4.3.3), she argues that all vowel-shift alternations must be produced on stratum 1 – on the one stratum (in her model and mine), that is, where SCE is operative. The underlying vowels in morphologically simple forms (*Mendel* and *serene* in (15)) must then be surface-identical. (Like McMahon, I ignore here the vowel 'reduction' found in the former.) And while the shift of the vowel in *Mendel*, tensed/lengthened by *CiV*-Tensing, is accounted for by the familiar rule of (Tense) Vowel Shift, given in (14) above, a new rule of (Lax) Vowel Shift, the downward-shifting mirror-image of (14), is needed to produce the surface [ɛ] in *serenity* out of the underlying /iː/ of *serene*, laxed/shortened to [ɪ] through TSS. The new rule is given in (16), after McMahon (1990: 220):

(16)   *Lax Vowel Shift*

$$
\begin{bmatrix} V \\ -\text{tense} \end{bmatrix} \rightarrow
\begin{Bmatrix}
[-\alpha\ \text{low}]\ /\ \begin{bmatrix} \underline{\hspace{1.5em}} \\ \alpha\ \text{low} \\ -\text{high} \end{bmatrix} \\[2em]
[-\beta\ \text{high}]\ /\ \begin{bmatrix} \underline{\hspace{1.5em}} \\ \beta\ \text{high} \\ -\text{low} \end{bmatrix}
\end{Bmatrix}
$$

Below are sketches of the derivations of *Mendel – Mendelian* and *sincere – sincerity*, following McMahon's account:

(17)   a. Mendel – Mendelian

/ɛ/	/ɛ/	Underlying Vowel	
(n/a)	[eː]	*CiV-Tensing*	(Stratum 1)
(n/a)	[iː]	Tense Vowel Shift	(Stratum 1)
(n/a)	*(n/a)*	Lax Vowel Shift	(Stratum 1)
[ə]	*(n/a)*	Vowel Reduction	(Stratum 2)

   b. sincere – sincerity

/iː/	/iː/	Underlying Vowel	
(n/a)	[ɪ]	Trisyllabic Shortening	(Stratum 1)
(n/a)	*(n/a)*	Tense Vowel Shift	(Stratum 1)
(n/a)	[ɛ]	Lax Vowel Shift	(Stratum 1)

Note that SCE makes precisely the right predictions regarding the application of the two rules of Vowel Shift. First, Lax Vowel Shift fails to apply, in the vowels under discussion, in *Mendel* (17a) and Tense Vowel Shift fails to apply in *sincere* (176): these vowels are underived. Second, neither Vowel Shift applies in the first vowels of either form, which are equally underived; nor does, third, any vowel in the by-now-infamous free-ride cases of the SPE analysis, such as those in *free, ride, name* etc., qualify for a derivation from any sort of surface-remote underliers. And fourth, in cases which constitute lexical exceptions to, for example, TSS (*obese – obesity*), SCE prevents (Tense) Vowel Shift from applying. The tense /iː/ in both *obese* and *obesity* are equally underived. Given that the two rules of Vowel Shift have tense and lax vowels, respectively, as inputs, only vowels whose tenseness/laxness has been produced by rule on the same cycle can undergo either Shift. The overall picture is, then, that all tenseness adjustments are triggered by the concatenation of morphemes (that is, by suffixation processes) and all instances of Vowel Shift are triggered by such tenseness adjustments. Ultimately, Vowel Shift can only occur therefore in morphologically complex forms. Morphologically simple forms, whether they form part of an alternating pair or not, must have surface-true underliers. In any alternating pair, the underlying vowel is provided by the surface vowel of the morphologically simple form. This is, then, an analysis that removes at a stroke all the unwarranted abstractness of previous accounts.

The price McMahon pays for this analysis is, however, substantial – so substantial that SPE was unwilling and, in fact, unable to pay it. What is at issue here is not the re-formulation of a rule that in historical terms raised tense vowels into one that synchronically lowers lax vowels: not only is such 'rule inversion' well-established as a form of linguistic change (Vennemann 1972b); Chomsky and Halle themselves are said to have contemplated this version prior to the publication of SPE (McCawley 1986). McMahon's analysis is not just a revision of a technical detail of the phonology of English but a downright challenge to one of the fundamentals of 'standard' generative phonology, namely Occam's Razor. Her account involves, as we have seen, the mirror-image duplication of rules – (14) and (16). Moreover, this duplication would be avoidable if we were to keep Vowel Shift, with all its abstractness problems, on stratum 2 in the form established by SPE and discussed in Section 4.3.1 above. The merits of Occam's Razor have to be weighed against the utterly implausible, yet inevitable, predictions made by its application. The Razor-driven account implies that speakers of English either store forms such as *free, ride, name* etc. in their pre-vowel-shift representations as /freː/, /riːd/, /naːm/ and give them free rides through the Vowel-Shift derivation, or that they store such non-alternating forms (the vast majority of words containing tense vowels in English) in their surface representations but marking them individually as exceptions to Vowel Shift. (Without such exception marking, *free* stored as /friː/ would of course surface as *[fraɪ].) Neither alternative has any psycholinguistic plausibility; nor is it the case that an analysis which rigorously applies Occam's Razor has greater inherent 'psychological reality' than an analysis that does not (see, for example, Linell 1979: 73ff.). Indeed, Occam's Razor is largely discredited as a psycholinguistic evaluation measure (Derwing 1973; Jaeger 1986).

It is impossible, then, not to accept McMahon's analysis of Vowel Shift as the preferable one. Both hers and the predecessor analysis, discussed in Section 4.3.1, are possible under the present two-strata model: the first stratum has SCE but the second does not. There can be little doubt that

SCE is the appropriate constraint to avoid the undesirable side-effects of the 'standard' account of vowel-shift alternations. The question that remains is, however, how the choice between the two competing analyses is to be made if both analyses are permissible in the grammar. I turn to this question in the following section.

4.3.3   SCE and the Alternation Condition

Recall the Alternation Condition, briefly discussed in Section 4.1.1 above and stated (simplified for present purposes) in (18):

(18)   *Alternation Condition (AC)*
        Structure-changing rules cannot apply to all occurrences of a given
        morpheme.

I noted in Section 4.1.1 that AC (Kiparsky 1973), succeeded in the literature by SCE/SCC, faces the major problem of not being interpretable as a formal condition on grammars. It is impossible to ascertain in advance whether or not a given rule will apply to all instances of a given morpheme. Given that the only way of ensuring that a given rule satisfies AC is a trawl through its entire output, AC is possibly an evaluation measure for existing grammars (I return to this point below); but it cannot be formally part of Universal Grammar or of individual grammars. As we saw, this observation was the main reason for replacing AC by SCE/SCC in phonological theory: the latter will block any offending derivations in advance, rather than (like the former) merely being able to stigmatise them *a posteriori*. It is for that reason alone that AC must be (and has been) abandoned in favour of SCE, which (as we also saw in Section 4.1) is, moreover, derivative of EC. (For a fuller discussion of the shortcomings of AC see Kiparsky (1982: 36ff.; 1993: 227ff.).)

But let us pretend, for the moment, that AC can be imposed on the grammar; in particular, let us assume that stratum 2, while not subject to SCE, is constrained by AC. Strikingly, AC will then adequately constrain the Vowel Shift analysis in its old (pre-McMahon) form, banning free-ride derivations in non-alternating forms while allowing the shifting of tense vowels to take place in all cases where alternations occur (the *sincere – sincerity* as well as the *Mendel – Mendelian* type). Notice that AC allows the vowel-shift derivation of *sincere* to go through as long as *sincerity* exists: AC is in this respect weaker than SCE in that it indiscriminately allows a given rule to apply in derived and underived environments as long as the rule does not affect all instances of the morpheme. Kiparsky (1982: 37) makes this point in connection with TSS, arguing that AC wrongly predicts the existence of pairs such as [ɒ]*rigin–**[oʊ]*riginal*, displaying TSS in the underived form on the strength of the derivative, in which TSS is bled by the stress rule. If it is only 'a certain type of rule, of which Trisyllabic Shortening is an example' (Kiparsky 1982: 37) in which such alternations systematically fail to occur, then this type of rule can in the present model be characterised as 'the stratum-1 rules'. But, as we have seen, it is by no means clear that Vowel Shift is not of this type: under McMahon's (1990) analysis it is. We are left, then, with the situation that we identified above, where the 'standard' vowel-shift derivation, sited on stratum 2, is adequately constrained by AC while McMahon's (1990) analysis, sited on stratum 1, is adequately constrained by SCE.

But if the grammar cannot, as we have seen, impose AC formally, what is the status of that constraint? We may take the view that, although the grammar cannot enforce AC, the speaker can:

> The only sense that can be made out of . . . [AC] is as a strategy of language acquisition which says that a learner analyzes a form 'at face value' unless he has encountered variants of it which justify a more remote underlying representation. (Kiparsky 1982: 36)

Under this interpretation (for which see also S. Anderson 1981), AC is in the first instance not a condition imposed in whatever way on the grammar but a generalisation concerning the acquisition of underlying representations. It predicts, for a vowel-shift analysis of the pre-McMahon kind, that a speaker learning items such as *free, bean, leaf, obscene* etc. will store these with the underlying vowel /iː/ until such time as he or she acquires *obscenity*. Internalising the [iː]/[ɛ] alternation, he or she will re-structure the entry for *obscene* so as to derive that alternation by rule (drawing on other vowel-shift alternations in the process of establishing the full generalisation). But the speaker will not impose the new underlying vowel resulting from such re-structuring on other, non-alternating forms, maintaining instead a '[–VSR]' diacritic in each such case unless/until such a form becomes part of an alternating pair. This would mean, as we saw earlier, that the speaker will avoid the free rides predicted by the rule by resorting to widespread exception marking in his or her lexical entries.

Consider now the relationship between SCE and AC. Any phonological rule that is subject to SCE – any structure-changing rule sited on stratum 1, that is – will automatically conform with AC: as we have seen, SCE is stronger than AC in that it allows rule application only in derived environments (ultimately only in morphologically complex forms) while AC fails to specify which member of an alternating pair is allowed to undergo a given rule. Such rules can be assumed to be optimally learnable (subject to their inherent complexity, of course) at least in the sense that their acquisition involves no re-structuring of previously acquired underlying representations and no exception-marking for the purpose of avoiding free rides. In contrast, a rule that is not subject to SCE (a stratum-2 rule) does not automatically conform with AC; nor can the grammar enforce AC-compliance for such a rule, given that AC is not a formal condition on the grammar. Apart from being a descriptive generalisation about the acquisition process, AC is an informal evaluation measure for the learnability of rules: a rule that conforms with AC is more easily acquired than a rule that does not. Under AC, a grammar that contains structure-changing rules on stratum 2 is under learnability pressure to transfer those rules to stratum 1, where they will be appropriately constrained: in formal terms, the only way for a rule to conform with AC is to be subject to SCE. Given that SCE is stronger than AC, in that it tolerates no rule application in morphologically simple forms, this means that in transferring to stratum 1, rules are typically inverted (in the sense of Vennemann 1972b). As McMahon (1990) has shown, the case of the Vowel-Shift transfer to stratum 1 is a particularly complex one in that it involves the duplication of rules (the uninverted transfer of the old rule to stratum 1 and the addition of a new inverted version); such transfer may, therefore, incur substantial additional cost. In Chapter 5 below, I shall argue for an analysis for alternations of schwa with full vowels in English (*atom – atomic, Mendel – Mendelian*) that invokes the spirit of McMahon's vowel-shift analysis by inverting the historical process of 'reduction' (and by incurring additional cost of an unprecedented kind).

To illustrate the principle of AC-driven rule transfer to stratum 1 with inversion, I conclude this section with the brief discussion of another rule whose plausibility is enhanced if it is inverted and sited on stratum 1. This is the rule of *mn*-Simplification, held responsible for alternations such as *damn, damning* (without [n]) vs. *damnation* (with [n]). Below is a (probably complete) list of the relevant morphologically simple forms, with some of the derivatives. The nasal [n] is absent in (19a) and (19b) and present in (19c).

(19)   a. autumn   b. autumny   c. autumnal
           column   columny   columnar

a. condemn	b. condemning	c. condemnation
contemn	contemning	contemnible
damn	damning	damnation
hymn	hymning	hymnology
limn	limning	limner
rhamn	—	rhamnaceous
solemn	solemner (*colloquial*)	solemnity

The facts presented in (19) are consistent with the interpretation, proposed by Mohanan (1986: 22), that the /mn/ sequence is simplified morpheme-finally on stratum 2 (see also Kaisse and Shaw 1985: 23; Kiparsky 1985: 89f.):

(20)   *mn-Simplification* (Stratum 2)
         /n/ → ∅ / /m/ ____]

At first sight, this is an appealingly simple (and hardly disputable) analysis, given that the Bracket Erasure Convention ensures that internal brackets of stratum-1 complex forms (*condemnation*), but not of forms produced on stratum 2 (*condemning*), are deleted prior to the operation of the rule. But rule (20) has at least the following problems. First, final *mn*-sequences are unsyllabifiable; the assumption of an underlying /n/ therefore necessitates the assumption that English has morphologically simple words that cannot be syllabified without the prior operation of the deletion rule (20). With syllabification operating on stratum 1 and (20) on stratum 2, this means that the syllabification process runs into problems necessitating a rather powerful version of extrametricality. Second, and more seriously, if (20) is a stratum-2 rule then it is entirely unconstrained, predicting free-ride derivations from underlying /mn/ sequences for all forms surfacing with final [m] except those which demonstrate the absence of such [n] in stratum-1 derivatives (e.g. *atomic*, not **atomnic*). The [m] in *ham*, *lamb* (!), *ram*, *some*, *come*, *hem*, and many more such items which are not subject to stratum-1 morphology at all, would be predicted to be derivable from underlying /mn/ sequences. While under AC there would in this case not be a need for exception marking of the kind we found in the case of Vowel Shift (speakers would simply not store non-alternating forms as /mn/), the problem remains that a stratum-2 account fails to recognise the fact that [mn] sequences only occur in a small number of stratum-1 derivatives, and that such occurrence is reliably reflected by (and arguably predicted by) the orthographic representation.

A stratum-1 formulation of the process would then look like this:

(21)   *n-insertion*   (Stratum 1)

$$\text{ø} \rightarrow [\text{n}] \ //\text{m}/ \ \underset{\overset{<\text{mn}>}{\rule{0.8cm}{0.4pt}}}{} \ V$$

I discuss the status of orthographic representations in some detail in Chapter 5, showing that the derivation of phonological properties from orthographic ones is not unreasonable in cases such as the present one, and completely unavoidable (if such properties are to be shown to be rule-governed at all) in others. As regards the present case, we may note that *n*-Insertion may alternatively be a rule whose inputs (all of nine roots) are individually listed. Such listing would not be unprecedented by other properties of stratum 1 (neither on the morphological nor on the phonological side); nor would it lead to a critical loss of generalisation.

The *mn*-alternations constitute another case, then, where a historical process (clearly one of deletion) is inverted, surviving in the synchronic phonology of Present-day English as a sporadic process of insertion. Especially in the light of further, similar phenomena to be discussed in Chapter 5 and *passim*, we seem to have uncovered the synchronic motivation for rule inversion, a well-established mechanism of historical change (first discussed by Vennemann (1972b)). If, in diachronic terms, Vowel Shift and *mn*-simplification started their life-cycle as postlexical rules (a not unreasonable assumption[3]), then the final lexical stratum may simply serve to provide a temporary home for them in the process of lexicalisation before they undergo inversion (under pressure from AC) and move onto an earlier stratum.

In more general terms, we have seen that in the present model structure-changing rules can apply in underived environments only on the final stratum: while all earlier strata have SCE, the final stratum is predicted not to be so constrained. But AC as a learnability measure exerts pressure on structure-changing stratum-2 rules to be reformulated so as to apply on an earlier (SCE-bound) stratum, undergoing inversion (as well as becoming more costly in certain cases). The optimally learnable grammar is then the one that has no structure-changing rules on stratum 2. But to impose a point-blank ban on such rules from the final stratum (which in any case would have to be done, in the present model, in a costly way: by independent stipulation) would be to claim that all grammars are optimally learnable – a claim that has been rejected by S. Anderson (1981) and refuted in more detail by Dresher (1981). Such a grammar would probably be too much for the learner to hope for.

5 Phonology and the literate speaker: orthography in Lexical Phonology

5.1 The problem of schwa-vowel alternations

5.1.1 Preliminaries

In this chapter I deal with a range of derivational relationships among English words that are well known and at face value quite straightforward, and that have to my knowledge never attracted any controversy in the phonological literature beyond the discussion of minor technical details. I shall demonstrate that these relationships are in reality far from straightforward. Indeed, their statement in the 'standard' format of feature-changing phonological rules is highly implausible in psycholinguistic terms and simply impossible in terms of a phonological theory that makes full use (as does the version of Lexical Phonology developed in Chapter 4) of well-established derivational constraints. The relationships in question are those exemplified in (1):

(1) a. real – reality
        totem – totemic
        hostile[1] – hostility
        atom – atomic
        autumn – autumnal

     b. deter – deterrent
        myrrh – myrrhic
        recur – recurrent

What characterises these derivational relationships is that all the morphologically simple forms share the same surface vowel in their final syllables – unstressed [ə] in (1a) and, in RP, its stressed variant [ɜː] in (1b), assumed to be featurally identical with the former (and henceforth referred to as 'stressed schwa') – while in the morphologically complex forms a member of the set of lax vowels [aɛɪɒʌ] surfaces in the same position.[2]

There is thus no one-to-one relationship between the surface vowels of morphologically simple and complex forms in such cases, a fact that puts this kind of derivational relationship on a different footing from that found, for example, in the Vowel Shift alternations (*divine – divinity, serene – serenity, profane – profanity* etc.). In that class of alternations, the speaker is in principle (if perhaps not in practice; see Jaeger 1986; Wang and Derwing 1986) able to compute the various surface vowels in the complex forms on the basis of those found in the respective simplex forms. The surface contrasts in the simplex forms are reflexes of underlying contrasts, from which in turn the surface forms of any given pair are derived by means of an ordered set of rules contained in the grammar: Trisyllabic Shortening, Vowel Shift (in one of several possible forms; recall Section 4.3.2 above) and possibly more. The discussion regarding Vowel Shift alternations in the framework of Lexical Phonology, conducted in Section 4.3 above, is of relevance to the account of schwa-vowel alternations presented in this chapter; let us briefly recollect the gist of that discussion before turning to the additional problems posed by the cases exemplified in (1).

The problem with the Vowel Shift alternations is, as we saw, that they are amenable to two alternative analyses in the present, two-strata model. Under the 'traditional' analysis – Halle and Mohanan (1985), after SPE and Halle (1977) – tense vowels are raised, as in (2) for *divine – divinity* and *vary – variety*.

(2)   a. /dɪviːn/ – /dɪviːn+ɪtɪ/   b. /væɪ/ – /væɪ+ɛtɪ/   UR
           (n/a)   ɪ   *(n/a)*   *(n/a)*   TSS
           (n/a)   *(n/a)*   *(n/a)*   iː   V–V
            aɪ   *(n/a)*   *(n/a)*   aɪ   VSR etc.

(where 'UR' = underlying representation, 'TSS' = Trisyllabic Shortening/Laxing (SPE: 180), 'V–V' = Prevocalic Lengthening/Tensing (SPE: 181), 'VSR etc.' = Vowel Shift Rule and Diphthongisation (SPE: 187, 183). Vowel Reduction is omitted.)

Under this analysis, VSR must be free to operate in either the morphologically simple or the morphologically complex member of any given pair, as shown in (2a) and (2b) respectively. VSR therefore cannot be subject to the Strict Cyclicity Effect; it must consequently be sited on a stratum that is exempt from SCE, that is, stratum 2 in the present model. The problem is that VSR, if exempt from SCE, will produce free-ride derivations in all non-alternating forms that contain tense vowels: *ride* must be derived from /riːd/, *free* from /freː/ etc. As I argued in Section 4.3, such free rides are devoid of psycholinguistic justification: the grammar is under pressure (through the informal 'Alternation Condition') to re-formulate its rules so as to avoid abstract underliers where they are not warranted through alternations.

The alternative account, first proposed by McMahon (1990) and adopted in Section 4.3, systematically avoids such free rides by placing VSR on stratum 1 and thereby subjecting the derivation to SCE. The analysis of *vary – variety* remains as stated in (2b): here, VSR operates in a derived environment. But along with all free-ride derivations, the analysis of *divine – divinity* (as well as, of course, *sincere – sincerity, profane – profundity* etc.), involving VSR in an underived environment (2a), is now blocked by SCE. A second VSR is necessary for such cases: the mirror-image of the original rule, lowering lax vowels. This derivation is sketched in (3); for technical details see Section 4.3.2 above and McMahon (1990):

(3)   /dɪvaɪn/ – /dɪvaɪn+ɪtɪ/   UR
       (n/a)   a   TSS
       (n/a)   ɪ   VSR

The net gain of this alternative account of such alternations is a ban on free rides in all derivations involving Vowel Shift; indeed, no morphologically simple form, whether alternating or not, is eligible for Vowel Shift and attendant rules. The underlying representations of vowels in morphologically simple forms are surface-true. The loss incurred is one of generality and simplicity: the new account requires both SPE's rule of Tense Vowel Shift and a complementary rule of Lax Vowel Shift, thus turning both /ɪ/ into [aɪ] (*variety*) and /aɪ/ into [ɪ] (*divinity*). While such mirror-image duplication of rules is expressly rejected by SPE (p. 180), it clearly is a small price to pay for the avoidance of spurious free-ride derivations, where abstract underliers, devoid of psycholinguistic support, merely serve to create the illusion of regularity in a system that would otherwise be littered with exception features.

I shall, in this chapter, propose a highly constrained analysis of the schwa-vowel alternations exemplified in (1) above that owes its principles to McMahon's account of Vowel Shift. Like that account, it will crucially involve stratum 1 as the natural site of the relevant constraint (*viz.* SCE): as we saw in Section 4.3, stratum 1 is the only stratum (and SCE the only constraint) available in the present model to implement the Alternation Condition. Like that account, mine will be more costly, in terms of rules, than its predecessor in the literature was, involving both a version of the original vowel 'reduction' and its inverted counterpart. I shall show that this new account is not only more plausible than its predecessor was but actually predicted by the model of Lexical Phonology pursued in this study. Moreover, the new account will both demonstrate and justify, in psycholinguistic terms, the relevance of orthographic representations to phonological analysis: I hope to show that alternations such as those in (1) above are amenable to an unambiguous formal analysis only if the relevant phonological rules are given formal access to orthographic representations, which must therefore be independent in status from underlying phonological representations. This re-assessment of the status of orthography in the phonology of English, tentatively anticipated in Section 4.3.3 above in connection with the rule of '*mn*-Simplification', will perhaps be the most important outcome of this chapter.

5.1.2   Problems of derivation and representation in SPE

Consider the examples in (4):

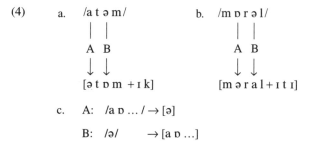

In each of the pair of forms in (4a) (4b), schwa figures in two different relationships with full vowels, labelled 'A' and 'B'. In relationship A, a full vowel in the morphologically simple form corresponds to schwa in the derived form; conversely in relationship B, schwa in the morphologically simple form corresponds to a full vowel in the derived form. These relationships are stated as rules in (4c), assuming for the moment that the segments that underlie the derivation are in each case identical with the surface vowels of the morphologically simple forms.

In the literature on the subject within Generative/Lexical Phonology, only the derivational relationship of the type A has been permitted, expressed by a rule of Vowel Reduction, which turns unstressed lax vowels into schwa (SPE: 111; Halle and Mohanan 1985: 100). For reasons that will become clear presently, type B has been treated as inadmissible; instead, the relationships holding in pairs such as those in (4) are expressed in terms of

the derivations sketched in (5) below, where schwa in each instance derives
from a full-vowel underlier:

(5)   a. /a t ɒ m/ – /a t ɒ m + ɪ k/
               ↓   ↓
              [ə]   [ə]

      b. /m ɒ r a l/ – /m ɒ r a l + ɪ t ɪ/
               ↓   ↓
              [ə]   [ə]

The reasons for employing this strategy rather than that of (4) are not discussed in SPE; but they are easily divined. First, to recognise both derivational relationships A and B (see (4c) above) is to admit to the grammar two
separate rules that are mirror-images of each other. As I reported earlier,
SPE expressly concluded that a comparable strategy in accounting for
vowel-shift alternations was 'surely in error' (SPE: 180). Second, while
McMahon (1990) has presented reasons for overturning such a conclusion
in the case of Vowel Shift (as discussed in Sections 4.3 and 5.1.1 above),
for alternations involving schwa the SPE analysis seems inevitable.
Relationship B cannot be stated as a phonological rule, given that the
quality of the output vowel is entirely unpredictable in phonological terms:
we get [ɒ] in *atomic*, [a] in *morality*, as well as [ɛ] in *totemic*, [ɪ] in *hostility*
(recall footnote 1) and [ʌ] in *autumnal*.

Third, the 'reduction-only' approach illustrated in (5) has the rather
attractive side effect of enabling SPE, apparently, to dispense with schwa as
an underlying segment: all instances of schwa are derived, through Vowel
Reduction, from underlyingly full lax vowels.[3] Schwa is not included in the
inventory of segments found in the underlying representations of English
morphemes (SPE: 176f.). Indeed, the central vowel [ə] is incapable of
specification in terms of the SPE feature system, which includes [± back]
but not [± front]: to specify a vowel that is neither back nor front, both features would be needed. But by excluding schwa from the underlying inventory, SPE side-steps rather than solves what is clearly a representational
problem for that framework: there is still the question of how surface schwa
is to be specified in terms of features. SPE's somewhat cavalier answer is
merely that:

> [t]he exact phonetic realisation of [ə] does not concern us. . . . For ease of
> exposition, we will simply make the assumption here that [ə] is distin-
> guished from all other vocalic segments. (SPE: 110)

This representational problem is only one of several to arise from the standard-generative treatment of schwa. It is not, as we shall see, beyond solution. But the second problem is that in many instances of schwa in English words – indeed, in what seems to be the vast majority of cases – the reduction-only approach cannot be motivated through observed alternations of schwa with full vowels in morphologically related pairs. In *among*, *about*, *agenda*, *account*, *camera*, *pedestal*, *mathematics*, for example, schwa does not engage in such alternations (whose absence from the derivational morphology of English is in the case of prepositions such as *among* systematic rather than accidental). It is, thus, impossible to determine a full-vowel underlier for such schwa in a reduction-only account; and as we have seen, the SPE feature system makes it equally impossible to assume schwa underlyingly. Interestingly, SPE occasionally employs the symbol 'V' in such underlying representations (SPE: 211, 228, 231, 235); but its use is unsystematic and its status unexplained. As an abbreviation convention it is clearly illegitimate within the SPE framework, given that that framework does not explicitly recognise any form of underspecification, and (more importantly) given that a 'V' short for a fully specified segment can neither stand for an unambiguous abstract underlier nor for schwa (Gussmann 1991).

These facts create an independent derivational problem. Assume that SPE's representational problem can be solved in a suitably enriched theory of phonological representations – that schwa, in other words, can be given a representation in both underlying and surface representations. I return to this issue below. Then SPE's derivational framework allows two options. Either, schwa in *among* etc. can be derived, on a free ride, from an underlying full vowel. But the underlying representation of that vowel cannot be unambiguously determined: any one of the inputs to Vowel Reduction – /aɛɪɒʌ/ – will give rise to schwa in the first syllable. Or the surface form may be derived, without change, from underlying schwa. No derivational constraints are available to the SPE model to block spurious derivations from indeterminate underliers; nor is that framework able to enforce, as is evidently desirable, surface-identical underliers (here /ə/) in cases where no abstract derivation is motivated through alternations. In fact, as we saw in Section 4.3, the principle of Occam's Razor, one of the overriding concerns of early Generative Phonology, perversely encouraged analyses involving free-ride derivations.

A third problem of the reduction-only approach relates to the speaker's acquisition of alternating forms such as *moral – morality*. Assume for the moment (as does S. Anderson 1981) that speakers store *moral* as /mɒrəl/ until such time as they acquire *morality*, at which point they restructure the underlying representation into /mɒral/ but then use the replacement vowel only in *morality*. This restructuring hypothesis is in itself far from plausible in psycholinguistic terms, as I shall argue in Section 5.5. For the moment we note in addition that the notion of restructuring within the SPE framework immediately raises the first, representational problem again: before their first encounter with *morality*, speakers are left with a non-alternating schwa, to which they are unable to attribute an underlying representation under a reduction-only approach. Clearly, this is unreasonable.

The SPE account of schwa, then, is flawed in both representational and derivational terms. I shall show in the next section that more recent work, while successfully dealing with the representational problem, has made no progress on the derivational side of the analysis despite the fact that post-SPE work on the nature of phonological derivations (notably that on Lexical Phonology) has been rather preoccupied with the development of derivational constraints. Just as much effort has gone into developing ways of bypassing these constraints, it seems.

5.1.3   Later developments

A new account of the representation of schwa in English was developed by Gussmann (1991), with ingredients taken from Underspecification Theory (Archangeli 1984, 1988) as well as, more importantly here, from Non-Linear/Autosegmental Phonology (in particular from Halle and Vergnaud 1982 and Clements and Keyser 1983). The subject of phonological representations (especially at the syllable level) will be developed further in Chapter 8; a brief exposition will suffice here. (On German schwa in a representational framework similar to Gussmann's see Giegerich 1987; Wiese 1988: Chapter II.2.)

Let us assume, with most post-SPE work on phonological representations, that the traditional notion of 'segment' (which, along with morphological boundaries, constituted the only unit of phonological representation in the strictly linear SPE model), is represented on two separate (but linked) tiers. The 'melody tier' consists of feature matrices excluding featural information regarding length and, within the specific model of 'CV-Phonology' (Clements and Keyser 1983; Wiese 1988), consonantality. Length (and possibly consonantality) is represented on the 'skeleton tier', whose elements are essentially abstract timing units represented by 'x' (Levin (1985); see also Giegerich (1992a) for a textbook exposition), which are in the CV-model further differentiated as 'C' and 'V'. I adopt here the simpler model in which the only units of the skeleton tier are 'x', without further specification.

The association of the x-slots of the skeleton tier and the feature matrices of the melody tier may be two-to-one (in the case of long segments), one-to-one (for short segments) or one-to-two (as, for example, in the case of affricates). These configurations are exemplified in (6a), (6b) and (6c) respectively:

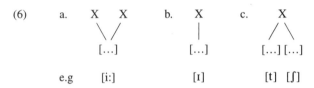

(6)   a.   X   X   b.   X   c.   X

e.g   [iː]   [ɪ]   [t] [ʃ]

Following Gussmann (1991), we may represent schwa in such a representational framework by an x-slot (occupying the nucleus position on the syllable tier) that is associated with an empty melody. Without making further demands on the theory of segmental representations,[4] such a notion gives recognition to the occurrence of neutral vowel melodies in positions defined by suprasegmental structure. In terms of Underspecification Theory, this is a melody that bears no specifications at least regarding those features that differentiate 'full' vowels (*viz.* the tongue body features): see (7) below.

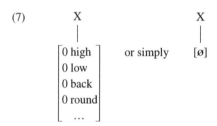

(7)   X

$$\begin{bmatrix} 0 \text{ high} \\ 0 \text{ low} \\ 0 \text{ back} \\ 0 \text{ round} \\ \dots \end{bmatrix}$$ or simply   [ø]   X

In such a framework the equivalent of SPE's rule of Vowel Reduction may be stated as a rule which severs the association of a nuclear x-position with a melody – a rule that de-links the skeleton and (at least part of) the melody in unstressed position.[5]

(8)   *Delinking*

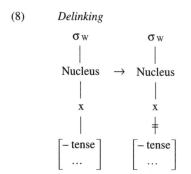

A late Default Rule (Archangeli 1984; Giegerich 1987) fills any melodically empty nuclear x-slots with the default melody [ə]:

(9)   *Default Schwa*

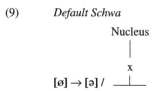

The deployment of these notational devices solves the representational problems encountered by the SPE treatment of schwa, discussed in Section 5.1.2 above. The 'V' used by SPE (illegitimately, as we have seen, in a framework that does not operate either with suprasegmental representations or with the device of underspecification) may then be interpreted as a skeletal position associated with an empty melody. Such a melodically empty segment may be present in the underlying representation of a morpheme; or it may arise derivationally through Delinking (8). And the featural specification of the default melody [ə] will, depending on other characteristics of the framework employed, be provided by a suitably revised feature system (which may, if it is binary, contain the feature [±front]); or the Default Rule (9) may be sited in a component of the phonology where features are no longer binary – in Lexical Phonology, at the postlexical stage. We may assume here that (9) is indeed postlexical (Giegerich 1987; Wiese 1988: Chapter II.2).

This raises the question of the stratal association of the Delinking Rule (8) – the successor to the Rule of Vowel Reduction found in SPE and Halle and Mohanan (1985). In returning to such derivational issues, let us briefly review the possibilities of deriving alternating pairs such as *atom – atomic*, *moral – morality* from single underlying representations.

As we saw in Section 5.2.1, there are two options, sketched respectively in (4) and (5) above. Option one, given in (4), assumes underlying representations that are surface-true for the morphologically simple member of any given pair (/atəm/ for example), from which the morphologically complex form is derived by means of two rules (A and B in (4) above): Delinking (8), which (together with the rule of Default Schwa) turns lax vowels into schwa, and its mirror-image turning schwa into full lax vowels: [ətɒm+ɪk]. The latter rule has not been discussed here; the SPE account does not use it and adopts instead the second option.

Option two, (5) above, posits underlying representations containing full vowels only (such as in /atɒm/), from which the surface forms [atəm] and [ətɒmɪk] are derived by invoking Delinking of the second vowel in the former, and of the first vowel in the latter form. Halle and Mohanan (1985), without discussion (but probably for the reasons given in Section 5.2.1 in connection with the SPE account), adopt the same derivational strategy.

We observed in Section 4.3 what the consequences are if, in a lexical phonology, structure-changing rules are posited in such a way as to operate in underived environments. The cases discussed there were that of Mohanan's (1986) '*mn*-Simplification' as well as Halle and Mohanan's (essentially SPE-based) version of Vowel Shift (see also Section 5.1.1 above), which derives the vowels in *divine, serene* etc. from underlying /iː/, /eː/ etc. Such rules cannot be subject to SCE; they must therefore be sited on stratum 2 of the present, two-strata model. (In Halle and Mohanan's four-strata model, it was similarly stratum 2 that was exempt from SCE – if, unlike the present model, by stipulation.) On that stratum, however, structure-changing rules will produce free-ride derivations due to the well-known impossibility of invoking the Alternation Condition as a formal constraint on derivations. It follows from the constraints of the model that any attempt to derive the *atom–atomic* alternations by means of Delinking alone must accommodate that rule on stratum 2 (Halle and Mohanan's and mine alike), where the rule is not only free to operate in the underived member of any given pair (as is of course desirable) but also in non-alternating forms. And this side effect is, as we have seen, highly undesirable, not only producing free-ride derivations in what seem to be the majority of schwa-instances in the phonology of English but also leaving the grammar with the problem of being unable to specify the underlying vowels in such cases beyond the feature [–tense]. We are faced with the somewhat depressing result, then, that no progress has been recorded in the literature on the lexical phonology of English in the analysis of schwa-vowel alternations. Halle and Mohanan's 'Vowel Reduction' is yet another rule that, located on stratum 2, is as unconstrained as the SPE version of the same rule was.

5.2   The limits of phonological derivation

5.2.1   Delinking vs. blank-filling

In the light of the highly undesirable side effects produced by a 'Delinking-only' account of alternations of the type *atom – atomic, moral – morality*, let us pursue what was identified above ('option one') as the only alternative account within Lexical Phonology. To constrain the rule of Delinking (8), we place it on stratum 1, where (as a structure-changing rule) it is automatically subject to SCE. This step, as we saw above, not only blocks all free-ride derivations of schwa from indeterminate underliers at a stroke; it also rules out an analysis whereby the schwa in the second syllable of *atom* is derived, through (8), from an underlying /ɒ/. Under the assumptions that stress assignment in English is structure-building on the first cycle (but – at least in part – structure-changing on subsequent cycles), and that the results of structure-building rules do not constitute derived environments (Chapter 4 above; Giegerich 1987), Delinking must be blocked in *atom*. In turn this must mean that the underlying representations of *atom, moral* etc. must be /atØm/, /mɒrØl/ etc. (where 'Ø' stands for a skeletal position associated with an 'empty' melody, as in (7) above). The underlying representation of the second vowel in *atom* cannot be /ɒ/; nor can that in *moral* be /a/, that in *totem* /ɛ/ etc. This means that the qualities of the second vowels of morphologically complex forms, such as the [ɒ] in *atomic* and the [a] in *morality*, cannot be encoded in the underlying representations of the respective morphologically simple forms but must be supplied by rule. We noted this as early as in the initial exposition of the relevant derivational relationships ((4) above) – a position to which we are now forced to return.

(10)   a.   /a t ø m/   b.   /m ɒ r ø l/

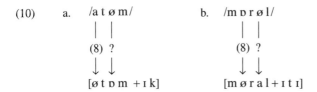

The rule in question, marked '?' in (10), fills empty nucleus melodies with the vowel qualities [aɛɪɒʌ]. Below is a provisional statement of this blank-filling rule:

(11)   *Blank-filling* (provisional):

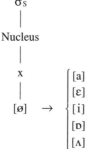

A more comprehensive list of examples than that in (1) above is given in (12):

(12)   [a]:   morality, reality, regularity, metallic
        [ɛ]:   totemic, torrential, essential, prudential
        [ɪ]:   hostility, mobility, fertility (footnote 1 above)
        [ɒ]:   atomic, personify, Miltonic, motoric
        [ʌ]:   autumnal, molluscoid, fecundity

As a blank-filling rule that makes available five distinct vowel qualities without specifying five distinct phonological contexts for them, (11) states point-blank that there are no phonological grounds on which the second vowels in forms such as *reality, torrential, mobility, personify* etc. can be predicted from the morphologically simple forms *real, torrent, mobile, person*. As we have seen, the vowels in question cannot be part of the under-lying representations; nor are they unambiguously predicted by rule. In purely phonological terms, then, alternations such as *real – *re[ɒ]lity, torrent – *torr[a]ntial* etc. would be no less grammatical than are the forms that actually exist.

The vowel qualities in question must, in this account, be listed with the individual lexical items. Let us assume for the moment that every morpho-logically simple form containing /Ø/ is individually specified for the particu-lar subrule of (11) that will apply when stress is shifted onto the relevant syllable. The necessity to list the range of applicable rules with a given lexical item is far from unprecedented in the present model and does not, therefore, constitute an independent argument against this particular account within the model. Stratum 1, as we saw in Section 3.3, is in any case characterised by the widespread listing of individual lexical items with regard to individual rules: roots are listed as to whether they undergo the Root-to-Word Conversion, whether they undergo certain phonological rules as well as to what affixes attach to them; affixes are listed as to which particular base allomorphies and phonological rules they trigger (or fail to trigger); and so forth.

It is, moreover, quite clear for independent reasons that (11) itself must be a stratum-1 rule. While it would be in principle conceivable that the empty melodies discussed here are filled on a stratum later than the first – so long as (11) applies before the postlexical Default Rule (9) – even when they have received stress in the course of a stratum-1 derivation, it is clearly more plausible to assume that (11) is triggered by stress assignment to the relevant syllable (the phenomenon of 'stress shift', confined to stratum 1) – I return to the link between (11) and stress below.[6] But the decisive argument in favour of the stratum-1 status of (11) is provided by alternations such as the following:

(13)   a. Milton   [ə]   b. Miltonic   [ɒ]   c. Miltonian   [oː]
          category [ə]   categoric   [ɒ]   categorial   [oː]
          marginal [ə]   marginality [a]   marginalia   [eɪ]
          Mendel   [ə]   ?Mendelic   [ɛ]   Mendelian   [iː]
          manager   [ə]   ?   [ɛ]   managerial   [iː][7]

The items in (13a) confirm the presence of /Ø/ in the underlying representations, which is in (13b) filled with one of the vowels available through rule (11). Three-way alternations such as these are accounted for if we recognise that the vowels provided by (11) may be subject to further derivation: in the items in (13c) the vowel in question undergoes the rule of 'CiV Tensing' (SPE: 181; Halle and Mohanan 1985; McMahon 1990), which, for example, turns [ɒ] into [ɔː], and subsequent (Tense) Vowel Shift (McMahon 1990), which produces the surface form [oʊ]. The other alternations in (13) are accounted for in the same way. Given that both rules following (11) in these derivations are stratum-1 rules and subject to SCE (McMahon 1990), (11) itself must be sited on stratum 1 – a conclusion that is both plausible and consistent with its essentially unpredictable (listed) output, as we saw above.

Given that (11) fills empty melody slots, it is clearly a structure-building rather than structure-changing rule, and as such not constrained by SCE. This is consistent with the behaviour of the outputs of (11) in further derivation: if (11) were structure-changing then it would itself create derived environments for Lax Vowel Shift (McMahon 1990; Section 4.3 above):

(11) is responsible for all the feature specifications of the vowel in question, including that for [– tense]; and Lax Vowel Shift is a context-free structure-changing rule affecting 'derived' lax vowels. Hence any vowel melody filled by (11) would undergo Tense Vowel Shift: [ɛ] provided by (11) would surface as [a] etc. Note that the candidacy of the outputs of (11) for CiV Tensing (*Miltonian* etc. in (13c) above) is explained through the fact that it is in that case the 'CiV' context itself that constitutes the derived environment; and this context is indeed provided by a (morphological) rule on the appropriate cycle. Rule (11) is, then, a stratum-1 rule that is, due to its structure-building nature, not subject to SCE.

The question now arises how rule (11) is to be barred from filling empty melodies on the first cycle; that is: in the second syllable of underived /atØm/, as well as in the various instances of such empty slots in non-alternating forms (*about, camera* etc.). Similarly, on later cycles the rule must be prevented from undoing the effect of Delinking (8), such that the first vowel in *atomic*, turned into [Ø] by (8), must remain empty until the Default rule (9) fills it with schwa on the postlexical stratum. Note again that the prevention of (11) in all these instances can have nothing to do with SCE, given that some such instances are derived and others underived. The most straightforward solution to this problem is the one already adopted in the formulation of rule (11): the rule affects only vowels in stressed syllables. Underlying empty melodies occur in unstressed positions only; and Delinking similarly produces such empty melodies only in unstressed positions. Rule (11), confined to stressed vowels, cannot fill empty slots coming from either source. I return to this issue, in relation to the Structure Preservation Condition (Kiparsky 1985; Borowsky 1989) in the following section.

The analysis of schwa-vowel alternations proposed in this section, involving Delinking as well as the blank-filling rule (11), has the advantage over its predecessor in the literature that it avoids free rides (which, moreover, involve indeterminate underlying representations) on principled grounds. Clearly it makes no sense to treat the schwa in *about*, for example, as derived from an underlying full vowel whose quality cannot be determined. This is achieved by placing both rules on stratum 1, thereby making full use of SCE, a constraint that is predicted by the present two-strata version of Lexical Phonology to operate on stratum 1 but not on stratum 2. But the price paid for this plausibility has once again been a hefty one: while its predecessor in the literature (Halle and Mohanan 1985) operated with Delinking only, the present account needs Delinking and an additional blank-filling rule, the mirror-image of Delinking, which in addition requires individual listing in that it makes available a context-free range of possible vowels, only one of which is appropriate in any given derivation. This is, then, another case of partial rule inversion prompted by a move of what was in historical terms clearly a postlexical rule of vowel reduction onto the final lexical stratum, and from there onto stratum 1 (which is when the inversion and multiplication of rules took place). The picture is, then, similar to that of Vowel Shift discussed in Section 4.3. If the reasoning presented there was correct then the present stratum-1 analysis of schwa-vowel alternations is encouraged by the fact that, despite its apparent cumbersomeness, its stratum-2 alternative must be riddled with exception features in order to meet the Alternation Condition (which, as we saw, is an acquisition strategy rather than a formal constraint on (stratum 2 of) the grammar).

The parallels with the Vowel Shift analysis go even further: it has to be acknowledged that, in formal terms, the grammar is unable to choose between Halle and Mohanan's account of schwa-vowel alternations and the present one, just as it permits both Halle and Mohanan's account of Vowel Shift and McMahon's (1990). Structure-changing rules can occur on stratum 2: there is no way of banning Vowel Shift or Delinking from that stratum, however plausible (for example in terms of AC) such a ban may be.

In the remainder of this chapter I shall put forward two further arguments in favour of the present analysis of schwa-vowel alternations. One argument will involve a similar set of alternations: those of the type *deter – deterrent*, first presented in (1b) above. I shall show that those (unlike the ones discussed so far) can only be handled on stratum 1: the Delinking analysis on stratum 2, possible for *atom – atomic*, is unavailable for them. The problematic blank-filling rule (11) must therefore be sited on stratum 1 for independent reasons.

The second argument will produce a formaliseable context specification of the subrules of (11). The status of rule (11) is in fact not as problematical as it has appeared so far: under a realistic view of the nature of lexical entries, the vowel-quality options provided by rule (11) are not as unpredictable as they appear to be.

5.2.2 'Stressed schwa'

I turn now to the discussion of vowel alternations involving [ɜː], first exemplified in (1b) above. The vowel [ɜː] is (near-)identical in quality (if not in length) to [ə] but occurs in stressed syllables only, a complementary distribution that makes the two segments non-distinct in phonemic terms. To determine the distribution of [ɜː] further, consider the following set of alternations (for Received Pronunciation), where the examples in (14a) are morphologically simple (ignoring prefixes), those in (14b) constitute stratum-1 derivations (in the *sir – sirrah* case of a somewhat tenuous nature) and those in (14b) stratum-2 derivations.

(14)   a. deter   [ɜː]   b. deterrent   [ɛ]   c. deterring   [ɜː]
           err   [ɜː]   error   [ɛ]   erring   [ɜː]
           refer   [ɜː]   referral   [ɜː]

           myrrh   [ɜː]   myrrhic   [ɪ]   ?myrrhy   [ɜː]
           sir   [ɜː]   sirrah   [ɪ]

           recur   [ɜː]   recurrent   [ʌ]   recurring   [ɜː]
           occur   [ɜː]   occurrence   [ʌ]   occurring   [ɜː]
           demur   [ɜː]   demurrer   [ʌ]   demurrer   [ɜː][8]

As a first approximation regarding the distribution of [ɜː], we may state that the vowel occurs in the context of (historic) tautosyllabic /r/[9] (as in (14a)) as well as before heterosyllabic [r] in stratum-2 derivatives (14c). A more detailed account of the distribution is complicated by a number of side issues, of which the first regards syllabification. An account of the lexical derivation of English syllable structure will be given in Chapter 8; here we treat the tautosyllabicity of the putative /r/ in (14a) and its heterosyllabicity in (14c) as uncontroversial.

The second problem is that in non-rhotic varieties such as Received Pronunciation (RP), historic /r/ in syllable rhymes is no longer present but synchronically reflected in the length of the vowel in question: in both [dɪtɜː] deter and [dɪtɜːrɪŋ] (deterring), for example, the vowel is long. This length, and especially its maintenance in the latter form (where [r] actually surfaces in RP), will be discussed in a fuller account of non-rhoticity that will be given in Chapter 6. I assume here that the variable of (non-)rhoticity and the length of the vowel in question may be ignored for our present purposes; the present account will conveniently refer to /R/ as the context of [ɜː], even where [r] is no longer present in phonetic representations. Awaiting revisions in Chapter 6, /R/ here stands for historic or actual /r/. That I nevertheless do not subscribe to a straight '/r/-Deletion' analysis for non-rhotic varieties, of the kind advocated by Mohanan (1985), will become clear in that chapter.

The first thing to note is that, similar to unstressed [ə] (Section 5.1 above),

[ɜː] is commonly found in non-alternating forms. Parallel to the alternations in (14a) and (14b) above, the historic /ε/–/ɪ/–/ʌ/ contrast is suspended
in non-alternating forms before historic tautosyllabic /R/, as in (15a) below,
while it is maintained before heterosyllabic (and therefore surfacing) /R/, as
in (15b). Notice that most of the items in (15a) not only fail to engage in the
relevant alternations but are unable to alternate as a matter of principle:
only in word-final position can the vowel-plus-/R/ sequence become heterosyllabic.

(15)   a. her   b. berry
            herd   ferret
            hermit   heron

            fir   squirrel
            firm   miracle
            myrtle   lyric

            burr   hurry
            church   turret
            murder   courage

Non-alternating forms such as those in (15a) outnumber alternating
forms by far. The derivational strategy whereby schwa in the items in (14a)
is derived, via a suitably modified version of Delinking (8), from the full
vowels in the corresponding forms in (14b) is therefore as problematical as
was its counterpart for unstressed schwa, discussed and rejected in Section
5.1. The appropriate Delinking rule would have to be situated on stratum 2
in order to be operative in the underived environments of (14a); and on that
stratum the rule could not be constrained so as to prevent free-ride derivations of [ɜː] from underlying full vowels, where once again the quality of
those underliers would be impossible to determine. In the *atom – atomic*
cases, a Delinking-only account (however inferior to the alternative involving Blank-filling) is not in principle barred from the grammar: as we saw
above, stratum 2 offers no constraints that would prevent free-ride derivations on that stratum. I shall demonstrate in the remainder of this section
that a Delinking-only account of the *deter – deterrent* cases is not only inferior to a Blank-filling analysis but actually impossible within the present
version of the lexical phonology of English.

A stratum-2 rule of 'tautosyllabic Delinking', producing [ɜː] in *deter* and
deterring while leaving [ε] in *deterrent* intact, would have to be cyclic. It
would refer to the context of tautosyllabic /R/ – a context that is present in
the underived form but undone in *deterring*. Therefore, such Delinking

must happen before the stratum-2 morphology; but such ordering of the rule is impossible under the assumption that stratum 2 is non-cyclic, as we saw in Chapter 4.

Under non-cyclic application, the rule would have to refer to the linear context 'vowel-plus-/R/' in order to affect the tautosyllabic /εR/ sequence in *deter* and the heterosyllabic sequence in *deterring*. But such a formulation would be too powerful, failing to leave the full vowels in (15b) – *berry* etc. – unaffected. In any case, in order to preserve the [ε] in the stratum-1 derivative *deterrent*, a morphological boundary would have to follow the linear /εR/ sequence in the rule's structural description: the boundary in *deterrent* would suitably be deleted (through the Bracket Erasure Convention) before that form's entry into stratum 2. But the presence of such a boundary would in turn fail to trigger Delinking in those examples in (15a) where a consonant rather than a boundary follows the /R/: *herd, firm, church* and many others. Note that a consonant following the /R/ would also (correctly) trigger Delinking in certain stratum-1 forms such as *detergent, emergence* etc. So, a stratum-2 formulation of the process would have to delink the melodies [εɪʌ] before /R/ followed by either a morphological boundary or a consonant, without reference to syllable structure. The boundary/consonant disjunction fails to constitute a natural class, of course, and has been known since Kahn (1976) to disguise syllable-structure (to be precise: syllable-rhyme) conditioning wherever it occurs in phonological rules. Such a rule – the only possible stratum-2 account of the facts (given that stratum 2 is non-cyclic) – is therefore unacceptable. In view of *detergent, emergence*, it is in any case intuitively obvious that syllable-structure conditioning must be decisive in any account of these alternations.

Let us return briefly to the option of locating Delinking on stratum 1. It is interesting to note that under the mechanics of cyclic rule application developed in Section 4.2, it is at first sight possible to produce the *deter – deterrent* alternation through Delinking. Consider the derivational paths of the two forms:

(16)   [deter] → $\begin{cases} \text{[[deter]ent]]} \\ \text{[[deter]}_V \end{cases}$

Example (16) shows the first-cycle morphology for *deter*, on which either *-ent* is attached to the root, or the root is converted into a verb through the Root-to-Word rule. There is, as we saw in Section 4.2.1, no phonological cycle prior to the first morphological operation; a rule delinking /ε/ before tautosyllabic /R/ would therefore operate after the conversion of *deter* into a verb (and not before it), leaving *deterrent* unaffected due to its incompatible syllabification. But the problem remains that in such a case, Delinking would have to operate in an underived environment: no component of the structural description of the rule (neither the following /R/ nor its tautosyllabicity) is the result of a structure-changing rule on the same cycle (or elsewhere). While the placement of the rule on stratum 1 would appropriately block the free-ride derivation of [ɜː] in the forms listed in (15a) from full underliers, such a placement would in addition wrongly block Delinking in *deter* etc. This situation is thus similar to that found in regard of the *atom – atomic* cases; what is different here is that pre-/R/ Delinking cannot be a stratum-2 rule either. The lexical phonology of English therefore cannot contain such a rule as long as stratum 2 can be assumed to be non-cyclic.[10]

Having rejected the derivation of [ɜː] from full underliers, we conclude that this segment (more precisely, in view of the Default Rule (9), /∅/) must itself be part of underlying representations. Let us turn to the blank-filling alternative account of the *deter – deterrent* alternations. It is a phonotactic fact of RP (as well as of American English) that [ɛɪʌ] cannot occur before tautosyllabic /R/ – hence the suspension of the historic lax-vowel contrasts in (14a)/(15a). The /ʊ/–/ʌ/ contrast *(put – putt)* is independently neutralised before *any* /R/ (there is simply a linear filter ruling out the /ʊR/ sequence); and given also that the lax vowels /a/ and /ɒ/ display different derivational behaviour before /R/ (see Chapter 7 below), the phonotactics of lax vowels before tautosyllabic /R/ is governed by the following filter:

(17)   * Rhyme

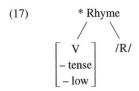

In other words, a tautosyllabic sequence of the form (17) cannot be syllabified and is therefore ruled out.

The empty melody /∅/ is free to occur in this context; hence *deter* has the underlying form /dit∅R/, *herd* has /h∅Rd/, and so forth. But /∅/ is in turn subject to phonotactic constraints: while free to occur in unstressed syllables, it is sanctioned in stressed syllables only in the presence of a following tautosyllabic /R/. I postpone further discussion of this matter until Chapter 7: the account obviously depends crucially on the (thus far undiscussed) underlying characterisation of /R/ in non-rhotic varieties – in fact, on the entire analysis of the [r]-vowel alternations in such varieties. Also postponed is the discussion of why in *deterring* etc., /∅/ is maintained before heterosyllabic /R/, in apparent violation of the constraints governing that segment.

Consider now the derivation given in (16) above in the light of the constraints on /ɛɪʌ/ as well as /∅/ – which hold at least throughout stratum 1, thanks to Structure Preservation (Kiparsky 1985; Borowsky 1989). Due to (17), the form *deter*, output of the Root-to-Word Rule, cannot be syllabified if it contains any one of /ɛɪʌ/ in its final syllable; and *deterrent* cannot be syllabified if it contains /∅/. Given the impossibility of the Delinking account, it is clear that the underlying representation must contain /∅/. This means that stratum 1 in English must contain rule (11) – a fact that provides independent support for the analysis of the *atom – atomic* alternations proposed above. Rule (11) need not be specially postulated for the purposes of that account (even if, as we have seen, the range of vowels available to such alternations is larger than that occurring in the pre-/R/ cases).

If we take the view that Structure Preservation has the power of triggering remedial rules in cases where the derivation unavoidably faces ill-formed configurations (a view suggested by Goldsmith 1990: Section 5.1.3), then the rule of Blank-Filling (11) is automatically triggered by the syllabification of *deterrent* and *atomic*. Moreover, Structure Preservation constrains rule (11) further in that it restricts the range of possible feature combinations constituting the rule's output: only such melodies can be inserted by (11) as are also found in underlying representations: given the severe limitations that this model imposes on the abstractness of underlying representations, this means that the outputs of blank-filling rules such as (11) effectively have to be established phonemes of the language.

Recall, however, that (11) by its very nature fails to specify which particular vowel out of its output range is inserted into any particular derivation. Such specification, as we saw above, lies beyond what the lexical phonology of English can predict on purely phonological grounds. Neither underlying representations nor rules provide an unambiguous derivational path from *atom* to *atomic* or from *deter* to *deterrent*. The inserted vowel quality has to be separately listed with the relevant stratum-1 derivation in each case. We noted above that such listing is not particularly problematic given that morphological stratum-1 derivations have to be listed individually in any case.

This would be the end of the story if there were not a degree of productivity, or predictability, in such alternations that is belied by the outright denial of a phonological relationship between their members. Speakers do 'know' such pair-wise relationships, judging the vowel in each of the derived forms in (1) above as the only correct one and, more importantly, producing one-off or nonsense derivations such as [pɛtálɪk] and [batónɪk], from *petal* and *baton*, without great difficulty. There is more to be said about the form in which the vowels in question are stored in the mental lexicon: clearly, they are not separately learned but already contained in some representation of the lexical item (which, as we have seen, cannot be the phonological representation). I shall argue in what follows that this is the orthographic representation.

5.3 Interlude: on the relationship between phonology and orthography

5.3.1   A principle of English orthography

As is well known, alphabetic writing systems tend not to conform to the 'phonemic principle' in that they fail to perform a simple one-to-one mapping of phonemes onto letters of the sort found, for example, in a phonemic transcription. Among the features that disrupt such a (seemingly desirable) bi-unique mapping are, among others, the frequent occurrence of one-to-many correspondences between sound and spelling (as, for example, in *she, see, sea, Pete, key, quay, people, amoeba, machine* in the case of /iː/), as well as the equally frequent occurrence of many-to-one correspondences. *Rough* vs. *bough, love* vs. *move* vs. *stove* are frequently cited examples, as well as the fact that the letter <c> may stand for [k], [s] or [ʃ] (as in *electric, electricity, electrician* respectively). While it is beyond dispute that many such cases of bi-uniqueness failure are in synchronic terms simply random, and perhaps exceptional deviations from default spellings, the example of <c> is not random (Carney 1994: 18), serving instead to illustrate a principle of orthography that is arguably more pervasive in English than is the phonemic principle (which this particular language implements in a remarkably inconsistent fashion). The principle in question is the one

> which, while admitting many exceptions, is what governs and systematizes many of the apparent inconsistencies of our writing system: The English writing system tends to employ a single combination of graphemes to represent a given morpheme, disregarding for the most part all but the grossest phonemic differences between allomorphs. (Francis 1958: 468)

This principle of 'morphemic spelling',[11] shows up impressively in the orthographic representation of the regular past tense morpheme in English (see (18a) below), and its failure – equally impressively – in that of the regular plural morpheme: (18b) (after Carney 1994: 19).

(18)	a.		\<ed\>	b.		\<(e)s\>
		/-ɪd/	matted		/-ɪz/	masses
		/-ɪd/	mated		/-ɪz/	maces
		/-t/	hopped		/-s/	hops
		/-t/	hoped		/-s/	hopes
		/-d/	planned		/-z/	plans
		/-d/	planed		/-z/	planes
		/-d/	hurried		/-z/	hurries
		/-d/	radioed		/-z/	radios
		/-d/	vetoed		/-z/	vetos/vetoes

Note that in regular past tense forms, the invariable addition of \<ed\> to the stem is disrupted only by the deletion of stem-final \<e\>, by the doubling of a single stem-final consonant where it follows a short vowel, as well as by the replacement of stem-final \<y\> through \<i\>. All three disruptions of the pattern are in themselves regular. In plural forms, on the other hand, the \<es\> spelling occurs only with the /-ɪz/ allomorph while the other two allomorphs (/-s/, /-z/) are spelt \<s\> with the exceptions of the *hurries* type, optionally *vetoes* and, obligatorily, *potatoes*. See Carney (1994: 19f.) for further discussion. But such disregard of the principle of morphemic spelling on the part of one of the most popular English morphemes does not alter the fact that the principle is otherwise remarkably consistent in English, in particular within the section of the vocabulary in which alternations of the *atom – atomic* and *deter – deterrent* type occur.

In addition to cases like *electric – electricity – electrician*, noted above, the invariable spelling of morphemes shows up in pairs displaying vowel-shift and related alternations such as *divine – divinity, serene – serenity* etc., where spelling discrepancies occur only in the [aʊ]–[ʌ] pairs (*profound – profundity, pronounce – pronunciation* etc.; but note *South – Southern*). And in the alternations at issue in this chapter (*atom – atomic, deter – deterrent* etc.), the principle is exceptionless. It is at least plausible to suggest that it is this principle of morphemic spelling which enables the speaker who knows *atom* to produce [ətómɪk] without having heard that form before; but such a suggestion is at odds with the commonly held and somewhat doctrinal view in linguistics whereby orthographic representations are derived from phonological representations and not possibly *vice versa*. If that view is correct then orthographic representations have no independent status; there can, therefore, be no information in the orthographic form of a given item that is not also present in its phonological form. I hope to show in the following sections that this view – which culminated in SPE's claim that orthographic representations are identical with, and therefore represent (SPE's version of), underlying phonological representations – is supported by little other than a long, if misguided, tradition in linguistic theory.

5.3.2 The 'standard' view

According to SPE, 'English orthography, despite its often cited inconsistencies, comes remarkably close to being an optimal orthographic system for English' (SPE: 49; similarly SPE: 184). This claim, repeated and further elaborated by N. Chomsky (1970a) and C. Chomsky (1970), has two parts. First, it contains the assertion that the implementation of the principle of morphemic spelling, at the expense of the phonemic principle, serves to optimise the orthographic system. On this, SPE (p. 49) is unequivocal: 'an optimal orthography would have one representation for each lexical entry.' As we are not concerned here with the question of how good the English spelling system really is, we need not evaluate this particular assertion beyond confirming that the orthography of English can indeed be characterised as having, normally, one representation for each lexical entry.

The second optimising characteristic of English orthography is, in SPE's view, the fact that the system not only displays morpheme invariance but that the actual spelt representations of English morphemes are in a large number of cases remarkably similar to what Chomsky and Halle choose to postulate as their respective underlying phonological representations. In the vowel-shift alternations noted above, the spelt representation of the alternating vowel (except the <ou> in *profound* etc.) regularly corresponds to what SPE postulates as the underlying vowel: /iː/ in *divine*, /eː/ in *serene* etc. *Neptune* has a final /e/ in its underlying phonological representation for stress assignment purposes, to be deleted after stress assignment. And the penultimate stress in *rubella, madonna, confetti* and many other words is regularised through SPE's (p. 148) assumption of a geminate consonant in the phonological underlier exactly where the spelt form has it: in this way the penultimate syllable becomes heavy and receives stress in the regular way before the geminate is simplified later in the derivation. The similarity between many of SPE's underlying representations and their orthographic forms is indeed striking (for further examples, see Carney 1994: 23); but, before any questions regarding the optimality of either representation or their mutual psycholinguistic support can be addressed, one has to ask how this similarity came about. It might, after all, be coincidence.

The fact that both the orthographic and the phonological system operate with invariable representations for each lexical entry is quite possibly coincidental (although reasonable claims regarding psychological reality can be made for both). In the latter system, morpheme invariance follows from the objective pursued by Generative Phonology and its successor models (including Lexical Phonology) to derive all surface forms of a given morpheme from a common underlier. In the former system, morpheme invariance may be the result of the speech community's (or the norm-setters') implicit recognition that such orthographic systems are optimal for native speakers (see SPE: 49f.); but it is also largely subject to historical explanation: the spelling system was fixed at (or, at least, with reference to) a stage of the language at which alternations of the vowel-shift type, for example, had not yet arisen. Letters representing long vowels in English words tend to reflect the pre-vowel-shift stage simply because orthographic norms have not changed substantially since. Such stability is in any case consistent with the fact that English has tended not to change the spellings of loan words substantially even regardless of whether morpheme invariance was at stake. In *moral, atom* etc. the relevant phonological alternations may have helped in retaining the etymological spellings; but the <p> in *psyche*, retained from the donor language despite the loss of the /p/ in the English form, cannot be justified by any orthographic principle except inertia.

The fact that underlying representations chosen in SPE are in many cases identical to standard orthography is due, partly, again to the fact that their vowel derivations are based on an underlying system that is largely that of a period predating the Great Vowel Shift (i.e. late Middle English), and partly to SPE's unconstrained diacritic use of phonological features and entire segments. It is coincidental that both should be reflected in the orthography with such reliability; and in any case, more recent derivational phonology (notably Lexical Phonology) has abandoned many of those abstract underliers for which SPE observes similarity or identity with the orthography. We saw above that the underlier of the stressed vowel in *serene* should in fact be /iː/ and that the second vowel in *atom* must be /∅/. *Madonna* cannot have an underlying consonantal geminate because the grammar cannot contain the degemination rule needed to produce the surface form. Such stress patterns, borrowed wholesale from Italian (which does have consonantal geminates) constitute a fairly large but nevertheless synchronically exceptional class in English; in an adequately constrained phonology, they cannot be brought into line with the stress rule that stresses penultimate syllables in nouns if they are heavy. Similarly, the underlying representation of *Neptune* cannot possibly contain a final /e/ in an appropriately constrained phonological derivation. While it is clear that both phonology and orthography operate with invariant representations for morphemes, there is no reason to suppose that the representations of both systems should be identical as a matter of principle. They are, in fact, not identical at the underlying level; nor is it clear, therefore, that the orthographic representation should be synchronically derived from the underlying phonological form. This is what SPE implied, and N. Chomsky (1970a) as well as Bierwisch (1972) subsequently argued within the same theoretical framework. Bierwisch does note that the outputs of early phonological rules may be of relevance to the derivation of orthographic representations, a view shared and further developed by Klima (1972), Hellberg (1974) and Kohrt (1987). These authors also note that exceptional spellings (obviously) have to be listed. Within Lexical Phonology, Wiese (1989) and Prinz and Wiese (1990) have argued similarly that orthography derives from phonological representations within the lexicon, not necessarily from the underlying representation (which would of course be impossible within Lexical Phonology given that that level would fail to provide orthographies for morphologically complex items).

But any debate about the particular level of phonological representation from which orthographic forms derive leaves unquestioned an assumption that is as old as modern linguistics itself: that in the synchronic grammar, orthography derives from phonology at all. We are faced here with an instance of the doctrine that spoken language is the primary object of linguistic study (or even the only one). Saussure (1916/1959: 23f.) had laid down the law on this issue by stating that 'spoken forms alone constitute the object [of linguistic study. HG].' This was a perhaps overstated reaction on Saussure's part to his Neogrammarian predecessors in the field; but subsequent theorists followed suit – Bloomfield (1933), Sapir (1921) and many others – often invoking the spurious argument that all languages have a spoken form but not all have a written form: this observation of course tells us nothing about the relationship between spoken and written form in languages that have both. (Coulmas (1981); see Householder (1971: Chapter 13) for a discussion of Saussure's position, and for some voices of dissent.) I noted above that Generative Phonology neither requires nor positively supports this traditional assumption. In the next section we shall see arguments against it.

5.3.3   *Accessing the mental lexicon*

It was one of the central assumptions of early ('Standard') Generative Phonology that any morphophonemic alternation (*divine – divinity, atom atomic*) is derived from a redundancy-free phonological underlier which contains all the information idiosyncratic to the item in question, enabling the production of surface forms by means of maximally general rules. The lexicon was viewed at that stage of the evolution of Generative Grammar (N. Chomsky 1965; SPE) as a repository of the idiosyncratic properties of lexical items: it was understood to be a mere list of redundancy-free (hence underlying) phonological representations of morphemes (containing also the syntactic and semantic features idiosyncratic to morphemes); any characteristics of surface forms that could possibly be derived by rule had to be so derived, and the appropriate rules placed in the grammar (e.g. the phonological component) rather than contained in the lexicon. As we saw above, orthographic representations were similarly assumed to be derived from phonological underliers (N. Chomsky 1970a; Bierwisch 1972): such representations were assumed to make no contribution to the lexical entries of morphemes.

This strategy placed heavy demands on both rules and underlying forms in terms of the power (and abstractness) of the devices deployed in both. But it was enforced theory-internally by Occam's Razor; theory-externally it was motivated by the assumption that linguistic competence is structured in such a way that storage (the sole remit of the 'standard' theory's lexicon) is minimised while at the same time an unlimited capacity exists for maximising the computing of generalisations.

While the 'standard' theory was in principle intended to be a theory of linguistic competence rather linguistic performance (in whatever way such a distinction may be defined), its proponents did not entirely refrain from making claims concerning the theory of performance:

> '[t]he only clear suggestions that have been put forth concerning the theory of performance . . . have come from studies of performance models that have been based on assumptions about underlying competence. (N. Chomsky 1965: 10)

It is clearly implicit in such a claim (which is similarly expressed in SPE 3ff. and *passim*) that any hypothesis concerning the mental lexicon in a theory of performance has to be based on the assumptions that Generative Grammar makes regarding the 'competence' lexicon, which in turn implies that the generative view of the lexicon as a redundancy-free list must be subject to empirical falsification.

The problem is that the consequent view of the mental lexicon as a list of redundancy-free representations of morphemes was never substantiated. Indeed, it has been falsified by psycholinguistic research; see Derwing (1973), Linell (1979) and others. It is patently not the case that speakers access lexical items by drawing exclusively on non-redundant phonological information. Rather, lexical access takes place through a variety of channels and with reference to various features. Speakers may draw on semantic, syntactic and phonological features of the item they are searching for; such features may be non-redundant ('underlying') but they may also be redundant and hence, under the 'standard' view, not part of the lexicon at all. Lexical access through orthography, for example, is well documented (Forster 1976; Marshall 1976; Matthei and Roeper 1983; Garman 1990).

Notably, the range of phonological characteristics of lexical items that is drawn on in lexical access includes information that is assumed to be redundant: in the 'tip-of-the-tongue phenomenon' (Brown and McNeill 1966), for example, speakers may recall the number of syllables, or the stress pattern, or other possibly non-underlying characteristics of a lexical item while experiencing an inability to find the lexical item itself. Nathan (1979) has given persuasive examples of lexical items being accessed through their spelling. His 'tip-of-the-tongue' example of a speaker remembering that somebody's name begins with a <p> without recalling the actual name (*Philip*) clinches the point: here a lexical item is accessed through information that is not only patently absent from what 'standard' generative theory assumes to be the underlying representation of the item (namely the phonological form /fɪlɪp/) but that is also not directly derivable from any phonological representation, underlying or not. The speaker recalled <p> rather than <ph>, where the latter might derive from an underlying /f/ but the former clearly does not. Such results and others (Linell 1979) clearly suggest that speakers memorise complete words (rather than morphemes), in a form that closely resembles classical phonemic representations (rather than more abstract underlying representations), enriched by relevant suprasegmental structure, orthographic information etc. Linguistic performance – real-time ('on-line') processing – draws on lexical entries of this, not 'optimally' redundancy-free form while the computation of phonological alternations and morphological relationships among words constitutes a more remote ('off-line') form of linguistic competence that is drawn on in the construction and recognition of words that were previously unknown to the speaker and that may be committed to memory, ready for real-time access at a later stage (Jaeger 1986; Mohanan 1986).

It would appear on these grounds alone, then, that Lexical Phonology provides a more appropriate model of the mental lexicon than that implied by 'Standard' Generative Grammar. Following Mohanan (1986: Section 2.6), we may assume that it is the output representations of the lexical derivation – the 'lexical representation' – that is stored in memory and available for real-time processing, and not the underlying representation. The lexical representations of words are not redundancy-free, containing as they do all information derived by lexical rules: they may be morphologically complex; their segmental abstractness is roughly that of classical phonemic representations; and they contain suprasegmental information such as syllable and foot structure. And if Wiese (1989) and Prinz and Wiese (1990) are correct at least in that orthographic representations are lexical, then such representations too are available for real-time access even if, as (Prinz and) Wiese argue, they are of a derived nature.

As regards the *atom – atomic, deter – deterrent* alternations under discussion in this chapter, the discussion of orthographic representation has so far produced the following results. First, the fact that *atom* and *atomic* share the same spelling is no coincidence but a matter of principle. Second, such a spelling does not of necessity tell us anything about the underlying phonological representation of the item. And third, spelling information is available to the speaker when accessing lexical items (for example *atomic*). These are important steps towards the (so far undelivered) argument that the full vowel in *atomic* is made available to the speaker by the orthography; but the three points made so far are also consistent with the old claim that orthography derives from phonology, and not *vice versa*. The opposite claim, whereby orthography is in principle able to inform phonology, is no less consistent with these three points; but it has to be substantiated.

5.3.4   Spelling pronunciations

In historical linguistics (notably in the history of English), examples supporting the view that spelling may at least partially determine phonological representations are not hard to find. These are the so-called 'spelling pronunciations' (Koeppel 1901; Luick 1903; Coulmas 1981), instances of words whose pronunciation has, through historical change, deviated from that normally represented by the spelling, but where a phonological form closer to that suggested by the spelt form is later reinstated. A classroom example is *waistcoat*, a form which (during the time when waistcoats were first fashionable) reduced (in diachronic terms) to the obscured compound /wéskət/, but where that phonological form is now obsolete and replaced by the transparent form (Faiss 1978: 183f.). Such spelling-based reinstatement of older pronunciations that correspond more closely to the orthography may especially be expected for words that have declined in use and have become confined to the written register (Luick 1903: 304)[12] – a point that will below be relevant to our discussion of *atomic, deterrent*.

While many instances of spelling pronunciations are isolated, one-off developments affecting individual lexical items, others are of a more general kind. Word-initial /h/, for example, appears to have been lost in most varieties of late Southern Middle English (Jordan 1968: Section 293); and loans such as *hostel, hotel, humour, hour* etc. certainly entered English, from French, without initial /h/ (Pope 1934: Section 185). It is reasonable to assume that the later reinstatement of /h/ in such loan words (with few exceptions: *hour, honour, honest*, American English *herb*) is due to the normative force of the spelling conventions. Notably, words such as *hostel* acquired /h/ in their phonological form, rather than dropping <h> from their orthographic form. These are clearly cases where the phonological representation was, at some point in the history of the word, derived from (or at least adjusted to) the orthographic representation, which must therefore have had independent status at the time. The only way of maintaining the SPE position regarding the status of orthography in the face of such cases would be the assumption that *hostel* had an underlying /h/ that was synchronically deleted during the [h]-less period in the history of the word. The reinstatement of the initial [h] would then have to be interpreted as the loss of the deletion rule – an analysis that would, as far as I can see, have no synchronic support during any of the relevant periods except for serving to maintain the spurious claim that orthography derives from phonology in every case.

Such cases are too frequent in the history of the language to be dismissed as insignificant; they are, moreover, a common occurrence in synchronic terms: erroneous pronunciations such as /siːn/ for *Sean* are obviously spelling-based; and they occur not only when reading aloud but may well be memorised and repeated without direct reference to the written form. This is precisely what happens in cases where the pronunciation of foreign names (for example place names) has been anglicised while the orthographic form has been left intact: *France, Paris, Reims* etc. A phonological form may be constructed on the basis of the default phonological value of the spelt form. It is reasonable to suggest that the derivation of orthographic forms from phonological forms is reversible at least in such a way that a spelling symbol can predict the phonological segment that figures in the default sound–spelling correspondence. Not only exceptional spellings but also regular ones must, then, be available to the speaker in a form that is independent from the phonological representation.

Perhaps more significantly regarding the question of orthographic conditioning in synchronic derivations, Moskovitz (1973), Jaeger (1986) and Wang and Derwing (1986) have shown that the vowel-shift alternations in Present-day English are productive only among literate speakers. While stateable in purely phonological terms even within the constraints of Lexical Phonology, such vowel relationships appear to require the independent support provided by the orthographic representation if they are to be fully productive. Such support can only be provided by orthographic representations if they have independent status from the phonology, a status supported by the existence of spelling pronunciations. As I noted above, such status is fully consistent with both the theory of Lexical Phonology and the psycholinguistic evidence; and it will be assumed in the discussion of the derivation of *atomic, deterrent* etc., to which I now return.

5.4   Beyond the limits: spelling-driven phonological rules

The conclusion reached in Section 5.2 regarding *atomic, deterrent* etc. was that the relevant vowels are provided not by the underlying phonological representation (which contains /∅/) but by the stratum-1 blank-filling rule (11), which offers the range of vowels [aɛɪɒʌ] without being able to specify a particular vowel for any given derivation. The fact that *atomic* contains [ɒ] rather than [ɛ], for example, is beyond what the phonology can predict. Such information must be separately listed; but while listing is by no means unprecedented in stratum-1 derivations (recall Chapter 3), it is inconsistent with the observation that speakers are actually able to judge nonsense formations such as [batɒnɪk] (from *baton*, possibly pronounced [batən]; D. Jones 1991) as grammatical, as well as being able to produce such forms quite freely. I return to this issue of productivity below, with further examples.

The vowel values in question are made available to the (literate) speaker by the spelling. First, the principle of morpheme invariance in orthography (C. Chomsky's (1970) principle of 'lexical spelling') holds without exception in the relevant alternating forms. Second, the sound-spelling correspondences obtaining in the relevant cases are invariably such that every [aɛɪɒʌ] corresponds to <a e i o u> respectively. The section of the vocabulary of English in which the relevant alternations occur displays remarkable uniformity in the sound–spelling relationship (Michaels 1980): the well-known irregularities of English orthography (recall *see, sea, Pete* etc.) are confined to non-alternating and mainly monosyllabic words. I return to the fact that certain tense vowels correspond to the same spelling symbols (*marginalia, Miltonian* etc.; (13) above) later in this section, recalling here merely that such tense vowels are derivationally linked with their lax counterparts in pairs such as *marginality – marginalia* etc.

The final version of the blank-filling rule, provisionally stated as (11) above, derives the vowel qualities [aɛɪɒʌ] from the orthographic representation. It is a Spelling–Pronunciation Rule (henceforth 'SP-rule'), and is almost certainly not the only one operative in English.

(19)   *Spelling–Pronunciation Rule*

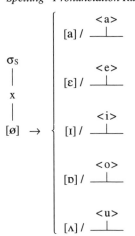

Note that the addition of orthographic context specifications[13] to the rule originally stated in (11) does not affect its status in the lexical phonology of English. Notably, it affects neither its stratal affiliation nor the constraints that it is subject to. Rule (19) is a stratum-1 rule like its predecessor (11); it is a structure-building rule and as such not subject to SCE. Its outputs provide inputs to CiV-Tensing in appropriate contexts (namely the attachment of a suitable suffix – see below); and it is subject to the Structure Preservation Condition. Under that condition, whose validity on stratum 1 is beyond any dispute in the model, the outputs of rules cannot contain configurations (features, feature combinations or phonological structures) that are not attested in the underlying representations of the language. In brief, (given that underliers in the present model are either surface-true or underspecified) SP-rules can only introduce members of the inventory of established phonemes of the language. Structure Preservation makes the prediction that English spelling pronunciations of non-native words (recall *France, Paris, Reims* etc.) are essentially 'English' in their phonological make-up.

I return now to the tense vowels that sometimes surface in places where the SP-rule predicts lax vowels. As I noted in Section 5.2 this happens, for example, in morphologically complex forms containing the suffix -*ian*, giving rise to three-way alternations such as *Milton – Miltonic – Miltonian* etc. As I noted above, such alternations are accounted for by the rule of CiV-Tensing (SPE: 181; Halle and Mohanan 1985; McMahon 1990), which tenses the vowel specified by the SP-rule and makes it a candidate for Tense Vowel Shift. Such a derivation is consistent with the independent conclusion that the SP-rule must be sited on stratum 1: CiV-Tensing and Vowel Shift are themselves stratum-1 rules, and the SP-rule provides the input to this derivational chain. The derivation of the tense vowel in *Miltonian* constitutes no problem for the present analysis (and indeed supports it); but what makes it worthwhile to return to the -*ian*-derivatives here is the fact that such forms frequently derive from surnames – a part of the English vocabulary where spelling idiosyncrasies (often among homophones, as in *Britten – Britton – Brittan – Britain*) are particularly widespread.

In a small survey (first discussed in Giegerich (1992c)), I asked 10 native speakers of English[14] to form de-nominal adjectives with -*ian* from the 11 names given in (19a) below. Subjects were given *Newton – Newtonian* as a model, followed by the eleven names, and asked to give the simplex names and their -*ian*-derivatives in phonemic transcription. The transcription task of the simplex names confirmed without exception that all the names contain schwa (or, in some cases, syllabic sonorants in free variation with schwa-plus-sonorant sequences) in their underived forms.

The results are given in (20b), where the numbers of responses conforming with the predictions made by the present account are underlined. All 10 subjects, for example, gave [oʊ] in the stressed syllable of *Andersonian*; six had [iː] and four [eɪ] in that of *Mendelian*, and so on. Where numbers do not add up to 10, subjects had declined to perform the task; their reasons were not specifically queried but several subjects commented that -*ian* formations are not always possible and in many cases rather forced.

(20) a. *Newton*   b. *Newtonian*   c. *SP*   *CiV*   *VSR*

			SP	CiV	VSR
Anderson	[oː] 10		[ɒ]	[ɔː]	[oʊ]
Mendel	[iː] 6, [eː] 4		[ɛ]	[eː]	[iː]
Gussmann	[a] 8		[a]	–	–
Britton	[oː] 8		[ɒ]	[ɔː]	[oʊ]
Andersen	[iː] 2, [ɛ] 4		[ɛ]	[eː]	[iː]
Pearlman	[eː] 2, [a] 5		[a]	[aː]	[eɪ]
Lendl	[lɛndliən] 4, [ɪ] 1		–	–	–
Britten	[iː] 2, [ɛ] 2		[ɛ]	[eː]	[iː]
Penzl	[pɛntsliən] 4, [ɪ] 1		–	–	–
Hurford	[ɒr] ~ [ɔː]		[ɒ]	–	–
Handel	[iː] 6, [ɛ] 2, [eː] 1		[ɛ]	[eː]	[iː]

The responses display considerable variation (as has also been noted for such formations by Bolinger (1981)); but (disregarding the qualities of the response vowels for the moment), the comparison of *Penzl, Lendl* with *Mendel, Handel* suggests immediately that orthography is the source of any vowel occurring in the derived form. There can be no doubt that the final syllables in the last three of the four names are phonologically identical and that the different onset in *Penzl* is irrelevant; yet four of five responses gave derived forms without the vowel in the former pair (and the remaining five subjects declined to use the suffix altogether), while in the latter pair ten and nine, respectively, contained a vowel.

Turning now to the qualities of the response vowels, we find that the derivations sketched in (19c) are followed in the majority of cases. The first vowel listed in (19b) is, in each case, the one predicted by the derivation. Again the results speak largely for themselves – contrast in particular *Andersonian* and *Andersenian*, where *Anderson/Andersen* are again homophonous. In the former, all ten subjects offered the predicted vowel [oʊ]; in the latter, none offered that particular vowel while two (out of six) offered the predicted quality [eɪ]. *Britton/Britten* yielded a similar result.

In *Hurfordian*, CiV-Tensing is blocked by the /Rd/ sequence: the rule operates only before single consonants (SPE: 181). All ten subjects conformed with this prediction; the [ɒr] ~ [ɔː] variation found in the responses is due to rhotic/non-rhotic variation among the subjects.

Compare now *Pearlman* and *Gussmann*. In the former, two subjects followed the predicted derivation while five offered [a] (where perhaps recognition of the morpheme |man| inhibited further derivation of the vowel), while in the latter none offered the predicted [eɪ], eight subjects using instead the SP-vowel in unmodified form. The reason behind this lies probably again in the orthography (which constitutes the only difference between the two forms): <n> in the former, <nn> in the latter. While CiV-Tensing is blocked by a consonant sequence in *Hurfordian*, there is no independent evidence to suggest that *Gussmannian* contains a geminate consonant in the phonological representation. SPE notes the similar case of *Maxwellian*, stating that:

> [n]onapplication of the rule can just as well be marked, as in orthography, by a double consonant. (Recall that clusters of two identical consonants simplify [later in the derivation. HG] . . .) (SPE: 182)

By invoking reference to orthographic representations in phonological derivations, we can avoid such diacritic (non-)solutions just as we did in the cases of the type *madonna*, *rubella* noted above: the double consonant spelling simply signals that the form in question behaves as if it had two consonants in the relevant position, thereby attracting the stress to the penultimate syllable in *madonna* and blocking CiV-Tensing in *Maxwellian*, *Gussmannian*. As I noted above, the stipulation of a geminate consonant in such forms would necessitate a degemination rule, which would have to be sited on stratum 2 in order to be applicable in underived forms. But it is precisely on stratum 2 that any arising geminates are maintained (*keenness* etc.). Such an analysis using geminates as diacritics is, then, not only highly undesirable for obvious reasons but actually impossible in the present model.

Apart from considerable variation in the responses, for whose detailed study the sample is too small (but see Bolinger (1981)), this survey shows clearly the influence of spelling on the phonetic form of the -*ian*-derivation. Orthography is responsible for the presence or absence of a vowel in the relevant position; it accounts for the quality of the vowel (assuming a derivation of the form given in (19c)); and the orthographic context of the vowel further determines its phonological derivation. Out of 110 potential (and 82 actual) responses to the task, 62 conformed with the spelling-based derivation proposed here.

5.5   Conclusions and implications

I conclude this argument with a few remarks regarding the acquisition of alternations of the form *atom – atomic*, *deter – deterrent*, attempting to show that the derivation proposed here is superior to the 'Standard' one not only in formal terms (as we have seen) but also in terms of its psycholinguistic implications.

It is of course impossible to provide direct psycholinguistic evidence for underlying representations. However, in the present case the question of how alternations such as these are acquired provides a window into their psycholinguistic status, and into the mental lexicon in general. Consider first the hypothesis – now abandoned on formal grounds – that English schwa-vowel alternations have full-vowel underliers, such as /atɒm/ etc. The first point to note here is that speakers, on acquiring the simplex form *atom* by hearing it as [atəm], are unable to determine the quality of the putative underlier. Nor do they have any motivation at all for positing a non-surface-identical underlier for this form: they do not know that later in their linguistic career they might involve this schwa in an alternation with another vowel while those in *baton*, *petal* they probably will not.

There are only two possibilities of resolving this dilemma. First, it might be assumed that *atomic* is acquired first, providing a surface-identical underlier for the complex form, from which speakers then derive the surface form for the simplex *atom* by means of Delinking (8). This would mean that all those forms that we have treated as morphologically simple (*atom* etc.; (1) above) must instead be treated as synchronic back-formations (see, for example, Bauer 1983: Section 7.7) – an analysis too preposterous to form the basis for any kind of argument. Or, second, it might be (and has been: S. Anderson 1981) argued that speakers acquiring *atom* analyse that form as /atØm/ and then, on acquiring *atomic*, re-structure the underlying representation into /atɒm/. In other words, speakers acquire the /ɒ/ when they first hear *atomic*, transfer the vowel to *atom* but actually implement it only in *atomic*. There is no independent reason for them to associate /ɒ/ with *atom*; the re-structuring hypothesis is supported by nothing except the assumption – a false one, as we have seen – that the full-vowel underlier is the only way of linking *atom* and *atomic* derivationally.

Moreover, the assumption of re-structuring fails to account for the productivity of such pair-wise relationships that was noted earlier. How can a speaker who is unfamiliar with the adjective derived from, say, *totem* nevertheless judge [toːtémɪk] as grammatical? How is he or she able to produce the (surely novel) form [batónɪk] from *baton* (but not from *batten*)? Only knowing the respective simplex forms [toʊtəm] and [batən], the speaker has no way of predicting the relevant vowel qualities in the derived forms and, therefore, does not know what to re-structure his or her previous underliers into. The re-structuring hypothesis makes the false prediction, then, that the only way for the speaker to acquire the *atom – atomic* alternation is that of hearing somebody else say *atomic*.

In contrast, the analysis based on empty underliers and a stratum-1 blank-filling rule whose only access to individual vowel qualities is through orthographic representations is plausible in specific as well as general terms. Specifically, it makes the prediction that the illiterate speaker who knows [atəm] has no way of predicting the vowel quality in the derived form. On hearing the derived form, the speaker may establish the morphological and semantic link and might, for the phonological link, implement the blank-filling rule without the orthographic context specification ((11) above). This would fail to establish a non-arbitrary derivational relationship in that the rule would merely say 'insert any one of the vowel melodies [aɛɪɒʌ]'. Any more specific information has to be listed with the individual lexical item; and any listing is a diagnostic of stratum-1 processes in the present model. This prediction is clearly correct.

The literate speaker, on the other hand, will automatically associate [atəm] with the orthographic form <atom>; and having also internalised (through the acquisition of literacy) the orthographic principle of English whereby the allomorphs of a given morpheme share the same orthographic form, the speaker will construct [atɒmɪk] from <atomic>, a spelt form that he or she is able to produce without problems (and without having ever heard it). Only the literate speaker can establish a regular derivational path from *atom* to *atomic*. This prediction for the acquisition process, made only by an analysis in which the formal link between such forms is provided by the orthography (only), is again surely correct.

In general terms, an analysis that involves SP-rules[15] constitutes a first step towards giving formal recognition to a number of well-known facts, all of which point towards the existence of independent orthographic representations in the lexicon: that the establishment of many morphophonological relationships is spelling-driven in the acquisition process (Jaeger 1986; Wang and Derwing 1986), that spelling pronunciations occur in diachronic terms (Koeppel 1901; Luick 1903; Coulmas 1981) as well as synchronic terms (Nathan 1979), and that orthographic information in many cases facilitates speakers' access to items stored in the mental lexicon (see Garman (1990) and references). I hope to have shown in this chapter that the theory of Lexical Phonology, in the version advocated in this study, is not only fully consistent with the (somewhat unorthodox) assumption that orthographic representations are independent from phonological representations and therefore able to inform those, but that the theory actually requires such independent representations in order to account for a number of derivational phenomena in English phonology.

6 [r]-*sandhi and liaison in RP*

6.1 *Explananda*

6.1.1 [r]-*sandhi: linking and intrusion*

My main concern in this chapter and the following will be [r]-sandhi: the phenomenon of 'linking [r]' and 'intrusive [r]' in RP and its synchronic derivation within Lexical Phonology. The singular form, 'phenomenon', is appropriate here. While the descriptive accounts (for example Wells 1982; Giegerich 1992a; Gimson 1994) and many of the more formal analyses found in the literature (Kahn 1976; Mohanan 1984, 1985; Nespor and Vogel 1986; Broadbent 1991; McCarthy 1991, 1993; Scobbie 1992; McMahon, Foulkes and Tollfree 1994; Harris 1994; Kamińska 1995; McMahon 1996) tend to draw the well-known distinction between 'linking [r]' and 'intrusive [r]' (see the examples in (1) below), reporting that RP speakers freely use the former but often shun the latter, it is also clear from the descriptions that the avoidance of [r]-intrusion does not come naturally to those speakers: it is brought about and maintained only thanks to continuous enforcement by a strong intrusion stigma (Gimson 1994: 263f.). It may well be more natural for the RP speaker to have both linking and intrusion than it is to have the former but not the latter. The deliberateness of intrusion-avoidance alone suggests that linking and intrusion may, in purely synchronic-phonological terms, be nondistinct (and stronger arguments to this effect will be given below); but any account dealing with the phenomenon also has to address the question of how it is that at least some speakers (especially those of 'speech-conscious adoptive RP' Wells 1982: 284f.) succeed in implementing the intrusion stigma with remarkable reliability.

Below, (1a) gives a list of the vowels after which linking [r] and intrusive [r] occur. Examples are given at (1b) and (1c) respectively. The difference between linking [r] and intrusive [r] is that in the former, the vowels in question are the residue left behind after the loss of historic /r/ (which is, without exception, still manifested in the spelling), while those in the latter do not derive from historic vowel-plus-/r/ sequences.

(1)   a. bar   ɑː   b. barring, bar is   c. baaing, Shah is
           store   ɔː   storing, store is   drawing, draw it
           cure   ʊə   curing, cure it   skua is
           hear   ɪə   hearing, hear it   idea is
           hair   ɛə   hairy, hair is   Eritrea is
           fur   ɜː   furry, fur is   (*unattested*)
           feather   ə   feathery, feather is   vanilla-y, vanilla is

No cases of intrusive [r] after [ɜː] exist: this vowel melody has only arisen in historic-/r/ contexts.[1] Similarly, the centring-diphthong contexts [ʊə] and [ɛə] are questionable in the absence of historic [r] (*skua*, *Eritrea*), given the normally heterosyllabic citation forms of such sequences: [uː.ə] and [eɪ.ə] respectively. The case of *idea* is somewhat unusual, given that historically comparable items (*diarrhoea*, *urea*, *trachea*) are likely to maintain the heterosyllabic sequence [iː.ə] rather than displaying the result of its contraction – the (tautosyllabic) centring diphthong [ɪə] – in the citation form. Such (diachronic) contraction of heterosyllabic sequences into centring diphthongs has occurred sporadically in certain lexical items, probably driven by word-frequency criteria. Clearly, it is not an active synchronic process.

Despite the possible failure of intrusive-[r] attestation in certain instances it is worth noting at this point that intrusive [r] occurs in no contexts other than those also displaying linking [r]: linking-[r]-attracting nuclei also attract intrusive [r] wherever such nuclei have diachronically also arisen without the involvement of historic [r]. Clearly, linking and intrusion are one and the same phenomenon except in terms of the (diachronic) origin of their contexts, a difference which is synchronically reflected in the spelling only (Gimson 1994: 263).

This observation gives rise to a further claim, made or implied in the relevant literature and here equally subscribed to: that both linking and intrusion are systematically confined to non-rhotic varieties of English – varieties in which [r] is maintained in syllable onsets (*rye*, *try*, *shrink*, *herring*, *story*) but no longer present in rhymes (*hear*, *beard*). In the case of linking [r] this claim is trivial: given that in rhotic varieties 'historic' [r] is pronounced in all contexts, there cannot be any [r] alternating with zero of the type shown in (1a) and (1b) above. What is more interesting is the fact that in rhotic varieties, intrusive [r] is absent:[2] forms such as those in (1c) never contain (a-historic) [r] in, say, General American or Scottish

Standard English. Unless this fact is treated as accidental it can only mean, in line with earlier observations, that linking and intrusion are one and the same phenomenon, which is moreover systematically connected with non-rhoticity.

It may be argued here that the [r]-zero alternation found in linking [r] (1a, 1b) is not the effect of an active phonological process in the synchronic phonology of present-day RP but, rather, the fossilised leftover from past diachronic change: while forms such as *hear, hair* lost their [r], in pre-pausal and preconsonantal contexts, in the development of non-rhoticity, prevocalic [r] in *hearing, hairy* has simply been retained. Diachronic [r]-loss in *hair* etc. was, of course, a highly natural change, involving the lenition and vocalisation of a consonant in the rhyme position that was, by virtue of its high sonority and low degree of constriction, particularly susceptible to such development (C. Jones 1989: 298 ff.; Lutz 1991; McMahon 1996).

This view effectively denies [r]-sandhi the status of a regularity in the synchronic phonology that is worth explaining: the occurrence of [r]-sandhi is, under that view, no more in need of a synchronic explanation than is, say, the non-occurrence of [t]-sandhi. Numerous phonological changes of the past have given rise to synchronic alternations: our strategy has been to state those – as generalisations aiming to be descriptively adequate but not necessarily explanatory – somewhere in the lexical phonology and most likely on stratum 1.

My view is that we are dealing here with a different kind of phenomenon, and that the grammar has to be more ambitious than merely aiming for descriptiveness at the risk of arbitrariness. If (as I noted above) the diachronic development of non-rhoticity was a natural process then the outcome of that development may well be amenable to synchronic explanation, rather than just description. One indication of the difference involved is the fact that [r]-sandhi takes place not only within words (which may have survived in that form through the diachronic period of [r]-loss) but also between words (*hear it, hair is* etc.): [r]-sandhi is, therefore, perhaps among other things, a postlexical regularity in present-day RP whose 'across-the-board' occurrence demands acknowledgement as a fully productive process. This is clearly not just detritus from a past change.

And there are further indications suggesting that the process is not only productive but also utterly natural. Intrusive [r] (1c) is in itself a problem for diachronically oriented accounts, which have to appeal to the strictly diachronic notion of 'analogous extension' in this case, whatever that may mean for the shape of the resulting synchronic grammar. What exacerbates this problem is the fact that this analogous extension, in terms of both linking and intrusion, is still going on. Both linking and intrusion occur regularly, in RP and other non-rhotic varieties, in new formations (clippings, acronyms; see (2a) below), in foreign forms (2b), as well as in phrases where the appropriate context has been produced by other (in some cases non-RP) phonological processes such as Cockney [h]-dropping or the (diachronic) reduction of unstressed final vowels (2c):

(2)   a. UNProFor is, IFor is   b. the junta[r] in Chile
       NASA[r] and   the Stella[r] Artois[r] event
       BUPA[r] is   gloria[r] in excelsis
       c. hear him [ʔɪərɪm]
       I tell you how [tɛljəræ]
       tomato[ər] and cucumber

(Examples partly from Wells 1982: 226f.; McMahon 1996)

Such examples clearly show, then, that [r]-sandhi is a fully productive process in the phonology of RP and other non-rhotic varieties, liable to occur whenever its triggering context arises. A natural synchronic explanation of the phenomenon is clearly needed. I turn to the characterisation of this context – another *explanandum* – in Section 6.1.2; here I complete the exemplification of [r]-sandhi with a survey of forms containing linking [r] and, unlike those in (1b) above, additional vowel alternations:

(3)   a. [ɜː~ɪ]   myrrh – myrrhic
                     sir – sirrah
          [ɜː~ɛ]   deter – deterrent
                     err – error
          [ɜː~ʌ]   occur – occurrence
                     demur – demurrer
       b. [ɑː~a]   isobar – isobaric
                     tartar – tartaric
                     Bulgar – Bulgaric
          [ɔː~ɒ]   abhor – abhorrent, horror
                     meteor – meteoric
                     (poly-)histor – historic
       c. [ɪə~ɛ]   sincere – sincerity
                     austere – austerity
          [ɛə~ɛ]   compare – comparison
                     declare – declarative
          [ɪə~a]   clear – clarity
          [ɛə~ɛə]   rare – rarity

Vowel alternations such as those in (3a) have already been discussed in Chapter 5. (3b) contains parallel cases containing the low vowels [ɑː ɔː] in

their base forms; and (3c), finally, gives some of the more 'standard' alternations, seemingly involving synchronic Vowel Shift (*sincere, compare*), its
alleged twice-over application in *clear* (SPE: 202) and the absence of the
alternation (presumably through the exceptional failure of Trisyllabic
Shortening) in *rare*.

In the face of such a motley collection of vowel alternations (all of which
involve, notably, the stratum-1 morphology), the question of productivity
arises again. While it is clearly conceivable that every one of these alternations might be fossilised in Present-day English, listed with individual items
in the way many of the quirks of stratum-1 derivation are, it is impossible to
take the opposite view whereby all these alternations are considered synchronically regular, accounted for by fully productive synchronic rules.
Clear – clarity vs. *sincere – sincerity* alone (where both [a] and [ɛ] in the
derivative correspond to [ɪə] in the morphologically simple form) make a
convincing case for the listing of one or the other alternation; but the question is, which? This is not a question that can be decided *a priori*: its answer
depends on the derivational details of those alternations that are considered
regular and synchronically productive (see (1) above).

Such vowel alternations will be discussed in Chapter 7; here I merely note
the obvious (and little noted) relevance of lexical stratification to the study
of [r]-sandhi and related (vowel-alternation) phenomena in English. The
more straightforward cases of linking and intrusion (see (1) above) obviously affect the shape of the stratum-2 and postlexical phonologies within
the present model; those given in (3) raise questions about the corresponding regularities (if any) contained in stratum 1.

6.1.2   Contexts for [r]-sandhi: a natural class?

We saw in Section 6.1.1 that [r]-sandhi occurs after the low vowels [ɑːɔː]
(*bar/Shah, store/draw*), the centring diphthongs [ʊə ɪə ɛə] (*cure/skua,
hear/idea, hair/Eritrea*), [ɜː] (*fur*) and [ə] (*father/banana*). [ɜː], provisionally
referred to as 'stressed schwa' in Section 5.2.2, groups with the centring
diphthongs and [ə] in that it has the roughly the same, central quality that
characterises the latter and the second elements of the former. [r]-sandhi
occurs, then, after low vowels and central vowels.

The problem with this characterisation of the inputs to [r]-sandhi is that
they do not at face value constitute a convincingly natural class: while the
input vowels have in common that they are non-high, central vowels
group strictly speaking no more naturally with the low vowels than they do
with the high vowels [i] and [u], or indeed with front or back vowels: the

characterisation of the input vowels as non-high does little to dispel the arbitrariness of that grouping. The perhaps most obvious solution to this problem would be to revise the featural analysis of [ə] (in its various manifestations ranging from the centring diphthongs to schwa itself). Indeed, Gimson (1994: 118, 132) places the relevant positional allophones of this vowel (though not the final elements of centring diphthongs) in the bottom third of the vowel diagram, almost on a par with the low vowels. So, the class [ɑ ɔ ə] is perhaps more natural than the characterisation of [ə] as simply 'central' would suggest. But note that such a revision of the featural specification of [ə] is of no help in solving the natural-class problem under the synchronic analysis of schwa pursued here. This analysis, proposed in the earlier literature (Gussmann 1991; Giegerich 1992b) and further developed in Chapter 5 above, assumes that schwa is underlyingly represented not as [– high] but as a melodically 'empty' nucleus [∅], filled by the melody [ə] by a late (postlexical) default rule. The lexical class [ɑ ɔ ∅] is no more natural than are the classes [i u ∅] or [e o ∅], for example. I intend to uphold this synchronic analysis of schwa here, and to elaborate it further. It will in fact be central to my analysis of [r]-sandhi. There are three possibilities of avoiding the natural-class problem, under an analysis that treats [ə] as an underlyingly empty nucleus.

The first possibility is one whereby [r]-sandhi is itself treated as a 'default' sandhi, which simply applies where other sandhi phenomena do not apply (and which is therefore under no apparent obligation to occur in a natural class of contexts). I discuss this possibility later in this section.

The second possibility avoids the natural-class problem by treating RP as underlyingly rhotic, synchronically deriving *hear*, for example, from underlying /hiːr/ in rhotic and non-rhotic varieties of English alike (Mohanan 1984, 1985; Kamińska 1995). This possibility I shall discuss in Section 6.2.1 below, showing that it is untenable for RP in the present model of Lexical Phonology.

The third possibility is one which revises the underlying representations of the 'long' low vowels [aː ɔː] so as to bring those into line with [∅] and, in particular, with the centring diphthongs, thus defining a natural class of [r]-sandhi contexts. Such an analysis treats [aː ɔː] as the surface reflexes of underlying centring diphthongs, whose representation (/a∅ ɔ∅/) parallels that of the surface centring diphthongs in RP ([ɪə ɛə ʊə]). It requires the assumption that a synchronic monophthongisation rule for centring diphthongs with low first elements is active in present-day RP. I shall explore the arguments in favour of this somewhat abstract analysis in Chapter 7 below, both in synchronic and in recent-diachronic terms. These arguments will turn out to be not only advantageous to the analysis of [r]-sandhi but, in fact, compelling on quite independent grounds. The analysis of [r]-sandhi presented in this chapter will ignore the low vowels [aː ɔː] except for occasional reference.

Consider now the possible analysis of [r]-sandhi as a simple default option, applicable in cases where other sandhi segments do not occur. As is well known (see, for example, Gimson 1994: Section 12.4.7), [r] is one of three sandhi 'segments' occurring in intervocalic juncture; the other two are [ʲ] and [ʷ], exemplified in (4a) and (4b) respectively:

(4)   a. seeing, see it   [siːʲɪŋ]   b. doing, do it   [duːʷɪŋ]
             laying, lay it   [leɪʲɪŋ]   showing, show it   [ʃoʊʷɪŋ]
             trying, try it   [traɪʲɪŋ]   allowing, allow it [əlaʊʷɪŋ]
             boyish, boy is   [bɔɪʲɪʃ]
             burying, bury it   [berɪʲɪŋ]

The distribution of [ʲ] and [ʷ] and [r] is complementary in that [ʲ] occurs after high front vowels (including diphthongs with high front second elements), [ʷ] occurs after high back vowels (including again diphthongs ending in such elements); and [r] occurs, as we saw, after low vowels and vowels ending in central elements. Given that the melodies [ɛ ʌ a ɒ] do not occur in the relevant contexts in the form of either short vowels or second elements of diphthongs, (4) completes the list of possible intervocalic sandhi contexts begun in (1) above.

The contexts of both [ʲ] and [ʷ] sandhi constitute natural classes in surface terms (and it may at least be argued that all such sandhi phenomena are postlexical). Moreover, given the well-known phonetic similarity of [j w] with high front and high back vowels respectively, the whole process seems utterly natural. [r]-sandhi (in whatever form it may be stated in the phonology) may then simply be treated as the default option applicable wherever the other two are impossible. However, such an analysis would be arbitrary in two respects. First, it would fail to account for the fact that it is precisely [r], of all segments, that constitutes the default sandhi: [l] for example would be equally conceivable.[3] Second, the default sandhi happens in an apparently heterogeneous set of contexts (namely low and central vowels) – a problem that has been noted before. Without a solution to the natural-class problem of inputs, a situation where different sandhi segments occur in the subsets of these contexts would strictly speaking be just as plausible. This approach to [r]-sandhi is, then, not fully explanatory.

Nevertheless, the complementary distribution of [r], [ʲ] and [ʷ] sandhi must form part of any non-arbitrary account of linking and intrusive [r]. I shall suggest below that such sandhi is in turn part of a more general feature of syllabification in English which governs also the placement of syllable boundaries as in *fee*[.l]*ing, fee*[.l] *it*. Notably, such strings have 'clear [l]' in RP while rhymes have 'dark' [l] (Gimson 1994: 182). If this generalisation about the distribution of the /l/-allophones is correct, as it undoubtedly is, then the /l/ in *feeling, feel it* must occupy syllable onsets just like any [r] that appears in RP must occupy that position in the syllable. This point, yet another *explanandum* connected with [r]-sandhi, will be taken up again in Section 6.3.1.

6.2   Previous accounts: [r]-deletion and insertion

6.2.1   The deletion analysis

I consider in this section the possibility of a synchronic derivation of non-rhoticity and [r]-sandhi which assumes that RP is underlyingly rhotic, and that non-rhoticity (the failure of [r] to surface in syllable rhymes) is the surface effect of a synchronic [r]-deletion rule in appropriate contexts. Such an analysis, proposed for Lexical Phonology by Mohanan (1984, 1985) and, in modified form, by Kamińska (1995), incorporates the essential stages of the history of non-rhoticity in RP into its synchronic phonology. It has, possibly for that reason alone, been the favoured option of accounting for the relevant facts in the 'standard' generative framework (see, for example, Gussmann 1980: 34ff.), given that framework's tendency to posit underlying representations that mirror the surface forms of earlier stages of the language. Recall, for example, the SPE account of vowel alternations caused historically by the Great Vowel Shift (discussed in Section 4.3 above). Linguistic change was in that period of generative linguistics viewed as largely confined to the rule system (King 1969): the grammar of RP would have acquired a rule of [r]-deletion, which effectively served to make surface forms more remote from their underliers than they had previously been.

This analysis also holds the apparent advantage of relegating dialect differences (here that between rhotic and non-rhotic varieties) to the rule systems of the dialects involved, rather than setting up different underlying inventories or different individual underlying representations (Thomas 1967; G. Brown 1972): rhotic varieties may have the breaking rule, to be dis-cussed below – as do the English West Country and some American varieties (Wells 1982) but, by and large, not Scottish English (McMahon 1996) – but they do not have the deletion rule. This apparent advantage, which in fact exemplifies a fundamental (if informal) principle of early generative dialectology, is known to be spurious; and so is the (rather less principled) reliance of that kind of phonology on past stages of the language in setting up synchronic underliers (as we saw in Chapters 4 and 5). But, given the informality of those 'principles', their decline in more recent phonological theory does not automatically invalidate the [r]-deletion analysis of non-rhoticity. The flaws of this analysis lie elsewhere.

In its broad outline, such an analysis runs as follows. Items such as *hear, bear, sure, car, sore* have underlying representations containing long vowels plus /r/. For non-low vowels, a rule of pre-[r] breaking produces centring diphthongs; and the /r/ is subsequently deleted, by a rule that is extrinsically ordered after the breaking rule, in syllable rhymes but not in onsets. For reasons that will become clear presently, the precise form of the rules involved is unimportant here: the flaws in this analysis (apart from its need for extrinsic ordering) again lie elsewhere. Below is a sketch of a sample derivation:

(5)   *hear*: /h iː r /   *hearing*: /h iː r ɪ ŋ /   UR (except Vowel Shift)
         [h ɪə r]   [h ɪə r ɪ ŋ]   Pre-/r/ Breaking
         [h ɪə]   *(n/a)*   /r/-Deletion

If we add synchronic Vowel Shift (in its SPE version) into this derivation (which would make the underlying form of *hear* /heːr/), the alternations *sincere – sincerity, declare – declarative* (see (3c) above) become regular, following the pattern *obscene – obscenity, profane – profanity*. This takes care of some of the problematic stratum-1 alternations given in (3c) above: under the deletion analysis, these alternations are regular and predictable. Those in (3a) (*myrrh – myrrhic* etc.) and (3b) (*isobar – isobaric* etc.) are, as far as I am aware, not discussed in the literature; but they could be handled under a deletion account. The former group would presumably have full-vowel underliers (/mɪr/ etc.), the surface [ɜː] in *myrrh, myrrhy* being produced by a reduction rule followed by some sort of lengthening (also applicable in *isobar*). And if the deletion account were to form part of a lexical derivation of the form proposed in Chapter 5, where the derivation of *myrrh* from a full-vowel underlier is technically impossible, then the alternative (spelling-based) derivation proposed in Section 5.2.2 could be adapted so as to be consistent with a deletion analysis for [r]. The spelling-based analysis of that class of vowel alternations before historic [r] is in that sense neutral with respect to the analysis of the [r] problem itself, although I shall argue in Section 7.5 that it opens up interesting possibilities for the alternative account of [r]-sandhi that will be offered below. I shall show there that an analysis that posits full-vowel underliers for cases such as *myrrh* would preclude the analysis of [r]-sandhi proposed below for independent reasons.

The deletion analysis has the immediate advantage of avoiding the natural-class problem discussed in Section 6.1.2. It does so by positing /r/ in underlying representations true to the history of individual forms – I return to this point presently – and by producing centring diphthongs (as well as, if not crucially, schwa and [ɜː] – see Chapter 5 above) derivationally from otherwise-attested members of the pure-vowel inventory, which need not then contain centring diphthongs. The resulting reduction of the inventory of underlying vowels is of course welcome, in that kind of analysis, under Occam's Razor (but see again Section 4.3 for discussion).

However, once again the elimination of centring diphthongs from the underlying inventory can only be achieved at the price of free-ride derivations. Centring diphthongs have to be synchronically derived from vowel-plus-/r/ sequences also in those cases where the putative /r/ is followed by a tautomorphemic consonant that prevents it from alternating: cases such as *weird, fierce, laird, scarce* – by no means scarce – would have to have /wiːrd/ etc. as underliers, disregarding (the SPE version of) Vowel Shift. We saw in Chapter 4 that such free rides do not present a technical problem for Lexical Phonology as long as the rules involved need not apply on stratum 1 of the derivation: on that stratum (alone), they would be blocked by SCE. Given that [r] is maintained in, say, *hear it*, the [r]-deletion rule must in fact be postlexical (Mohanan 1985; Kamińska 1995) and therefore will not be constrained by SCE. Under the deletion analysis, RP is rhotic throughout the lexical derivation. But even though this analysis is technically possible in the present framework, the necessity of free-ride derivations highlights its abstractness, with the well-known learnability problems in its wake: there is no independent evidence for /r/ being synchronically present, in RP, in non-alternating forms like *weird*. Attempting to avoid such free rides by positing underlying centring diphthongs for such non-alternating forms (recall here the discussion of the Alternation Condition in Section 4.3.3 above) would of course mean losing one of the major attractions of this analysis: the exclusion of underlying centring diphthongs from the RP inventory.

It may be argued that there is phonotactic support for an analysis of *weird* etc. that derives the centring diphthong from a long vowels plus /r/ in

the underlying representation: consonants following the centring diphthongs are (with few exceptions) coronal obstruents:

(6)   beard   laird   gourd
        weird   scarce   Lourdes
        fierce   bairn
        pierce   cairn

This apparent phonotactic restriction on consonants following centring
diphthongs (ignoring items from the 'Celtic fringe' such as *cairn*) may be
said to support an analysis whereby such nuclei occupy three skeletal slots:
in the phonotactics of English it is the fourth slot in the rhyme that is
restricted to coronal obstruents (see Section 8.5.4 below; Kiparsky 1981;
Giegerich 1992a: Chapter 6).

Note, however, that coronal obstruents are free to occur in the third skeletal position of the rhyme. Under a two-slot analysis for centring diphthongs, the items in (6) therefore do not violate the phonotactics of English.
Such an analysis would therefore at worst result in the loss of a minor
phonotactic generalisation.[4] More likely, all that is shown by this apparent
restriction is the uncontroversial point whereby such centring diphthongs
originate historically from sequences occupying three skeletal slots. I return
to matters of syllabification in Chapter 8; here I merely note that considera-
tions of the synchronic phonotactics of RP are of no help in establishing the
underlying status of centring diphthongs.

The deletion account would, albeit at the price of incurring unacceptable
abstractness in the form of free-ride derivations, make correct empirical
predictions were it not for the existence of intrusive [r]. For that, two analyses are possible within the deletion account, suggested by Mohanan (1984,
1985) and Kamińska (1995) respectively. I deal with each in turn.

In Mohanan's analysis, intrusive [r] is the product of an independent [r]-
insertion rule which operates (optionally, in order to cater for the intrusion
stigma), after low vowels and surface schwa, in pre-vocalic contexts. The
stratal affiliation is not entirely clear; the rule would certainly have to be
present postlexically (to handle cases such as *I saw*[r] *it*); and it might also
operate on stratum 2 (*draw*[r]*ing*) if it were to be linked with the
syllabification process. Alternatively, such onsets might be left empty until
the postlexical stratum. Such a possible account (anticipated by Kenyon
(1958) and rejected by Johansson (1973)) was defended, in the SPE framework, by Gussmann (1980). There are arguments of three kinds against
such an analysis, in addition to the abstractness problem of the deletion
rule, already discussed.

First, the rule of (intrusive) [r]-insertion is arbitrary in two respects: in its selection of [r] as the inserted segment – this is a problem faced by all insertion analyses, discussed in more detail below – and in terms of the contexts in which it applies: the natural-class problem, discussed in Section 6.1.2 above. (I shall show in Chapter 7 that the context problem can be overcome.)

Second, the insertion rule is the mirror image of the deletion rule, operating (by sheer accident, in synchronic terms) in contexts exactly identical to those left behind by the deletion rule for underlying /r/. This is admittedly a drawback of a kind that we have tolerated in the cases of McMahon's (1990) Vowel Shift (Section 4.3 above) and the schwa-vowel alternations discussed in Chapter 5. Recall, however, that those analyses had rather strong arguments in their favour: both were subject to SCE (which in fact enforced the mirror-image duplication) and resulted in the absence of free-ride derivations. The combined deletion-and-insertion analysis of [r]-sandhi yields no such results and is not enforced by the grammar.

Third, an account that operates with two unrelated rules makes no predictions regarding their coexistence within a single grammar except for one, which is false: it predicts, on the grounds of simplicity, that a speaker is more likely to have just one of the rules than he or she is to have both. In detail, the prediction is that speakers may have either /r/-deletion and no insertion, or [r]-insertion and no deletion. This prediction is false on both counts: non-rhotic speakers have to learn, on entirely non-phonological grounds, the suppression of intrusive [r], not its use. And there are no rhotic speakers that have intrusive [r]. This account fails to express the intimate empirical connection between [r]-linking and [r]-intrusion.

It is, in fact, the occasional failure of [r]-intrusion in RP (as opposed to the obligatoriness of linking) that has led researchers such as Gussmann (1980) and Mohanan (1984, 1985) to suppose that linking and intrusion are distinct processes. In the face of the facts set out in Section 6.1.1, this position is untenable: the possible absence of [r]-intrusion is not subject to synchronic phonological explanation and cannot therefore have a bearing on any phonological account.

Here is an apparently more sensible alternative account of intrusive [r] within a deletion model. Let us say that, instead of applying a rule of [r]-insertion to implement intrusive [r], speakers extend the underlying /r/ to items that in historical terms do not contain it, and then treat it derivationally in the same way in which they process words which do have historic /r/.

This is, in essence, the analysis proposed by Kamińska (1995: Chapter 5); like the previous one it was anticipated and criticised by Johansson (1973). I omit certain aspects of Kamińska's intricate analysis here, and will return to them later.

Such an analysis apparently presents no problems regarding the low vowels: *draw*, *Shah* are stored by intrusive-[r] speakers as /drɔːr/, /ʃɑːr/. For such speakers, items ending in schwa (*vanilla*, *Brenda*) similarly contain an underlying /r/ after the vowel (Kamińska 1995: 160f.). The first problem arises in the case of centring diphthongs, not discussed by Kamińska. Items like *idea* (admittedly somewhat isolated; see Section 6.1.1 above) would have to have underlying (heterosyllabic) /iː.ər/, to be contracted in the synchronic derivation, or, at the price of introducing centring diphthongs into the underlying inventory, /ɪər/. The latter, more surface-true option saddles the grammar with indeterminate underliers in two sets of cases. In *cereal*, *Mary, fury* the surface centring diphthong may then be either underlying or derived through pre-[r] breaking (although this is a problem also faced by alternative analyses; see Section 7.5 below). And, more seriously, in linking-[r] cases like *hear* etc. the motivation for positing /iːr/ disappears: having introduced centring diphthongs into the inventory, we might as well set up such forms as /ɪər/, too, and dispense with the synchronic breaking rule. This would considerably change the analysis (for the better actually, as we shall see below). As regards the original analysis, the basic problem is this: the extension of /r/ to a-historic contexts cannot be done on the grounds of analogy with other underliers but must work on vowels derived to the point just before /r/ deletion operates. The putative underlier of *hear*, /hiːr/, resulting in [hɪə(rɪŋ)], cannot serve as the model for the analogous extension of the /r/ simply because such an extension would then be expected to affect items like *see*, resulting in *[sɪə(rɪŋ)]. This problem can be technically overcome, of course, by allowing the /r/ to spread only to such items as have precisely those vowels in their underlying representations that are, in words that do contain historic /r/, the result of synchronic derivation. But the notion of the 'analogous' extension of rhyme-/r/ would in such cases be far from plausible; it would in fact not even be analogous.

There are further problems. The first of these is perhaps a minor one, given the well-known irregularities of stratum-1 formations: how can a speaker who uses intrusive [r] in *drama*[r] *is*, and who therefore presumably has an underlying /r/ in that item, produce *dramatise*, *dramatic* (similarly *aromatic*, *Asiatic*, *stigmatise*)? There should be no need for that speaker to insert hiatus-breaking [t] before such suffixes, given that the base already has the final consonant /r/. *Dramarise* would be the expected regular form.

The second problem relates, again, to the model's predictions regarding the productive use of intrusive [r]. Concentrating on the otherwise (at least at this point) unproblematic low vowels, we have no problems with speakers who implement intrusive [r] without inhibition, in *draw*[r]*ing* and *draw*[r] *it*, *baa*[r]*ing* and *Shah*[r] *is*. Such items would simply have a-historic underlying /r/. The problem is that RP speakers tend to stigmatise word-internal intrusive [r] (in *drawing*, *baaing*) very strongly, while being more tolerant towards intrusion between words (*draw it*, *Shah is*) (Gimson 1994: 264). A lexical derivation cannot accommodate such speakers; in fact, it makes the opposite prediction: if a speaker has *draw* as /drɔːr/, he or she can maintain the /r/ in *drawing* and delete it before he or she reaches the postlexical phonology (*draw it*), or can maintain it throughout the derivation. But there is no way that the speaker can have stratum-2 *drawing* without [r] (which would indicate either the absence of /r/ in that item, or its deletion prior to stratum 2 – another indeterminacy), and then resurrect such [r] in the postlexical phonology so as to produce intrusion in *draw*[r] *it*. The model predicts point-blank that such speakers do not exist. They do.

I recalled in the previous section that early 'standard' Generative Phonology assumed diachronic change to be largely a matter of rule addition or loss, leaving underlying representations largely intact through long periods in the history of a language. Under that tradition, the diachronic loss of rhyme-/r/ in RP must be interpreted as the addition of an [r]-deletion rule to the synchronic phonology; but we have seen that this strategy fails to model accurately the synchronic facts of RP. It would arguably work (if at the cost of free rides and other hallmarks of non-explanatory abstractness) if RP had linking [r] only; but the problem that none of the history-copying accounts can handle is the occurrence of intrusive [r] and its possible failure through varying degrees of stigmatisation. Vennemann's (1972) proposal whereby 'rule inversion' (already invoked at various points in earlier chapters) is one of the possibilities of linguistic change has put paid to the doctrine of the diachronic longevity of underlying representations: if a given rule 'A → B / ____ C' inverts diachronically to 'B → A / ____ ~ C' then the underlying representation changes from A to B. Non-rhoticity is in fact one of the cases discussed by Vennemann. The idea is that synchronic [r]-deletion in one set of contexts switches diachronically into synchronic insertion in complementary contexts. I shall explore this possible development in RP in the next section.

6.2.2   The insertion analysis

The analysis of RP [r]-sandhi by means of an insertion rule, put forward by
Vennemann (1972), Johansson (1973), Wells (1982), Nespor and Vogel
(1986), McMahon (1996) and others, is strikingly simple and appears to
solve the various problems encountered by the alternative deletion account
at a stroke. A basic version of the only rule this account needs is given
below:

(7)   [r]-*Insertion*

$$\emptyset \rightarrow [r] / \left\{ \begin{array}{l} [\text{ə}] \\ [\text{ɜː}] \\ [\text{Və}] \\ [\text{ɑː}] \\ [\text{ɔː}] \end{array} \right\} \underline{\quad\quad} V$$

The insertion site will, of course, always be preceded by a morphological
boundary: in lexical phonology, by a '|' within morphologically complex
words (*hearing* etc.) or by '||' between words and within compounds (*hear
it, tour operator*). If we assume that (7) is linked to the syllabification
process, which makes empty onsets available, filled by the inserted [r]-
melody, then the rule is possibly operative on both lexical strata as well as
postlexically – note that, as a structure-building rule, (7) is not subject to
SCE on stratum 1 (where in any case the following vowel would constitute
an appropriate derived environment for a structure-changing rule to
operate in). Alternatively, (7) may be postlexical, the relevant onsets being
left empty throughout the lexical derivation. Note also that (7) does not distinguish between [r]-linking and intrusion, predicting in its basic form that
these are not distinct processes.

The analysis proposed by Kamińska (1995) argues for abstract (rhotic)
underliers and postulates synchronic weakening of /r/ to schwa in syllable
rhymes, followed by a postlexical rule like (7) which inserts sandhi-[r] after
such schwa. The advantages of such a combined weakening-plus-insertion
analysis are hard to discern: they appear mainly to lie in its ability to accommodate a SPE-type Vowel Shift derivation – now discredited (McMahon
1990; Section 4.3 above) – as well as in the possibility of distinguishing derivationally between schwa reflecting underlying /r/ and schwa allegedly
resulting from synchronic 'vowel reduction' (*America*), so that for those
RP speakers who have no intrusive [r] (**America*[r] *is*), rule (7) can be

extrinsically ordered so as to apply before the final vowel in *America*, presumably /a/, is reduced to schwa in the postlexicon. But recall from Chapter 5 that there is no synchronic vowel reduction in items like *America*. Recall also that there is no reason to suppose that linking and intrusive [r] are distinct phonological phenomena. Kamińska also values the fact that similar /r/-weakening is found in some varieties of Scottish English, which is rhotic, so that underliers as well as parts of the derivation can be shown to be shared by different (and disparate) varieties of English. Such identity of underliers across dialects is, as we saw above, not a feature that necessarily lends merit to the analysis that postulates it.

In more general terms, Kamińska's weakening-plus-insertion analysis runs into exactly those abstractness problems that the /r/-deletion analysis faces. Indeed, the apparent advantages of her analysis turn out on closer inspection to constitute such problems. The real advantages of an insertion analysis over the deletion account are lost for the simple reason that they all relate to the fact that rule (7) is capable of operating on surface representations with respect to the vowels after which it applies. No abstract underliers are therefore required for centring diphthongs, for example. Such an analysis, which by its very nature is extremely 'concrete', automatically accounts for intrusive [r] in cases like those listed in (2) above (*NASA*[r] *is* etc.); indeed it predicts their occurrence in that it does not connect its triggering contexts, as stated in (7), with any particular kind of putative abstract underlier. And the various versions of the intrusion stigma found among RP speakers can be built into the rule by making orthographic <r> part of its structural description (as precedented by rule (19) in Chapter 5) for some or all of the input vowels. The existence of speakers who avoid intrusion in *drawing* but have it in *draw it* points to a postlexical location for rule (7) with a morphological bracket built into its structural description: word-internal brackets such as that in *drawing* are erased at the end of the lexical stratum on which they arise.

What, then, are the drawbacks of an analysis that treats linking and intrusive [r] as the effect of a synchronic [r]-insertion rule of the form, roughly, (7) above? I enumerate them here in increasing order of importance.

First, such an analysis faces major difficulties in dealing with the stratum-1 alternations listed under (3) above: while there is no problem in accounting for the [r] itself, in such alternating pairs, the accompanying vowel alternations become rather mysterious. This may or may not be a problem, given the fact that stratum-1 derivations are particularly characterised by their unpredictability. Recall from Chapter 3 that the individual listing of such alternations constitutes one of the characteristics of stratum 1. Note also that cases like *drama – dramatic* are comparatively straightforward in a model that, like the insertion account, does not postulate an underlying /r/ in syllable rhymes: such cases would be listed for having [t], rather than [r], as a hiatus-breaker.

Second, the insertion analysis faces the natural-class problem of its input vowels, discussed at length in Section 6.1.2 above and left largely ungeneralised in the formulation given in (7): [r] is inserted after schwa, /ɜ:/, centring diphthongs and low vowels. The solution to that particular problem – to be proposed in Chapter 7 and involving an analysis of low vowels as underlying centring diphthongs (so that [r] occurs after (all and only) underlying nuclei ending in schwa) – will be equally available to the straight-insertion analysis. This is not a problem specific to this particular account; nor is it insurmountable.

Third, and anticipating that analysis of the relevant underliers, the insertion analysis has the problem of arbitrariness that essentially all synchronic insertion rules face. Why, of all segments, [r]? Several researchers have observed the phonetic similarity between schwa and RP's particular version of [r] (Johansson 1973; Kahn 1976; McMahon 1996); but the fact that the putative insertion rule operates in a context that is, in that sense, natural (as well as, of course, historically motivated at least in the linking-[r] cases) does not alter the fact that any synchronic insertion is arbitrary (Broadbent 1991). In terms of its formal properties, an insertion rule producing natural results is not fundamentally different from one whose output is highly unnatural. This is of course a problem faced by all rule-based theories, but here it shows up with particular force.

Fourth, recall the observation made in Section 6.1.2 whereby [r] is not the only sandhi phenomenon found in vowel hiatus: others are [j] (*see*[j]*ing*, *see*[j] *it*) and [w] (*do*[w]*ing*, *do*[w] *it*), occurring in complementary distribution with [r] in that [j] and [w] follow high front and high back vowels respectively, and [r] central (and low) vowels (Stene 1954; Gimson 1994: 264). Those, too, might of course be interpreted as inserts (where they would raise the same problem of arbitrariness noted for [r]-insertion above). An alternative interpretation would be that the relevant melodies, [j] and [w], are already present in the string, in the form of the high vowels, front and back respectively, 'after' which [j] and [w] occur, and that all that happens is some sort of autosegmental re-alignment of existing melodies so as to fill otherwise empty syllable onsets. Such an analysis, which will be developed in the following sections, would avoid the problem of arbitrariness; it would moreover tie in with a similar re-alignment of domain-final consonants in that position: the /l/ of *feel* is realised 'clear' in both *feeling* and *feel it*, suggesting that not only (uncontroversially) in the former but also in the latter case, the /l/ constitutes a syllable onset. An account of this phenomenon of 'liaison' (Gimson 1994: Section 12.4.7) will form part of the new analysis of linking and intrusive [r] that will be offered below.

We have seen, then, that both the deletion and the insertion analysis have to be rejected. The former is unacceptable because of its excessive abstractness and of course because it fails to handle the facts; the latter is unsatisfactory because of the arbitrariness that is inherent in all analyses that rely on the insertion of segments into strings. The one point that is clear already is this: centring diphthongs must figure in the underlying inventory of nuclei in RP: the only alternative, whereby surface centring diphthongs are synchronically derived from (sequences of) other members of the inventory is the deletion account, which has been dismissed. In line with the analysis pursued in Chapter 5, and to be developed further below, I shall analyse [ə] as the surface reflex of the underlying 'empty' melody /∅/. Centring diphthongs will then be /ɪ∅ ɛ∅ ʊ∅/; and the analysis of the long low vowels [ɑː ɔː], postponed until Chapter 7, will be modelled to the same pattern. Schwa in its underlying form /∅/ will, in each case, be the crucial trigger for [r]-sandhi.

6.3   An alternative account of [r]-sandhi

6.3.1   *Liaison and the* [ə]/[r] *allophony in RP*

I shall make two separate (but connected) points in this section. First, I shall argue that 'liaison', as roughly described in the preceding section and discussed here in more detail, plays a crucial part in the synchronic account of [r]-sandhi. Second, I shall argue that in RP (and probably generally in non-rhotic varieties of English), [r] and [ə] are underlyingly non-distinct, even in the sense of classical phonemics, and therefore derived from the same underlier in Lexical Phonology. I shall argue that [r] is not inserted after schwa but, instead, that the underlier common to both is simply realised as schwa in rhymes and as [r] in onsets. The fact that in *hearing* both schwa and [r] surface will be shown to be a specific effect of liaison, comparable for example to the fact that both the final [ɪ]-melody of the surface diphthong and [ʲ] occur in *say*[ʲ]*ing*.

As exemplified in (1) above, [r]-sandhi (both linking and intrusive) occurs in RP in two different contexts: word-medially before vowel-initial suffixes (*hearing, hairy* etc.), and between words where again the second word begins with a vowel (*hear it, hair is* etc.). In both contexts, [r]-sandhi is paralleled by [ʲ] and [ʷ] sandhi (*say*[ʲ]*ing, say* [ʲ]*it, do*[ʷ]*ing, do* [ʷ]*it*), as well by allophonic phenomena such as clear [l] (*feeling, feel it*; Gimson 1994: 182), which point towards an analysis whereby the consonantal melodies in question fill onsets. The former, word-medial context, and associated consonantal phenomena (sandhi and allophony) are found in all varieties of English (as well as in German, to be discussed briefly below); the latter context – onset formation across word boundaries – is not common to all varieties of English and absent in German. It is the latter, across-word-boundary context that constitutes 'liaison' in the strict sense (Gimson 1994). But I take the view that liaison is, in syllabification terms, a postlexical parallel of the word-medial phenomenon of onset formation across the base-suffix boundary (*hea.ring, fee.ling*); the difference is merely that liaison is language- and indeed accent-specific whereas its word-medial equivalent is not. Kiparsky (1979), Mohanan (1985) and others have argued that such association of final consonants with onsets is the result of a re-syllabification rule; but I postpone the formal account of the phenomenon until Chapter 8. Here I state informally that in RP, triplets (morphologically simple vs. suffixed vs. connected speech) such as *Ealing – feeling – feel it, bucket – bucking – buck it* and, notably, *eerie – hearing – hear it* have identical surface syllabifications, in whatever way those may be brought about in derivational terms.

Nespor and Vogel (1986: 64f.) make the notable claim that there is no liaison in English. But what undermines their argument is the fact that the phrases they give to exemplify liaison failure – *call Andy, Anne ate* – have in common that the following word begins with a stressed syllable. In such contexts (across foot boundaries), liaison is indeed known to be absent:

> it is unusual for a word-final consonant to be carried over as initial in a word beginning with an accented vowel, the identity of the words being retained . . . Thus, *run off, give in, less often*, are rarely /rʌ'nɒf, gɪ'vɪn, . . . /; more particularly, the voiceless plosives do not acquire aspiration such as would accompany their shift to an accented syllable-initial position, e.g. *get up, look out, stop arguing* . . . (Gimson 1994: 264)

Gimson also notes that instead of liaison, an audible pre-vocalic glottal stop may occur in this context, 'in careful speech' (Gimson 1994: 155), again most commonly before a stressed syllable. (See also Giegerich (1992a: Section 9.4.1.) We conclude tentatively here, then, that the domain of liaison is the foot. Across foot boundaries, liaison is at best optional. Hence in Nespor and Vogel's examples, *call Andy* etc., there may indeed be no liaison (and the /l/ will be dark), while in cases like *call it, call America* (not mentioned by Nespor and Vogel), the /l/ will be clear in RP, thanks to liaison.[5] Similar cases can be observed which exemplify that, *ceteris paribus*, [r]-sandhi is obligatory foot-medially and optional between feet. In (8a) below, linking [r] is obligatory; in (8b) a glottal stop may occur in its stead:

(8)   a. hear[r] it   b. hear[r/ʔ] Andy
          roar[r] incessantly   roar[r/ʔ] angrily

There is, then, a case for a causal link between liaison and [r]-sandhi in RP. The converse case can, moreover, be made unequivocally in South African English and German.

In South African English, [r]-sandhi is the norm within words (*hearing* etc.) but it is uncommon between words, where instead prevocalic glottal stops (*hear* [ʔ]*it*) tend to occur (Giegerich 1986: 95ff.; Lass 1996). Given that this glottal stop also blocks the other sandhi and allophonic phenomena mentioned above, it makes sense to suggest that South African English has no liaison, and that the absence of [r]- and other sandhi is an effect of a connected-speech syllabification pattern (perhaps due to Afrikaans contact) whereby word-final consonants do not, as they do in RP, supply melodies for following onsets.

Similarly, German has no liaison: the pre-vocalic glottal stop (*fester Vokaleinsatz* 'firm vowel onset') occurs regularly not only in morpheme-medial vowel hiatus (*The*[ʔ]*ater* 'theatre', *O*[ʔ]*ase* 'oasis')[6] but also between words, as in [ʔ]*in* [ʔ]*einer* [ʔ]*O*[ʔ]*ase* 'in an oasis' (Krech 1968; Giegerich 1989: 62ff.; Kohler 1994). Moreover, Standard German – the variety described by Duden (1990) – is non-rhotic at least to the extent that it vocalises rhyme-/r/ after long vowels; hence *Heer* [heːɐ] 'army' vs. *Herr* [hɛr] 'gentleman' (Ulbrich 1972; Hall 1993). In *Heere* [heːrə] 'armies', the /r/ is in the onset and remains unvocalised. But no linking [r] is found between words, in phrases like *das Heer* [ʔ]*ist* 'the army is' or in fact anywhere else.[7]

So, while German has alternating [r] in word-medial contexts exemplified here by *Heer* – *Heere*, it has no linking [r] between words. The more general fact that German has no liaison between words provides an explanation, beyond reasonable doubt, for this absence. While non-rhoticity is a condition for [r]-sandhi as defined here, the presence of liaison in the language is another.

If this reasoning is correct, then (as is intuitively plausible and uncontroversial in any case) alternations such as RP *hear – hear*[r]*ing* and German *Heer – Hee*[r]*e* are due to the mechanisms of word-internal syllabification. In RP (and most other varieties of English), these mechanisms also hold postlexically, producing liaison as well as specifically the same type of alternations involving [r]: *hear – hear*[r] *it*. The absence of postlexical liaison in German ([ʔ]*in* [ʔ]*einer* [ʔ]*O*[ʔ]*ase, Heer* [ʔ]*ist* etc.) is then responsible for the absence of [r]-sandhi between German words. Moreover, the occurrence of prevocalic [ʔ] in German, as well as in English wherever liaison fails to happen, suggests that onsets may be assumed to be obligatory constituents (they are always associated with a surface melody) so that [ʔ] may be treated as the default melody for onsets.

The relevant representations for RP are given in (9) below; I shall return to their derivational properties in Chapter 8.

(9)

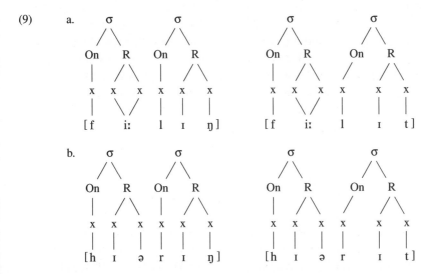

It is quite clear that the onset-/l/ in (9a) is not the result of any kind of insertion rule: the empty skeletal position supplied by the syllabification process simply absorbs the consonantal melody immediately before it. (Whether or not this melody is previously attached to the preceding syllable, its association with the onset in (9a) being performed by a resyllabification rule (Kiparsky 1979; Levin 1985; Mohanan 1985), is a separate question, to be addressed in Chapter 8.)

Let us turn to parallel cases where there is no final consonant, as in *saying, say it* [seɪʲɪŋ], *showing, show it* [ʃoʊʷɪŋ], noted in Section 6.1.2

above. We saw there that the distribution of these hiatus-breaking 'glides' is such that [ʲ] occurs after nuclei ending in surface high-front(-unrounded) melodies, and [ʷ] after nuclei ending in surface high-back(-rounded) melodies. It might be argued here that these hiatus-breakers, unlike the /l/ in *feel it*, are supplied derivationally by an insertion rule that selects a consonantal segment (given that onsets must contain consonants) phonetically similar to the preceding vowel. But such an analysis is both undesirable and unnecessary. It is undesirable because, as was noted in Section 6.1.2 in connection with the insertion analysis of [r]-sandhi, it is entirely arbitrary (see also Broadbent 1991): a synchronic insertion rule of this (or indeed any) kind essentially fails to explain the fact that the segment 'inserted' in either context is not, for example, [p]. And it is unnecessary because the melody that serves as a hiatus-breaker, [ʲ] or [ʷ], is in fact already present in the string, just as is the /l/-melody in *feel*. This, as I noted in Section 6.1.2, is the decisive argument against the insertion analysis.

As is well known, the segments [j] and [w] are nondistinct from [ɪ] and [ʊ] respectively in melodic terms (see for example Giegerich 1992a: Section 6.5.3) except perhaps in regard of the degree of their constriction. They are, moreover, in complementary distribution: the 'semi-vowels' [jw] are confined to onsets while the vowels [ɪʊ] are syllable nuclei. The feature [±consonantal], which serves to express degrees of constriction, is in a redundancy relationship with the melody's position in the syllable in such a way that onset melodies must be [+consonantal] and nuclei [−consonantal]. It is therefore possible to derive [jɪ] (and [wʊ]), as allophones, from a common underlier even within the strict confines of a phonemicist framework, provided that framework recognises syllable structure in a fairly uncontroversial form: the melody in question acquires the feature specification [+consonantal] in onsets and [−consonantal] in nuclei. (See Lass and Anderson (1975: Section 3.2) for similar results in a non-syllabic framework, and Clements and Keyser (1983) for a parallel CV-analysis.) In phonological terms, the distinction is one of notation only, which is not even shared by all transcription systems – note, for example, the American Structuralist tradition and its representational successors where complex nuclei are treated as vowel-plus-glide sequences (Trager and Smith 1951; SPE).

We may take the view, then, that the empty onset provided in the syllabification of a vowel-initial item, as in *saying, say it, showing, show it*, automatically imposes the feature [+consonantal] on any melody that is to fill that onset. I spell out the appropriate rule in Section 8.4. Now, just as in *feeling, feel it,* such onset-filling is clearly not the result of epenthesis; in *saying* etc. it is clearly not the result of a re-syllabification rule which takes the final segment out of the preceding rhyme association and links it with the onset. If that were the case then the surface form *[sejɪn], rather than [seɪʲɪŋ], would be predicted. I suggest that what happens instead in this case is that the empty onset automatically imposes the specification [+ consonantal] on its melody, and that it shares the rest of the melody with the preceding, [consonantal] slot.

(10)

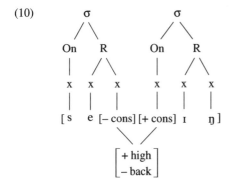

The resulting melody, specified as [+ consonantal, + high, − back], then surfaces as the seemingly 'epenthetic' [ʲ] while the melody [− consonantal, + high, − back], associated with the previous skeletal position, surfaces as [ɪ]. Hence [seɪʲɪŋ]. The same obviously happens in *seeing, doing, showing* etc., as well as in the parallel cases involving liaison across words (*say it* etc.), which is specific to (most varieties of) English but does not, as we have seen, happen in German or South African English. In German, something like (10) only occurs word-medially: *Partei*[j]*en* 'parties' etc. (Vennemann 1982), while in *Partei ist* 'party is', the hiatus breaker is [ʔ]. The [+ consonantal] onset melody surfaces as the minimal consonant [ʔ] by default, rather than sharing further features with the preceding melody as in (10). I postpone a more general discussion of this issue and its derivational aspects, including the syllabification of *feel it,* to Chapter Eight; here I return to [r]-sandhi.

I claim here that [ɪ]/[j] and [ʊ]/[w] are not the only phonemic melodies in RP whose allophones straddle the vowel-consonant divide in a syllabic framework: [ə]/[r] is the third pair of such segments that share an underlier. The arguments in favour of such an analysis are virtually the same as those for the other two. First, [ə] and [r] are in complementary distribution in non-rhotic varieties of English: the former occurs in rhymes only, the latter in onsets only. Second, as has been reported in much of the literature (for example by Kahn 1976: 95ff.; McMahon 1996), RP's typical [r] and schwa are phonetically similar to a remarkable degree. McMahon specifically notes their acoustic similarity:

> Spectrograms for schwa and approximant [r] indicate that the spectral shapes for the two sounds are rather similar, except that F3 for [r] is kept low by some fairly complex articulatory manoeuvres. If this articulatory effort is relaxed at all, then F3 will raise, and the resulting spectral shape will resemble the shape for schwa very strongly. (McMahon 1996: 80)

These observations not only confirm that RP [r] and schwa are clearly similar enough to qualify for an allophonic relationship in phonemicist terms (given also their complementary distribution); they also support the prediction that any weakening of rhyme-[r] should result in schwa (which is of course exactly what has happened diachronically in the development of non-rhoticity).

Recall now the argument presented in Chapter 5 whereby the underlying representation of [ə] is an 'empty' melody, /Ø/, associated with a skeletal position in the syllable nucleus. Such an analysis is not only warranted by various schwa 'epenthesis' phenomena (Gussmann 1991; Giegerich 1987), which frequently have prosodic motivations involving the creation of nuclear skeletal positions in the syllable structure (to be discussed in Chapter 8). /Ø/ also figures crucially in the account of alternations of the type *atom – atomic* that I gave in Chapter 5. In diachronic terms, schwa is commonly the result of the weakening and loss of articulatory gestures – of the reduction of historically full vowels (Minkova 1991), as well as of [r]-loss in non-rhotic accents, as I noted above. It makes sense for all those synchronic and diachronic phenomena, then, to treat schwa synchronically as an empty nuclear melody, which may be the result of the creation of vacant nuclear positions in the suprasegmental structure or of the diachronic loss of articulatory information in an underlyingly existing melody. If that is the case then the [ə]/[r] allophones may be treated, exactly in parallel to the [ɪ]/[j] and [ʊ]/[w] allophonies discussed above, as the surface reflexes of underlying /Ø/, where the former is non-consonantal, occupying a nuclear skeletal position, and the latter is consonantal, occurring in the onset. Details to account for [r] can now be added into the analysis of schwa proposed in Chapter 5.

I anticipate here a model of syllable structure, to be developed in Chapter

8, whereby syllables branch into onsets and rhymes but where only the latter has categorial status. (I continue to use the term 'onset' informally in what follows.) Moreover, I shall argue there that 'nucleus' and 'coda' are not phonological categories. Given, then, that [ə] occurs in rhymes and RP [r] in onsets only, the basic complementary distribution of the two can be stated in a straightforward 'elsewhere' relationship (with surface melody details to be filled in by default rules to be given below).

(11)   [ə]/[r] *Allophony*

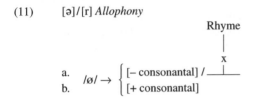

I turn now to the rules predicting surface [ə] and [r]. We have to assume that the /∅/ stated in (11) and previously is not an entirely empty melody. There are two independent reasons for this perhaps problematic assumption. First, onset-[r] is not the default consonant of English in that position: that role is played by [ʔ], as has been known for a while (Rapp 1836: 53). [r] is merely the onset version of the [r]/[ə] pair, whose members have in common not only the underlying absence of tongue-articulation specifications but also the presence of sonorancy. [r] is then the consonantal default sonorant; and /∅/ must have the underlying specification of [+ sonorant] to distinguish it from [ʔ]. Second, I shall argue in Chapter 7 that the melodic entity /∅/ is subject to manipulation by phonological rules; it cannot therefore be a completely empty melody, in the sense of 'nothing'. I return to this question below.

(12)   *Sonorant Default*

a.
$$\begin{bmatrix} - \text{consonantal} \\ + \text{sonorant} \\ \emptyset \end{bmatrix} \rightarrow [\text{ə}]$$

b.
$$\begin{bmatrix} + \text{consonantal} \\ + \text{sonorant} \\ \emptyset \end{bmatrix} \rightarrow [\text{r}]$$

It is at this point that the question of 'why [r]?' arises again. This question has been partially answered by the observation made earlier whereby [r] is the most schwa-like consonant in RP, distinct from the latter perhaps only in that it is [+ coronal] (SPE: 177; Kamińska 1995: 130). Rule (12b) is, then, natural and predictable for RP inasmuch as coronality can be relied on as being the default place of articulation. (See here Paradis and Prunet (1991) and Hall (1997); but also McCarthy (1993) for a rejection of this position.)

I give the configuration of *hear*[r] *it*, resulting from (11) under liaison, in (13) below, although the mechanism of liaison itself still has to be established (Section 8.6 below). What emerges is two, partially shared melodies: [− consonantal, + sonorant, ∅] and [+ consonantal, + sonorant, ∅]. Of these, the former is interpreted by (12a) as schwa and the latter, by (12b), as [r].

(13)

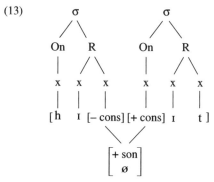

Rule (12b) is effectively the rule responsible for [r]-sandhi, assuming the more general mechanisms of liaison. Note that it is only through liaison – the onset's association with the preceding melody – that the hiatus breaker emerges as [r]. In the absence of liaison, say in the somewhat exceptional (but possible: Gimson 1994: 155) string *hear* [ʔ]*it*, the association line between the onset-[+ consonantal] melody with the [+ sonorant, ∅] of the preceding segment is absent. While [r] is the default melody for (onset) sonorant consonants, [ʔ] is the more general default melody for (onset) consonants. This is of course also the situation found in German, *ceteris paribus*. The default rule which associates the melody [ʔ] with empty onsets is given in (14) below; I assume the specification [+ consonantal] to be the automatic consequence of syllabification (see (14) in Chapter 8 below). This rule ought to bear the name of 'Rapp's Law', after Karl Moritz Rapp (1836), who was to my knowledge the first to argue that all syllables have obligatory (consonantal) onsets, and to identify explicitly the default status of prevocalic glottal stops in that context.[8] (See Giegerich 1989: 62ff. for discussion.)

(14)   *Default Onset ('Rapp's Law')*

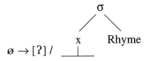

ø → [?] /

6.3.2   *The intrusion stigma and the lexical status of* [r]*-sandhi*

I argued in the preceding section that [r]- and complementary [ʲ ʷ]-sandhi are conditioned by syllable structure: an empty (onset) skeletal position attracts part of the preceding rhyme melody and imposes a consonantal interpretation on it. I shall here, finally, address the question of where in the derivation this happens. We may assume that the appropriate syllable-structure contexts arise during the lexical derivation. Then, while there is no doubt that external sandhi (as in *hear it, do it* etc.) is postlexical, the identical phenomenon found word-medially (*hearing, doing*) may either be lexical, or the onsets in question may remain empty in the lexical derivation, to be filled postlexically. I shall tentatively argue here that the sandhi phenomena in question are both lexical (in the word-medial cases) and postlexical (between words). One set of arguments in favour of that position will arise from linking [r], another from the varying stigmatisation patterns of intrusive [r].

For the moment I ignore intrusive [r]. It is clear from the descriptive accounts (Gimson 1994; Wells 1982) that linking [r] is obligatory within words (within stratum-2 forms like *hearing*, that is). But between words, this and other sandhis may occasionally fail, so that [?] materialises instead. This variability is clearly not in turn due to variability in the occurrence of the conditioning syllable-structure context: wherever [r] sandhi does not occur, [?] does. Between words, linking [r] may be driven by non-structural factors such as speech tempo etc., which are of no relevance whatsoever where word-internal [r]-sandhi is concerned. This difference in applicability alone suggests that there is obligatory lexical and optional (albeit likely) postlexical [r]-linking. In South African English, liaison (and hence [r]-linking) within words is obligatory but between words it is highly uncommon, giving rise instead to *hear* [?]*it* etc., under Rapp's Law (14). Without wishing to invoke the facts of one variety of English to explain those of another, I note that South African English clearly has lexical [r]-sandhi while its postlexical version is possibly entirely absent. It is, then, at least possible for [r]-sandhi to be lexical: this much (although not more) of the South African facts is relevant to RP.

If this reasoning is correct then it is likely that not only internal [r]-sandhi but also internal [ᶨʷ] sandhi, with which the former is in complementary distribution, are lexical. (See further Section 7.2.5 below.) And from this it possibly follows, further, that the diphthongisation at least of the underlying tense melodies /e o/ into surface [eɪ oʊ], providing contexts for the sandhi, should be lexical.[9] On the other hand, the surface diphthongisation of the high tense vowels (e.g. of /i/ into [ɪi]) may well be postlexical: those provide the appropriate sandhi contexts in undiphthongised form (and are in any case more variable on the surface).

I turn now to intrusive [r] and the stigma associated with it. The view taken in this study has been that in purely phonological terms, linking and intrusion are nondistinct; the argument presented above rested crucially on that assumption. Any RP speaker who makes the distinction (by shunning intrusive [r] but not linking [r]) does so on non-phonological grounds – either by referring to the spelling or, in the unlikely case that he or she is illiterate, by imposing arbitrary exception markers on forms that would otherwise be inputs to [r]-sandhi. Given the reliability of the spelling, and the arbitrariness of exception marking, an account of the phenomenon that characterises [r]-sandhi (and hence the avoidance of intrusive [r]) as spelling-driven predicts, surely rightly, that literate speakers can avoid intrusion reliably if they so choose, while illiterate speakers implement the stigma at best unreliably, and probably not at all. For a speaker who avoids intrusion, then, [r]-sandhi is triggered by the presence of <r>.

Such a model will account for speakers who have linking and intrusion indiscriminately, as well as for speakers who have linking but avoid all intrusion. And speakers who avoid word-internal intrusive [r] only (*saw[r]ing), while implementing it between words (saw[r] it), will have the <r> condition in the lexical version of the rule but not in the postlexical version. This appears to be the commonest of the three patterns in RP (Gimson 1994). Notably, the converse pattern, whereby RP speakers systematically avoid intrusion between words while allowing it within words, does not seem to exist: recall Section 6.2.1. The obvious explanation for this absence is, clearly, that in such a hypothetical variant of RP, speakers would impose no *lexical* marking (of the form '<r>') on forms that do attract [r]-sandhi but would have to impose such markers postlexically. No mechanisms for such late imposition of exception markers exist, of course: exception marking has to be part of the underlying representation of a given lexical item and would therefore be expected to come into play earlier than the postlexicon. And as I showed in Chapter 5, the exception marking under discussion here derives from the orthographic representation (which I there showed to be of independent underlying status).

Moreover, the absence of speakers who have word-internal intrusion but avoid it between words is consistent with the assumption that the postlexical phonology has no exceptions (Mohanan 1986); but the notion of 'exception' in the postlexical phonology has to be clarified here. Consider, again, the second of the three patterns – that where all intrusive [r] is avoided. I noted above that in such a grammar, [r]-sandhi is only implemented where the relevant (lexical and postlexical) liaison, in appropriate contexts, is sanctioned by <r>. There is of course no alternative to treating [r]-sandhi between words (*abhor it, saw it*) as postlexical. There is also no doubt that the feature <r>, associated with certain words but not with others, is part of the lexical representation (the output representation of the lexical derivation), originating derivationally from independent orthographic representations. What is interesting here, in connection with the assumption that postlexical rules are said to be exceptionless, is that any speaker who avoids intrusive [r] between words can only do so by referring to orthographic information in the postlexical phonology. And in the unlikely case that such a speaker is illiterate, we are faced with arbitrary (genuine) exceptions in the postlexicon. If the assumption is correct whereby postlexical rules have no exceptions, then illiterate speakers may perhaps, on the grounds of arbitrary exception marking, be expected to avoid word-internal intrusion but they cannot avoid intrusive [r] between words. In any case, the facts clearly suggest that this assumption has to be modified with respect to orthographic information: it is clearly possible to carry orthographic information from the lexicon into the postlexical phonology and to refer to such information there. Given that orthographic representations are, as I argued in Chapter 5, not only lexically present but actually part of the underlying (stored) representations of all lexical items, it is not unreasonable to accord them a status that differs from 'genuine' exception marking to certain, specified, phonological processes.

Let us summarise the findings of this section. First, I hope to have shown that [r]-sandhi in RP is a phenomenon that is exactly paralleled by the [j]-sandhi found in *say it* and the [w]-sandhi in *show it*. (This point was also made by Broadbent (1991).) All three are effects of liaison, whereby empty onsets absorb melodic material contained in the final segment of the preceding rhyme. [r]-sandhi is therefore not the surface effect of the non-application of a putative /r/-deletion rule (a possibility that I rejected on independent grounds in the preceding section); nor is it the result of an arbitrary [r]-insertion rule. There is no insertion for the simple reason that the relevant melodies, in all three cases of sandhi, are already present in the string.

Second, [r] and schwa are surface realisations, in complementary distribution, of the same melodic underlier. Following the arguments presented
in Chapter 5 above, this underlier must be an 'empty' nuclear melody. The
surface qualities [r] and schwa are predicted by straightforward blank-
filling rules.

In more general terms, the account of [r]-sandhi as it has been developed
so far makes the following predictions. First, it predicts that the phenomenon only occurs in the presence of the more general mechanism of liaison.
This mechanism applies within words without fail; but between words it
may be absent. Varieties of English, or languages, that do not have postlexical liaison are predicted not to use [j w r] as a hiatus-breaker in such contexts even if they are non-rhotic. This prediction is likely to be correct, as is
shown by South African English and Standard German as well as by the
occasional failure of liaison in RP: in all these cases, [ʔ] occurs as the hiatus-
breaker instead. Second, this account predicts [r]-sandhi to occur only in
non-rhotic varieties of English. Rhotic varieties have no [r]-sandhi (which
would, by definition, be 'intrusive' [r]) even if they have liaison. The reason
for this is that in rhotic varieties, [r] and schwa (however phonetically
similar they may or may not be) are not in complementary distribution
(*Leda* vs. *leader*, *piston* vs. *cistern* etc.) and, hence, cannot have a common
underlier. In such varieties, rhyme-[r] has not historically merged with
schwa and must therefore be synchronically distinct from it.

This analysis is consistent, then, with the assumption that in RP schwa
and centring diphthongs have underlying melodic representations associated with skeletal positions as given in (15a) and (15b) respectively. A
syllabified example (*hear*) is given in (15c):

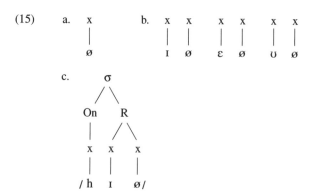

Liaison will be discussed again in Chapter 8, in more formal terms and
connected with the more general question of (re-)syllabification. What is

clear at the present point, however, is that RP, for obvious diachronic reasons connected with the emergence of non-rhoticity, has centring diphthongs (as in (15b)) in its underlying inventory. Such an analysis is possible within the present framework as long as similarly concrete underlying representations are set up for *myrrh – myrrhic, deter – deterrent, occur – occurrence* etc. (see (3a) above): if these were synchronically derived from full-vowel underliers then those underliers would be unavailable for the surface centring diphthongs. In fact I showed in Chapter 5 that items such as *myrrh* etc. do not have full-vowel underliers. I return to the underlying status and derivational properties of the [ɜː] found in RP *bird, myrrh, deter* in Chapter 7, as part of a more general discussion of the input vowels to [r]-sandhi.

7 Input vowels to [r]-sandhi: RP and London English

7.1 Introduction

7.1.1 The representation of centring diphthongs

Recall the assumption whereby RP [ə], occurring for example as the second element of centring diphthongs, is the surface effect of a skeletal position associated with a melody that is underlyingly specified only as [+ sonorant], all other specifications being empty. If that skeletal position is syllabified in the rhyme, perhaps as part of a complex nucleus (Wiese 1986; Giegerich 1987; Gussmann 1991), it will surface as schwa. Attendant to the syllabification process (which is here, uncontroversially, assumed to be automatic; see Chapter 8 below), this segment acquires the feature [− consonantal] in rhymes and [+ consonantal] in onsets. I shall continue to represent the relevant melody simply as 'Ø': it is underlyingly empty for present purposes in the sense that none of the feature specifications that it either has underlyingly or acquires derivationally matter to the analysis. But given that this melody carries at least one specification (namely [+ sonorant]) throughout its derivational history, it is to be (and will be) treated as a representational object that can be manipulated by rules.

Centring diphthongs such as those under discussion here will then be underlying sequences of vowel-plus- 'Ø', structured as in (1):

(1)

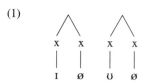

In diachronic terms, such a representation of schwa, in centring diphthongs and elsewhere, stands to reason: schwa is commonly either the residue of the diachronic reduction (feature loss) of originally full vowel melodies (Minkova 1991), or the melody associated with a skeletal ('x') slot

198

supplied by the mechanisms of syllabification (as in *little*, where the final /l/ surfaces either as syllabic or as the sequence [əl]; Gussmann 1991). And in centring diphthongs, schwa is in non-rhotic varieties such as RP often (if not always)[1] the historic residue of /r/. I give further, synchronic arguments in favour of representations such as (1) for the centring diphthongs, and in particular also for the underliers of present-day [ɔː ɑː], in Section 7.3 below, noting here merely that it is reasonable to suggest that the processes noted above should give rise to 'empty' melodies (in the sense defined above).

7.1.2 *The monophthonging of* [ɛə]

There is a sound change going on in RP and related non-rhotic varieties of English which subjects the centring diphthong [ɛ:], but not [ɪə ʊə], to 'monophthonging' (Wells' term (1982: 216)): Gimson (1994: 133), for example, notes that '[n]owadays a long monophthong [ɛː] is a completely acceptable alternative in General RP.' Exactly when this sound change began is unclear; certainly it has been underway since at least the turn of the century. At that time, Jespersen (1909: 422) comments that in /ɛə/, 'the [ə] position . . . is held only for a short time', a comment that is conspicuously absent from his description of the other two centring diphthongs, /ɪə ʊə/. The monophthonging of [ɛə] to [ɛː], completed for some speakers in present-day RP, had clearly begun at that time.

Nothing is said in the literature about any possible allophonic distribution of the resulting present-day monophthong [ɛː], nor has it – yet? – found its way into the relevant handbooks, in terms of standard pronunciation or phonemic symbolism. (See, for example, Wells 1990; Jones 1992; Gimson 1994.) What makes this process interesting in the present context, and suitable as an introduction to the rather more complicated phonology of the long low vowels in RP that will take up the bulk of this chapter, is the fact that such monophthonging appears to remove the context that was in Chapter 6 identified as the crucial trigger of [r]-sandhi, namely the 'empty' melody [∅]: despite the possible change of the surface melody from [ɛə] to [ɛː], relevant items continue to attract [r]-sandhi (*bearing, bear it* etc.) in all non-rhotic speech, behaving just as if the schwa were still present. In terms of the behaviour of that vowel in the phonology, there is no reason to suppose that the '∅', underlier of schwa, has disappeared from the underlying representation, even for speakers that have the surface monophthong [ɛː]. If the underlying form of that vowel had been restructured to /ɛː/ then

[r]-sandhi could not be synchronically motivated after that vowel. I shall argue here that the degree of abstractness required for the phonology of speakers that have monophthonged '/ɛə/' but retain (as they all do) full use of [r]-sandhi is well within the limits of what the framework permits. Indeed, the framework predicts such behaviour: I shall argue in Section 7.2.5 that, for independent reasons, all long non-tense vowels have underlying representations of the type (1) above. That of [ɛː] should therefore remain unchanged as long as the vowel remains non-tense.

This is, then, a case where a recent sound change has affected only the surface representation of the segment in question: its surface-phonetic make-up has changed, but its behaviour in the phonology of the language has remained unaltered. In synchronic terms, it is a case of a possibly context-free process that probably has not established itself in the lexical phonology yet. There is in fact no reason to suppose that the phenomenon is a lexical one: it does not appear to have lexical exceptions and apparently does not interact with the morphology. And it is likely to be variable even for individual speakers. In (2a) below I give a formulation of the process reflecting the situation at Jespersen's time; (2b) describes the completion of the process, achieved by some speakers in present-day RP.

(2)   a. [ɛə]-*Monophthonging*: turn of the twentieth century (postlexical)

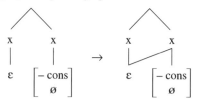

     b. [ɛə]-*Monophthonging*: present-day RP (postlexical)

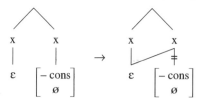

Spreading rules of this kind are well attested in the literature (Itô 1986; Goldsmith 1990), as is the assumption that they may or may not involve attendant delinking of the second element (see again Itô 1986). Both possibilities – spreading with and without delinking – are exemplified in (2).

(2a) describes the spread of the first melody, [ɛ], at the partial expense of the second; the right-hand skeletal position is then shared by [ɛ] and [∅]. Such a configuration may be interpreted as a diphthong with a relatively long first element, in line with Jespersen's (1909: 422) observation. This early-twentieth-century version demonstrates an early stage of the gradual implementation of a sound change that was later to result in a spread-and-delink rule: the complete monophthongisation of the vowel – in formal terms, spreading with delinking – is achieved (for some speakers) in present-day RP, shown in (2b) above.

Let us turn now to the technical aspects of spreading and delinking. I assume (with Itô 1986) that the delinked melody is not automatically deleted but remains available (as a 'floating' melody in the sense of Harris (1994: Chapter 5)) for docking onto another skeletal position. How long such floating melodies remain available to the subsequent synchronic derivation is a question to which I return below; the point here is that they *are* available, thus preserving a melody for subsequent derivation although it does not surface. In the present, postlexical, instance of delinking we may uncontroversially assume the postlexical absorption of the floating melody into the following empty onset: its delinking from the rhyme and its absorption into the next onset are not even subject to any kind of ordering. (3) below presents a picture parallel to (13) in Section 6.3.1 above, giving *hair is* in a monophthongal pronunciation. Liaison is unaffected by the question of whether the relevant melody is delinked from the preceding rhyme (by (2b) above) prior to or after its attachment to the following onset; indeed, it is unaffected by delinking altogether. If Jespersen's version (2a) operates, then there simply is no delinking of that melody. And of course there are speakers who do not delink that melody at all.

(3)

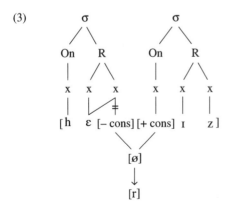

The ∅-part of the de-linked melody specified as [− consonantal, ∅] will automatically be absorbed by the empty onset of the next, vowel-initial syllable in the string (*hairy, hair is*) through the liaison process discussed in Chapter 6; the onset node imposes the [+ consonantal] specification on that melody, which surfaces as [r]-sandhi. This is what (3) above shows for *hair is* [hɛːrɪz]; in cases like *hair was*, or indeed simply *hair*, the melody de-linked by (2b) is deleted subsequently.

I noted above that (2), in both its early-twentieth-century and present-day versions, is probably postlexical: there is no reason to suggest otherwise. This diagnosis has no bearing on the stratal affiliation of [r]-sandhi itself: while it is clear that external [r]-sandhi (*hear it, hair is* etc.) must be postlexical, its internal counterpart (*hearing, hairy*) may either be produced on stratum 2, where the appropriate forms arise, and attendant to the syllabification process, or the empty onsets arising there might be left empty until the postlexical phonology. If the *hair* vowel is a centring diphthong that is levelled as late as postlexically then internal [r]-sandhi can still be lexical, operating on the unlevelled sequence [ɛ∅] and produced by the liaison shown in (13) of Chapter 6. Both derivational paths are motivated here in their own right; both must therefore be available.

But this is not to say that rules of the form (2a) and (2b) cannot be lexical. In the two-strata lexicon advocated for English in this study, the spread-and-delink version (2b) would be constrained on stratum 1 by SCE (delinking is a structure-changing operation), but not from stratum 2. And the spreading part of the rule is barred from any stratum that is subject to Structure Preservation – again, certainly from stratum 1 but not, if we follow Borowsky (1990), from stratum 2. Indeed, we shall come across lexical (that is, stratum-2) instances of such rules in the remainder of this chapter.

7.2   The low 'monophthongs': rule inversion in progress?

7.2.1   The problem

I turn now to the low vowels [ɔː] and [ɑː]. As I noted in Section 6.1.2, these constitute a problem for the phonology of [r]-sandhi in that they fail to constitute an unambiguous natural class with schwa, notably under an analysis that assumes /∅/ to underlie that vowel. As regards the account of [r]-sandhi presented here, this problem is a particularly pressing one given that

that account is committed to /∅/ as the crucial input to the synchronic process that results in surface linking/intrusive [r]. It has to be shown, then, that [ɔː] and [ɑː] derive synchronically from melodic configurations that are centring diphthongs, /ɔ∅/ and /ɑ∅/.

The argument that I shall present here will be different in nature from those presented, on various topics, earlier in this study. It will be diachronic in that it will derive much of its substance from developments in the twentieth century, starting with the synchronic status of the vowels in question at the turn of the twentieth century: I shall show that at that stage, these vowels were indeed surface (and underlying) centring diphthongs. Then I shall argue that there is conclusive evidence to suggest that in London English, those underliers have since turned into monophthongs but that there is no evidence to support the same claim of re-structuring in RP. Such a claim would not only be entirely speculative; it would also (as I shall show) adversely affect the synchronic analysis of [r]-sandhi after [ɔː] and [ɑː] (*bor*[r]*ing*, *bore*[r] *it* etc.). Like the analysis of [ɛː] given in Section 7.1.2, the present analysis would then be compelled to treat [r]-sandhi after low vowels as a fossilised and essentially irregular phenomenon despite the fact that it happens, with a degree of productivity that is on a par with that of [r]-sandhi after schwa, in the postlexical phonology (and possibly on stratum 2 of the lexicon). Moreover, the surface-monophthongal character of these sounds can be accounted for within the constraints of the model. Such an argument involves the postulate of abstract synchronic underliers that reflect obsolete surface forms – a form of argumentation, reminiscent of SPE's approach, that I have consistently rejected in earlier chapters. What makes me adopt such argumentation here is not so much the fact that the underliers that I shall posit hark back a mere ninety years or so and not, as does the SPE analysis of the tense vowels of English, half a millennium. Rather, I shall show that no rule inversion can possibly occur until a synchronic derivation of the kind proposed here is in place: rule inversion can only happen when the synchronic facts are simultaneously amenable to both a given analysis and its inverse. Rule inversion has demonstrably happened in London English, but the phonology of RP has not progressed to that point.

Later in this chapter I shall look at the behaviour of relevant items on stratum 1, arguing that once again the model of the lexical phonology of English presented here makes the right predictions. But let us start by going back some ninety years.

7.2.2   Synchronic facts

7.2.2.1   Early-twentieth-century RP

[ɔː] in present-day RP has a number of historical sources;[2] some (but notably not all) of those involve historic rhyme-/r/. The three principal sources are Early Modern English /ɔː/ (*thought, flaw, law*), /ɒr/ (*north, short, corn*) and /oːr/ (*floor, source, lore*). Let us first establish the early-twentieth-century (RP) pattern by considering some contemporary accounts. I shall draw here on the NED (1888–), Sweet (1908) and Jespersen (1909).

The pronunciations given in the NED (here represented in IPA notation) clearly suggest that the three-way merger into [ɔː] was not completed at the turn of the century: *source, floor, lore* etc. (historically /oːr/) are given as [oːᵊ]; but historic-/ɔː/ and historic-/ɒr/ forms (e.g. *thought, north* respectively) are represented as [ɔː].

Sweet's (1908) roughly contemporary account similarly implies that the merger is not completed, and that forms deriving from historic /oːr/ are still distinct from forms deriving from other sources. Below are his descriptions – I include that of /ɑː/ for comparison, but the argument that follows will mainly be based on the behaviour and history of [ɔː].

> ɔ. Low-back-narrow-round + mid-mixed-wide-round [ɔö]: *awe, saw, all, story, pause, cough, broad; order, court, warm.* . . . . ɔə: *boa, bore, oar, more, door, four.*' (p. 73)

> aa. Mid-back-wide + mid-mixed-wide [aë]: *baa, fast, half, bar, barred, bard, starry, clerk, heart.* (p. 70)

Notice that (unlike the NED) Sweet regards all the vowels under discussion as surface centring diphthongs; yet he regards the vowel deriving from historic /oːr/ as distinct. Elsewhere in the same work, he comments in more detail (without, however, saying more about the [ɔə] of *bore*):

> It is to be observed that the English ɔ is generally slightly diphthongic, which is the result of the tongue being allowed to slip into the mid-mixed-wide-round position at the end of the vowel, so that it may also be written [ɔö]. (p. 32)

> Our aa also differs from that of most other languages in being slightly diphthongic: it generally ends in the mid-mixed-wide vowel, so that it might be written aə. (p. 35)

> *Father* and *farther* are both pronounced alike; and the r which many unphonetic observers persist in hearing in the latter word is, of course, only the ə which is just as distinct in *father*. ɔ also ends in a mixed vowel; but as this vowel is rounded, there is no difficulty in adding an ə to it. (p. 64)

Sweet's observation that all of the early-twentieth-century equivalents of present-day [ɔː ɑː] are centring diphthongs (and not just the historic-/oːr/ cases) is important and surprising. In the knowledge of their subsequent history (which is monophthongal) as well as particularly of their historic sources, one would expect these mergers to have resulted in long monophthongs. A centring diphthong arising through the loss of historic /r/ is unsurprising (compare present-day RP [ɪə] (*beer*) etc.); but Sweet's diphthongal description of *saw, all, father* etc. raises the question of why those vowels, too, should have had in-glides. For the moment we conclude that they did, however slight such diphthongisation may have been, even in the absence of similar statements in contemporary descriptions: the NED gives in-glides only in historic-/oːr/ cases, as we have seen; and Jespersen (1909) follows suit.[3]

But what is more surprising than Jespersen's (1909) failure to note the in-glide is the fact that he also omits mention of the continued distinctness of historic-/oːr/ forms, which both Sweet and the NED record. Unlike those, Jespersen regards not only explicitly the merger of all sources into [ɑː] as completed – '*farther* = *father* [faːðə]' (Jespersen 1909: 427) – but also, implicitly, the parallel merger into [ɔː]. It has been suggested by commentators that the NED represents a pronunciation standard that was conservative at its time, both in general terms and specifically regarding the contrast in question (Horn and Lehnert 1954: 491; see also MacMahon 1985). Sweet (1908), synchronic-descriptive and probably not subject to that charge, simply recorded what occurred,[4] even if – and this may well have been the case – the occurrence of this contrast was by then restricted to certain speakers and perhaps obsolescent.

For the centring diphthong associated with present-day [ɔː] (not deriving from /oːr/), Sweet (1908: 64) observes allophonic variation, noting that some speakers drop the in-glide (which in standard pronunciation he assumes to be invariable) in pre-consonantal position. The same allophonic distribution of [ɔː] (*lord, laud*) vs. [ɔə] (*floor, flaw*) occurs today in London English, to be discussed below. Notably, neither the distribution in Present-day London English nor that reported by Sweet depend in any way on the different historic sources of the sounds in question. In this respect, Jespersen (1909) does follow Sweet (1908), acknowledging a-historic allophony, for some speakers, involving the pre-consonantal and pre-pausal positions.

> Before a pause, the sound in a frequent pronunciation, represented by Sweet and others, ends in a short and not too distinct [ə]-glide, which is

found not only where the vowel is formerly followed by *r*, as in *nor*, but also in other instances, as in *law*. Before a consonant, no [ə] is heard in standard pronunciation, which makes *lord= laud* [lɔ·d] (Jespersen 1909: 435)

I turn now to the present-day situation in RP and London English, before attempting an interpretation of these partially conflicting descriptions.

7.2.2.2   *Modern RP and London English*

In the standard descriptive work on modern RP (Gimson 1994), the monophthong [ɔː] is treated as standard (unlike [ɛː]); the slightly diphthongal character of this sound, recorded by Sweet, has disappeared. But a diphthongal pronunciation of historic-/oːr/ items, giving rise to a phonemic contrast, is still possible, if clearly obsolescent: 'Until relatively recently there was a contrast between /ɔː/ and /ɔə/ in RP, so that *saw* and *sore* were pronounced differently. Nowadays this contrast is generally not made, except by some older speakers' (Gimson 1994: 110).

The continued presence of [ɔə] in historic-/r/ forms, among older/conservative speakers of RP, is also noted by Trudgill and Hannah (1985) and Hughes and Trudgill (1987). And Wells (1982: 235f.), who similarly writes off the contrast for mainstream RP, notes that in the EPD the contrast persisted longest in word-final position. Noting the possible influence of the orthography he reports that in the last (12th, 1963) edition of that work edited by Daniel Jones himself, [ɔə] is given as a (less usual) pronunciation in, for example, *store, four, core, door* (as well as in some pre-consonantal cases where homophony may be at stake: *court, board, coarse, hoarse, sword, source*). All these cases conform with what the NED (1988–) gives as the standard pronunciation, as I noted above. In fact, the same occurrence of [ɔə] in historic-/r/ forms is still recorded (again as less likely) in the more recent (14th, 1991) edition of the EPD, regularly in word-final position and sporadically elsewhere.

Equally, the a-historic [ɔː]/[ɔə] allophony of /ɔː/, noted by Sweet (1908) and Jespersen (1909), continues to occur: [ɔː] pre-consonantally (*lord, laud, pause*) and [ɔː] word-finally (*saw, sore*). Wells (1982: 293) characterises this distribution as 'perhaps a near-RP Londonism'.

In London English proper, a similar (if more complex) pattern of distribution occurs (Sivertsen 1960: 75; Wells 1982: 304). Examples are given in (4):

(4)   a. [oʊ]   b. [ɔə]   c. [ɔə]

board	bore	bored
pause	paw, pore	paws, pores
Crawley	poor	poorly

This pattern differs from the 'near-RP Londonism' noted above in two respects. First, [ɔə] occurs not only word-finally (4b) but, more generally, morpheme-finally (4c), giving rise to 'minimal pairs' (in Harris's (1990) terms, a 'derived contrast') such as *board/bored* etc. The precise character-isation of the contexts exemplified in (4c) will concern us later. Second, the pre-consonantal vowel in (4a) is [oʊ] rather than RP-[ɔː], reflecting a perhaps recent raising of that vowel in London English which is also found, if to a lesser extent, in modern RP (Gimson 1994: 111). This is perhaps again due to the influence of London speech, where the raising appears to have originated. Wells states that '[t]he vowel /ɔː/ has been getting less open over the last half-century. Newsreels from the thirties often evidence a cardinal-6-like quality which now seems dated' (Wells 1982: 293).

7.2.2.3 Interpretation

The pattern of distribution found in the modern language, surveyed in Section 7.2.2.2, is fairly straightforward. While in mainstream RP the vowel surfaces as [ɔː] in all contexts, its centring-diphthong variant [ɔə] occurs, in different contexts, with two distinct sets of RP speakers. Older (conserva-tive) RP speakers maintain [ɔə] sporadically in forms deriving historically from long-vowel-plus-/r/ (*store, court* etc.). I shall refer to this [ɔə] as 'his-toric [ɔə]'. And London-influenced RP speakers have [ɔə] word-finally, regardless of its historic origin (*saw, sore*). This I shall refer to as 'a-historic [ɔə]'. For (non-RP) London speakers, this a-historic [ɔə] occurs more gen-erally before morpheme boundaries (*bore, bored*).

The early-twentieth-century picture, surveyed in Section 7.2.2.1, is more complex. There are three different (but overlapping) patterns. The first (henceforth 'mainstream') pattern has in common with present-day main-stream RP that '/ɔː/' has no monophthong/diphthong allophony that might be of relevance here. But that variety differs from present-day mainstream RP in that, on Sweet's (1908) testimony, that vowel (as well as '/ɑː/') is a cen-tring diphthong, if only slightly, in all contexts. This clearly means that for the turn of the twentieth century we must posit centring diphthongs as underlying representations for the long low vowels; but it remains to be seen whether the same analysis can be justified for modern RP and related varieties.

Both historic and a-historic [ɔə] are on record, the former unsurprisingly. Regarding the former – the second pattern to be noted here, under the tentative assumption that historic [ɔə] was already obsolescent in the mainstream variety of the time – the contrast is one between what Sweet (1908) gives without further comment as [ɔə] (in forms deriving from historic /oːr/ (*bore* etc.)), and [ɔː], also slightly in-gliding (in forms from other sources (*sort* etc.)). Recall now that the NED gives historic [ɔə] as [oːə]. No detailed phonetic description beyond this symbol is available; but this difference in notation may well mean, in line with the history of such forms, that this vowel had recently lowered at Sweet's time. The NED symbol is closer to the vowel's undisputed historical source, and recall that that work is reputed to be conservative in its transcription (Horn and Lehnert 1954: 491).

Regarding a-historic [ɔə] – the third pattern – it is perhaps not unreasonable to suggest that the (unspecified) speakers to whom both Sweet (1908) and Jespersen (1909) refer may have been London English(-influenced) speakers (Ward 1939: 96ff.). A-historic (London English-influenced) [ɔə] is, then, at least 90 years old. Those London speakers have a-historic [ɔə] word-finally and a pure monophthong [ɔː] in complementary contexts. I have found no early-twentieth-century records of the modern (London English-specific non-RP) [ɔə]/[oʊ] distinction (*bored*/*board*), which would confirm the distribution given in (4) above.

In the following sections I shall present a formal synchronic analysis of these various distributions at the turn of the twentieth century, before turning to present-day RP and London English.

7.2.3   *Synchronic analysis: the turn of the twentieth century*

Three questions arise from the summary of the early-twentieth-century situation given in Section 7.2.2.1. These concern, first, the underlying and surface representations of the slight centring diphthongs in the mainstream variety of Sweet's (1908) time, second historic [ɔə] as in *sore*, whose contrast with *saw* (although possibly already obsolescent at the time) is still recorded by the NED (1888–) and Sweet (1908), and third a-historic [ɔə] in word-final position. I shall deal with each of these questions in turn.

7.2.3.1 The mainstream variety

There can be little doubt that in the principal variety described by Sweet (1908), the 'long' low vowels were phonetically centring diphthongs throughout their synchronic distribution. In the absence of arguments to the contrary, it is plausible to suggest on these grounds alone that their underlying representations were of the form exemplified in (1) above: complex nuclei whose second elements were 'empty' melodies. There are strong diachronic arguments in favour of such an analysis in those cases where the relevant nuclei had arisen, quite recently at the time, from sources involving the weakening of rhyme-/r/. But it is intriguing that /r/-less sources (*thought, flaw; grasp*) should equally have resulted in this configuration, as is clearly shown by Sweet. I return to this issue in Section 7.2.5, offering a synchronic explanation involving more generally the representation of long vowels.

It is equally clear that the centring diphthongs /ɪə ʊə/ (*hear, sure*), clearly established at the time (Sweet 1908: 72f.), had the same kind of underlying representations. But their surface forms differed from those of Sweet's long low vowels in that they were, as is still the case, not subject to monophthonging: as we saw above, the in-glide in the low vowels was considerably shorter and less noticeable at the time than that of the former.

The low vowels were subject, then, to a spreading rule that was similar to that affecting /ɛə/ (see (2a) above). The complete monophthongisation of the low vowels is achieved in present-day RP, as it is, for some speakers, in the case of /ɛə/. Sweet's variety demonstrates for the low vowels the gradual implementation of what was later to result in a spread-and-delink rule. The relevant rule is given in (5):

(5)   *Low vowel monophthonging: Sweet's version* (postlexical)

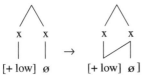

Like (2), (5) results in a configuration where the low vowel melody occupies the first skeletal slot while sharing the second with the melody 'Ø'. Again, we may interpret such a configuration as a centring diphthong with a relatively long first element. I assume that at this early stage, monophthonging is still a postlexical phenomenon, concerned with fairly low-level phonetic detail. While there is no evidence to suggest that (5) is lexical at Sweet's time, I shall argue below that the present-day successor of this rule must be lexical – a familiar route for a sound change to follow (Harris 1990).

The phonetic detail provided by Jespersen (1909) suggests that the monophthonging of /ɛə/ was less extensive than that of the low vowels but more so than that of /ɪə ʊə/ (which did not monophthong). A parallel situation holds in present-day RP, where /ɪə ʊə/ are still resistant to monophthonging while /ɛə/ may and the low vowels must undergo that process. We have the onset of a sound change, then, that results in progressive monophthonging of centring diphthongs from the low nuclei upwards. The formal notation employed here does not allow for the expression of such detail: spreading either does or does not take place; delinking at that stage does not, for any of the vowels in question (Sweet 1908). I shall suggest in the next section that the two rules, (2) and (5), can be collapsed (at the expense of such inexpressible detail). The gradient nature of the monophthonging rule (2)/(5) points once more towards the postlexical location of the rule (Mohanan 1986).

7.2.3.2 *Historic* [ɔə]

Recall that the NED (1888–) gives [oːᵊ], and Sweet (1908) [ɔə] (in his broad transcription), for forms originating from historic /oːr/ (*source, floor, lore*), giving rise to contrast with respect to *sauce, flaw, law*. This contrast, not recorded by Jespersen (1909), was possibly obsolescent even at that time (Horn and Lehnert 1954: 491); it certainly is now. Let us represent this vowel as underlyingly /o∅/ (see (6) below), as opposed to the /ɔ∅/ in other cases, with which /o∅/ was set to merge.

(6)

There are several reasons for positing this underlier. First, it is well motivated in terms of its diachronic development: the change from /oːr/ to eventual [ɔː] is likely to have passed through that stage. Second, the merger of historic /oːr/ and other relevant sources into present-day [ɔː], which happened in mainstream RP at the latest between Sweet's time and now, and for some speakers perhaps even before Sweet, may then be stated in the form of a synchronic rule lowering /o∅/ to [ɔ∅], which neutralised the contrast, with subsequent loss of the distinct underlier (6). I return to this putative lowering rule in (8) below. Third, the underlier (6) is, as its subsequent history shows, evidently unstable. I shall argue in Section 7.2.5 that (6) expresses this instability: while diachronically well founded, it is structurally anomalous in synchronic terms. Its forthcoming merger of /oØ/ with /ɔØ/ is predicted by the grammar.

I tentatively suggest (on the somewhat insecure basis of its NED transcription as [oːᵊ]) that the nucleus given in (6) is subject to spreading, as expressed in rules (2)/(5). This means that the structural description of the three rules can be collapsed into [− high]:

(7)   *Non-high vowel monophthonging: Sweet's version* (postlexical)

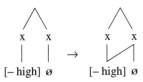

7.2.3.3 A-historic [ɔə]

Recall Sweet's (1908: 64) observation whereby some speakers (reasonably assumed to be Londoners) drop the in-glide of [ɔə] in pre-consonantal contexts (*lord, laud*) but maintain it in word-final position (*lore, law*). This allophonic distribution is not historically-motivated (affecting /r/-ful and /r/-less sources alike), nor does it apparently affect [ɑə]. Given also that Jespersen concurs with (in fact, draws on) Sweet in this respect, I suggest that those speakers monophthonged [ɔə] in pre-consonantal contexts by spreading the first and delinking the second melodic element before consonants in the same word:

(8)   *A-historic [ɔə]/[ɔː]: Sweet's version* (postlexical)

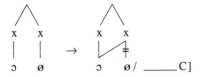

This is, again, a postlexical rule – a classic case of allophony, which is unproblematic on the standard assumption that word brackets (the outermost brackets of any morphological construction) are available for reference on the postlexical stratum. Note that the converse statement of this distribution, whereby monophthonging is blocked word-finally, is not possible in the theory. Such a statement would have to employ the word-final bracket ']' to block the rule; but, while morphological brackets are well attested to trigger rules, they cannot block them (Mohanan 1986: Section 5.2.1). This point will become relevant in Section 7.2.5 below.

In conclusion, the facts suggest that three (RP/near-RP) systems existed side by side at the turn of the century: Sweet's variety, which had rule (7); another (presumably London) variety, which additionally had rule (8);[5] and an obsolescent variety which had the underlying nucleus (6) in its inventory. All three varieties had in common that their low vowels derived synchronically from centring diphthongs, and that the rules involved in these derivations were postlexical.

7.2.4   *Synchronic analysis: present-day RP*

7.2.4.1   *The mainstream variety*

Recall from Section 7.2.2.2 that present-day mainstream RP, as described by Wells (1982) and Gimson (1994), has neither historic nor a-historic [ɔə]. This variety is, in this respect, the direct successor of Sweet's variety; but the difference is that the in-glide, reported for both low vowels by Sweet, is no longer in evidence.[6] This raises the question, alluded to before, of whether a re-structuring of the underlying representations of these vowels has taken place since Sweet's time, or whether a synchronic monophthonging rule has been added to the grammar. The latter possibility would imply that the underliers have over time become more remote from the surface – an analytical strategy that is not dissimilar from that followed by SPE, although of course the time-span in question is merely one of some 90 years (at a stretch within the life expectancy of a single generation of speakers) and not, for example, one harking back to pre-Vowel Shift times, as does the SPE analysis of the Present-day English vowel system. Despite the potential abstractness problems that the latter type of analysis brings with it, I pursue that analysis here for reasons that will become clear in Section 7.2.5 below. I shall argue there that re-structuring and the inversion of the relevant rules (Vennemann 1972b) has taken place among some speakers but that no such re-structuring can occur until a synchronic monophthonging rule is in place, as it is in present-day mainstream RP.

One argument in favour of the at least temporary maintenance of centring-diphthong underliers for the monophthongs [ɑː] and [ɔː], in mainstream RP, is that the rule involved in the derivation of these surface forms constitutes the completion of a process that, as we saw in Section 7.2.3.1, was already underway at Sweet's time. This rule (see (9) below) – the spreading of the first melodic element given in (5) above, to which now the delinking of the second element has been added – is not only of a type that is well attested in the literature (see again Goldsmith 1990); it can also be accommodated within the known constraints of Lexical Phonology. As a structure-changing rule operating in an underived environment, it is barred (by SCE) from stratum 1 but neither from stratum 2 nor from the postlexical phonology. I take the view here that (9) has not only become more radical in its effect than its early-twentieth-century predecessor was, but that it has also moved into the lexicon (where, by virtue of SCE, it is automatically confined to stratum 2). As I shall argue in the next section, its lexical status is enforced by the existence of lexical exceptions. This rule, then, monophthongises the centring diphthong underliers of the long low surface vowels in mainstream RP.

(9)   *Low-vowel monophthonging: mainstream RP* (lexical)

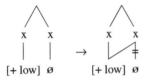

7.2.4.2 Historic [ɔə]

Recall that this diphthong, residue of old /oːr/ (*floor, source, lore*) and transcribed by the NED (1888–) as [oːə], is still occasionally found in the pronunciations of older speakers of conservative RP (Gimson 1994: 110; Hughes and Trudgill 1987: 27ff.; Wells 1982: 235f.). I suggested in Section 7.2.3.2 that the contrast was still active (*contra* Sweet, notably) for some speakers at the turn of the twentieth century, with /oØ/ as the underlier of *floor, source, lore* and /ɔØ/ as that of *flaw, sauce, law*. But it is hard to see how in present-day RP the status of diphthongal pronunciations of *source* etc. can be anything other than exceptional. The principal reason for this judgement (and the issue is clearly a judgemental one) is that the surface quality difference between this vowel and its mainstream-RP counterpart has disappeared: NED [oːə] has changed to present-day [ɔə], whose quality (ignoring surface monophthonging) is identical with the counterpart of this vowel in mainstream RP. Moreover, its distribution overlaps with the 'near-RP Londonism' of a-historic [ɔə] (Wells 1982: 293; Section 7.2.2.2 above) in word-final position: *sore* etc.

Here is the pattern that emerges if historic [ɔə] is assumed to have a separate underlier:

(10)   a. (conservative RP)   /o∅/   →   [ɔə]   *source, sore*
                                /ɔ∅/   →   [ɔː]   *sauce, saw*

        b. (mainstream RP)   /ɔ∅/   →   [ɔː]   *source, sore, sauce, saw*

        c. (near-London RP)   /ɔ∅/   →   [ɔə]   *sore, saw*
                                /ɔ∅/   →   [ɔː]   *source, sauce*

I shall here give two possible synchronic analyses of historic [ɔə] and subscribe to the second. Under the first analysis, the early-twentieth-century underlier of historic [ɔə] is preserved (although somewhat depleted in terms of incidence):

(11)   *Historic*-[ɔə] *lowering* (postlexical)

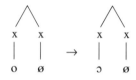

In formal terms, (11) is unobjectionable. As a postlexical rule it is free from any constraints affecting context-free structure-changing rules; its postlexical status, moreover, automatically means that relevant items are not candidates for (lexical) monophthonging (see (9) above), which only affects low vowels. The surface contrast given in (10a) above is, then, produced by rules (9) and (11) affecting separate underliers at different derivational stages.

But the problem with such an analysis is that it does effectively nothing more than side-step exception-marking, artificially prolonging the life of a phonological contrast that was in its dying days, possibly even in Sweet's time. Given the regular synchronic derivation of surface [ɔː] from underlying /ɔ∅/, that of (historic) [ɔə] from underlying /o∅/ through the context-free lowering rule (11) merely expresses what may far more simply be described as the failure of items such as *source* to undergo rule (9) above.

The second, preferred analysis of historic [ɔə] is, then, one whereby items such as *source, floor* etc. constitute lexical exceptions to rule (9), which must for that reason alone be a lexical rule. Rule (11) is no longer active in the synchronic phonology, having effected (at some point between the turn of the twentieth century and the late 1990s) the merger of /o∅/ with /ɔ∅/. It is only with conservative speakers that these exceptions to (9) are likely to occur. Given that it is of course more 'normal' for phonological rules not to have lexical exceptions, it is unsurprising that the incidence of such exceptions should decline over time, and that mainstream (non-conservative) RP should have none.

It is possible that the failure of (9) to be implemented in certain items in conservative RP, may be due to orthographic influence. This possibility, suggested by Wells (1982: 235f.), was noted in Section 7.2.2.2; and I argued in Chapter 5 that certain seemingly-regular phonological processes in the synchronic phonology of English may in reality be spelling-driven (for example the quality of the stressed vowels in *atomic, reality, deterrent* etc.). But in the case of (9), the expression of such orthographic conditioning is by no means straightforward. While it is certainly true that all exceptions to (9) contain <r> in their orthography, the items that do undergo the rule may or may nor contain <r>. Like the NED (1888–), the EPD (1991) gives (optional) centring-diphthong pronunciations in certain forms deriving historically from /ɔːr/ (*floor, source, lore* etc.) but not in any forms deriving from historic /ɒr/ (*north, short, corn* etc.) or historic /ɔː/ (*thought* etc.). Assuming that the examples are representative of the spelling patterns of the two <r>-ful sources in question, orthographic conditioning blocking the rule would have to be of the form '<r> preceded by a vowel digraph and/or followed by <e>'. The more plausible analysis whereby (9) is triggered by orthographic features, for conservative RP speakers, would be no less complex: in that case (9) would operate 'either in the absence of <r> or in the presence of <rC> not preceded by a vowel digraph'. A spelling-driven analysis of the present-day distribution of historic [ɔə], then, does not convince through simplicity. It is more likely that we are dealing simply with synchronically-random lexical exceptions.

7.2.4.3 *A-historic* [ɔə]: *'near-RP' and London English*

I noted in Section 7.2.2.2 that a-historic [ɔə] occurs, in different distributions, both as a 'near-RP Londonism' (Wells 1982: 293) and in London English (Wells 1982: 304; Sivertsen 1960: 75). In the former variety, [ɔə] occurs word-finally (*sore, saw* etc.) but not elsewhere. In the latter, its occurrence is more generally morpheme-final, followed possibly by stratum-2 suffixes: *bore, bored*; *paw, paws*; *pore, pores*; *poor, poorly* etc. (see (4) above).

The synchronic account of the former, in present-day London near-RP, is by and large unchanged from Sweet's time. In more detail, it can be assumed that the centring-diphthong underlier of this nucleus has remained unchanged in this variety, and that the speakers in question still have rule (8), and a version of the context-free rule (7) affecting [+ low, − round], i.e. for /a∅/ only. Both of these rules qualify at face value for post-lexical status; but I assume that the whole apparatus of rules handling these nuclei has moved into the lexicon since Sweet's time. This assumption is, as we have seen, crucial to the account of mainstream and conservative RP; it will be further strengthened by the distribution found in London English proper, to be discussed below. If both in mainstream RP and in London English the processes in question are lexical, then they should plausibly be of the same status in London-influenced RP.

As I noted in Section 7.2.2.2, London English proper differs from the London-influenced variant of 'near RP' discussed above, in the respects here relevant, in that first it has [ɔə] not only word-finally in *pore, paw, poor* but also in stratum-2 morphologically complex forms such as *pores, paws, poorly*; and second in that the monophthongal congener of the vowel is not [ɔː] but [oʊ] (*pause* etc.). This distribution was tabled in (4) above. I deal first with the distribution of [ɔə] and then turn to the quality of [oʊ].

It is self-evident that this distribution can only be accounted for by a (stratum-2) lexical rule, given that it crucially involves stratum-2 suffixes. It is also clear that this rule must make crucial reference to morphological brackets: compare *paws* and *pause*. (See Harris (1990: Section 6.1), Borowsky (1993: Section 6.3) for discussion.) But the problem is that, under the assumption that the relevant underlier is /ɔ∅/ (as it is in RP), such a rule would have to state that the monophthonging of that nucleus is blocked by the presence of the morphological bracket ']'. Morphological brackets are well-attested as triggers of phonological rules; but there cannot be rules that require the absence of morphological brackets in their structural descriptions: brackets cannot block rules (Mohanan 1986: 130). Rather than overturning this well-founded principle in an *ad hoc* decision, we must here conclude that the nucleus that underlies [ɔə]/[oʊ] in London English cannot be /ɔ∅/. Instead of London-influenced RP's rule (8), which monophthongises /ɔ∅/ before consonants, London English must then have the mirror-image rule which diphthongises an underlying monophthong before ']'. Anticipating arguments that will be given in the next section, I shall assume here that the underlier is /oː/ and state the rule, in an obviously provisional form, in (12) below. Rule (12) is automatically blocked on stratum 1 by SCE.

(12)   *A-historic* [ɔə]: *London English* (lexical)

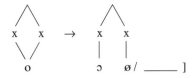

ɔ   ø / _____]

If we compare this aspect of London English with RP (and its London-influenced variant), it becomes obvious that, assuming that both varieties ultimately stem from the same historical source, one of them must have undergone a rule inversion in the sense of Vennemann (1972b): a rule of the form 'A → B / _____ X' has turned into 'B → A / _____ ~ X'. The historical evidence suggests that it is London English that has been subject to the inversion. I have found no records predating Sivertsen (1960) that give [ɔə] in forms such as *paws* etc.; but such lack of recorded (or discovered) evidence obviously cannot serve to date the phenomenon. What is more telling is that the present-day RP underlier /ɔØ/ was, as I have shown, in place at Sweet's time, and that in turn it is strongly motivated by the more remote historical development. Given that several of the sources of /ɔØ/ involve historic /r/-loss, it is clearly more plausible to suggest that /ɔØ/ was or is an intermediate stage in the development of a long monophthong, than it would be to claim that the loss of /r/ first gave rise to a monophthong which later diphthongised into /ɔØ/. Further arguments to the same effect will be given below; here I state that the variety of English in which the rule inversion has happened must be London English.[7] In the following section I shall argue that this rule inversion was connected with the raising of the underlying vowel to /oː/.

7.2.5   Rule inversion and the raising of [ɔː]

Let us assume that in English, tense vowels (and only those) are automatically associated with two skeletal positions while nontense vowels are associated with one such position, as in (13) below.[8]

(13)   a.   x   x   b.   x

  \ / |

  [+ tense]   [− tense]

This association automatically gives rise to a pattern whereby tense vowels are redundantly long while lax vowels are redundantly short; but it faces the well-known problem that among low vowels the feature [±tense] is by all accounts ill-defined, and perhaps devoid of phonetic correlates (Wood 1975; Halle 1977). If we follow Halle's (1977) analysis whereby the low vowels in English are underlyingly unspecified for tenseness then we need an alternative way of producing, for those vowels, the long–short distinction in terms of skeletal associations.

There appear to be only two other ways of expressing long–short contrasts among low vowels in the absence of a tenseness specification. The first involves geminate melodies (on the assumption, presumably, that (only) low-vowel melodies can occur as geminates in underlying representations), as in (14a) below; but this structure is ruled out by the Obligatory Contour Principle. (See Goldsmith (1990: Section 6.4) for discussion.) The second way of expressing long low vowels is given in (14b).

(14)   a.   *   b.

The melody in (14b) is associated with a single skeletal slot, which in turn forms part of a two-x nucleus.[9] This structure may either have the status of an underlying complex segment, or it may be built, by rule, on a melodic /ɔØ/ sequence. In that case the grammar would have a phonotactic filter permitting /Ø/ to form nuclei only with single-x non-consonantal melodies. This filter is obviously of a more general nature, disallowing three-x nuclei. Whichever solution is adopted, the structure (14b) is consistent with that given in (2) above. This means that structures like (2) are the only way of representing length among non-tense vowels. Such structures are hence not only motivated diachronically, having in many cases arisen through the weakening and loss of their second (originally consonantal) melodies; they are also independently motivated in synchronic terms. Moreover, an analysis whereby tense vowels are associated with two skeletal positions in the normal (default) case identifies structures such as (6) above (where tense /o/ forms part of the structure /oØ/, similar to (14b)) as marked, and hence likely to change. Such a structure has to form an underlying complex nucleus, overriding any rule-governed association of melodies with suprasegmental structure. The analysis of present-day historic [ɔə] suggested above indeed implies that early-twentieth-century /oØ/ has merged with /ɔØ/.

Given that the empty melody in (14b) (previously represented as 'Ø') is also the underlier of schwa (Giegerich 1992a; Section 2.1 above), such an analysis makes the prediction that, in the absence of rules affecting structures of the kind (14b), long non-tense vowels will be expected to have in-glides. Such structure-changing rules, of which several have materialised in this chapter, are in obvious violation of the Structure Preservation Condition as well as (if they apply in non-derived environments) of Strict Cyclicity. They cannot therefore be located on stratum 1, where both conditions hold; but they are free to apply on stratum 2 or postlexically (Borowsky 1989).

A further property of non-low long vowels, in addition to that of being tense, is their tendency in many varieties of English (including those discussed here) to surface as off-gliding diphthongs. Low vowels do not behave in this way. Such dissimilation, pictured in (15) below, again represents a violation of both conditions noted above. It is irrelevant here whether structural changes like (15) are lexical (i.e. stratum 2) or postlexical; but recall relevant remarks in Section 6.3.2. Nor is the precise form the relevant rules of concern here.

(15)   *Tense vowel dissimilation* (example)

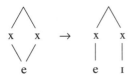

With these points in mind, consider again the distribution of [ɔə]/[oʊ] in London English, first discussed in Section 7.2.4.3. I stipulated there that the nucleus underlying these surface forms is /oː/, a stipulation that is supported by Ward (1939: 96) and Sivertsen (1960). Two further points will support this stipulation and illustrate its effects. First, given that /oː/ is long and non-low, it can be expected to be tense and therefore to form part of a structure of the form (13a), as well as to surface with an off-gliding diphthong. Indeed, the default surface form (arising in non-rule-(12) contexts) is [oʊ] in London English. Second, the mystery surrounding the structural change of (12) disappears if we interpret this rule's output as the ultimate effect of a lowering process, which automatically affects the tenseness specification. If that is the case then the resulting [ɔØ] structure is the automatic consequence of the fact that the lowered (and hence laxed) melody cannot any longer be associated with two skeletal positions.

Recall now that in mainstream RP, too, this vowel 'has been getting less open over the last half-century' (Wells 1982: 293), perhaps due to the influence of London speech on RP. And recall also that the statement of a-historic [ɔə] for London-influenced RP, given in (8) above, was the inverse of the statement of the corresponding rule for London English (12). That analysis assumed that the system of London-influenced RP is identical with the RP system in regard to the underlying quality of [ɔə] – assumed to be /ɔØ/ in both varieties. In the light of the ongoing raising of the vowel, London-influenced RP may well have inverted rule (12) by now; or the inversion may be in progress, so that the 'derived contrast' [ɔə]/[oʊ] (*paws*/*pause*) may be expected to occur there if the rule, once inverted, retains its lexical status. If it is postlexical then the rule inversion will have no surface effects whatsoever.

Rule inversions can of course only occur at times when the synchronic facts are equally, and simultaneously, amenable both to a given analysis and to its inverse (Vennemann 1972b). For mainstream RP this means that the possibility of rule inversion could not have arisen until the grammar acquired the synchronic monophthongisation rule (9) above: the surface monophthongisation of the (synchronically underlying) centring diphthongs in question is a prerequisite to any re-analysis whereby the underliers become monophthongs. In London-influenced RP, the distribution given in (10c) above – [ɔə] (*sore, saw*) vs. [ɔː] (*source, sauce*) – can be accounted for by a postlexical rule that diphthongises an underlying monophthong in pre-bracket position (i.e. the inverse of rule (8) above): that variety, too, is possibly amenable to an inverted analysis. Given also the observed raising of the surface monophthong in RP (if to a lesser extent than in London English and without off-gliding diphthongisation), we can conclude that the conditions for rule inversion are in place in both present-day mainstream RP and London-influenced RP. But it is only in London English that rule inversion can be shown to have happened between the turn of the twentieth century and now: as I showed in Section 7.2.4.3, the distribution of [oʊ] (*pause*) vs. [ɔə] (*paw, paws*) cannot be accounted for without the assumption of monophthongal underliers.

What I have been trying to show here is this: the empirical effects of rule inversion, from underlying diphthong monophthongised on the surface to underlying monophthong subject to surface diphthongisation, are clearly evidenced in London English; but they do not (yet?) show up in RP. Any suggestion on the grounds of present-day surface vowels that rule inversion has happened in RP, resulting in the abandonment of diphthongal underliers for the long low vowels, would be entirely speculative, and hence unacceptable.

And consider again the facts of present-day [r]-sandhi, first in RP and then in London English. In RP, the delinking of the [∅] melody takes place on stratum 2; there can be little doubt that this process is lexical. If [r]-sandhi is postlexical (as its external version must be: *bore*[r] *it*) then the delinked [∅] must be preserved beyond the lexical derivation so as to be available for docking onto the syllable onset in the postlexicon. In Harris's (1994: Chapter 5) terms, it is a 'floating melody'. In London English, where the vowel in question is an underlying monophthong, diphthongisation resulting in the emergence of [∅] similarly takes place on stratum 2: again, the empty melody is available from then onwards (and particularly in the postlexicon). What is important here is that under an alternative analysis which assumes rule inversion to have happened in RP (to the effect that Sweet's underlying centring diphthongs have turned into the underlying monophthongs /ɔː/ and /ɑː/) no [r]-sandhi can be motivated: the derivations of those vowels would then go, uneventfully, from underlying /ɔː/ and /ɑː/ to surface [ɔː] and [ɑː] without the emergence of [∅] anywhere in the derivation. The continued and productive occurrence of [r]-sandhi after low vowels independently supports the analysis, then, whereby rule inversion has not happened in RP.

In the next section, the analysis of the input vowels of [r]-sandhi will be completed by an account of the phonology of [ɜː]. This analysis will be the continuation of the discussion of cases such as *recur – recurrent* begun in Chapter 5 above, therefore also addressing the stratum-1 aspects of this vowel's derivational path. This is a topic that also has still to be addressed in connection with [ɔː] and [ɑː], as indeed with [ɪə], [ɛə] and [ʊə].

7.3   The representation and derivation of [ɜː]

We have seen so far that in the present model of the lexical phonology of RP, the surface centring diphthongs must have the underlying representations /ɪ∅ ɛ∅ ʊ∅/, and the long low vowels /ɑ∅ ɔ∅/. The former must be so because a synchronic derivation from the more abstract underliers /iːr/ etc., involving the synchronic breaking of the vowel and deletion of the /r/, is not viable: I showed in Section 6.2.1 that such an analysis breaches the limits of abstractness that the theoretical framework can tolerate, quite apart from the fact that it also makes incorrect empirical predictions. I argued for the latter analysis, posing underlying /ɑ∅ ɔ∅/, because there is no evidence in RP to suggest that these underliers have changed since the turn of the twentieth century, when the relevant vowels were centring diphthongs on the surface. That analysis, which is also somewhat abstract but clearly less so than the rejected derivation of [ɪə] from /iːr/, is strongly supported by the fact that the long low vowels continue to attract [r]-sandhi, which could not be explained under an underlying-monophthong analysis. I turn now to the representation of [ɜː] and its derivation through the lexical strata.

In phonetic terms, [ɜː] surfaces as long (occupying therefore two skeletal positions). It is, moreover, phonetically similar to schwa but confined to stressed syllables. In diachronic terms it has in relevant items no sources other than historic /r/, in every case preceded by historic /ɪ ɛ ʌ/ (Section 6.1.1 above). It occurs in non-alternating forms (when followed by a tautomorphemic consonant), as in (16a) below; it engages, moreover, in a range of vowel alternations, in which the historic source vowels re-surface when involved in pre-stressing suffixations on stratum 1 (16b). And of course it attracts linking [r] both word-medially and between words, as in (16c).

(16)   a. [ɜː]   bird   herd   curse
                     first   stern   church
                     third   pearl   churl
                     firm   merge   burn
                     myrtle   kernel   murder
         b. [ɜː ~ ɪ] myrrh – myrrhic
                     sir – sirrah
            [ɜː ~ ɛ] deter – deterrent
                     err – error
            [ɜː ~ ʌ] occur – occurrence
                     demur – demurrer
         c. [ɜːr]   myrrhy, myrrh is
                     deterring, deter it
                     erring, err and
                     recurring, recur and
                     demurring, demur and

In Section 5.2.2 I began to characterise the underlying representation of [ɜː]. Vowel alternations of the type exemplified in (16b) were of particular concern at that point. Provisionally referring to the melody occupying the second skeletal position of [ɜː] as /R/ ('historic /r/'), I argued against the type of derivation that one would have expected to inherit from standard Generative Phonology, whereby the underlying representation of, say, *err* would be /ɛR/, true to the historic source of the vowel and surfacing unaltered in *error* but subject to some sort of reduction or de-linking in the surface forms *err, erring*. (Similarly /mɪR/ for *myrrh* etc.) I argued that this kind of analysis is not only undesirable in the light of the free-ride derivations involving indeterminate underliers in non-alternating forms (see (16a) above), but that it is actually impossible in the present model of the lexical phonology of English as long as stratum 2 can be assumed to be non-cyclic. In brief, the structure-changing rule that de-links the full-vowel melody, required by that sort of account, can be sited neither on stratum 1 (because it would have to apply in underived environments: *err*) nor on stratum 2 (because it would have to be cyclic, applying before the formation of *erring*). The alternative analysis presented in Section 5.2.2 formed part of a more general argument in favour of spelling-driven synchronic derivations, which is of no concern in the present chapter. But what is of concern here is that the underlier for [ɜː] predicted by the present model was identified as the sequence /ØR/.

We have since seen that what was left behind by the loss of historic rhyme-/r/ (provisionally '/R/') is suitably represented as the 'empty' nuclear melody /Ø/. This means that the underlying representation of surface [ɜː] is the sequence given in (17):

(17)   x   x

          | |

          ø   ø

We are now in a position where we can discuss the syllabification properties of the sequence (17), as well as of those in (16b) above, in some more detail (albeit still provisionally, awaiting the fuller account to be given in Chapter 8): labels such as 'Nucleus', 'Rhyme' etc. still have provisional and informal descriptive status, requiring clarification.

I argued in Section 4.2.1 that there cannot be a phonological cycle prior to the morphological operations on stratum 1. This assumption was there shown to be crucial to the derivation of the 'Strict Cyclicity Effect' from the Elsewhere Condition. Here it gives rise to a derivational pattern in which, say, *myrrh* and *myrrhic* are syllabified separately: the syllable *myrrh* does not constitute an input to the phonological structure *myrrhic*.

(18)   [myrrh] →   { [[myrrh]ic]] → ...   (a)
                      { [[myrrh]]ₙ   (b)

The input to the derivation, *myrrh*, has the phonological form /mØØ/. In (18a), this form is (after the suffixation of -*ic*) syllabified as in (19a) below. In (18b) the root is converted into a word (a noun), ready to exit from stratum 1. Its syllabification is as in (19b) below.

(19)   a.   b.

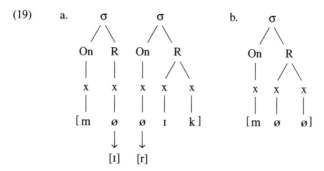

In (19a), the onset-[r] is produced by rule (14) of Chapter 6, and the [ɪ] by the Spelling Pronunciation Rule (19) of Chapter 5. Note that in (19b), the 'ØØ' sequence becomes a rhyme prior to entering into stratum 2. The specification [− consonantal] automatically arises in both instances of 'Ø'. This is, then, the form in which *myrrh* enters into stratum 2, to yield [mɜː] as well as, possibly, [mɜːrɪ] (*myrrhy*). I turn to the stratum-2 derivation of such forms presently, concluding here that (given the constraint discussed in Chapter 5 whereby schwa syllables are unstressable) the model of lexical phonology proposed here produces stratum-1 alternations of the form (16b) automatically. My next point will be that the further derivation, resulting in stratum-2 *myrrh* [mɜː], *myrrhy* [mɜːrɪ], is equally automatic.

Consider again the structure for *myrrh* produced on stratum 1 (see (19b) above), where the two skeletal positions associated with 'ØØ' form a rhyme. I noted before that 'Ø' is not truly empty: it has the underlying feature [+ sonorant] and acquires [− consonantal] through rule (11) of Chapter 6. 'Ø' therefore constitutes a representational object that can be manipulated by rules. A configuration such as 'ØØ' is subject to the Obligatory Contour Principle ('OCP': Leben 1973; McCarthy 1986): identical melodies in the same constituent must merge. The rhyme melodies in (19b) above are identical; hence they will merge. To the extent to which OCP forms part of Universal Grammar, such merger of melodies is automatic as soon as the grammar permits it, so that the structure (19b) is expected to change as in (20) below, producing the long (two-x) non-consonantal melody that surfaces as [ɜː], on stratum 2:

(20)

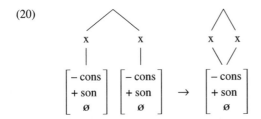

Such a change is clearly structure-changing, involving as it does the loss of a melody. It happens, moreover, in an underived environment, given that structure-building operations such as syllabification do not create derived environments. (20) is therefore blocked on stratum 1 by SCE. But it will be automatically triggered as soon as the constraints on derivations permit it. As we saw in Chapter 4, stratum 2 (in the English two-strata lexicon) has no SCE. Since I assume (with Borowsky (1989)) that Structure Preservation turns off after stratum 1, nothing stands in the way of the melody merger on stratum 2. Alternations such as [ɪr]/[ɜː] (*myrrhic – myrrh*) are therefore automatic in the present version of the theory.

I turn now to [r]-sandhi: this too follows a path that is already established. The derivation of [r]-sandhi after [ɜː] proceeds along that of surface centring diphthongs such as [ɪə], which is in any case plausible given that [ɜː] contains exactly the melody that produces [r]-sandhi. I give the structure resulting from the second analysis of [ɜː] below, for *myrrhy*:

(21)

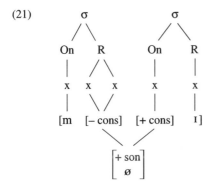

Arguably (and more speculatively), the absence of Structure Preservation on stratum 2 (and its presence on stratum 1) is also of relevance to the fact that the sequence [ɜːrV] (as in *furry, myrrhy*) cannot be monomorphemic in English. I noted in Section 2.2.6 above that complex forms such as *Toryish*,

containing hiatus vowels, are impossible on stratum 1 (as are morphologically simple forms of that structure): stratum-1 formations must conform
with the phonotactic constraints operative in morphologically simple
forms. If my analysis of the stratum-1 alternations in (16b) is accepted, and
if the ban on hiatus in morphologically simple forms as well as in stratum-1
formations is also true, then stratum 1 in English does not have the liaison
mechanism discussed in the previous sections: while (as a structure-building operation) permissible on that stratum under SCE, it is barred by
Structure Preservation. A structure like [ɜːrV] cannot then on stratum 1
have the form (21) for two reasons: the melody merger (20) cannot happen
there, as we saw earlier; and the third skeletal position (resulting in [r])
cannot 'liaise'. The alternative way of producing monomorphemic [ɜːrV]
would be the sequence (22):

(22)   *   x   x   x
              | | |
              ø   ø   ø

This sequence is ill-formed in English: it cannot be syllabified unambiguously. Note that the segmental sequence *[rɜː] is equally impossible.

So, owing to OCP, [ɜː] groups with the centring (surface) diphthongs.
It is subject to liaison on stratum 2 (and postlexically) but cannot arise,
as a biskeletal melody, on stratum 1. The picture presented here accounts
automatically for the alternations given in (16b) above as well as for the
production of [ɜː], with the possibility of [r]-sandhi, later in the derivation. Also accounted for is the impossibility of [ɜːrV] in monomorphemic
forms.

7.4   More on stratum 1: /ɔØ/, /ɑØ/ and the nature of stratum-1 'regularity'

I return once more to the analysis, proposed in Section 7.2, whereby the
long low vowels in RP are underlying centring diphthongs. We have seen
that the stratum-2 and postlexical characteristics of that analysis fit in
with the analysis of [r]-sandhi: the natural-class problem of the vowels
triggering [r]-sandhi is avoided. But nothing has been said about the
stratum-1 behaviour of these vowels. I shall show here that this analysis of
the long low vowels is able to account for a number of stratum-1 alternations in a way that closely mirrors the stratum-1 behaviour of surface [ɜː],
discussed in the preceding section. This will raise the question of how the

presence of such stratum-1 regularity figures in the overall evaluation of the analysis.

Consider the following alternating forms:

(23)   a. [ɑː ~ a]   isobar – isobaric
                        tartar – tartaric
                        Bulgar – Bulgaric
                        Feldspar – Feldsparic
                        quasar – quasaric

       b. [ɔː ~ ɒ]   abhor – abhorrent, horror – horrible etc.
                        meteor – meteoric
                        (poly-)histor – historic

Examples of this kind are scarce, mainly because items expected to be candidates on historical grounds tend to have lost the full-vowel quality in the final syllable in modern RP, and for most speakers now end in schwa instead (for example *Pindar, sonar* as well as the agent suffix *-or*). Indeed, even of *tartar* the more common RP pronunciation is [tɑːtə]. Such cases involving schwa, if they alternate in the way here relevant, follow the *metal–metallic* pattern established in Chapter 5. Moreover, probably all cases involving root-final [ɑː ɔː] not deriving from historic-[r] sources are non-Latinate in origin (*shah, saw*) and therefore fail to attract the relevant stratum-1 suffixes under the [±Latinate] constraint. For that reason, no stratum-1 cases involving intrusive [r] after these vowels are available, while stratum-1 linking [r] (accompanied by vowel alternations) is attested by the examples given in (23). The same is true for surface [ɜː]: I noted before that this vowel has, with few exceptions (*colonel*, here irrelevant), only arisen in historic-[r] contexts. Note that these accidental gaps allow no conclusions to be drawn regarding the possibility in principle of intrusive [r] occurring on stratum 1.

Three observations may be made about the examples in (23). First, and unsurprisingly, all these forms attract linking [r], in the normal way, between words and before stratum-2 suffixes (*isobar is, abhorring* etc.). Second, the vowel alternations listed here are strikingly parallel to those given in (16b) above (*myrrh – myrrhic* etc.). In historical terms, the difference is accounted for by the fact that comparatively early in the development of non-rhoticity (in the fifteenth century, according to Horn and Lehnert (1954: 444); see also Lutz (1991: 161)), the non-low short/lax vowels merged into [ɜ], here denoted '∅', before rhyme /r/ (which had not been lost by then). But the low short vowels remained distinct while the following tautosyllabic /r/ was still present, as well as of course after its loss. The diachronic loss of the melodies [ɪ ɛ ʌ] in the same context has resulted in the synchronic opacity of alternations of the type *myrrh – myrrhic* (except through the spelling), as we have seen. But the parallel low-vowel alternations are transparent, as I shall show below.

The third observation is in itself twofold. On the one hand, it is notable that all alternating forms listed in both (23) and (16b) involve suffixes attached, either generally or in the relevant specific cases, on stratum 1. Alternations of the form *myrrhic – myrrhy, abhorrent – abhorring* vindicate therefore the version of lexical stratification given in Chapter 2; in fact they constitute an argument in favour of lexical stratification that has, to my knowledge, not been put forward in the literature. On the other hand, many of the suffixes involved in these stratum-1 alternations have in the literature been associated with vowel shortening (SPE: 180; Myers 1987; Yip 1987). It may be argued, therefore, that the long–short alternations displayed by these examples are the result of synchronic shortening rules, rather than (as I shall argue) the automatic effects of stratification. Note, however, that the case for the shortening-by-rule of the preceding vowel has not been made for all the suffixes listed in (23) (compare *audible* vs. *horrible*, for example, both of which must be stratum-1 formations) and that, moreover, this shortening is by no means exceptionless: in the case of *-ic*, which dominates those lists, *scenic* always and *systemic* often has a long vowel, which in the latter case is not even underlying. If the cases listed in (23) can (as they will) be shown to be derived without a synchronic shortening operation then the putative existence of synchronic shortening effects will not invalidate the derivation proposed here. In fact, the case for shortening rules triggered generally by certain suffixes (or generally on stratum 1) will be weakened by free rides through the shortening rule in the forms discussed here.

The stratum-1 derivations of the forms given in (23) above (*tartar* etc.) are parallel to that of *myrrh – myrrhic*, discussed under (18) in the preceding section. The only difference is that in the *tartar* cases no vowel melody needs to be supplied by a spelling-driven rule. The absence of a pre-morphology cycle ensures that *tartar* and *tartaric* are syllabified separately, resulting in different configurations where the '∅' is associated with a rhyme in the former and with an onset in the latter form, where it gives rise to [r]. (24a) below gives the syllable structure of the relevant part of *tartaric*; (24b) that of *tartar*. (*Abhorrent – abhor* obviously follow the same pattern.)

(24)   a.

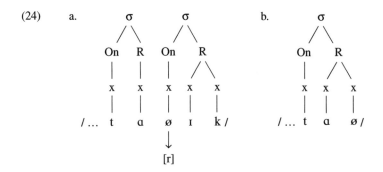

Stratum-1 alternations of the type *tartar – tartaric, abhor – abhorrent* are, then, regular in terms of this model's version of the characteristics of that stratum. Equally, the form *Bulgarian* is produced by a transparent synchronic derivation: the vowel is subject to 'CiV-Tensing' and subsequent Vowel Shift (SPE: 181; Halle and Mohanan 1985; McMahon 1990). (I return to the centring diphthong [ɛə] in *Bulgarian* below.) But we have to bear in mind that the availability of a regular derivational path producing such forms, however interesting and perhaps welcome, does not 'prove' the correctness of other aspects of this analysis; in fact, it supports that analysis only weakly. Stratum 1, as I showed in earlier chapters, is the lexicon's repository for irregular derivations and listed information; the synchronic irregularity of a given alternating pair on stratum 1 should therefore be neither surprising nor disturbing. Indeed, pairs that appear similar to *abhor – abhorrent*, involving vowel-plus-∅ underliers, do not follow regular derivational paths (any longer) in RP: consider the following.

(25)   a. myrrh – myrrhic   b. sincere – sincerity
        deter – deterrent   compare – comparative
        occur – occurrence

For derivations of the type (25a), we have seen that no derivation on purely phonological grounds is available that would predict the vowel qualities in the morphologically complex forms. The relevant information is made available by the orthographic representation only (which, however, has a regular input into the stratum-1 phonology, as I showed in Chapter 5). For illiterate speakers, such alternations are entirely irregular. They were entirely regular, of course, prior to the neutralisation of the [ɪ ɛ ʌ] contrast before tautosyllabic /r/; and they still are regular in conservative Scottish Standard English, where that neutralisation has not occurred (Giegerich

1992a: 63). The point is that their phonological regularity, in the sense of transparency, has now disappeared from RP.

Cases of the type (25b) would be synchronically regular if surface [ɪə ɛə] were synchronically derived from underlying /iːr eːr/: only then can the vowel alternations be produced by known level-1 rules (Trisyllabic Laxing, Vowel Shift etc.; McMahon 1990), parallel to cases such as *obscene – obscenity, profane – profanity* etc. But while, *ceteris paribus*, /iːr eːr/ are still synchronic underliers of *sincere, compare* etc. in rhotic varieties of English, RP [ɪə ɛə] are no longer so derived, as we have seen. What has happened in *sincere – sincerity* etc. is that the morphologically simple member of the pair has changed so as to revise the underlying representation while the other member has not changed. The diachronic change of underliers from /iːr eːr/ to present-day /ɪØ ɛØ/ in RP and other non-rhotic varieties has clearly put paid to any synchronic regularity: under the analysis proposed by McMahon (1990) and here adopted (recall Section 4.3), vowel shift of lax vowels is subject to SCE and affects only vowels whose laxness is the result of a rule. As the /ɪ/ in *sincere* does not constitute an environment so derived, it is not subject to Vowel Shift. The [ɛ] of *sincerity* must, therefore, be listed with that form. Such listing is not unusual, as we have on several occasions noted before; it is, moreover, predictable once again through the spelling. For any analysis of productive (stratum-2 and postlexical) regularities, the synchronic derivability of related stratum-1 alternations is an additional bonus (given empirical support for their regularity); but such alternations do not constitute the main agenda for the analysis. If any analysis is left with a residue of synchronic irregularity then that residue must be, in English, located on stratum 1. Note that this strategy, itself predicted by the present model of lexical stratification, differs sharply from that of early Generative Phonology, which concerned itself predominantly with the regularisation of (in our terms) stratum-1 alternations.

To return, one more time, to [ɔː]: once the underlier of this vowel has been revised (as it patently has been in London English /oː/), this stratum-1 alternation, too, joins the irregular ranks of *sincere – sincerity, myrrh – myrrhic*, as well as *clear – clarify, drama – dramatic* etc. The point made here is that stratum-1 processes by their very nature must be expected to become less regular, rather than more regular, over time, and that (as predicted) the rule inversion witnessed above in London English results in the irregularisation, rather than regularisation, of associated stratum-1 alternations.

7.5   Concluding remarks: on the RP vowel inventory

In the course of the preceding chapters, the set of underlying vowels assumed for RP has undergone almost constant revision, and indeed expansion. I summarise the results in this section, as well as going into one or two unexplained details.

I have been making two central assumptions in the preceding chapters. The first has been that there is a tense/lax dichotomy among the vowels of RP, whereby tense vowels are associated with two skeletal positions (thereby surfacing as long) and lax vowels with one skeletal position. The recognition of this well-known dichotomy does not in itself imply that the tense/lax distinction is underlying and the skeletal association derived by rule, but I tentatively follow this path of derivation. There are in fact no details in the analyses presented here that could not be produced by the alternative derivational strategy whereby the skeletal association is underlying and the tenseness specification redundant. What was more important to the argument was that tense vowels surface as off-gliding diphthongs in RP; I argued in Chapter 6 that at least the diphthongisation of the mid vowels into [eɪ oʊ] may be lexical (to be precise: stratum 2).

Tenseness is, however, defined only among non-low vowels (Halle 1977; Wood 1975). Low vowels cannot be tense; they cannot therefore be associated with two skeletal positions early in the derivation. This point was important in the analysis of [ɑː ɔː], which for that reason alone must be underlying centring diphthongs.

The second assumption that has proved central to the overall picture is that [ə] and [r] have been recognised as 'allophones' of the same underlier, represented as the 'empty' melody /Ø/. This, as I argued in Chapter Six, is the crucial point in our understanding of [r]-sandhi. And it is an insight that has knock-on effects throughout the system of centring diphthongs and related vowels and vowel sequences.

The next relevant point, made as early as in Chapter 5, was that [ɜː], despite its occasional involvement in alternations with full vowels (*myrrh – myrrhic, deter – deterrent* etc.), cannot be derived from full-vowel underliers (in our terms, */ɪØ εØ/ etc., where the use of 'Ø' is independently motivated). Instead, the full vowels in derived forms such as *myrrhic, deterrent* must be listed (or gleaned from the orthographic representation). The underlier shared by this set of vowels must then be /ØØ/.

This analysis had important, in fact crucial, repercussions in the overall system: it facilitates in turn the analysis of the surface centring diphthongs [ɪə ɛə ʊə] as /ɪ∅ ɛ∅ ʊ∅/. These underliers are independently enforced by my rejection of the derivation of these vowels from underlying /iːr/ etc., through the synchronic breaking-and-/r/-deletion analysis advocated by Kamińska (1995), as well as independently by my rejection of /r/ as an underlying segment in RP. So, the stipulation of /iː∅/ etc. as the underlier of [ɪə ɛə ʊə] is also rejected. Importantly, /ɪ∅ ɛ∅ ʊ∅/ are available as under-liners for [ɪə ɛə ʊə] only if they do not figure in the analysis of [ɜː], which, as I showed, they do not. The model of Lexical Phonology developed here rules out the derivation of [ɜː] from full-vowel underliers; and it also rules out the derivation of the surface centring diphthongs from abstract underli-ers. The analysis of the centring diphthongs presented here, where underli-ers are surface-true (except for the stipulation of /∅/), is therefore predicted by the model.

　　There is, in fact, a further reason why the analysis summarised above is inescapable, apart from the arguments already presented. This analysis now frees the sequence /iː∅/ for being the underlying sequence in *trachea* and perhaps *theatre, theory* etc. (in citation-form trisyllabic pronunciations). These, as will become clear in Chapter 8, emerge as [iː.ə], through the mecha-nisms of syllabification, in a straightforward way. Once again, if we had adopted the /iː∅/ analysis for the centring diphthongs then we would not be able to account for the sequence in *trachea* etc. without having to abandon the crucial insight that [r] and schwa are underlyingly identical.

　　One question that remains to be settled is that of the underlying represen-tations of the stressed vowels in forms such as *cereal, fairy, fury*. In this (tau-tomorphemic) context, the long/tense vowels [iː eː uː] fail to contrast with the centring diphthongs [ɪə ɛə ʊə]; but the handbooks (such as Gimson 1994) transcribe them phonemically as the latter. Consider the (RP) distri-bution of vowels before tautomorphemic [r] given in (26) below, with transcriptions adapted from D. Jones (1991):

(26)　　a. [ɪr]　　　b. [ʌr]　　　c. [ɛr]　　　d. [ɒr]
　　　　　mirror　　　hurry　　　herring　　　moral
　　　　　squirrel　　currant　　merry　　　sorrow

　　　　e. [ɪər]　　f. [ʊər]　　g. [ɛər]　　h. [ɑːr]
　　　　　cereal　　　fury　　　Mary　　　safari
　　　　　era　　　　curia　　　vary　　　harem

　　　　i. [ɔːr]　　j. [aɪər]　　k. [aʊər]　　l. [ɔɪər]
　　　　　story　　　pirate　　　Lowry　　　Moira
　　　　　chorus　　tyrant　　　Maori

In this context, the whole vowel inventory of RP is attested with the exceptions of [ɜː] (already discussed), the *put/putt* and *flow/flaw* contrasts (there are no *[ʊrɪ], *[oʊrɪ]), which I ignore here, and the contrast between tense vowels and centring diphthongs (with the sole exception of the loan form *Beirut*, pronounced like *bay root* despite the absence of a morphological boundary[10]).

Two analyses are available to account for the occurrence of centring diphthongs before tautomorphemic [r]. The first is simply to posit /ɪØ ɛØ ʊØ/ in this context, with a filter that rules out tense vowels before [r]. The second is to posit underlyingly tense vowels and to produce the surface diphthongs through a synchronic breaking rule. No such rule has materialised in this study so far; in fact I argued in Section 6.2.1 against its synchronic involvement in the production of surface *hear* [hɪə]. But note that in the present case, breaking would be a postlexical rule with strong phonetic motivation, affecting vowels before actual (surface) [r], while the argument against breaking in the *hear* cases formed part of the rejection of the /r/ deletion analysis of non-rhoticity. In the present set of cases, on the other hand, breaking is independently needed to account for the schwa in (26j), (26k) and (26l) above. But in order to avoid indeterminacies in setting up underlying representations for *cereal* etc., a filter of a rather strange form, referring to a heterosyllabic construction, would in turn be needed to ban underlying centring diphthongs in this context. In fact, the complementary filters needed by both alternative analyses would have to refer crucially to information across syllable boundaries, given that surface [r], which is really the crucial segment in the offending string, materialises derivationally far later than the point at which the filter has to apply, and given also that the mere sequence tense-vowel-plus-/Ø/ is not to be ruled out: it occurs in *trachea*.

This is a particularly interesting case of indeterminate underliers, and one that I do not propose to resolve. The view taken here is, in fact, that both analyses are available to the speaker, and that neither of the filters mentioned above actually exists. The reason why relevant minimal pairs do not occur is simply that if the speaker has an underlying tense vowel in such a context then he or she is still forced to implement the breaking rule, which I regard as postlexical and automatic (given the retroflex quality of RP [r]). At least the availability of the second analysis is supported by the fact that there are many speakers who in both contexts – *cereal* and *pirate* – implement breaking only very weakly. The effect of postlexical breaking does not necessarily amount to the same degree of surface diphthongisation as the underlying centring diphthong does. This view is supported, although not specifically for R P, by Wells (1990: xiii), who notes the possibility of 'vowel qualities closer to iː uː than to ɪə ʊə in words such as *periodic, purity* [. . . for . . .] many British English educated non-RP speakers'. And those speakers who have a stronger in-glide in *cereal* than they have in (triphthongal) *pirate* may well have a centring-diphthong underlier in the former. This indeterminacy may be regarded as a shortcoming of the model presented here. On the other hand, it may be a fact of life that does not lend itself to simple formal treatment: speakers may simply maintain comparatively strong breaking in *cereal* because the centring diphthong pronunciation is known to them from other items, while the surface triphthong in *pirate* is not otherwise contrastively attested. (The 'triphthong' in *fire* is heterosyllabic.) Whether such analogy is sufficient reason to revise an underlying representation, in the presence of a perfectly natural phonetic rule that is capable of producing the same effect, is a question that to my knowledge has not been settled in phonological theory. And the phonetic facts, whether the [ɪə] in *cereal* is the same as that in *beer*, or indeed in *beerier*, are far from clear.

A further argument in favour of the presence of a synchronic breaking rule in RP is provided by the occurrence of centring diphthongs in forms such as *Bulgarian*, mentioned in the preceding section: in such cases, the centring diphthong must be produced derivationally. Consider some further examples (from Lehnert 1971) which show the same pattern:

(27)   a. ether – etherial   b. secretary – secretarial
            psalter – psalterial   Caesar – Caesarian
                                        bursar – bursarial

In these cases, a lax vowel melody is specified in the derivation by the Spelling Pronunciation Rule (19) of Chapter 5, which is then subject to 'CiV-Tensing' and Vowel Shift, as was also discussed there in connection with alternations such as *marginality – marginalia*. Such alternations are parallel to the *Bulgaric – Bulgarian* pair discussed here, differing from the latter only by their failure to display surface centring diphthongs. While the tensed and shifted pre-[r] vowel – [iː] in (27a) and [eː] in (27b) – surfaces as [ɪə ɛə] respectively, the corresponding vowel in *marginalia*, not preceding [r], does not break. It has to be acknowledged, of course, that (as in earlier cases) stratum-1 forms provide only weak support for any given analysis that may result in their regularity. But there is no reason to believe that in *Bulgarian* etc. breaking itself happens on stratum 1. The centring diphthongisation found in these examples is the entirely automatic, and certainly exceptionless, reflex of tense vowels that may have arisen in the derivation before [r]. This is the same postlexical rule that also accounts for the surface centring diphthongs in (26e), (26f) and (26g) above. While we cannot have such an abstract derivation in *sincere*, as I have shown, the breaking of a tense vowel is likely to be synchronically present in the context of surface-[r]: in *cereal* and, as we see now, in *etherial*.

8   Syllables and strata

8.1   Introduction

This chapter, concerned with the predictions regarding syllable structure that are made by the present model of stratified phonology–morphology interaction, will focus on two kinds of issues. The first of these is the interaction of syllabification with the processes of the morphology. This is both a theory-internal matter, dealing with the mechanics of the lexical and post-lexical derivation, and an empirical matter, concerning the generalisations that are available regarding syllable structure and the position of syllable boundaries in the vicinity of morphological boundaries. And it is of course connected with the issue of liaison: the various sandhi phenomena – [r], [ʲ ʷ], prevocalic [ʔ] – and more generally the effect of morphological boundaries on the organisation of the speech continuum into syllables. The second issue concerns the possible existence of stratum-specific characteristics of syllable structure. While it is not inconceivable that syllabification may follow a uniform pattern throughout the derivation (in that case, the relevant mechanisms would simply not be stratum-sensitive), the opposite case whereby the syllable patterns found on different strata have different characteristics would lend valuable support to the stratification model proposed in this study. I shall show here that syllabification does indeed have a number of stratum-specific features, although the basic mechanisms are the same throughout the lexical derivation.

Obviously, stratum-specific and morphology-sensitive syllable patterns can only be defined against the background of a specific model of syllable structure, developed in turn with regard to the present derivational framework. This is the third (in fact, arguably the first) item on the agenda of this chapter. I intend to pursue here a theme, pervasive in the preceding chapters, that may be described as 'derivational realism': an approach that has led me earlier in this study to reject unwarranted synchronic structure changes – vowel shift in underived environments in Chapter 4 (following

236

McMahon 1990), similarly vowel reduction in underived environments in Chapter 5, synchronic /r/-deletion in Chapter 6, and so on. Here I shall argue that there is no synchronic resyllabification: syllable structures, once assigned, are not dismantled later in the derivation. No segments – and this argument will mainly concern domain-final and syllabic consonants – change their association with syllables during the derivation.

8.2   Syllabification and morphological structure: some facts

8.2.1   Morphologically simple words: maximal onsets and the Law of Initials

I present in this section briefly the main patterns of English syllabification, highlighting aspects that will be referred to later in this chapter. Possible overlap of syllables (ambisyllabicity) is here disregarded as far as possible.

In polysyllabic words, syllabification follows the Sonority Sequencing Generalisation ('SSG') (Selkirk 1982a, 1984), whereby sonority in onsets increases and in rhymes decreases from left to right, and the Maximal Onset Principle ('MOP'), whereby single consonants as well as consonant sequences form onsets wherever possible. Under the Law of Initials ('LOI') (Vennemann 1972a; Anderson and Jones 1974), only such consonant sequences can form morpheme-medial onsets as can also form morpheme-initial onsets in the language. Examples are given in (1):

(1)   a. a.ro.ma   b. pen.tath.lon
            ma.tron   e.nig.ma
            di.sci.pline   Ed.na
            a.gen.da   at.las

In (1a), single consonants as well as the sequences [tr pl] form onsets due to MOP; the [nd] sequence in *agenda* is barred by SSG from becoming an onset. Examples in (1b) contain consonant sequences that cannot be word onsets and that are therefore barred by LOI from becoming word-medial onsets. Syllabifications such as these are supported by stress regularities (the penultimate syllable in *pentathlon* is heavy and hence stressed while that in *discipline* is light and unstressed), as well as by allophonic phenomena: in the [tl] sequence of *atlas*, the [t] has glottal reinforcement and the [l] is fully voiced, while in the [pl] sequence of *discipline*, no glottal reinforcement is present and the [l] tends to devoice (Anderson and Jones 1974).

It would appear, then, that the three principles named above are operative in English. Of these, however, at least LOI is not necessarily universal

(Vennemann 1972a): it is possible, at least in principle, for a language not to implement LOI. In a non-LOI language, constraints on morpheme-initial onsets are not valid as constraints on morpheme-medial onsets. Following Clements and Keyser (1983) and Fudge (1969), I assume such constraints to have the form of 'filters' – negative well-formedness conditions that rule out onsets such as *[θl] in English (*pentathlon*). It follows that in a LOI language, onset filters have the form (2a) below while in a non-LOI language they have the form (2b), where the preceding morpheme-initial bracket '[' ensures that morpheme-medial onsets are unaffected by a given filter that constrains morpheme-initial (and, by implication, word-initial) onsets.

(2)   a.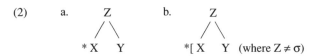

German is an interesting case in point here: Usually LOI is obeyed, but in certain instances the standard language (as described by Duden (1990)) disobeys LOI, while the colloquial variety implements this constraint without exception. *Adler* 'eagle', *Segment* 'segment' and other items syllabify as [.dl .gm] in Standard German but as [t.l k.m] colloquially, as is shown by the voicing behaviour of obstruents (Giegerich 1992b; but see Rubach (1990) for an alternative analysis).

It is possible, then, for the filters of a given language to be a mix of both kinds. (There may be 'partially-LOI languages'.) Note that in a LOI language, onset filters are of a simpler form than they are in a non-LOI language in that their operation is not restricted to any particular morphological context. In terms of relative markedness, non-LOI languages should therefore be more highly marked despite the fact that their onsets are less highly constrained (Anderson and Ewen 1987: 60). It is plausible, therefore, that the highly formal Standard variety of German should be non-LOI while the colloquial variety obeys LOI. (See Giegerich (1992b) for more detailed discussion.) For English, I take the view here that LOI is obeyed except for some very occasional violations, which will materialise below. I turn now to the effect that the presence of morphological brackets, first '[' and then ']', may have on the syllabification of a string of segments.

8.2.2   *Prefixes, compounds and syllabification: the impact of '['*

Recall from Chapter 2 that, following Kiparsky (1982), morphological bracketing is here assumed to have the following form. Prefixes enter the

derivation as '[P', suffixes as 'S]' and roots as '[R]'. A morphological operation places a set of brackets round the resulting morphologically complex
forms, so that (ignoring here the distinction between roots and words) compounds have the form '[[R][R]]', prefixations the form '[[P[R]]' and
suffixations the form '[[R]S]]'. Recall also, although this will not be relevant
here, that the transition from Root to Word (in English) results in a further
pair of brackets, hence '[[W]]', which means that typical (word) compounds
(*green-house*, *pop art*), as well as stratum-2 affixations, contain more brackets than were indicated above. Such proliferation of brackets has no effect
on syllabification (in fact, possibly no phonological effects of any kind);
what is relevant is the presence of either '[' or ']', not the depth of embed-
ding.

Below is a sample of prefixed forms.

(3)   a. V[V   b. V[C
           re-invest   reproduce
           pro-active   amoral
           de-escalate   becalm

        c. C[V   d. C[C
           ineligible   sublunar
           misinform   disproportionate
           uneven   misplace

The general pattern here is that in such forms, syllables are not formed
across the morphological bracket, '['. Indeed, [ʲ ʷ]-sandhi, caused by liaison
(Section 6.3.1 above), is absent in (3a) in the slow, 'citation form' pronunciation that is here assumed to reflect the relevant aspects of lexical representations. In (3a), (3b) and (3c) a prevocalic glottal stop may occur at the
boundary in slow pronunciation; voiceless stops in (3b) have aspiration;
and the consonant sequences straddling the bracket in (3d) do not form
onset clusters although the principles of onset formation given above
(including LOI; compare *blue*, *spray*, *split*) would permit them to do so.

D. Jones (1991) gives some examples for *in-* where the preferred (though
not exclusive) pronunciation has onset-[n] before a vowel-initial base
(*inebriation*, *inept*, *inert*). As these involve bound 'cranberry' bases, I
suggest that such forms are commonly stored as morphologically simple
items (see Chapter 3 above) and treated as such – that is, without the relevant bracket – in syllabification.[1] Such cases do not conclusively demonstrate stratum-sensitive differences in the aspect of syllabification here
discussed (although cases like *inept* must be stratum-1 forms, if they are
complex at all, for morphological reasons alone: Chapter 4 above). I show

below that, insensitive to lexical stratification, no onset formation takes place across '[' in the lexical phonology.

The apparent blocking effect of '[' on syllabification is confirmed by the behaviour of compounds: again, the citation form pronunciation shows no liaison:

(4)   a. V][V   b. V][C
           zoo animal   shoe shop
           eye ointment   fee payment
           sea elephant   tea-cup

        c. C][V   d. C][C
           pop art   camp leader
           talk assessment   bird reserve
           school inspector   off-licence

The pattern is the same as in (4) above: in citation forms, prevocalic glottal stops are possible in (4a), (4b) and (4c); voiceless stops in (4b) have aspiration; and in (4d), onsets are not maximised across '][' although LOI would permit the resulting clusters.

As I noted, such syllabification patterns will be found in slow 'citation form' pronunciation. In the more normal performance conditions of connected speech, liaison is found in (3a/4a), in the form of sandhi-[ʲ ʷ], and in (3c/4c). Indeed, such liaison is (near-)obligatory where the syllable following '[' is unstressed (*inappropriate, uneventful*). This aspect of liaison is identical with what happens between words in connected speech, and (as I show in Section 8.6 below) I regard it as part of the more general phenomenon of postlexical liaison, rather than as specific to lexical syllabification.

8.2.3   *Suffixes and syllabification: the impact of '].'*

(5)   a. V]V   b. V]C
           Maoist   clueless
           denial   freedom
           employee   boyhood

        c. C]V   d. C]C
           sincerity   glibly
           feeling   helpless
           keeper   booklet

The syllabification pattern found in (5), which again contains stratum-1 and stratum-2 forms, differs sharply from that found in (3/4) above – in a way, moreover, that does not immediately appear to form a pattern in itself.

In (5a), (5b) and (5c) liaison is obligatory: there is not even the option of a prevocalic glottal stop at the morphological boundary. Linking [r] (*sincerity*) is obligatory in this context, as we saw in Chapter 6. The [l] is clear in *feeling* and the [p] aspirated in *keeper*. While such cases clearly show onset formation across ']', this generalisation does not hold in (5d): there, the syllable boundary coincides with the morphological bracket despite the fact that, again, onset maximisation across the bracket would produce the phonotactically well-formed onsets /bl pl kl/. The only available generalisation for (5) is this: in the context of ']', onsets are associated with single melodies, which may be located on either side of ']', and no onsets remain empty (in the sense in which they do in (3a), (3b) and (3c), for example). There are, notably, no English suffixes that begin with consonant sequences; the syllabification of hypothetical constructions of the form 'V]CCV' cannot therefore be attested.

This generalisation about the syllabification of suffixes may be pursued in two different directions. We may conclude that the different morphological categories Root, Suffix and Prefix obey different phonotactics and are therefore subject to different syllabification devices.[2] This would effectively result in the morphological labelling of the prosodic category 'σ' – a perhaps not unreasonable strategy, but not one that is required here: the relevant information is encoded in the morphological bracketing. Instead we may therefore account for the behaviour of 'suffix syllables' by making the syllabification mechanisms sensitive to morphological bracketing. This approach, to be pursued in this chapter, will have to take account especially of the behaviour of final consonants before ']': why do these go with the next syllable if, and only if, the following suffix is vowel-initial, as for example in *feel – fee.ling, divine – divi.nity*? I review previous approaches to this question in the next section, before presenting my own analysis.

8.3 Domain-final consonants and the size of the rhyme: extrametricality and resyllabification

The perhaps most obvious approach to alternations such as *feel – fee.ling, divine – divi.nity* involves resyllabification. This implies exhaustive syllabification of the affixation base prior to the attachment of the suffix, followed by the removal of the base-final consonant from its coda position after the attachment of the suffix, and its incorporation (as onset) in the newly formed following syllable. This resyllabification analysis was suggested for the lexical phonology of English (without a full analysis) by

Mohanan (1985), who stipulated a specific rule of consonant resyllabification. A fuller study along similar lines by Levin (1985), developed for German by Rubach (1990), treated the resyllabification of domain-final consonants after the attachment of a vowel-initial suffix as the effect of a universal 'CV rule', which accounted for the universal CV shape of the basic syllable (see Section 8.2.1 above for English) and, in addition, had resyllabifying power so as to re-associate domain-final consonants. We should note here that such an analysis would not pose technical problems for the lexical derivation in the present framework. While the CV rule is evidently structure-changing whenever it resyllabifies previously syllabified consonants, it does so only in derived environments: the rule resyllabifies only where a vowel has been introduced on the right of the consonant in question, as part of a morphological operation for example. Note, moreover, that in stratum-1 cases like *divi.nity* etc., the lexical derivation proposed in Chapter 4 (discussed further in Section 8.5.1 below) has no need for resyllabification under Levin's or indeed anybody's analysis of prosodic structure: in the absence of a pre-morphology cycle, *divinity* and *divine* are syllabified separately, in each case from scratch.

The problems of the resyllabification analysis are, then, not of a technical or theory-internal nature; they are more general (and more important) than that. If it is the case that syllable structure alternations in the context of 'l', like *feel – fee.ling*, are universal then universal grammar is saddled with a structure-changing rule that applies in identical contexts in all languages. The cost of such an operation is in part offset by the fact that the CV rule, which executes the structure change in this context, is deployed elsewhere without changing structure; but the power that this rule must be endowed with is rather suspicious: clearly, compelling arguments are needed in favour of such a device. Such arguments would be expected to have the form of significant generalisations, depending crucially on the short-term derivational association of the consonant in question with the preceding syllable, prior to its resyllabification. And it would appear that there are no such generalisations to be had. On the contrary: there are significant regularities in the structure of syllables and higher-order prosodic units that become apparent only when domain-final consonants are excluded from domain-final syllables, rather than being associated with them. The arguments (again in the shape of generalisations regarding syllable and higher-order structure) are well known; in some instances they pre-date the resyllabification approach.

Hayes (1982) demonstrated conclusively that domain-final consonants are 'extrametrical' in that they do not figure in the calculation of syllable weight for the purposes of stress placement. The basic (if not exceptionless) generalisation is that in nouns the penultimate syllable is stressed if it is heavy, and the antepenult if the penult is light (see (6a) and (6b) below), while in verbs the final syllable is stressed if heavy and the penult if the final syllable is light ((6c and (6d)):

(6) a. aróma   CVː   b. cámera   CV
        agénda   CVC   América CV
     c. maintáin CVː<u>C</u>]   d. édit   CV<u>C</u>]
        usúrp   CVC<u>C</u>]   márry   CV]

A uniformly valid calculation of syllable weight (resulting in the definition that a syllable is heavy if and only if its rhyme branches) is possible only if domain-final consonants (underlined in (6)) are excluded from that calculation. The stress generalisation itself is not exceptionless – stress rules seldom are. *Bádminton* and *rubélla* etc. violate the stress rule for nouns and in *cadét, hotél* – independently exceptional for their final stress (Giegerich 1992a: 183) – the stressed syllable is light under this calculation of syllable weight if the final consonant is extrametrical; but the more relevant sub-generalisation of verb stress expressed in (6c) and (6d) is remarkably free from exceptions. Hayes (1982) was concerned with foot structure and did not offer a model of syllabification that would account for consonant extrametricality in terms of syllable structure. As was argued in Giegerich (1985: 48ff.; 1986: 18ff.), such a model would have to bear out the point that domain-final consonants are excluded from syllabification not only for the purposes of stress assignment but also in a more general way. Recall the starting point of the present argument: whenever a consonant is extrametrical for stress purposes it is also unstable in terms of syllabification, going with the next syllable whenever an opportunity arises, in terms of the morphological derivation. While the alternative resyllabification analysis handles this instability, it has to abandon Hayes' stress generalisation given that under a resyllabification analysis, exhaustive syllabification must precede both resyllabification and stress assignment.

For different reasons (and, as we shall see, in not necessarily identical contexts), the device of extrametricality to account for the behaviour of domain-final consonants was also invoked by Borowsky (1989). Concerned with rhyme phonotactics rather than foot structure, as Hayes was, and drawing on earlier work by Itô (1986), Borowsky employs extrametricality in accounting for the fact that rhymes containing three skeletal positions are common only in word-final position: both long vowels plus single consonants and short vowels plus consonant clusters are possible there (*dream*, *help*, *usurp*); but in medial position such sequences are (near) impossible. Typically in morpheme-medial position, vowels are short in closed syllables, and tautosyllabic consonant clusters absent. In Borowsky's account, the ill-formedness of hypothetical forms like **areelba*, **agelmda* is due to a constraint on stratum-1 syllabification whereby rhymes can only contain two skeletal positions. In similar form, this point was also made in Giegerich (1986: Section 2.3; 1989: Section 1.3.1) as well as, again similarly, by Rice (1989), who also advocates consonant extrametricality. The exceptions to this generalisation, such as *an.gel*, *shoul.der*, *poul.try*, conform by and large with the sub-generalisation whereby the melody in the third rhyme position and that in the following onset are homorganic. In terms of autosegmental representations, the third skeletal position therefore partially shares a melody with the following position and is thus licensed within the structure. Borowsky then argues that this generalisation about syllable structure only holds on stratum 1, and that on stratum 2 (where the Structure Preservation Condition no longer operates) the syllabification of domain-final stray consonants is possible and rhymes can grow to three skeletal positions.

In this way Borowsky also accommodates the regularity among the irregular (stratum-1) morphology whereby the addition of a single-consonant suffix induces vowel shortening. Following Myers (1987), she argues that the shortening of the vowel in *kept*, *left*, *dealt*, *dreamt* etc., as well as that in *width* etc., is due to a stratum-1 shortening rule triggered by the addition of the (irregular) past-tense suffix *-t* or derivational *-th*. Constrained by Strict Cyclicity, this shortening does not affect morphologically simple forms of similar segmental composition (*traipse*, *coax*, *count*); nor does it operate on stratum 2 (*seemed*, *cokes*). This generalisation can be maintained in the account of stratum-1 syllabification to be presented in this chapter; and it constitutes a nice example of a stratum-1 structure-changing rule and its constraints (similar to Trisyllabic Shortening, which under Myers' (1987) account is in fact part of the same regularity). But, as we have come to expect of stratum-1 rules, there is nothing 'natural' about such shortening. This descriptive generalisation provides no more support for any model of syllable structure in English than Trisyllabic Shortening provides evidence for foot structure: *traipse* and *dreamed* are possible English syllables, just as *nightingale, mightily* (and indeed *obesity*) demonstrate the language's ability to form trisyllabic feet with long stressed vowels. Indeed, the consonants that the morphology procures to induce this shortening are, with striking regularity, coronal obstruents and hence extrametrical on quite separate grounds. Such consonants are 'appendices', supernumerary to the rhyme in addition to the third skeletal position found, for example, in *keep*: recall *traip͜se* etc. (Fujimura 1979; Kiparsky 1981; Giegerich 1992a: Section 6.4.5). Given also that forms like *kept* are the sporadic residue left behind by a roughly thousand-year-old sound change, and that the derivational morphology of nominalising *-th* is clearly unproductive, nothing much would be lost if such vowel alternations were simply listed on stratum 1 as are, in any case, the forms that are subject to such irregular inflection and, in the case of *width*, to nominalisation through *-th*.

Borowsky claims, then, that morpheme-medially and inside stratum-1 formations, rhymes can have two skeletal positions only; one or more further skeletal positions can occur only at the edge of the domain (*traipse* etc.) and remain stray until the stratum-2 syllabification mechanisms attach them. I shall subscribe to the basic argument below, without however making the same claim regarding a putative difference in the syllabification devices of the two strata. One argument against proposing such a difference is that three-position rhymes (other than those involving homorganic clusters mentioned above: *angel* etc.) do occur sporadically inside simplex forms (*Kingsley, Grimsby, Orkney* etc.: Borowsky 1989: 154) and stratum-1 derivatives: *absorption, sculpture* etc. Borowsky's account predicts that such forms cannot be syllabified, which is patently false. It is difficult to see how her model can tolerate a single exception. Such exceptions are in fact not as scarce as Borowsky claims: under a model that is appropriately restrictive on the morphological side, the cases that she puts down to stratum 2 without further argument (*ordnance, vestment, harpsichord* etc.) must be stratum-1 formations, if they are morphologically complex in Present-day English at all. *Ad hoc* stratal affiliations of particular forms are no longer possible here. As we shall see below, a number of such forms are obscured compounds; the point is that the phonology is evidently able to syllabify them. Supernumerary ('stray') consonants are not strictly confined to the edge of the domain. The view I shall take below is that such items are amenable to a unified definition referring to their historic origin as morphologically complex forms, and marked synchronically merely in the sense that they require the operation, and incur the derivational 'cost', of an additional rule.

Another argument against confining the relevant constraint to stratum 1 emerges when we attempt a unified account of the three aspects identified so far of the behaviour of domain-final consonants: unstable syllabification (*feel – fee.ling*), Hayes' extrametricality for stress purposes (*edit, usurp*) and Borowsky's phonotactically motivated version of extrametricality. Hayes' version of extrametricality affects possibly all and certainly only those consonants that also show unstable syllabification; but Borowsky's account of extrametricality notably fails to capture all of them: for final consonants occupying the second skeletal position in the rhyme (*edit, develop* etc.), extrametricality is not predicted by Borowsky's account and 'must be marked in some way or another' (Borowsky 1989: footnote 8). As it happens, Hayes' extrametricality has fewer relevant exceptions (if indeed any) than Borowsky's account does; and the phenomenon of unstable syllabification has none at all. While Hayes' extrametricality is only needed on stratum 1, where the rules of foot formation operate, unstable syllabification is found throughout the suffixation morphology: *divi.nity* (stratum 1), *fee.ling, war.mer, wri.ter, sweetne.sses* (stratum 2). A unified account of all the behavioural aspects of domain-final consonants must, therefore, posit identical syllabification mechanisms for the entire lexical derivation: Hayes' extrametricality will be an automatic by-product; and Borowsky's findings regarding restrictions on rhymes will have the status of preferred syllable shapes, rather than that of obligatory stratum-1 shapes. Before going into this, let us review yet another aspect of the behaviour of domain-final consonants.

As I noted above, the only kind of evidence that would justify a resyllabification analysis has the form of generalisations that crucially depend on the final consonant's attachment, as (part of) the coda, to the preceding nucleus. Extrametrical consonants, on the other hand, do not form part of the syllable structure. It follows that any restrictions on the possible range of such consonants cannot refer to syllable structure (to be precise: to coda structure, if indeed there is such a constituent under such a model). I subscribe to the latter view here: there is, to my knowledge, no incontrovertible evidence – phonotactic or otherwise, and *pace* Hall (1994) – to suggest that final consonants form part of the preceding syllable at any point of the derivation. But 'extrametrical' cannot be taken to mean that, where the feature composition of such consonants is concerned, anything goes. What does go is one or more coronal obstruents (which, as 'appendix', need not conform with SSG: *books, texts*) and/or, preceding any appendix, a consonant that is less sonorous than the one before it. *Alp, lilt, bulk, film, earl* etc. are monosyllabic because the final consonant sequence conforms with SSG; the final, 'extrametrical' consonant in fact constitutes a relative sonority minimum in the sequence (albeit flanked only on the left). Compare *apple* [apl] and *little* [lɪtl], disyllabic because the sonority trough is on the penultimate segment. It is this sonority-trough status that characterises the 'extrametrical' consonant (ignoring appendices) and restricts its melodic range. There are ways other than the coda-SSG of imposing this restriction.

I argued in Giegerich (1985: Section 2.2.1) that the extrametrical consonant has the structural status of onset to a following 'zero syllable', showing elsewhere (Giegerich 1986: Section 2.3; 1989: Section 1.3.1) for German that any phonotactic restrictions holding between the final consonant and the one preceding it (i.e. the 'coda', as in *alp*) are of two kinds. They are either due to SSG, and hence equally well expressed by an analysis that employs a generalised version of MOP in treating the final consonant in *alp* (and the final sequence in *apple* [apl]) as onset; or they are strictly linear, often referring to place features and making no reference to suprasegmental structure at all. This analysis, including the postulate of a following zero ('degenerate') syllable, has since been adopted by Government Phonology (Kaye 1990; Kaye, Lowenstamm and Vergnaud 1990; Harris 1994; Harris and Gussmann 1998). Taking the form of an 'empty nucleus', this postulate is in fact central to the theory of phonological government. Harris (1994: Chapter 4) investigates 'coda' phonotactics in detail, concluding that:

> (a) In failing to induce closed-rhyme shortness, final consonants behave quantitatively like word-internal onsets rather than like internal codas. (b) The final consonant position enjoys more or less the same degree of distributional freedom as an internal onset. (c) The systematic phonotactic dependencies observable within final two-consonant clusters are more or less identical to those operating in internal coda–onset clusters. (Harris 1994: 161)

The present study is concerned neither with foot structure (my original motivation for positing the 'zero syllable': Giegerich 1981; also Burzio 1994) nor with phonological government: short-cuts will be taken in both areas of analysis. For that reason alone I choose here not to pursue the idea of empty nuclei or degenerate syllables. Without having to invoke such empty positions in the analysis of final consonants, the analysis of syllable structure presented below will be compatible with a model that does invoke them.

8.4   Syllabification without resyllabification

8.4.1   Preliminaries

In this section I present a model of syllabification that is structure-building throughout the derivation, dispensing therefore with resyllabification rules of the kind advocated by Levin (1985) and Mohanan (1986), and indeed with any processes that dismantle previously erected parts of syllables in the course of the derivation. The basic principles, which owe much to the 'extrametricality' (Itô 1986; Borowsky 1989; Rice 1989) and Government (Harris 1994) accounts reviewed above as well as drawing on Giegerich (1986, 1989, 1992b), are discussed here; further details, amendments and supplements follow later in this chapter.

I have been assuming throughout this study that in phonological representations, 'segments' are expressed on two tiers: the melody tier and the skeleton tier (Levin 1983, 1985). This representational model and its variant, 'CV-phonology' (Clements and Keyser 1983), are widely accepted; what is worth highlighting for present purposes is the nature and status of the skeleton tier. Phonological elements on that tier, here represented as 'x', are the terminal elements of the constituency structure that characterises a syllable; they have no other formal status. A statement regarding the number of skeletal elements associated with a given melody is a statement about the number of nodes immediately dominating that melody. Epenthesis on the skeleton tier (for example 'prosodic' schwa epenthesis; Giegerich 1987) is short for the causation of branching in the relevant constituent (in this case the rhyme). The function of skeletal elements as 'timing slots' (Clements and Keyser 1983) is a side effect of this basic status. While it can be assumed that in the default case, there is a simple one-to-one correspondence between melodic elements and skeletal elements, there may occasionally be a two-to-one correspondence between whole or partial melodic units and skeletal elements (as in the case of the English affricates /tʃ/ and /dʒ/ (Ewen 1980, 1982; Giegerich 1992a: Section 10.3), characterised probably by a sequence of manner melodies associated with a single (shared) place specification and in turn with a single skeletal element.

Moreover, as was discussed in Section 7.5 above, the tense–lax contrast found, in most varieties of English (including RP), among non-low monophthongs gives rise to a long–short distinction. Such lexical length distinctions are then expressed in such a way that tense vowel melodies are associated with two skeletal elements, and lax melodies (by default) with one.

The overall picture regarding the relation between melody and skeleton is, then, that the segmental contrasts of the language are, by and large, expressed on the melody tier and that the skeletal representation of a given melody is assigned by means of structure-building rules. This does not preclude the possibility that skeletal information may be stored underlyingly for certain melodies. One such case concerns the English affricates, noted above. Moreover it may well be the case that in varieties of English in which the long–short distinction among vowels is not accompanied by a straightforward tense–lax distinction (for example Australian English; Giegerich 1992a: Section 3.7), the inventory of vowel contrasts is underlyingly bifurcated into 'single-x' and 'double-x' vowels. Nothing hinges here, incidentally, on the question whether in RP the tense–lax distinction or the skeletal distinction is the underlying one. I assume the former (see Giegerich (1992a: Chapter 3) for discussion); but if the latter is found to be the case (as assumed by Halle and Mohanan (1985), among others) then in any given string, part of the melody/skeleton association is already defined before the relevant structure-building syllabification rules come into operation.

These rules of assigning skeleta to melodies are here incorporated into the mechanisms that build syllable structure: in stating the number of terminal nodes that a given melody is to be associated with in the structure, they constitute the obvious first step in the erection of syllable structure. The basic mechanism comprises three such steps, here called 'Onset' Formation, Rhyme Formation and Syllable Formation respectively. The first of those, however, does not actually assign a prosodic category; the intrasyllabic constituent 'Onset' will be shown to be relationally defined as the left daughter of the syllable node ('σ'). For that reason (and in fact for other reasons also, which will strike the reader presently), the use of the term 'onset' is here of mnemonic value only. It may be objected that if the onset is relationally defined then so is the rhyme (as the right-hand daughter of 'σ'). This is true. The reasons why Rhyme Formation nevertheless assigns a prosodic category (the Rhyme) will be given in Section 8.4.3.

8.4.2   'Onset' formation and the sonority minimum

Most theories of the phonological syllable rely on the assumption that syllables are associated with sonority peaks in strings of segments, and that in turn a given segment's sonority value ('relative loudness') can be read off a scale, probably universal, on which a given language's segments are ranked (Ladefoged 1983; Selkirk 1982a; Rice 1992; Zec 1995). Attention has traditionally focused on two aspects of this sonority-based definition of the syllable: first, on the peak itself, where in addition to its status as relative sonority maximum, local constraints come into play such that in English, for example, only vowels and, domain-finally (*little*, *button* etc.), sonorant consonants can be syllabic. I deal with the latter in Section 8.4.2. Second, the phonotactics of consonant sequences on either side of the nucleus is subject to sonority-based generalisations. The standard assumption here is that such sequences are subject to SSG (Selkirk 1982a), amended by statements of language-specific gaps in the range of sequences obeying the overall pattern (Fudge 1969, 1987; Clements and Keyser 1983; Giegerich 1992a: Chapter 6). As already noted in Section 8.2.1, such statements of gaps (ruling out, for example, onsets of the form */θl /dn etc.) are here assumed to have the form of negative well-formedness conditions (filters of the form (2) above), usually expressing LOI (Vennemann 1972a).

Here I focus on the second of these two aspects of the syllable in relation to the structure of onsets, and invoke a third one that has, in formal terms, received rather less attention. This is the generalisation whereby the positions of syllable boundaries can be predicted with reference to the sonority trough in the sequence. In sequences allowed as onsets by the relevant filters, MOP predicts the syllable boundary to occur immediately on the left of the segment whose sonority is smaller than that of its neighbours. (Recall the examples given in (1) above.) Given also the constraint whereby English onset sequences cannot contain more than two consonants (for example /pl kr/: *play*, *crew*) except where such a sequence is preceded by /s/ (as in *splay*, *screw*, disregarded for the moment) the principle governing the formation of onsets has the form given in (7) below. Note that the emerging constituent is maximally binary, given that English has no consonantal melodies that are associated with two skeletal positions.

(7)   'Onset' formation

In any domain [. . .], the consonantal melodies C_1 or $C_1 C_2$ form a maximal constituent from right to left, where C_1 is a relative sonority minimum.

In (8a) below, (7) selects single consonants; as noted above, the formation of constituents implies minimally (and here no more than) the association of these melodies with skeletal positions. In (8b), the sequences /pl br/ are selected, both able to form single constituents. In (8c), the affricate /dʒ/ has a single 'x', as a complex segment of the language, and in the /mfr/ sequence (*Humphrey*), (7) selects /f/ as the sonority minimum, excluding thereby the preceding /m/:

(8)

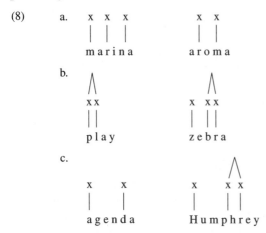

Recall now that the language has a number of phonotactic filters (of the form (2a) above) that bar certain consonant sequences from grouping into single constituents. The sequences /gm dn/, for example, can occur as inter-vocalic sequences but they cannot form onsets in English. This implies that words beginning with such sequences cannot be syllabified and hence cannot exist (Vennemann 1972a; Kiparsky 1982); and if such sequences occur medially then (7) ensures that the constituent's maximal extension to the left stops short of the first consonant in the sequence. Only the second members of such sequences can form constituents:

(9)

As we shall see, (7) predicts that sequences such as these are split by a syllable boundary: *e.nig.ma, Ed.na, pen.tath.lon, at.las* etc. Note that such syllabification is borne out by stress placement in relevant cases: in *enigma, pentathlon* the penultimate syllable is heavy and hence stressed. (Compare *di.sci.pline, pe.di.gree* etc., and see Anderson and Jones (1974) for discussion.)

Consider now the fact that a word may end in one or more consonants: unlike the morpheme-medial position (Section 8.4.3 below), the final (pre-']') position tolerates consonants after short or long vowels. I exclude here, for the moment, instances of 'extrametrical' coronal obstruents, as in *axe*, *text*, *mind* etc. (to be discussed in Section 8.5.4), as well as words ending in syllabic sonorants, as in *apple*, *little* etc. (see Section 8.5.2 below). All other cases end either in single consonants or in consonant sequences of decreasing sonority: *bean*, *keep*, *camp*, *film* etc. In each case, the final consonant (constituting a sonority minimum although flanked by only one segment) is subject to (7):

(10)

The full implications of this assignment of constituents will become clear shortly. For the moment we note, first, that these are the consonants that were identified in Section 8.3 as being subject to extrametricality under some proposals (Hayes 1982; Borowsky 1989[3]), and to resyllabification (in *kee.ping*, *hel.per*) in other models (Levin 1985; Hall 1994). Second, the inverted commas surrounding the term 'onset' in (7) are now accounted for: as I noted above, that notion has no categorial status here, being relationally defined as the left-hand daughter of 'σ'. In the contexts discussed in (10), these constituents do not function as syllable onsets. Recall also from Section 8.3 that Government Phonology (Harris 1994) treats such consonants in the same way.

8.4.3   *Rhyme formation and the sonority maximum*

The second step in the erection of syllable structure is the formation of rhymes (see (11) below), an operation whose details resemble those of 'onset' formation in a number of ways.

(11)   *Rhyme formation*

In any domain [. . .], the melodies V or VX form a maximally binary, maximal constituent labelled 'Rhyme' from left to right, where V is [− consonantal] and a relative sonority maximum and X [+ sonorant] or /s/.[4]

Let us return to some of the examples used in the preceding section.

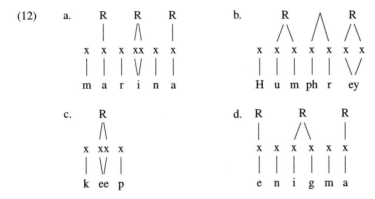

Like 'onset' formation, rhyme formation builds constituents from the melody tier upwards. As I noted before, its operation has default status, pre-empted in certain cases by specific melody-skeleton associations: 'long' vowels are (underlyingly or derived from melodic tenseness) associated with two skeletal slots. In such a case, (11) merely completes the structure by forming a single rhyme comprising those two terminal nodes (12a). The possibility that in English, a single vowel melody (but not a single consonant melody) may occupy two skeletal slots is also the reason why here the 'maximally binary' nature of the constituent has to be explicitly stated. The constituent formed by (7), too, is maximally binary; but in English, no single consonantal melody can occupy two (tautosyllabic) skeletal slots. While the maximally binary nature of 'onsets' is therefore predicted by the maximal input of two melodies, it has to be stipulated in the rhyme.

In word-final position, a long vowel may of course be followed by a consonant (*keep*, *help*). Such cases do not constitute counterexamples to the claim that rhymes are maximally binary: recall that, as a relative sonority minimum, the consonant at the edge of the domain ('l') is otherwise accounted for (12c) and will be discussed further below. But (11) does leave certain cases of (apparent) three-x rhymes noted by Borowsky (1989) (see Section 8.3 above) unexplained. While *areelba, *agelmda are as a rule impossible, long vowels can occur morpheme-medially before tautosyllabic consonants where such a consonant is homorganic with the next and licensed in that way (*angel, shoulder*), or where the lexical item is historically complex: *Grimsby, harpsichord* etc. This last class of exceptions will require further treatment. Here I merely note that only rhyme formation has such exceptions (there are no syllable onsets involving three skeletal positions except for the *splay* class), and that such exceptional three-x rhymes (if that is what they are) usually occur in items where the supernumerary consonant was once followed by a morphological bracket ']'.

Unlike 'onset' formation, (11) assigns a prosodic category. There are three reasons for this difference between the two operations. First, the constituent here labelled as 'rhyme' always surfaces as a syllable rhyme – in contrast to 'onset' formation where, as we saw, word-final consonants will not actually surface as syllable onsets (see (10) above). Second, the category Rhyme is relevant to the structure-building rules of stress assignment, where the branching or non-branching nature of rhymes (but not in English of onsets; Davis 1988) plays a decisive role. And third, as we shall see, the final step of syllable formation (Section 8.4.4 below) makes reference to that category.[5]

Under MOP (Section 8.2.1 above) a consonant that on sonority criteria alone may be either onset or part of the rhyme will become an onset: a sequence of the form CVCV is syllabified CV.CV rather than *CVC.V. Curiously, this principle is not derivative of any theory of the syllable that is essentially sonority-based but has to be stipulated separately in such theories (Giegerich 1992a: 135f.). In the present model, this ambiguity arises in such a way that, if (7) and (11) are regarded as separate structure-building rules, the application of (7) before (11) yields the correct result of maximised onsets whereas application in reverse order results in single intervocalic consonants becoming part of rhymes (hence *CVC.V) before the operation of (7). This ambiguity is of course easily resolved through the extrinsic ordering of (7) before (11): through no coincidence, the principle in question is also occasionally referred to as the 'Onset First' principle. Just as easily, the suspect device of extrinsic ordering can be avoided by stating a phonotactic filter (referring, interestingly, once again to the category Rhyme rather than 'Onset'):

(13)   *Maximal Onset Principle*

8.4.4   *Syllable formation and morphological structure*

The final step in the erection of syllable structure groups 'onset' and rhyme constituents (the former unlabelled) into syllables. This step is unproblematic; the only point to make beyond the obvious is that syllables are here regarded as having obligatory onsets. This implies that, for syllables such as *all*, onsets are present in the structure although they are devoid of melodic material. Direct phonetic evidence for empty onsets is of course impossible to adduce: only the presence of onsets that are not empty can be substantiated. The point that I am making here (and in more detail in Section 8.6 below) is that in items containing no underlying melodic material for the provision of onsets, such material is systematically provided by the phonology. The perhaps most obvious non-underlying (and hence epenthetic, onset-filling) melody of this kind is the prevocalic glottal stop ('Rapp's Law': see Section 6.3.1 above), famous for being both more salient and more widely distributed in German (Krech 1968; Giegerich 1987) than it is in English. In English, it has competition through liaison (compare *fee.l it* and German *fühl* [?]*es*); but it is at least optionally present at foot boundaries (*very* [?]*angry*) (Gimson 1994: 155, 264; Andrésen 1969), reaching the salience level of its German counterpart under emphatic stress, as in [?]*Out!*

The formation of syllables is, then, completed as follows:

(14)   *Syllable formation*

In any domain [. . .], binary constituents 'σ' are formed such that every right-hand daughter dominates a Rhyme and every left-hand daughter is [+ consonantal] aligned with available melodic material.

I return once more to some of the examples used in the preceding sections. In morphologically simple items, (14) predicts that domain-final consonantal melodies, elevated to constituent ('x') status by (7), remain outside the syllable. Such an unsyllabified segment is shown in (15a). (15b) shows the opposite: here a domain-initial rhyme gives rise to a syllable with an empty onset.

(15)   a.   σ   b.   σ   σ   σ

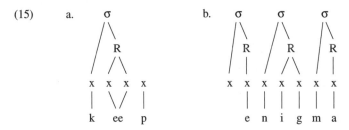

Notice how such items fit together in connected speech like pieces of a jigsaw puzzle. Liaison such as that found in *kee.p Enigma* appears to follow

naturally from such structural configurations. On the other hand, in German (where the relevant structures would be broadly the same: Giegerich 1992b), liaison English-style does not take place despite such favourable conditions and a prevocalic glottal stop would occur before *Enigma*. I shall show in Section 8.6 that liaison of this kind, of necessity postlexical, and largely restricted by foot boundaries, is indeed facilitated by the structural configuration shown in (15).

The one configuration of consonantal melodies that has not been discussed here is that of final clusters comprising a consonant plus a sonorant of greater sonority: *apple* /apl/, *kindle*, *button* etc. Such clusters will become single constituents through (7) provided they do not violate the relevant filters (as *kindle*, *button* do); but they do not achieve syllable status through (14), which can handle only vowel melodies. Nonetheless, such clusters become syllables in the course of the derivation (containing syllabic sonorants or epenthetic schwa). I postpone this discussion, which will necessitate stratum-specific amendments to the mechanisms developed so far, until Section 8.5.2.

I deal now with the syllabification of morphologically complex items, returning to the structure types and examples discussed in Sections 3.2.2 and 3.2.3. I shall demonstrate that the differences observed there between the syllabification of prefixed and suffixed items are accounted for through the operation of, specifically, Syllable Formation (14). But before details are discussed, a few more general remarks about the operation of the three steps, (7), (11) and (14), are in order.

All three steps contain the phrase, 'in any domain [. . .]'. The specific reasons for this restriction will become apparent presently; here its general implications are at issue.[6] I regard the three steps in the erection of syllable structure as structure-building devices. This is in line with the general assumptions underlying this study's theoretical framework; but it would equally be possible to regard (7), (11) and (14) as static ('declarative') wellformedness conditions on syllable structure. Under the provision of (13), these rules are intrinsically ordered: (7) operates before (11) (at least where they compete for inputs), and (14) cannot apply before both have operated.

Syllabification is, moreover, intrinsically cyclic. The specification 'in any domain [. . .]' means that in any domain of the form [[X]Y]], for example, a syllable is erected within the innermost set of brackets [X] before that structure is appropriately enlarged to cover [XY]. Similar assumptions are made, *ceteris paribus*, by Steriade (1982), Itô (1986) and others; and they would once again equally fit with an alternative 'declarative' interpretation of syllable structure. This assumption of 'intrinsic cyclicity' is unrelated to the question of whether a given lexical stratum is cyclic or not. I return to the specific syllabification characteristics of stratum 1 (which is cyclic), in Section 8.5 below. If syllabification is 'intrinsically' cyclic such that the three rules constitute a micro-cycle, as it were, and if the whole stratum is 'extrinsically' cyclic such that morphology and phonology constitute a set of macro-cycles, then the latter will automatically contain the former on the phonological side (without, however, causing structural changes from one cycle to the next, given the nature of the rules). If, on the other hand, a given stratum is 'extrinsically' non-cyclic (as stratum 2 of English is here assumed to be) then the micro-cycle of syllabification simply takes place within the single application of all phonological rules of that stratum, after the whole of the morphology. But given, again, the strictly structure-building nature of the rules, it is immaterial whether or not at the point of their operation the morphological construction is complete: nothing would change if stratum 2 were found to be a cyclic stratum.[7]

In the remainder of this section I shall first discuss the syllabification of words containing suffixes and then turn to prefixed and compound items. The relevant facts were set out in Section 8.2, where a structural difference between suffixation on the one hand and prefixation and compounding on the other was noted: items of the latter type, but not those of the former, contain a left bracket '['. I shall demonstrate that this structural difference gives rise to a difference in syllabification behaviour (without, however, being formally appealed to): the former syllabify across the internal bracket where the bracket is followed by a vowel (*kee.ping*), but in the latter, syllabification across the morphological bracket is blocked in citation-form pronunciation and a glottal stop may occur before the vowel: *un.[ʔ]even, pop.[ʔ]art* vs. **keep.[ʔ]ing*.

(16)   a.   b.

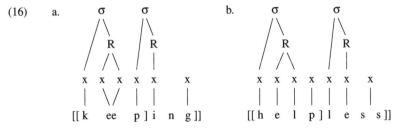

These analyses of two representative examples involving suffixes demonstrate the effect of the three-step erection of syllable structure. After the structure has been completed in the innermost domain **[. . .]**, as in (15)

above, that in the outermost [. . .] is built. (7) and (11) determine constituency for the melodies of the suffix. In (16a), the new rhyme node and its left-hand neighbour /p/, member of the same domain [. . .], become daughters of 'σ' through Syllable Formation (14). In (16b), the melodies of the suffix become constituents in the familiar fashion, and again (14) erects a binary 'σ' on top. Crucially, the final /p/ of *help* is uninvolved here: it has already become a constituent. At this stage of the operation, the initial /l/ of the suffix constitutes C_1 in the sense of (7). The mechanism of syllabification contains no instruction to adjoin new constituents to previously erected ones; therefore the /pl/ sequence (although a permissible onset in English) is predicted not to become a complex onset structure here.

In (17) below I give two representative analyses (omitting final syllables) involving prefixes with C[C and C[V configurations respectively, where the former once again contains a sequence that is permitted by the onset filters of English. Such cases are somewhat rare, but C[V cases are quite common. The remaining permutations of vowels and consonants, V[C (*reproduce*) and V[V (*amoral*), follow the same lines.

(17)   a.

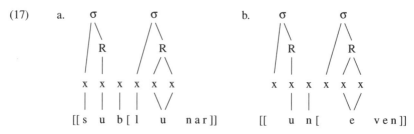

Working first within the innermost pair of brackets, the formation of onsets and rhymes shows nothing that has not been demonstrated before. (14) ensures that every rhyme is the right-hand daughter of a 'σ'. Under (14), every such 'σ'-node has a left-hand daughter, which will in (17a) automatically dominate the /l/ constituent on its left. For (17b), (14) predicts that the first syllable of *even* has an empty onset: recall that 'σ' must have two daughters.

Next, the prefixes are syllabified, again following familiar lines: note especially the exclusion of the final consonants (/b/ in (17a) and /n/ in (17b)) from the syllable. These melodies are subject to (7) but fail be incorporated within the prefix σ, for familiar reasons. Nor do they, in the lexical phonology, 'liaise' with their right-hand neighbours. For the 'stranded' /n/ in (17b) to be subsumed under the dangling onset of the following 'σ', and similarly for the stranded /b/ in (17a) to join the following /l/ to form a /bl/

onset, a special mechanism would have to be available in the lexical phonology: the mechanisms spelled out so far make no such prediction. There is no reason to believe that the lexical phonology contains such a mechanism. Such liaison is possible postlexically, as part of the more general liaison that also occurs between words: see Section 8.6 below. But citation-form pronunciations (which I assume to reflect lexical syllabification) place the syllable boundaries exactly where they are predicted by present mechanisms.

I turn briefly, and only for the sake of completeness, to compound words. One representative structure (*pop art*) will suffice to show that such items (more extensively exemplified in (4) above) share their syllabification behaviour with prefixed words: the elements of the compound are syllabified separately, there is no lexical liaison joining the 'stranded' final /p/ (on which see Section 8.5.3 below) and the 'dangling' onset node of the next syllable.

(18)

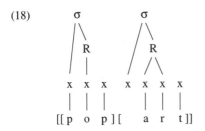

The account presented so far – the core of the mechanisms responsible for syllabification – predicts, then, that the syllabification of suffixed words is systematically different from that of prefixed words and compounds: *kee.ping* vs. *un.even*, *pop .art*. This syllabification difference is indirectly related to the presence of a '[' bracket in the latter type and its absence in the former; but, unlike Booij and Rubach's (1987) account, the present one does not formally appeal to morphological brackets as devices that block rules.

On the debit side, a number of questions have arisen. Perhaps the most interesting of those is that of the 'stranded' domain-final consonants. What happens, for example, to the unsyllabified final /p/ in *keep*? This question is linked with others. For example: English stress, assigned on stratum 1, is generally associated with branching rhymes ('heavy' syllables). But *pop* (see (18) above) is a light syllable bearing stress. More generally, how does stratum-1 syllabification work, given the derivational structure of that stratum (Chapter 4 above)? More specifically, how do we account for the syllabicity among final sonorants (where the final consonant is not the sonority minimum), and attendant syllabicity alternations such as *hindrance – hindering*? And, finally, there is the question of liaison, in various shapes and forms and giving rise to a number of sandhi 'segments' (most prominently linking [r], of course). I deal with these questions in the remainder of this chapter.

8.5   Syllabification and lexical strata

8.5.1   *Syllabification on stratum 1*

Recall from Chapters 3 and 4 that in the English lexicon, stratum 1 differs from stratum 2 in a number of ways, notably in that it is cyclic and that it displays SCE. I repeat a sample derivation in (19) below, which illustrates the main characteristics of a cyclic derivational path as well as showing one or two minor points of interest.

(19)   *Cycle 1*   *Cycle 2*   *Cycle 3*

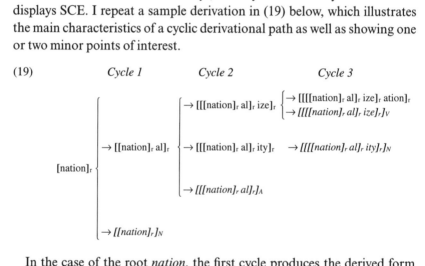

In the case of the root *nation*, the first cycle produces the derived form *national* and, as a result of the root-to-word rule, the noun *nation*. The latter exits to stratum 2: being a word, it is subject to no further stratum-1 derivation. *National*, a complex root, goes into the second cycle to produce *nationalise*, *nationality* and (again through root-to-word) the adjective *national* which again exits from the stratum. The 'free root' status, in standard terminology, of *nation* is reflected by the fact that this form is subject to the root-to-word rule: 'bound roots' are not. Indeed, as I argued before, it may well be the case that speakers take *nate-* as the underlying root and treat *nation*, alongside *innate* and *native*, as a derived form. Nothing depends on the depth of a given speaker's derivations on stratum 1; the point is – and here I turn to the phonological side of the derivation – that a speaker who has *nation* as a morphologically underived underlier (as in

(19)) must have an underlying /ʃ/ in that form: a synchronic derivation of [ʃ] from underlying /tɪ/ is blocked by SCE.

Under SCE, structure-changing phonological rules can only apply to *national*, in (19), but not to *nation*. Similarly, no further structure-changing rules can apply to *national* on the next cycle; and so forth. Recall now from Section 4.2.2 that there cannot be a pre-morphology cycle: no phonological rule (structure-changing or, relevant here, structure-building) applies to *nation* before this form has become a noun on the first cycle. This means that *nation* and *national* are syllabified separately – notably, the latter form is syllabified from scratch in a single operation – while the syllables of *national* do form an input into the syllable structure of *nationality* on the second cycle. I am unaware of any empirical differences in the syllable structures of first-cycle and second-cycle derivations in English that might correspond to this difference on the derivational side; and indeed the syllabification mechanisms of English, structure-building as they are, predict that there are none. The same syllable structure would be produced by the devices introduced earlier if the syllables of *nation* formed the input to the syllable structure of *national*. Syllabification from scratch on the first cycle is the phonological counterpart of the semantic non-compositionality typically found on stratum 1 between the root and the first suffix (Kiparsky 1982: 27). This matter deserves further, probably diachronic, study; it may be the case that the syllabification mechanisms proposed above take insufficient account of morphological boundaries on stratum 1 (beyond the first cycle).

A possible case in point is the non-syllabicity of root-final sonorants in forms like *baptismal, hindrance, cylindric*. Such non-syllabicity is produced in the present model throughout the morphology of stratum 1 regardless of the particular cycle on which the relevant context arises. *Hindrance* is clearly a first-cycle form while *baptismal* is formed on the second cycle for any speaker who makes a synchronic link between *baptise* and *baptism*, deriving both from the bound root *bapt-*. (20a) below gives the first-cycle syllabification (from scratch) and (20b) the second cycle:

(20)   a.   b.

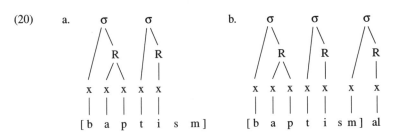

Further relevant examples are scarce. An apparent counterexample is *-able/-ible*, which attracts *-ity* on the second cycle. The form *-ability/-ibility*, however, is clearly irregular (not least in terms of the quality of the relevant vowel) and cannot serve as evidence for a syllabification difference between the first and second cycles on stratum 1.

I add two more observations here. One concerns forms such as the noun *kindling*, as well as a large number of similar forms that appear to be stratum-2 products, given their particular suffixes, but behave, in syllabification terms, like stratum-1 products. Recall from Chapter 2 that the non-syllabicity of final sonorants in the relevant contexts is one of the diagnostics of stratum-1 formations: I shall show in the following section that on stratum 2 the regular syllabification of such forms produces syllabic sonorants. The view taken here is that morphologically complex forms may move, in diachronic terms, to stratum 1 – prompted by the acquisition of non-compositional semantics (*kindling* 'small pieces of wood to start a fire', *crackling* 'roast pork fat' etc.) or perhaps merely by frequent usage. Such forms are then treated by the phonology, just as by the semantics (or in fact by the frequent user!) as morphologically simple forms. It is difficult to see an alternative analysis for this well-attested phenomenon. Postlexical syllabicity loss would have to happen across the board and could not possibly be restricted to specific lexical items. And a structure simplification on stratum 2, for certain items, would fail to account for the semantic change which in many cases gives independent motivation for that simplification of the phonological structure.

The second observation concerns again the forms *nation* and *national*. The latter should have been syllabified as *[naʃ.nəl]. But despite its stratum-1 provenance, this form has a syllabic [n] (or an [ən] sequence). This indeterminacy has been noted on various occasions before: the relevant final clusters can, in English, be either of the form consonant-plus-sonorant, or they may contain an underlying vowel separating the two consonants. The latter results in a stable root-final syllable even in stratum-1 complex forms, and it is the case in *nation*. In other cases, involving a stress difference between the simple and complex forms, the underlying vowel is evidenced on the surface by an unreduced vowel quality: recall forms like *totem – totémic*, amply discussed in Chapter 5. *Nation*, by accident, provides no such evidence in its subsequent derivational path. (But the hypothetical form *natiónic* would contain a full stressed vowel.) We have to conclude that *hindrance* and *national* exemplify two different patterns, the former involving a syllabicity alternation (*hinder*) and the latter not. As a means of diacritic marking, although disturbingly unconstrained, giving an underlying nuclear element (specifically, /Ø/) to the latter (as well as to *totem* and *-able/ible*) seems the best way of expressing this indeterminacy.

8.5.2 Syllabic consonants

8.5.2.1 Stratum-specific syllabicity in English

I showed in the preceding section that the derivational mechanisms of stratum 1 automatically syllabify forms such as *cylindric, baptismal, hindrance* in such a way that their root-final sonorants are non-syllabic, unlike in the morphologically simple surface forms. In English, syllabicity alternations of this type are confined to the stratum-1 morphology: I argued in Chapter 2 that this phenomenon is one of the diagnostics of stratum 1. The disyllabic noun *kindling* must be a stratum-1 form while the trisyllabic participle *kindling*, of compositional semantics, is the product of the stratum-2 morphology.

Note, however, that the syllabification model has had nothing to say so far about syllabic consonants such as those found in the root-final positions of *cylinder* (ignoring non-rhoticity), *baptism, kindle* etc.[8] Given that only vowel melodies can become rhymes under (11), the final /dr zm dl/ sequences in these examples can become syllables only in the presence of an amendment to Rhyme Formation (11) whereby certain consonants can become rhymes if they immediately precede a closing bracket ']'. In English, these are sonorant consonants. The rhyme condition stated below allows them to enter into Syllable Formation (14):

(21)   *English Rhyme Condition* (stratum 2)

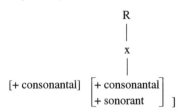

The sequences affected by (21) are of necessity such that sonority increases from left to right; all other sequences (*film, curl* etc.) automatically receive the standard treatment prescribed by (7) above, which takes stratal precedence; see below.

Obviously, (21) must be lexical: the syllable structure of items such as *cylinder*, *baptism*, *kindle* is entirely stable in the postlexical phonology regardless of what follows (*kindle it*, *kindle them* etc.). Indeed, it is stable as early as on stratum 2: *kindling* (the participle), *cylinderish* etc. have syllabic sonorants. I suggest, then, that (21) comes into play on stratum 2. In the absence of resyllabification rules (a central feature of the model proposed here), such syllables remain stable throughout the remaining derivation. Note that exactly the same effect could be achieved by placing (21) on stratum 1 (with the further condition that the bracket is not followed by a vowel). In that case, only the output of the root-to-word rule would be affected (*cylinder*) but not the form *cylindric*, which would still be syllabified in a single operation as if it were a morphologically simple form like *Humphrey* (see (12b) above). But by placing (21) on stratum 2, another generalisation can be captured: such 'vowel-less' syllables do not figure in the stress rules of English. They are not only unstressable but also invisible to any stress rule that counts syllables from right to left. *Cýlinder*, *cálendar*, *báptism*, *lávender* would have penultimate stress if the final syllable were included in the count. Such sub-generalisations are of course only as strong as are the major generalisations that they form part of, and any generalisation in English based on stress behaviour has the inherent weakness of potential exceptions. But this particular sub-generalisation regarding stress is fairly robust in English; and while it came easily to SPE (71ff.), whose stress rules counted vowels rather than syllables, it has prompted subsequent researchers to posit specific extrametricality or resyllabification devices (Liberman and Prince 1977; Hayes 1982; Mohanan 1985: in Mohanan's account even without reference to stress). In the present model we achieve the extrametricality effect without formally invoking that notion, just as we did in the case of final single consonants: if the relevant stress rules operate on stratum 1 (to be precise: on the output of the root-to-word rule, given that these rules make crucial reference to lexical category information) then the stress pattern of *cylinder* etc. becomes regular if the syllabification of the final sequence does not take place before stratum 2.[9]

8.5.2.2   *Sonorant syllabicity in German: strata and lexical categories*

I show in this section that German has a number of rhyme conditions in the place of the single one needed in English. My purpose for this renewed excursus into German is to demonstrate that the notion of rhyme condition is of considerable versatility: in German, these are sensitive to lexical categories and scattered over all three lexical strata, accounting for an intricate pattern of syllabicity alternations. Indeed, we are about to see further evidence in support of the three-strata model of the German lexicon – further support, by implication, of the base-driven stratification model that predicts three strata for German and two for English.

Syllabicity alternations involving stratum-1 forms, similar to English *cylinder – cylindric*, are also found in German: *Zylinder – zylindrisch,*[10] *Filter – filtrier(en)*, *Filtrat*. But the pattern of syllabicity alternations is rather richer than that found in English, affecting forms beyond stratum 1. A sample is given in (22) below. The syllabicity of a consonant (in variation with schwa-plus-sonorant sequences, similar to English [lɪtl̩] – [lɪtəl]) is indicated by <e> in German spelling.

(22) Atem 'breath'   dunkel 'dark'   trocken 'dry' (Adj)
      Atmung 'breathing' (N) die dunklen 'dark' (Adj pl) die trockenen 'dry'
                                                            (Adj pl)
      atmen 'breathe'   im Dunkeln 'in the dark'   Trockner 'drier' (N)

Alternations such as these have been extensively studied in syllabic frameworks similar to the present one (Féry 1991; Giegerich 1985, 1987; Hall 1992; Wiese 1986, 1987, 1996), as well as in earlier, SPE-inspired work (Wurzel 1970; Kloeke 1982; Strauss 1982). Rather than adding another (semi-)full analysis to the literature, I focus here on the possible implications of such an analysis for the present model of syllabification, as well as for the theory of lexical stratification: I hope to show that rhyme conditions similar to the one that handles the English cases are placed throughout the lexical derivation, referring crucially to lexical categories and progressively increasing the range of affected cases. I deal only with syllabicity alternations occurring within the root (which of course acquires stem and word status later in the derivation), such as *dunkel-* vs. *dunkl-*; schwa-zero alternations in the inflectional system (*-n* vs. *-en*: 'inflectional' schwa) are not an immediate matter of syllabification (Giegerich 1987).

My central assumption is here, as for English (Gussmann 1991), that any schwa occurring in the final consonant–sonorant context (recall English [lɪtəl]) is the result of epenthesis to the left of a previously erected rhyme consisting of a single ('syllabic') sonorant consonant.[11] It is the building of such rhymes that concerns me here. Recall that the mechanisms developed so far, which are in all relevant aspects identical to those developed above for English (Giegerich 1992b) make no provision for the syllabicity of consonantal melodies: only one syllable has so far been assigned to *Atem*, *dunkel* etc.; the final sequences are unsyllabified.

It is self-evident that the non-syllabic alternants given in (22) above (*atmen*, *dunklen* etc.) cannot be accounted for by the mechanisms of stratum 1. They are extremely unlikely to be stratum-1 formations: in a model of stratification that is appropriately restrictive on the morphological side just about the entire regular inflectional morphology would then have to be sited on stratum 1. I clarify this particular point by first looking at forms involving verbal bases in both derivation and regular inflection. As I argued in Section 3.3 above, this section of the morphology of German is stem-based and hence sited on stratum 2. Consider the following forms of the inflexional morphology – infinitive *-(e)n* in (23a) and past tense *-(e)te* in (23b):

(23)   a. atmen 'breathe'   b. atmete
           öffnen 'open'   öffnete
           widmen 'dedicate'   widmete
           segnen 'bless'   segnete

           umsegeln 'circumnavigate'   umsegelte
           besiedeln 'populate'   besiedelte
           vereiteln 'frustrate'   vereitelte
           wedeln 'wave'   wedelte

           erweitern 'extend'   erweiterte
           erläutern 'explain'   erläuterte
           meutern 'mutiny'   meuterte
           eitern 'fester'   eiterte

Stem-final liquids are syllabic in these contexts while nasals are not.[12] This pattern recurs in the deverbal derivational morphology, for example in *nomina actionis* involving *-ung*, a suffix attaching to verb stems with full productivity (Fleischer 1974: 168ff.), and in pejorative *nomina actionis* formed with *-(er)ei* (Fleischer 1974: 134ff.):

(24)   a. Atmung   b. Atmerei   *Atemei
           Öffnung   Öffnerei   *Öffenei

           Umsegelung   Segelei   *Seglerei[13]
           Besiedelung[14]   Besiedelei   *Besiedlerei

           Erweiterung   Erweiterei   *Erweitrerei
           Erläuterung   Erläuterei   *Erläutrerei

                              Lacherei 'laughing'   *Lachei
                              Singerei 'singing'   *Singei

Note that despite its final stress, *-(er)ei* is a stratum-2 suffix on morphological criteria: it attaches to verb stems with full productivity. The stress must, therefore, be marked on the lexical entry of the suffix. The relevant rhyme condition is stated in (25):

(25)   *German Rhyme Condition: verbs* (stratum 2)

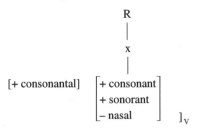

Through (25) the consonant–liquid sequence acquires syllable status during the completion of the syllable structure after affixation on stratum 2 (where the stem [ze:gl]$_V$, for example, will have emerged from stratum 1 with one syllable).

The distribution of -*erei* and -*ei* is a case of prosodically conditioned allomorphy, or 'prosodic morphology' (McCarthy 1984; McCarthy and Prince 1986, 1990). I adopt here the account offered by Wiese (1996: 85ff.) whereby the subcategorisation frame of -*(er)ei* (which, unlike Wiese, I regard as a single suffix with two allomorphs; Giegerich 1987) is specified for a monosyllabic final foot preceded by a disyllabic foot.

We see, then, that the verbal morphology displays a remarkably uniform pattern regarding the syllabicity of stem-final sonorants. The pattern whereby non-nasals become syllabic is clearly a case of morphological categories conditioning phonological structure – a case, moreover, in support of lexical stratification, as will become clearer below. Note also that (25) follows the sonority scale: it is not surprising that nasals, least sonorous among sonorants, should remain non-syllabic. While the rhyme condition for adjective stems, to be discussed below, shows some deviation from this phonetically natural pattern, the overall distribution of rhyme conditions in the lexicon will confirm the basic pattern.[15] What remains to be shown here is that (25) only holds for verb stems, and that it is relaxed on later strata (thereby supporting the model of stratification proposed here).

For adjective stems, the pattern differs in that laterals remain unsyllabified in the relevant contexts while non-laterals are syllabic. The following are adjectival plural forms.

(26)   offene 'open'   eitle 'vain'   heitere 'cheerful'
         trockene 'dry'   dunkle 'dark'   biedere 'conventional'

The relevant rhyme condition is given in (27) below. I suggest tentatively that, like its verbal counterpart, it is sited on stratum 2. While the verbal morphology is stem-based (recall Section 3.3) and cannot therefore happen later than stratum 2, adjectival inflection is by and large word-based. This means that it may be sited on stratum 3 or (given that every word contains a stem) on stratum 2. The main point is that an adjective (stem?) will behave differently from a verb stem with regard to sonorant syllabicity – we may speculate here that this difference provides a functional explanation for the deviation from phonetic naturalness shown by (27): only in this way can the language ensure that *dunkeln* 'to darken' and *dunklen* 'dark' are distinct.

(27)   *German Rhyme Condition: adjectives* (stratum 2)

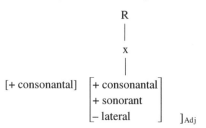

I turn briefly to nouns. It would appear that the noun morphology – by far the most complex part of the morphology of German – is distributed over all three strata (Wiese 1996: 132ff.). But what is more interesting for present purposes than the stratal siting of individual morphological processes is the fact that the only syllabicity alternations among final sonorants are those connected with the stratum-1 derivational morphology (*Zylinder – zylindrisch*). Apart from that, the syllabicity of all consonant–sonorant clusters is stable throughout the derivation. This means that German has a rhyme condition for nouns that syllabifies all such root-final clusters on stratum 1. Given that the condition is specified for nouns, it comes into play in the output of the root-to-stem rule (*Zylinder*) but does not affect *zylindrisch*. An interesting side effect of this condition is that it accounts for a recurrent stress difference between English nouns and their German cognates: compare English *cýlinder, calendar, lavender* and German *Zylínder, Kalénder, Lavéndel*. We saw in Section 8.5.2.1 that in English, such final clusters are unsyllabified on stratum 1. If the present brief description of the German facts regarding nouns is correct, then the relevant clusters are syllables at the point of stress assignment and stress is assigned to the favoured, penultimate syllable (Wiese 1996: 280ff.).

Let us look, finally, at the very end of the lexical derivation. In English, all relevant clusters are syllabified prior to their exit from the lexical phonology. The same is the case in German. Nouns are fully syllabified from stratum 1 onwards, as we have seen. But at the end of the lexical derivation, so are adjectives such as *übel* 'bad', *eitel* 'vain' etc., as well as verb stems in complex forms (*atembar* 'breathable'): this is a default mechanism affecting all relevant clusters that have not been syllabified earlier in the derivation.

(28)   *German Rhyme Condition: default* (stratum 3)

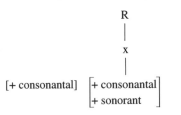

I summarise here briefly the findings of this section. Two results deserve highlighting. The first is that stratum 1 automatically produces alternations of the form *cylinder – cylindric, baptism – baptismal* in English and *Zylinder – zylindrisch, Filter – filtrier(en)* in German. The second result is that on later strata, such alternations do not automatically and unavoidably occur. In English, thanks to the rhyme condition (21), they never do: all relevant clusters are syllabified on stratum 2, and of course remain syllabified from then onwards. In German we have a more complex pattern, unsurprisingly given the richness of the inflexional paradigm. This richness of inflection is of course why German has retained the category Stem while English has dropped the stem stratum. And it is also why German, unlike English, imposes lexical category conditions on the formation of such rhymes. The discussion will have demonstrated that the diversification of rhyme conditions through the lexical derivation, driven by lexical categories as well as different natural classes of sonorant consonants, is at the root of alternations such as those sampled in (22) above. The general point made here has really been quite simple: final consonant–sonorant sequences alternate with respect to syllabicity; they are therefore unsyllabified in the beginning of the derivation. But they form patterns (for example: non-nasals are syllabic in morphologically complex forms involving verb stems); and these patterns remain stable throughout the rest of the derivation. Once a syllable has been formed in accordance with the relevant condition, it remains in place through the remaining lexical strata. Rhyme conditions are weakened later in the derivation, interestingly along the lines predicted by the sonority

scale. Even more interestingly, these rhyme conditions are never strengthened in the course of the derivation. Any strengthening of such conditions
(such that, for example, nouns might stop having syllabic sonorants beyond
stratum 2) would necessitate structure-changing syllabification rules. My
main point in this chapter is that no rules of structure-changing power are
needed for syllabification; indeed, as I noted before, the devices that I have
been informally referring to as 'rules' may equally well be viewed as conditions on syllable structure.

Note also that any ordering of these mechanisms in the derivation is here
taken care of by lexical stratification. This, I suggest, is consistent with the
analysis offered in Chapter 3 whereby English has two lexical strata and
German three; indeed, it gives phonological support to what at that point
was an essentially morphological argument. In English, the case is simple
and well known: *hindrance* vs. *hindering*, *cylindric* vs. *cylinderish* provide
standard arguments for the stratal split. In German, (25) cannot be sited on
stratum 1 and (28), as a default mechanism, must apply after (25). Such
ordering is in fact predicted by the Elsewhere Condition; but it would be
hard to see how it can be achieved if (25) and (28) are sited on the same
stratum.

8.5.3   Syllable weight and stress

I deal in this section with the well-known (if not trivial) correlation between
stress and syllable weight, without however going into the phonology of
English stress beyond subscribing to the claim that the domain of the stress
rules relevant here is stratum 1. Siegel's (1974) account of the distinction
between stress-shifting and stress-neutral suffixes (*totem – totemic, solemn –
solemnity* vs. *hesitate – hesitating – hesitatingly* etc.) serves to make this
point; and further arguments provided by Siegel (1974) and others have
resulted in consensus. In the present model, given that at least part of the
stress rules makes reference to lexical-category distinctions, the site of the
relevant stress rules is the output of the root-to-word rule: recall *nation*, (19)
above. But this is not to say that the entire set of stress rules is sited on
stratum 1: the evidence adduced by Siegel and others concerns the placement of feet and not the erection of higher-level structures. Indeed, it is
noteworthy that the standard version of the Lexical Category Prominence
Rule ('right-hand nodes are strong if and only if they branch'; Hogg and
McCully 1987: 86ff.) rather strikingly handles morphologically simple
forms (*mùlligatáwny*) and compounds alike (*làbour party finance commit-*

tee), where the latter are formed on stratum 2. There is, moreover, no evidence to suggest that the difference between primary and secondary stress (the main purpose of the Lexical Category Prominence Rule) is relevant in any stratum-1 regularities. The following argument will concern the foot level; no stance is taken here regarding the erection of metrical structure above the foot.

Heavy syllables – syllables with branching rhymes – attract stress in certain favoured positions: the penultimate syllable in nouns (*aróma, agénda*), and the final syllable in verbs: *maintáin, usúrp* (Hayes 1982; Hogg and McCully 1987; Halle and Vergnaud 1987). But not all heavy syllables are stressed (the penult in *níghtingàle* is not); and, more importantly, not all stressed syllables are heavy at the point of stress assignment. If a noun's penult or a verb's final syllable is light then stress is assigned to the preceding syllable regardless of its weight: *cámera, devélop* etc. Similarly, the first syllable of *píty* receives stress by default. But on the phonetic surface the correlation of stress and syllable weight is rather stronger. In *petrol*, for example, the /t/ is ambisyllabic, displaying the allophonic characteristics of both the syllable-final and syllable-initial positions: it is both glottalised and aspirated. Such ambisyllabicity – typically found among consonants that are (part of) permissible onsets and immediately follow short stressed vowels – is not only consistent with observable allophonic behaviour (Giegerich 1992a: 170ff.) but also broadly confirmed by experimental studies (Fallows 1981; Treiman and Danis 1988). Some examples of ambisyllabic consonants (underlined) are given in (29a) below; there is no ambisyllabicity in (29b):

(29) a. me<u>t</u>ric b. enigma
        a<u>pp</u>le   atlas
        pe<u>d</u>estal   decathlon
        la<u>b</u>rador   April
        mado<u>nn</u>a   maple

Ambisyllabicity is the effect of a conflict between Onset Formation (7), which maximises syllables towards the left, and a condition whereby stressed syllables must have branching rhymes and therefore maximise towards the right (Giegerich 1992a: 171f.; Ramers 1992). Given that ambisyllabicity is crucially conditioned by stress, it is not predicted by the mechanisms developed so far. On the well-founded assumption that stress is conditioned by syllable structure, ambisyllabicity must be brought about by an amendment to that structure caused by the assignment of stress (foot structure) to syllables: no syllable 'knows' in advance whether it will receive stress later in the derivation. The relevant condition has the following form; the subscript 's' indicates a foot-initial syllable:

(30)   *Syllable Weight Condition*

It is unsurprising that the regularity expressed by (30) should occur in a stress accent language such as English: the close correlation between stress and syllable weight has been well documented in the relevant literature (Hyman 1977a; Ritt 1996). Moreover, as Ramers (1992: 268ff.) notes, ambisyllabicity is a partial synchronic manifestation of 'Prokosch's Law' (Vennemann 1988, after Prokosch 1939: 140):

> In stress accent languages an accented syllable is the more preferred, the closer its syllable weight is to two moras, and an unaccented syllable is the more preferred the closer its weight is to one mora. (Vennemann 1988: 30)

Like the other mechanisms for syllabification, (30) has a strictly structure-building effect: it results in the spread of a rhyme so as to link with the skeletal position already associated with the following onset:[16]

(31)   Foot

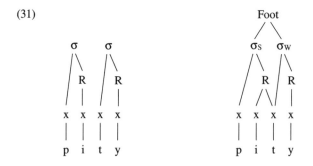

Is ambisyllabicity, of the kind discussed here, a lexical or a 'merely' postlexical phenomenon? The segmental evidence cited above does not suggest that it is lexical: allophonies such as glottal reinforcement and aspiration are postlexical. On the other hand, given that (30) is a well-formedness condition on stressed syllables, it is reasonable to suggest that this condition comes into play as soon as feet are formed – that is, as early as on stratum 1. Within the present model of the English lexicon, and specifically of English syllabification, the latter must in fact be the case. Structures resulting from (30) have formed inputs to a variety of lexical generalisations (see Chapters 5 and 7 above). More importantly, (30) is needed on stratum 1 to confirm the well-formedness of *pop*.

Pop art was the example given in (18) above to demonstrate that the components of compounds, like those of prefixed forms but unlike suffixed forms, are syllabified separately. What is relevant here is that *pop* is not a heavy syllable, at least not through the basic syllabification devices (7), (11) and (14): the final consonant is unattached to the syllable. But it is one of the more robust generalisations about English phonotactics that the minimal size of any lexical-category word is a single heavy syllable. No lexical word in English has the form */pɒ/. Given that all lexical words receive stress, (30) identifies putative items like */pɒ/ as ill-formed nouns, verbs, adjectives or adverbs. In a lexical derivation, such ill-formed items must be prevented from entering into the stratum-2 derivation (although they may under this analysis occur as 'bound' roots, not subject to root-to-word: see Section 4.2 1 above and Inkelas (1993)). This means that (30) must apply on stratum 1. If it is correct that foot structure is assigned to the root-to-word output (given that it refers to lexical categories) then (30) is a well-formedness condition on that output.

Note that the combined operation of (14) and (30) is responsible for ambisyllabicity arising in suprasegmental contexts identical to those discussed above even when they have been created through a stratum-2 suffixation; that is, after the operation of (30). Consider the derivation of *filling*. (32a) below gives *fill* as it enters into stratum 2. (32b) gives the complete structure after suffixation.

(32)   a.   b.

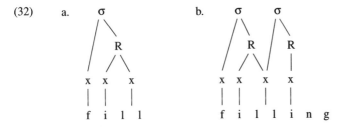

It is in derivations like this that the clause in (14) comes into play whereby the left-hand daughter of 'σ' is aligned with available melodic material. /l/ is a possible onset; it will therefore end up being both part of the rhyme of *fill* and onset to the following syllable. Like *feeling*, this is a case that I discuss further, under the heading of 'lexical liaison', in Section 8.6 below.

8.5.4   *Stray consonants*

We have so far identified onsets (relationally defined), rhymes and syllables
as the constituents of lexical syllabification. Onsets are the domain of filters
(see (2) above). Rhymes (distinguished only in terms of branching vs. non-
branching: the maximal expansion covers two skeletal positions) play a
part in foot assignment and other generalisations. And the syllable as a
lexical constituent not only ensures the alternate occurrence of onset and
rhyme constituents in the string; it also plays a part, through the postulate
of obligatory onsets, in the phonological structuring of morphologically
complex forms. Moreover, the account of syllabic sonorants relies crucially
on the syllable level of representation: note, for example, that /tl/ cannot be
an onset while it is a permissible final syllable: *little*. These points and others
substantiate the claim that syllables are lexical constituents; but despite the
presence of (30), certain segments have not so far been incorporated in the
syllable. First, domain-final consonants become part of rhymes only where
they immediately follow a short vowel and where the syllable is stressed, as
in *pop* (discussed in Section 8.5.3). They become onsets to the following syllable where a vowel-initial suffix follows. But where these conditions are not
met the consonant is unattached. In *help*, the /p/ is not neighbour to a short
vowel. In *helping* it becomes onset; but in *helpless* both the /p/ and the final
/s/ are stray. Note that both the nature and the distribution of such stray
consonants are tightly constrained by (7): they are less sonorous than their
left neighbour; they are single; and, at the point in the derivation where they
arise, they are immediately followed by ']'. Through (7) they are, moreover,
associated with a skeletal position. This association amounts to a permis-
sion to occur in a well-formed syllable, expressing simultaneously the regularity that domain-final syllables can have three-x rhymes, Hayes's (1982)
consonant extrametricality for stress purposes as well as the fact that their
incorporation into either rhyme or onset will vary depending on context.
Note that these generalisations are expressed without actually incorporat-
ing these consonants into the syllable structure; in fact, such incorporation
is clearly not warranted in regard to Hayes' extrametricality generalisation,
and (as we saw in Section 8.3) the fact of unstable syllabification would in
that case necessitate resyllabification after the attachment of a suffix. There
is, therefore, no need to adjoin such consonants except for the possible
expression of further generalisations.

It appears that no such further generalisations are lexical. Postlexically, however, a number of allophonies cannot be stated in a unified way unless final consonants are adjoined. Consider the occurrence of dark /l/ in RP: *little, fell, felt, feel, field*. In the first three examples, the /l/ constitutes (part of) the rhyme, in the last two it is stray. Given that the simplest possible context description for dark /l/ is the rhyme, I suggest that stray consonants are adjoined postlexically to the preceding rhyme:

(33)   *Stray Adjunction* (postlexical)

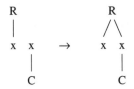

It is neither possible nor necessary to confine postlexical Stray Adjunction explicitly to consonants in the pre-'l' position. It is impossible because the relevant internal bracket in, for example, *helpless*, is erased at the end of the relevant lexical stratum (in this case, of stratum 2). And it is unnecessary because the bracket is in every case present at the point in the derivation of syllable structure where the stray consonant arises. As stray consonants can only arise at the right edge of the domain, there is no need for Stray Adjunction to refer to the bracket that marks that edge.

Consider now the exceptions, apparent or real, to the generalisation that stray consonants occur only at the domain edge. Borowsky (1989) distinguishes broadly three groups of cases. In the first group the relevant consonant is licensed autosegmentally through sharing its place of articulation with the neighbouring segment (*antler, angel, shoulder, poultry* etc.). These cases are, then, otherwise accounted for. The second class comprises items that Borowsky's account, but not this one, is able to handle on stratum 2: *vestment, harpsichord, ordnance* etc. In our model, stratum-2 syllabification cannot account for them in any better way than stratum 1 can. In any case, they clearly cannot be stratum-2 forms on morphological grounds; in fact, even the claim that they are morphologically complex on stratum 1 is in some cases unsafe. (Is *-sichord* an English suffix?) The third group comprises largely place names: *Orkney, Grimsby* etc. This group is of substantial size. A brief look at a map of Britain suggests that it is just as common for a disyllabic place name to begin with a 'super-heavy' syllable as is conformance with the 'regular' pattern. To name a few:

(34)   Laceby   Thornton   Barnsley   Chelmsford
        Raithby   Screveton   Berkeley   Neasden
        Ulceby   Barnton   Farnley   Wilmslow

It is striking that such patterns are found with such frequency among place names while they are exceedingly rare in the non-name vocabulary. A frequent historical characteristic of names, seldom shared by other lexical items, is that they may be obscured compounds. While there is no reason to suppose that such items are morphologically complex in synchronic terms, their segmental make-up and possibly 'irregular' syllabification are a residue from earlier complexity. This phenomenon is also found, for example, in plant names (*honewort, loosestrife, thalecress, groundsel*). For the same diachronic reason, personal names may display irregular syllabification: *Edward* should have an ambisyllabic /d/ (compare *dwell*) but syllabifies as *Ed.ward*. All these forms in fact contain (one or more) cranberry morphs.

The phonological behaviour of such items becomes regular if they are assumed to have retained an internal 'J' bracket (Allen 1980), which automatically licenses a preceding consonant – a diacritic solution, of course, but one that has strong diachronic motivation. Recall from Chapter 3 that it is in any case not only possible, but in certain instances necessary, to store historically complex items as simple forms on stratum 1. *Reckless, feckless, gormless*, which must be stratum-1 forms, display the same syllabification problems and lend themselves to the same solution: historically complex, they have simply kept the internal bracket.

I turn briefly to 'appendix' segments, such as those underlined in *min*d, *loun*ge, *boun*ce etc. Such segments, in all cases coronal obstruents and frequently introduced by the inflectional morphology (*book*s, *help*ed), are supernumerary to the syllable in addition to the consonants discussed above; moreover, unlike those consonants, they are free to violate SSG. And once again, they are confined to the right[17] edge of the domain. They pose a problem for any sonority-based theory of the syllable and constitute the classic case of 'extrametricality' in a theory-neutral sense (Sievers 1901; Fujimura 1979; Giegerich 1992a: Section 3.4.5; and many others). I assume here that a domain-final postconsonantal string of coronal obstruents (whose length is in principle unlimited: Kiparsky (1981) gives *(thou) estrangedst* as the somewhat archaic record) is automatically licensed (in the sense that they are eligible for skeletal positions). Later in the derivation they behave just like the domain-final consonants discussed above: they will become onsets if a vowel-initial suffix is attached (*min.der, boun.cing*);

otherwise they are attached to the preceding syllable. In the absence of evidence to the contrary, I assume that (33) handles such cases. Such an analysis will result in postlexical rhymes of considerable complexity, containing not only what was lexically identified as the rhyme but also all adjoined material. However, the rhyme is here analysed as a flat structure: there seems to be no postlexical (and certainly no lexical) motivation for constituency between the rhyme node and the skeletal position. This means that peaks and codas have no formal status in the phonology.

8.6   Liaison

I return, finally, to the subject of liaison, a phenomenon that includes the occurrence of sandhi segments such as [ʲ ʷ] (*seeing, do it*) and [r] (*hearing, banana*[r] *is*), as well as syllabification across morphological boundaries (*fee.ling, hel.p it*). This phenomenon appears to be heterogeneous in several respects. First, it seems to involve epenthetic sandhi segments in some cases and cross-boundary syllabification in others. But, as I argued at length in Chapter 6, [ʲ ʷ] and [r] 'sandhi' are no more the result of epenthesis than the [l] in *feel it, feeling* is: the relevant melodies, already present in the string, are merely subject to autosegmental re-alignment. Indeed, the present chapter has shown that the obligatory onsets procured by (14), left empty unless filled in those various ways, provide a unified structural context for liaison to occur. Second, liaison appears to be a heterogeneous set of different phenomena in that inside morphological structures involving vowel-initial suffixes it is strictly obligatory (*hearing, feeling*) while in all other contexts it is to varying degrees optional: in *re-invest, pop art, hear Arthur, feel ill* a glottal stop may occur, marking the absence of liaison. But this, as I shall argue below, does not mean that radically different kinds of processes are involved; rather, liaison is lexical – in fact, part of the syllabification process – in the former context and the result of a postlexical process to the same effect in the latter set of contexts. I shall deal with the lexical and postlexical versions of liaison in turn.

Recall that, through (14), every left-hand daughter of 'σ' is [+ consonantal] and aligned with available melodic material. This, as we have seen, automatically accounts for the obligatoriness of syllabification across the morphological boundary in *fee.ling, hel.per*. It is also responsible for ambisyllabicity in *filling* (Section 8.5.3 above). Moreover, we saw in Section 6.3.4 that certainly [r]-sandhi, and probably [ʲ ʷ]-sandhi, before vowel-initial suffixes are lexical for independent reasons: they are obligatory – glottal stops are ruled out – and they have spelling-driven lexical exceptions in the case of those speakers who avoid intrusive [r]. Such identity of both context and status would suggest that the sandhis and cross-boundary syllabification are part of the same lexical regularity. In fact, (14) already accounts for this: morpheme-internally and at the juncture of a suffixed construction, onsets must be consonantal, and they must be filled. While in *keeping* and *filling* ((16a) and (31b) above) the left branch of 'σ' simply associates with the base-final skeletal position (which is [+ consonantal]), in the case of sandhi (*hearing* etc.), (14) forces the creation of an additional consonantal position. Recall now that the surface consonants [r j w] have special status in the English segment inventory ([r] only in non-rhotic accents) in that they fail to contrast with the surface vowels [ə ɪ ʊ] respectively: their underliers are not specified for consonantality. This means that in a form such as *hearing* (see (35) below), the consonantal specification imposed on the onset node through (14) is able to align itself with the remainder of /∅/ (which makes a well-formed melody with both [+ consonantal] and [− consonantal]), giving rise to the sequence [ər]. This alignment will in fact automatically happen, given that Syllable Formation 'looks for' melodic material across ']'. If /∅/ becomes [− consonantal] in rhymes by virtue of syllabification (Section 6.3.1 above), then the provision of a skeletal slot specified as consonantal through (14) will automatically result in the [ər] sequence (and similarly in sequences such as *say*[j]*ing*).

(35)

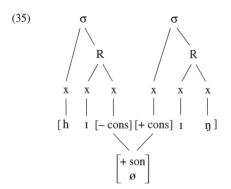

So, liaison at vowel-initial suffix junctures is obligatory through being part of the lexical syllabification process. The context in which this happens is characterised by a single ']'. All other liaison contexts involve a '[' bracket – prefixed constructions, compounds, and strings of words in the postlexical phonology. Even where this bracket is word-internal, no lexical syllabification takes place across it, as we have seen. I claimed above that these two kinds of liaison are essentially one and the same phenomenon although the former is obligatory and the latter optional especially (but not exclusively) across foot boundaries (see (37) below). To be precise, lexical and postlexical liaison produce the same structural configurations, although in the latter case the process involved links two previously erected neighbouring syllables across a '[' bracket.

(36)   *Liaison* (postlexical)

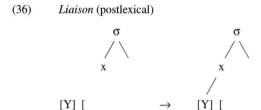

(where [Y] is a melody and 'x' empty except for [+ consonantal])

Postlexical liaison (which is absent in German as well as, probably, in South African English) results in structures identical to those shown previously for lexical liaison: *hear it* identical to *hearing* (35), *fill it* identical to *filling* (32), *keep it* identical to *keeping* (16a); and similarly in cases involving prefixes and compounds.

I add two points regarding the optionality of (36). The first point concerns the question of what happens when (36) does not. In such a case, the onset (empty except for consonantality) is filled by [ʔ] (under Rapp's Law: (14) of Chapter 6), which is assumed to be the default consonantal melody. The second point relates to the status of foot boundaries in liaison.[18] (37a) lists examples where the relevant juncture is foot-medial; in (37b) it coincides with a foot boundary:

(37)   a. inexperienced   b. unable
            disallow   disintegrate
            school inspector   phone operator
            care assistant   beer evening
            hear it   hear Isobel
            feel it   feel ill
            show it   low impact
            may arrive   may earn

There is no binary distinction here between obligatory and optional liaison. In (37a) liaison is highly likely, evidenced by clear [l], [r] and [ʲ ʷ]-

sandhi, and perceived cross-boundary syllabification, while in (37b) it is far less likely and the occurrence of [ʔ], accompanied by dark [l], the absence of [r]and [ʲ ʷ]-sandhi and such like, more common. If we can assume that post-lexical liaison (but not its lexical version) is driven by speech tempo and style variables, then greater tempo and lesser formality is required to trigger liaison in (37b) than is in (37a). (See Gimson 1994: 262ff.[19]). As an approximation, all that can be said regarding such varying optionality in a formal statement is that liaison is inhibited where the 'σ' in (35) is foot-initial. But this deserves further investigation (like much else of what has been said above).

Notes

1 A requiem for Lexical Phonology?

1 The term 'stratum' is used throughout the present study to refer to this derivational notion, not out of deference to its previous users (Halle and Mohanan
1985; Mohanan 1986) but in order to avoid confusion with prosodic 'levels' (of
representation): syllable, foot, etc.

2 This rule of 'stem-final tensing' (Mohanan 1986: 26ff.) suffers from an unreli-
able and unverified presentation of the observed facts (see Wells 1982: 291),
which is especially unfortunate in the light of the rule's relative importance for
Mohanan's stratification model. Moreover, those facts (if they stand up to
empirical validation) are also in all probability amenable to an alternative analysis that obviates the crucial reference to the stratal distinction proposed by
Mohanan – though not, in the present framework, to that suggested by Booij
and Rubach (1987), involving the use of brackets to block rules (see Chapter 7).
Such an analysis may appeal to both morphological and prosodic structure: the
[i] in, say, *happy hour* is foot-final while the [ɪ] in *happiness* is not.

2 Affix-driven stratification: the grand illusion

1 Curiously, the redundancy of boundary distinctions in the presence of 'levels'
escaped Siegel's (1974) notice.

2 Furthermore, SPE used a '=' boundary in certain prefixed constructions. Siegel
(1974) demonstrates that this boundary is nondistinct from '+'.

3 There are, incidentally, further reasons to doubt the assumption that all rules of
word stress are sited on stratum 1: if compounding is a stratum-2 operation then
the rules of compound stress must be stratum 2; and these are known to be identical to the devices that define prominence among feet within single words:
introdúction, etc. (Hogg and McCully 1987). See further Section 8.5.3.

4 Such syllabicity alternations are unrelated to the fact that a word-final syllabic
sonorant (as in *button*, *little*) may be replaced by a schwa-plus-sonorant
sequence (Gussmann 1991).

5 It would, moreover, be rather rash to reject this form out of hand. Committee
jargon ('to turn an idea into a formal proposal'?) is more versatile than
morphologists can imagine.

6 What obscures the issue is the fact that many *-able* forms attract (stratum-1) *-ity*
(*comparability*, *dependability*) without appearing to support an AOG. Given

that *ability* also figures as a free form, an analysis whereby *-ability* is a single suffix is not implausible.

7   The distribution of related *-ance/-ence* appears to support this analysis.

8   If *huggee* is possible then so is *cuddlee*, which would then probably have a syllabic [l], identifying it as a stratum-2 form.

9   See here also Kiparsky's (1982: 7) discussion of 'agent' vs. 'device' formations (*cook/cooker* vs. *driller/drill*) in terms of lexical stratification.

10 One case where *-er* behaves like *-or* in this respect (except for the quality of the vowel in the derived form) is *manager* (*– managerial*). *Manager* must therefore be formed on stratum 1, and the suffix phonologically represented as /Vr/. Note that spelling doublets are occasionally found: *convener/convenor*.

11 *Ravenry* – marked '?' in (19a) – on the other hand, is a well-formed word of English but the object so denoted does not exist in the real world. (Ravens lead solitary lives.)

12 Note that the suffix *-ian* (*Mendelian, Newtonian*), similarly attaching to proper names, is clearly confined to stratum 1 due to its stress-shifting behaviour. See Chapter 5 below for discussion.

13 Note again, in (25), the frequency of [t] before non-syllabic [r], resulting in the recurrent final string *-tress*. Marchand (1969: 287) observes that such diachronic contractions arose in the sixteenth century, where they were modelled after (and erroneously identified with) French *-trice*. Going further, Jespersen (1942: 314) treats *-tress* as an independent suffix that arose during that period and gave rise to forms such as *hermitress, hostress, poetress*. In synchronic terms such an analysis is not tenable (and the adequacy of Jespersen's treatment has to be doubted even for the relevant period): it would leave us either with bound roots of the form *hermi-, poe-*, or with a specific t-degemination rule along with the condition that *-tress* only attaches to bases ending in just that [t].

14 Note that adverb-forming *-ly* (clearly stratum 2) shows similar behaviour in the context of base-final /l/: *idly, doubly, trebly, quadruply*.

3 Principles of base-driven stratification

1   Recall from Section 2.4.12 that *-al* occasionally attaches to *-ment* forms not based on bound roots (*governmental, departmental*). Such forms are not counterexamples to what is said here: the point is that stratum-1 affixation may be based on bound roots (but does not have to be) while stratum-2 affixes must attach to words.

2   The Blocking Effect predicts *longness* to be grammatical if its meaning is distinct from that of *length*. Indeed, in discussing the longness of a vowel one assumes it to be long, while the discussion of its length implies no such assumption. Similarly *highness* vs. *height*.

3   It may be argued here that many names have the phonotactic make-up typical of Latinate words (polysyllabicity, stress pattern etc.) and that, therefore, forms like *Anderson* are synchronically 'pseudo-Latinate'. Then *Andersonian* may be a stratum-1 formation compliant with the [± Latinate] constraint, while mono-

syllabic *Jonesian*, displaying no stress shift, may be stratum 2 (where, as we saw before, the [± Latinate] constraint is largely suspended: *withdrawal*, *tenderize* etc.). Nothing depends on and no serious insight arises from this detail though.

4 Such alternations date too far back in the history of English to be 'regular' in terms of SPE vowel phonology (which continues to provide some sort of benchmark in the minds of phonologists regarding the notion 'regular'). Interestingly, *health* is commonly taken to derive synchronically from the verb *heal*, on the *serene – serenity* pattern (see, for example, Raffelsiefen 1993), rather than (as is diachronically the case) from the archaic adjective *hale* (as in *hale and hearty*). Vowel alternations will be discussed in Chapters 5 and 7.

5 Predictability of syntactic behaviour from semantic behaviour is by no means unprecedented in current linguistic theory. If, for example, the complementation patterns found with verbs are predicted from the semantics through formal mechanisms like θ-rôles, then it is equally plausible that morphosyntactic verbhood itself should be so predicted: see here Anderson (1997).

6 Noun/verb doublets differentiated by stress of the type *convict, digest* – diachronically verb-to-noun conversions – must under this model be roots marked for two subrules of (10); no item carrying a lexical category specification can be input to a morphological process on stratum 1. This analysis is more plausible than the one proposed by Kiparsky (1982) involving synchronic conversion on stratum 1, given that the underlying verbhood of such forms is by no means obvious. The opposite, more transparent and productive noun-to-verb conversion (*to table, to condition, to pattern*) can be assumed to happen on stratum 2 by rule, as in Kiparsky (1982).

7 Note that *maternality* (compare *mortality*) is blocked by *maternity* only under the same meaning; the form is possible for the meaning 'maternalness' and perhaps waiting to be coined.

8 While this model of stratum 1 makes no ruling as to whether *nation* is morphologically simple or complex, it does predict that only those speakers who have it as complex will derive the [ʃ] from underlying /tɪ/. The Strict Cyclicity Effect (Chapter 4 below) blocks such structure-changing rules in morphologically simple forms.

9 In the apparent doublet *Masseuse/Masseurin*, the latter has recently come into official use in response to sexual connotations developed by the former (not found with other *-euse* formations). This is another case where semantic change in a stratum-1 form un-blocks the stratum-2 competitor.

10 Note that the syncretism of these forms with imperative singular free forms is only partial (and clearly synchronically accidental): while *trink!* ('drink!') and others show imperative/stem syncretism in those varieties of German that have lost the final schwa in the imperative form, those varieties will still have *iß!* ('eat!'), *lies!* ('read!') as the imperative forms of *essen, lesen* (compare *eßbar, lesbar/Lesung*).

11 While the range of available *Fugenelemente* is a subset of the inflectional suffixes, their occurrence in compounds is not synchronically driven by the rules of the

inflectional morphology. Thus *Lammbraten* 'roast lamb' contains an apparent nominative singular, *Rindswurst* 'beef sausage' a genitive singular and *Rinderbraten* 'roast beef', *Schweinebraten* 'roast pork' nominative plural forms which are no more semantically motivated than is the plural in *Kinderbett* ('cot', vs. *Kindbett* 'confinement'). Moreover, in *Liebeslied* 'love song', *Liebes is not a possible word form: *-(e)s* is a genitive suffix of German but does not attach to *Liebe* (Wiese 1996: Section 5.3.3).

12   Possibly, adjective-forming *-ian* (*Andersonian*, *Mendelian*) constitutes such a case.

4   Deriving the Strict Cyclicity Effect

1   In other respects, Borowsky's (1993) model shares important features with the one presented here.

2   It is likely that certain structure-building rules of foot assignment – in particular of course those that are sensitive to lexical categories, such as Noun Extrametricality (Hayes 1982) – apply to the outputs of rule (4). This in turn implies, controversially, that word stress is probably non-cyclic (Selkirk 1980; Halle and Vergnaud 1987).

3   While Labov (1981) seems to class vowel quality changes as 'diffusing' rather than 'Neogrammarian', the initial raising of tense vowels that was to give rise to the Great Vowel Shift was probably postlexical ('Neogrammarian'). See also Harris (1989); McMahon (1991).

5   Phonology and the literate speaker: orthography in Lexical Phonology

1   Alternations of the kind [ə] – [ɪ] (as in [hɑstəl]) appear to be confined to American English. The [aɪ] – [ɪ] found in non-American varieties for *hostile* – *hostility* etc. is of course a straightforward Vowel-Shift alternation.

2   The account offered here deals with the form these alternations have in RP and, by and large, other non-rhotic accents. In rhotic accents the underived forms given in (1b) have either [ɜr] throughout (General American) or [ɛr ɪr ʌr] respectively (conservative Scottish Standard English).

3   Schwa has another (synchronic) source exemplified by items such as *little*, *bottle*, *button*, where it does not alternate with full vowels but is governed by low-level epenthesis rules (Gussmann 1991) or occurs in free variation with syllabic sonorants. This 'prosodic schwa' (Giegerich 1987) is irrelevant to the present discussion.

4   I do not assume full-scale underspecification, in whatever form, here; in fact, the reader will note that elsewhere in this study, structure-changing rules occupy a prominent place in the argument. The only kind of underspecified segment employed here is the 'empty' one, which as far as I can see makes no requirements regarding underspecification elsewhere in the system, and which is motivated in every case by prosodic structure. Questions arising from the use of this device (which I regard as uncontroversial beyond minor technical details) are left open for further investigation. See Mohanan (1991), McMahon (1992,

1993), Steriade (1995) on some of the problems encountered by underspecification in Lexical Phonology.

5 Certain melody features may maintain their link with the skeleton. I shall show in Chapters 6 and 7 that what is represented for the moment as '[∅]' and informally called 'empty' is not an entirely empty melody but one that has certain features associated with it by virtue of being 'nuclear'. This is not 'nothing' but a representational object that is amenable to manipulation by rules. The term 'nuclear', too, is here used informally (subject to revision in Chapter 8).

6 Note, however, that the Structure Preservation Condition, operative at least on stratum 1 (Kiparsky 1982; Borowsky 1989, 1990) bars schwa from occurring in stressed nuclei.

7 *Managerial* is irregular in other respects: recall note 10 of Chapter 2.

8 D. Jones (1991) glosses the [ʌ] form of *demurrer* as 'objection on ground of irrelevance' and the [ɜː] form as 'one who demurs'. This follows the model's predictions in that the stratum-1 *-er* form displaying [ʌ], here relevant, has non-compositional semantics while its stratum-2 counterpart is regular.

9 [ɜː] derives diachronically from lax-vowel-plus-/r/ in (I believe) every instance except *colonel*, here irrelevant.

10 I return to the question of (non-)cyclicity for stratum 2 briefly in Section 8.4.4. Should stratum 2 be found to be cyclic then the status of the *deter* derivation proposed here becomes identical to that of the *atom* derivation, and indeed to that of the Vowel Shift derivation. The stratum-1 version of the *deter* derivation will then be favoured by AC but not, as we have seen, the only one that is technically possible in the lexical derivation.

11 I use this term (in analogy to the principle of 'phonemic spelling') rather than 'lexical spelling' (C. Chomsky 1970; Carney 1994). See also Venezky (1970), Oswalt (1973), Emerson (1997) and Carney (1997).

12 Luick's two-sentence (!) explanation of spelling pronunciations and their causes is so concise that it is worth quoting in full.

> Nicht bloss haben sich [im Englischen. HG] die typischen lautwerte der buchstaben zum teil beträchtlich von denjenigen entfernt, welche in den anderen germanischen und den romanischen sprachen zumeist gelten, sondern es giebt auch viele wörter, welche gegenüber diesen spezifisch englischen lautwerten ausnahmen darstellen. Wenn solche wörter im mündlichen gebrauch selten sind, so dass sie vorwiegend gelesen und geschrieben, nur wenig gehört oder gesprochen werden, wenn also das schriftbild nicht ein vom gedächtnis festgehaltenes lautbild auslöst, sondern analogisch in ein solches umgesetzt werden muss, liegt es nahe, den buchstaben die gewöhnlichen, typischen lautwerte unterzulegen, und es entstehen neue lautungen, welche sich manchmal von den ursprünglichen beträchtlich entfernen. (Luick 1903: 304)

13 <y>, if representing a vowel, groups with <i> (*myrrhic*).

14 The survey was conducted in written form; subjects were competent users of IPA symbols but unfamiliar with the exercise's objective.

15 A precursor to the analysis presented here, in the SPE framework and treating tense vowels (such as the [oʊ] in *Andersonian*) as directly provided by the spelling, was offered by Michaels (1980). See also Hudson (1984: 250f.).

6   [r]-sandhi and liaison in RP

1   The sole exception is *colonel,* here irrelevant.

2   'Hyper-rhoticity', found in the rhotic areas of the English West Country in items such as *China* [tʃɒɪnɚ] (Wells 1982: 343), is not restricted to pre-vocalic environments and is therefore distinct from intrusive [r]. In *idea* (commonly [aɪdɪr] in rhotic varieties of English), the Structure Preservation Condition prevents the formation of a centring diphthong through the contraction into a disyllablic form (rhotic varieties have no underlying centring diphthongs) and the relevant sequence is re-interpreted (possibly aided by the speaker's passive knowledge of non-rhotic varieties).

3   Indeed, intrusive and linking [l] are reported to occur in some Carolinas varieties of American English. These varieties are fully rhotic but have vocalised historic /l/ in syllable rhymes. Hence *sore* [sɔːr] vs. *saw, Saul* [sɔː]; and *sore*[r] *is* (of course) vs. *saw*[l] *it, Saul*[l] *is* (Ash 1982; Gick 1991 and personal communication). The parallelism with RP, which vocalises historic /r/ but not /l/, is striking.

4   If the pattern in (6) were the effect of a synchronic constraint then hypothetical forms such as ?[bɛəg] (as well as of course *cairn!*) would be impossible words of English. This does not seem to be the case; the pattern is therefore accidental, in synchronic terms.

5   The observation that liaison is merely optional across foot boundaries further undermines Mohanan's (1985: 146) four-strata model of the English lexicon, as well as specifically his argument whereby the structural description of his 'l-resyllabification' rule may contain a morphological bracket in certain dialects.

6   Stress on the second of the hiatus vowels is a conditioning factor in German: compare *The*[ʔ]*óderich* and *Thé*[ʝ]*o* 'Theo(dore)'.

7   Note that here, unlike in English *hairy,* no centring diphthong precedes the [r] in the disyllabic form. The similar absence of word-medial intrusive [r] from the language can probably be attributed to the two facts that, first, pre-[r] vowels have no breaking, as noted above and, second, the [eːɐ] sequence has not arisen in the language from sources other than historic /r/. *Heere* [heːrə] and *Hefe* [heːfə] 'yeast', for example, constitute a minimal pair; the context [eː_ ə] is not unique to [r] and hence will not trigger this segment in other instances, such as *Seen* [zeːən] 'lakes'. (See, for discussion, Giegerich 1989; Hall 1993; Wiese 1996: Chapter 7.)

8   'Wenn ich ə sage, so hab' ich schon zwei Buchstaben ausgesprochen, das heisst neben dem Urvocal ist hier auch schon der Urconsonant gegeben. Es ist Gesetz: Kein Vocallaut kann laut werden, ohne einen Mitlaut, Mitlauer vorauszuschicken, denn irgendwo muss die Stimme, die beim Kehlkopf aus dem reinen Tongebiet in das Sprachgebiet herübertritt, irgendwo muss sie ansetzen, um als Laut vorzubrechen, und dieser Ansatz, wenn er am einfachsten, unmerkbarsten geschehen soll, producirt sich unmittelbar über dem Kehlkopf . . . Dieser Laut muss jedem Vocal, der die Rede anheben soll, noch vortreten, und er producirt sich überall von selbst, wo nicht ein anderer Consonant den Vocal einführt; er tritt also vorm Vocal überall ein, sobald der-

selbe nicht an einen unmittelbar vorangehenden Laut ohne Absatz der Stimme sich anschliessen kann (Rapp 1836: 53).

9 However, as Claire Sigsworth has pointed out to me (personal communication), [ʲ ʷ] sandhi appears to occur in Scottish Standard English although this variety does not diphthongise /e o/.

7 Input vowels to [r]-sandhi: RP and London English

1 Recall from Section 6.1.1 that another source of centring diphthongs, not involving historic /r/, is the diachronic contraction of an originally heterosyllabic sequence: compare disyllabic *idea* and (for most speakers) trisyllabic *trachea, urea* etc. (where the contraction of heterosyllabic [iːə] to tautosyllabic [ɪə] has not happened).

2 This account disregards earlier [ʊə] (*sure, poor*) as a source of present-day [ɔː] – the 'second FORCE merger' (Wells 1982: 237). Closer investigation of the diachrony of this still-ongoing merger is in order; here I assume that in items which exemplify the merger, the underlying representation of the vowel has switched from that of [ʊə] to that of present-day RP [ɔː] (Fry 1947; Strang 1970: 46).

3 Sweet notes elsewhere (1877: 111) that the diphthongisation of these sounds 'is not marked enough to be written', and in Sweet (1888: 277; 1904: 15f.) he has them as monophthongs. It is therefore unsurprising that the NED and Jespersen (1909) similarly fail to express the diphthongal nature of these sounds in their transcriptions.

4 The contrast is also noted in Sweet (1877: 277), a work of primarily diachronic orientation, and in Sweet (1904: 20), a text directed at foreign learners (and possibly adopting a conservative pronunciation model comparable to that of the NED).

5 Under EC, rule (8) is predicted to block the application of the more general rule (5) for London speakers. This prediction seems plausible, but the phonetic detail provided by the available sources – Sweet (1908) etc. – does not permit its empirical evaluation.

6 But see Kahn (1976: 69, 108), who claims that the long low vowels (at least word-finally) still have in-glides in modern RP. It is unfortunate for present purposes that Kahn fails to specify the variant of RP to which this claim relates.

7 The strong diachronic influence exerted by London English on RP is well known: Wells 1982: Section 4.2.1; Wyld 1920.

8 For present purposes, the feature [±tense] is assumed to underlie contrasts such as *bit – beat* etc. in RP and related varieties of English, the length (skeletal) representation being derivative. The opposite derivational strategy, where skeletal representations are specified underlyingly and tenseness is a redundant feature, is more cumbersome here but not impossible. I return to this issue in Chapter 8.

9 The fact that, in the analysis given here for RP, the second skeletal position is not truly empty but contains (at least) the specification [+ sonorant] does not affect

the argument, given that that specification is in any case part of any vowel melody.

10 I discuss further cases of similar nature in Section 8.4.5. See also Giegerich (1985: 116f.) on the notion of 'fictitious boundary' (there abused: Hayes 1986).

8 Syllables and strata

1 See the more detailed discussion of comparable cases in German (*su.blim* vs. *sub*[p].*lunarisch*, *sub*[p].*lingual*) in Giegerich (1992b).

2 The effect of left brackets was also observed by Booij and Rubach (1987), while Wiese's (1996: 65ff.) account of German syllabification appeals to the notion of the 'phonological word'. The account offered here makes no reference to that notion which, despite considerable longevity in phonological theory (see Szpyra (1989) and Wiese (1996) for discussion), continues to be disturbingly ill-defined (Isensee 1997).

3 *Discipline* is, like *edit*, *develop* etc. identified in Section 8.3, among those cases for which Borowsky's model fails to predict extrametricality.

4 The specification of 'X' as [+ sonorant] or /s/ expresses the generalisation whereby, in English, *alp*, *camp* and *lisp*, *rusk* are well formed (as well as of course *time* etc.: vowels are sonorants) while **lifp*, *lashf* are not. In these, the final consonant is handled by (7) and the penultimate consonant cannot be an obstruent other than /s/ (Giegerich 1992a: Section 6.5). Final coronal obstruents ('appedices' as in *axe*, *texts*, *width*) are here excluded; but see below. Recall also that /∅/ is a sonorant and hence free to be 'X'.

5 Note, for completeness' sake, that rhyme formation is like 'onset' formation subject to filters: RP does not, for example, have rhymes of the form /ʊ/ plus nasal. (See Fudge (1969) for details.) Such sequences then cannot be syllabified, and therefore cannot occur.

6 *Pace* anonymous reviewer: such a restriction does not in formal terms amount to brackets 'blocking' phonological rules, in the sense of Mohanan (1986: 19ff., 129ff.): the view taken here is that under Mohanan's prohibition, here adopted, there cannot be a phonological rule that applies only if no bracket is present in its structural description (see also Section 7.2.5 above). In the present case, the phrase 'in any domain [. . .]' defines a domain whose presence, in fact, triggers a rule. (See Mohanan (1986: 143 footnote 5.) The fact that in empirical terms, no syllabification takes place across '[' is a surface effect of the syllabification process, not the result of a rule that makes illegitimate use of brackets.

7 This study has in fact produced no evidence in favour of the non-cyclicity of the final stratum; notably, as we have seen, the absence of SCE on the final stratum is unaffected by that question. Given that the introduction of 'cyclic' processes on non-cyclic strata, witnessed in this chapter, is a rather powerful facility, one may well argue that the evidence from syllabification supports the assumption of cyclicity for the final stratum. (See also Inkelas 1993.)

8 To be precise, *cylinder* (but not *baptism*, *kindle*) already has a binary final constituent through (7), which however does not have syllable ('σ') status. The

mechanism proposed below will amend this constituent and accord it syllable status as part of a structure-building operation, rather than deleting it.

9 Even so, some irregularities remain. The form *Aristotelian* suggests that *Aristotle* ends in a syllable containing a vowel (Chapter 5), but that syllable is nevertheless ignored by the stress rules. Moreover, there are some cases where final /r/ appears to remain unsyllabified for stress and other purposes (Chomsky and Halle 1968: 181; Kiparsky 1979; Hayes 1982). Such cases are sporadic and confined to specific roots or suffixes, and subject to an essentially diacritic analysis; but it is nevertheless notable that they follow the sonority scale.

10 I follow Wiese (1996: 120) here in assigning *-isch* to stratum 1, unlike its English cognate *-ish*.

11 For some reason, this analysis is standard for English but not at all uncontroversial for German, where the phonetic facts are the same: Wiese's (1986) alternative analysis posits schwa epenthesis prior to syllabification, on the grounds that the string would otherwise be unsyllabifiable. See Giegerich (1987) for discussion.

12 The distribution of *-en* and *-n* in the infinitive and that of *-ete* and *-te* in the past tense are governed by prosodic conditions involving foot structure, such that disyllabic and trisyllabic feet respectively occur throughout the paradigm (Giegerich 1987).

13 The forms involving /l/ are ill-formed only for this particular meaning. The suffix *-erei*, without the allomorphy shown in (24), denotes a place, corresponding to the English suffix *-(e)ry* (*bakery*, *smokery*, *carvery*). Hence *Bügelei* is a *nomen actionis* ('ironing') while a *Büglerei* is an ironing service.

14 Interestingly, disyllabic *Siedlung* 'housing estate' is not a *nomen actionis*. Such non-compositional semantics suggests a stratum-1 form, for which a nonsyllabic /l/ is correctly predicted by the phonology. Another such doublet is *Verdunklung/Verdunkelung*, where again the (stratum-1) form displaying nonsyllabic /l/ tends to be semantically distinct from the *nomen actionis*: 'black-out' vs. 'darkening'. The same happens in English, as we have seen.

15 The naturalness of (25) is confirmed even by its exceptions. In the first person singular present, /l/ remains exceptionally nonsyllabic in the standard language: *ich segle* 'I sail', *vereitle* 'frustrate', *hoble* 'plain (wood)' etc. Here /l/, the second-most sonorous sonorant (ignoring approximants, here irrelevant), is nonsyllabic but the most sonorous one, /r/, is syllabic as predicted (*ich verweigere* 'I refuse'). Nasals are nonsyllabic, also as predicted: *ich atme, öffne*. In these cases, the inflectional suffix imposes a special condition on the phonological structure of its base, which results in the case of /l/ in a less-than-full exploitation of what (25) permits (and not in the violation of that condition). It is unsurprising that some colloquial German (for example my own, Rhineland variety) does without this specific condition: *ich segel(e), hobel(e)* etc. are possible but, notably, *ich *atem(e), *öffen(e)* are not.

16 This analysis of ambisyllabic consonants differs from the one proposed by Ramers (1992: 273) who (following Borowsky, Itô and Mester 1984) assumes the identity of ambisyllabic consonants with geminates and consequently associates

them with two skeletal slots. I take no firm position on this question here but note that, first, Middle English had consonantal geminates, which were distinct from ambisyllabic consonants (Anderson and Britton 1997) and, second, the 'length' suggested by Ramers' dual attachment of the segmental melody is belied by the fact that lenitions associated with intervocalic /t/, such as [ʔ] or [ɾ] in *pity*, are unaffected by this suprasegmental configuration.

17 The single /s/ that may precede 'core' onsets (*split, strike, screw*) is probably amenable to similar treatment. Alternatively, we may treat /sp st sk/ as complex segments (similar to affricates: Ewen 1980). This would simplify (11) in that *lisp, rusk* would no longer need special treatment, but it leaves the notion of 'complex segment' rather poorly constrained.

18 I assume here, perhaps oversimplifying matters, that lexical liaison is insensitive to foot boundaries. This predicts obligatory liaison inside *usherette, duet, oasis* etc. Matters are more complicated in German – compare *Thé*[i]*o* vs. *The*[ʔ]*óderich* ('Theodore'), *O*[ʔ]*áse, Du*[ʔ]*étt*.

19 Gimson (1994: 265) lists some examples of non-homophony at junctures: *a name* vs. *an aim, illegal* vs. *ill eagle*. All these involve foot boundaries, however, and therefore do not constitute counterexamples to this analysis. For independent reasons, word boundary information is needed to account for such subtle non-homophony, which is largely due to postlexical ('allophonic') lengthening before 'l' (Giegerich 1992a: 270ff.). Compare also Abercrombie's (1965) well-known case of *Take Grey to London* vs. *Take Greater London*. In any case, there is probably more to the distribution of liaison in suprasyllabic terms than the presence or absence of foot boundaries.

List of references

Abercrombie, David (1965a). 'Syllable quantity and enclitics in English', in: Abercrombie (1965b).

(1965b). *Studies in phonetics and linguistics*. London: Oxford University Press.

Allen, Margaret R. (1978). 'Morphological investigations'. Doctoral dissertation, University of Connecticut. Storrs, CT.

(1980). 'Semantic and phonological consequences of boundaries: a morphological analysis of compounds', in: Aronoff and Kean, eds. (1980).

Anderson, John M. (1997). *A notional theory of syntactic categories* (Cambridge Studies in Linguistics; 82). Cambridge: Cambridge University Press.

Anderson, John M. and Derek A. Britton (1997). 'Double trouble: geminate versus simplex graphs in the *Ormulum*', in: Fisiak, ed. (1997).

Anderson, John M. and Colin Ewen, eds. (1980). *Studies in dependency phonology* (Ludwigsburg Studies in Language and Linguistics; 4). Ludwigsburg: R.U.O. Strauch.

(1987). *Principles of dependency phonology* (Cambridge Studies in Linguistics; 47). Cambridge: Cambridge University Press.

Anderson, John M. and Charles Jones (1974). 'Three theses concerning phonological representations', *Journal of Linguistics* 10: 1–26.

Anderson, Stephen R. (1981). 'Why phonology isn't natural', *Linguistic Inquiry* 12: 493–539.

(1992). *A-morphous morphology* (Cambridge Studies in Linguistics; 62). Cambridge: Cambridge University Press.

Andrésen, Bjørn S. (1969). *Preglottalisation in English standard pronunciation* (Norwegian Studies in English; 13). Oslo: Norwegian Universities Press.

Anshen, Frank and Mark Aronoff (1981). 'Morphological productivity and phonological transparency', *Canadian Journal of Linguistics* 26: 63–72.

Archangeli, Diana (1984). 'Underspecification in Yawelmani phonology and morphology'. Doctoral dissertation, MIT. Cambridge, MA.

(1988). 'Aspects of underspecification theory', *Phonology* 5: 183–207.

Aronoff, Mark (1976). *Word formation in generative grammar* (Linguistic Inquiry Monographs; 1). Cambridge MA: MIT Press.

Aronoff, Mark and Marie-Louise Kean, eds. (1980). *Juncture: a collection of original papers*. Saratoga, CA: Anma Libri.

Aronoff, Mark and Richard T. Oehrle, eds. (1984). *Language sound structure:*

studies in phonology presented to Morris Halle by his teacher and students. Cambridge MA: MIT Press.

Aronoff, Mark and S. N. Srıdhar (1983). 'Morphological levels in English and Kannada, or Atarizing Reagan', *Papers from the parasession on the interplay of phonology, morphology and syntax*, Chicago Linguistics Society: 3–16.

Ash, S. (1982). 'The vocalization of intervocalic /l/ in Philadelphia', *SECOL Review* 6: 162–175.

Baker, C. L. and John J. McCarthy, eds. (1981). *The logical problem of language acquisition.* Cambridge MA: MIT Press.

Barnhart, Clarence L., Sol Steinmetz and Robert K. Barnhart (1973). *A dictionary of New English.* London: Longman.

Bauer, Laurie (1983). *English word-formation.* Cambridge: Cambridge University Press.

Bierwisch, Manfred (1972). 'Schriftstruktur und Phonologie', *Probleme und Ergebnisse der Psychologie* 43: 21–44.

Bloomfield, Leonard (1933). *Language.* New York: Holt, Rinehart and Winston.

Bolinger, Dwight (1981). *Two kinds of vowels, two kinds of rhythm.* Bloomington, IN: Indiana University Linguistics Club.

Booij, Geert (1977). *Dutch morphology: a study of word formation in generative grammar.* Lisse: Pieter de Ridder Press.

(1994). 'Lexical phonology: a review', in: Wiese, ed. (1994).

Booij, Geert and Jerzy Rubach (1987). 'Postcyclic vs. postlexical rules in lexical phonology', *Linguistic Inquiry* 18: 1–44.

Booij, Geert and Jaap van Marle, eds. (1988). *Yearbook of Morphology.* Dordrecht: Foris Publications.

Borowsky, Toni (1989). 'Syllable codas in English and structure preservation', *Natural Language and Linguistic Theory* 7: 146–166.

(1990). *Topics in the lexical phonology of English.* New York: Garland.

(1993). 'On the word level', in: Hargus and Kaisse, eds. (1993).

Borowsky, Toni, Junko Itô and Armin Mester (1984). 'The formal representation of ambisyllabicity: evidence from Danish', *Proceedings of the North-Eastern Linguistic Society* 14: 33–48.

Brame, Michael K., ed. (1972). *Contributions to generative phonology.* Austin, TX: University of Texas Press.

(1974). 'The cycle in phonology: stress in Palestinian, Maltese, and Spanish', *Linguistic Inquiry* 5: 39–60.

Britton, Derek A., ed. (1996). *English historical linguistics 1994: papers from the 8th International Conference on English Historical Linguistics.* Amsterdam: John Benjamins.

Broadbent, Judith (1991). 'Linking and intrusive *r* in English', *UCL Working Papers in Linguistics* 3: 281–302.

Brown, Gillian (1972). *Phonological rules and dialect variation* (Cambridge Studies in Linguistics; 7). Cambridge: Cambridge University Press.

Brown, Roger and David McNeill (1966). 'The "tip-of-the-tongue" phenomenon', *Journal of Verbal Learning and Verbal Behaviour* 5: 325–337.

Burzio, Luigi (1994). *Principles of English stress* (Cambridge Studies in Linguistics; 72). Cambridge: Cambridge University Press.

Carney, Edward (1994). *A survey of English spelling*. London: Routledge.

(1997). *English spelling*. London: Routledge.

Carstairs-McCarthy, Andrew (1992). *Current morphology*. London: Routledge.

Chomsky, Carol (1970). 'Reading, writing and phonology', *Harvard Educational Review* 40: 287–309.

Chomsky, Noam (1965). *Aspects of the theory of syntax*. Cambridge, MA: MIT Press.

(1970a). 'Phonology and reading', in: Levin and Williams, eds. (1970).

(1970b). 'Remarks on nominalization', in: Jacobs and Rosenbaum, eds. (1970).

Chomsky, Noam and Morris Halle (1968). *The sound pattern of English*. New York: Harper and Row.

Clements, George N. and S. Jay Keyser (1983). *CV phonology: a generative theory of the syllable*. Cambridge, MA: MIT Press.

Clyne, Paul R., William F. Hanks and Carol L. Hofbauer, eds. (1979). *The elements: a parasession on linguistic units and levels*. Chicago, IL: Chicago University Press.

Coulmas, Florian (1981). *Über Schrift* (suhrkamp taschenbuch wissenschaft; 378). Frankfurt am Main: Suhrkamp.

Cyran, Eugeniusz, ed. (1998). *Structure and interpretation: studies in phonology* (PASE Studies and Monographs; 4). Lublin: Wydawnictwo Folium.

Dalton-Puffer, Christiane (1996). *The French influence on Middle English morphology: a corpus-based study of derivation* (Topics in English Linguistics; 20). Berlin: Mouton de Gruyter.

Davis, Stuart (1988). 'Syllable onsets as a factor in stress rules', *Phonology* 5: 1–19.

Derwing, Bruce L. (1973). *Transformational grammar as a theory of language acquisition* (Cambridge Studies in Linguistics; 10). Cambridge: Cambridge University Press.

Dresher, Elan (1981). 'On the learnability of abstract phonology', in: Baker and McCarthy, eds. (1981).

Dressler, Wolfgang U., Oskar E. Pfeiffer and John R. Rennison, eds. (1981). *Phonologica 1980: Akten der vierten internationalen Phonologietagung* (Innsbrucker Beiträge zur Sprachwissenschaft; 36). Innsbruck: Institut für Sprachwissenschaft der Universität Innsbruck.

Duden (1990). *Duden Aussprachewörterbuch: Wörterbuch der deutschen Standardaussprache* (Duden; 6). 3. Aufl., bearb. v. Max Mangold. Mannheim: Dudenverlag.

Eisenberg, Peter and Hartmut Günther, eds. (1989). *Schriftsystem und Orthographie* (Reihe germanistische Linguistik; 97). Tübingen: Max Niemeyer.

Eisenberg, Peter, Karl-Heinz Ramers and Heinz Vater, eds. (1992). *Silbenphonologie des Deutschen* (Studien zur deutschen Grammatik; 42). Tübingen: Gunter Narr.

Emerson, Ralph H. (1997). 'English spelling and its relation to sound', *American Speech* 72: 260–288.

EPD = D. Jones (1963; 1991).

Ewen, Colin (1980). 'Segment or sequence? Problems in the analysis of some consonantal phenomena', in: Anderson and Ewen, eds. (1980).

— (1982). 'The internal structure of complex segments', in: van der Hulst and Smith, eds. (1982).

Fabb, Nigel (1988). 'English suffixation is constrained only by selectional restrictions', *Natural Language and Linguistic Theory* 6: 527–539.

Faiss, Klaus (1978). *Verdunkelte Compounds im Englischen: ein Beitrag zur Theorie und Praxis der Wortbildung* (Tübinger Beiträge zur Linguistik; 104). Tübingen: TBL-Verlag Gunter Narr.

Fallows, Deborah (1981). 'Experimental evidence for English syllabification and syllable structure', *Journal of Linguistics* 17: 309–317.

Féry, Caroline (1991). 'German schwa in prosodic morphology', *Zeitschrift für Sprachwissenschaft* 10: 65–85.

Fisiak, Jacek, ed. (1997). *Studies in Middle English linguistics* (Trends in Linguistics: Studies and Monographs; 103). Berlin and New York: Mouton de Gruyter.

Fleischer, Wolfgang (1974). *Wortbildung der deutschen Gegenwartssprache*. 3. überarb. Aufl. Leipzig: Bibliographisches Institut.

Forster, Kenneth L. (1976). 'Accessing the mental lexicon', in: Wales and Walker, eds. (1976).

Francis, W. Nelson (1958). *The structure of American English*. New York: Ronald Press.

Fry, Denis B. (1947). 'The frequency of occurrence of speech sounds in southern English', *Archives Néerlandaises de Phonétique Expérimentale* 20: 103–120

Fudge, Erik (1969). 'Syllables', *Journal of Linguistics* 5: 253–286.

— (1987). 'Branching structures within the syllable', *Journal of Linguistics* 23: 359–377.

Fujimura, Osamu, ed. (1973). *Three dimensions of linguistic theory*. Tokyo: TEC.

— (1979). 'An analysis of English syllables as cores and affixes', *Zeitschrift für Phonetik, Sprachwissenschaft und Kommunikationsforschung* 32: 471–476.

Garman, Michael (1990). *Psycholinguistics*. Cambridge: Cambridge University Press.

Gick, Bryan (1991). 'A phonologically motivated theory of consonantal intrusion and related phenomena in English'. Unpublished manuscript, Department of English Language, University of Edinburgh, Edinburgh.

Giegerich, Heinz J. (1981). 'Zero syllables in metrical theory', in: Dressler, Pfeiffer and Rennison, eds. (1981).

— (1985). *Metrical phonology and phonological structure: German and English* (Cambridge Studies in Linguistics; 43). Cambridge: Cambridge University Press.

— (1986). *A relational model of German syllable structure* (L.A.U.D.T. Series A; 159). Duisburg: Linguistic Agency, University of Duisburg.

— (1987). 'Zur Schwa-Epenthese im Standarddeutschen', *Linguistische Berichte* 112: 449–469.

— (1988). 'Strict cyclicity and elsewhere', *Lingua* 75: 125–134.

(1989). *Syllable structure and lexical derivation in German*. Bloomington, IN: Indiana University Linguistics Club.

(1992a). *English phonology: an introduction*. Cambridge: Cambridge University Press.

(1992b). 'Onset maximisation in German: the case against resyllabification rules', in: Eisenberg, Ramers and Vater, eds. (1992).

(1992c). 'The limits of phonological derivation: spelling pronunciations and schwa in English', *Linguistische Berichte* 142: 413–436.

(1994a). 'Base-driven stratification: morphological causes and phonological effects of "strict cyclicity"', in: Wiese, ed. (1994).

(1994b). 'Confronting *reality*: phonology and the literate speaker', in: Stamirowska, Mazur and Walczuk, eds. (1994).

(1997). 'The phonology of "/ɔː/" and "/ɑː/" in RP English: Henry Sweet and after', *English Language and Linguistics* 1: 25–47.

Gimson, A. C. (1994). *Gimson's pronunciation of English*. 5th edn., rev. by Alan Cruttenden. London: Edward Arnold.

Goldsmith, John A. (1990). *Autosegmental and metrical phonology*. Oxford: Basil Blackwell.

Goldsmith, John A., ed. (1995). *The handbook of phonological theory*. Oxford: Basil Blackwell.

Gussmann, Edmund (1980). *Introduction to phonological analysis*. Warszawa: Państwowe Wydawnictwo Naukowe.

Gussmann, Edmund, ed. (1985). *Phono-morphology: studies in the interaction of phonology and morphology*. Lublin: Redakcja Wydawnictw Katolickiego Uniwersytetu Lubelskiego.

(1988). Review of Mohanan (1986). *Journal of Linguistics* 24: 232–239.

(1991). 'Schwa and syllabic sonorants in a non-linear phonology of English', *Acta Universitatis Wratislaviensis: Anglica Wratislaviensia* 18: 25–39.

Hall, T. Alan (1997). *The phonology of coronals* (Current issues in linguistic theory; 149). Amsterdam: John Benjamins.

Hall, Tracy A. (1992). *Syllable structure and syllable-related processes in German* (Linguistische Arbeiten; 276). Tübingen: Max Niemeyer.

(1993). 'The phonology of German /r/', *Phonology* 10: 83–105.

(1994). 'Extrasyllabicity and resyllabification', in: Wiese, ed. (1994).

Halle, Morris (1977). 'Tenseness, vowel shift and the phonology of the back vowels in Modern English', *Linguistic Inquiry* 8: 611–625.

Halle, Morris and S. Jay Keyser (1971). *English stress: its form, its growth, and its role in verse*. New York: Harper and Row.

Halle, Morris and K. P. Mohanan (1985). 'Segmental phonology of Modern English', *Linguistic Inquiry* 16: 57–116.

Halle, Morris and Jean-Roger Vergnaud (1980). 'Three-dimensional phonology', *Journal of Linguistic Research* 1: 83–105.

(1987). *An essay on stress*. Cambridge, MA: MIT Press.

Hargus, Sharon (1993). 'Modelling the phonology-morphology interface', in: Hargus and Kaisse, eds. (1993).

Hargus, Sharon and Ellen Kaisse, eds. (1993). *Studies in lexical phonology* (Phonetics and Phonology; 4). San Diego, CA: Academic Press.

Harris, James W. (1983). *Syllable structure and stress in Spanish: a nonlinear analysis*. Cambridge, MA: MIT Press.

Harris, John (1989). 'Towards a lexical analysis of sound change in progress', *Journal of Linguistics* 25: 35–56.

(1990). 'Derived phonological contrasts', in: Ramsaran, ed. (1990).

(1994). *English sound structure*. Oxford: Basil Blackwell.

Harris, John and Edmund Gussmann (1998). 'Final codas: why the west was wrong', in: Cyran, ed. (1998).

Hayes, Bruce (1982). 'Extrametricality and English stress', *Linguistic Inquiry* 13: 227–276.

(1986). Review of Giegerich (1985). *Journal of Linguistics* 22: 229–235.

Hellberg, Steffan (1974). *Graphonomic rules in phonology: studies in the expression component of Swedish* (Nordistica Gothoburgensia; 7). Gothenburg: University of Gothenburg.

Hogg, Richard M., ed. (1992). *The Cambridge history of the English language. Vol. 1: The beginnings to 1066*. Cambridge: Cambridge University Press.

Hogg, Richard and C. B. McCully (1987). *Metrical phonology: a course-book*. Cambridge: Cambridge University Press.

Horn, Wilhelm and Martin Lehnert (1954). *Laut und Leben: Englische Lautgeschichte der neueren Zeit (1400–1950)*. 1. Band. Berlin: Deutscher Verlag der Wissenschaften.

Householder, Fred (1971). *Linguistic speculations*. Cambridge: Cambridge University Press.

Hudson, Richard (1984). *Word grammar*. Oxford: Basil Blackwell.

Hughes, Arthur and Peter Trudgill (1987). *English accents and dialects*. 2nd edn. London: Edward Arnold.

Hyman, Larry M. (1977a). 'On the nature of linguistic stress', in: Hyman, ed. (1977b).

Hyman, Larry M., ed. (1977b). *Studies in stress and accent* (Southern California Occasional Papers in Linguistics; 4). Los Angeles, CA: Department of Linguistics, University of Southern California.

Inkelas, Sharon (1993). 'Deriving cyclicity', in: Hargus and Kaisse, eds. (1993).

Inkelas, Sharon and Orhan Orgun (1994). 'Level economy, derived environment effects and the treatment of exceptions', in: Wiese, ed. (1994).

Isensee, Bettina (1997). Review of Wiese (1996). *Lingua* 102: 195–201.

Itô, Junko (1986). 'Syllable theory in prosodic phonology'. Doctoral dissertation, University of Massachusetts. Amherst, MA.

Jacobs, Roderick A. and Peter S. Rosenbaum, eds. (1970). *Readings in English transformational grammar*. Waltham: Blaisdell.

Jaeger, Jeri J. (1986). 'On the acquisition of abstract representations for English vowels', *Phonology Yearbook* 3: 71–97.

Jespersen, Otto (1909). *A Modern English grammar on historical principles. Part I: Sounds and spellings*. London: George Allen and Unwin; Copenhagen: Ejnar Munksgaard.

(1942). *A Modern English grammar on historical principles. Part VI: Morphology*. London: George Allen and Unwin; Copenhagen: Ejnar Munksgaard.

Johansson, Stig (1973). 'Linking and intrusive /r/ in English: a case for a more concrete phonology', *Studia Linguistica* 27: 53–68.

Jones, Charles (1989). *A history of English phonology*. London and New York: Longman.

Jones, Daniel (1963). *English pronouncing dictionary*. 12th edn. London: Dent.

(1991). *English pronouncing dictionary*. 14th edn., ed. by A. C. Gimson, rev. by Susan Ramsaran. Cambridge: Cambridge University Press.

Jordan, Richard (1968). *Handbuch der mittelenglischen Grammatik: Lautlehre*. 3. Aufl. Heidelberg: Carl Winter Universitätsverlag.

Kahn, Daniel (1976). *Syllable-based generalizations in English phonology*. Bloomington, IN: Indiana University Linguistics Club.

Kaisse, Ellen and Patricia Shaw (1985). 'On the theory of lexical phonology', *Phonology Yearbook* 2: 1–30.

Kamińska, Tatiana E. (1995). *Problems in Scottish English phonology* (Linguistische Arbeiten; 328). Tübingen: Max Niemeyer.

Kastovsky, Dieter (1992). 'Semantics and vocabulary', in: Hogg, ed. (1992).

(1996). 'Verbal derivation in English: a historical survey. Or: Much ado about nothing', in: Britton, ed. (1996).

Katamba, Francis (1993). *Morphology*. Basingstoke: Macmillan.

Kavanagh, James F. and Ignatius G. Mattingly, eds. (1972). *Language by ear and by eye: the relationship between speech and reading*. Cambridge, MA: MIT Press.

Kaye, Jonathan (1990). '"Coda" licensing', *Phonology* 7: 301–30.

Kaye, Jonathan, Jean Lowenstamm and Jean-Roger Vergnaud (1990). 'Constituent structure and government in phonology', *Phonology* 7: 193–231.

Kean, Marie-Louise. (1974). 'The strict cycle in phonology', *Linguistic Inquiry* 5: 179–203.

Kenyon, John S. (1958). *American pronunciation*. Ann Arbor, MI: Wahr.

King, Robert D. (1969). *Historical linguistics and generative grammar*. Englewood Cliffs, NJ: Prentice-Hall.

Kiparsky, Paul (1973). 'How abstract is phonology?' in: Fujimura, ed. (1973).

(1979). 'Metrical structure assignment is cyclic', *Linguistic Inquiry* 10: 421–441.

(1981). 'Remarks on the metrical structure of the syllable', in: Dressler, Pfeiffer and Rennison, eds. (1981).

(1982). 'Lexical phonology and morphology', in: Linguistic Society of Korea, ed. (1982).

(1985). 'Some consequences of lexical phonology', *Phonology Yearbook* 2: 85–138.

(1993). 'Blocking in nonderived environments', in: Hargus and Kaisse, eds. (1993).

Klemola, Juhani, Merja Kytö and Matti Rissanen, eds. (1996). *Speech past and present: studies in English dialectology in memory of Ossi Ihalainen* (Bamberger Beiträge zur englischen Sprachwissenschaft; 38). Frankfurt am Main: Peter Lang.

Klima, Edward (1972). 'How alphabets might reflect language', in: Kavanagh and Mattingly, eds. (1972).

Kloeke, W. U. S. van Lessen (1982). *Deutsche Phonologie und Morphologie: Merkmale und Markiertheit* (Linguistische Arbeiten; 117). Tübingen: Max Niemeyer.

Koeppel, Emil (1901). '*Spelling-pronunciations': Bemerkungen über den Einfluss des Schriftbildes auf den Laut im Englischen* (Quellen und Forschungen zur Sprach- und Culturgeschichte der germanischen Völker; LXXXIX). Strassburg: Karl J. Trübner.

Kohler, Klaus (1994). 'Glottal stops and glottalisation in German: data and theory of connected speech processes', *Phonetica* 51: 38–51.

Kohrt, Manfred (1987). *Theoretische Aspekte der deutschen Orthographie* (Reihe germanistische Linguistik; 70). Tübingen: Max Niemeyer.

Krech, Eva-Maria (1968). *Sprechwissenschaftlich-phonetische Untersuchungen zum Gebrauch des Glottisschlageinsatzes in der allgemeinen deutschen Hochlautung.* Basel: Karger.

Labov, William (1981). 'Resolving the Neogrammarian controversy', *Language* 57: 267–308.

Ladefoged, Peter (1993). *A course in phonetics.* 3rd edn. Fort Worth, TX and London: Harcourt Brace College.

Lass, Roger (1996). 'Glottal stop and linking [h] in South African English. With a note on two antique connections', in: Klemola, Kytö and Rissanen, eds. (1996).

Lass, Roger and John M. Anderson (1975). *Old English phonology* (Cambridge Studies in Linguistics; 14). Cambridge: Cambridge University Press.

Leben, William (1973). 'Suprasegmental phonology'. Doctoral dissertation, MIT. Cambridge, MA.

Lehnert, Martin (1971). *Reverse dictionary of Present-day English – Rückläufiges Wörterbuch der englischen Gegenwartssprache.* Leipzig: VEB Verlag Enzyklopädie.

Levin, Harry and Joanna P. Williams, eds. (1970). *Basic studies on reading.* New York: Academic Press.

Levin, Juliette (1983). 'Dependent levels of representation: the skeleton tier and syllable projections', *GLOW Newsletter* 10: 52–54.

—— (1985). 'A metrical theory of syllabicity'. Doctoral dissertation, MIT. Cambridge, MA.

Liberman, Mark and Alan Prince (1977). 'On stress and linguistic rhythm', *Linguistic Inquiry* 8: 249–336.

Lieber, Rochelle (1981). *On the organization of the lexicon.* Bloomington, IN: Indiana University Linguistics Club.

Linell, Per (1979). *Psychological reality in phonology: a theoretical study* (Cambridge Studies in Linguistics; 25). Cambridge: Cambridge University Press.

Linguistic Society of Korea, ed. (1982). *Linguistics in the morning calm: selected papers from SICOL-1981.* Seoul: Hanshin.

Luick, Karl (1903). Review of Koeppel (1901). *Beiblatt zur Anglia* 14: 304–307.

Lutz, Angelika (1991). *Phonotaktisch gesteuerte Konsonantenveränderungen in der*

Geschichte des Englischen (Linguistische Arbeiten; 272). Tübingen: Max Niemeyer.

Lyons, John (1970a). 'Morphology', in: Lyons, ed. (1970b).

Lyons, John ed. (1970b). *New horizons in linguistics.* Harmondsworth: Penguin.

MacMahon, Michael K. C. (1985). 'James Murray and the phonetic notation in the *New English Dictionary*', *Transactions of the Philological Society* 83: 72–112.

Marchand, Hans (1969). *The categories and types of Present-day English word formation: a synchronic-diachronic approach.* 2nd edn. München: C. H. Beck'sche Verlagsbuchhandlung.

Marshall, John G. (1976). 'Neuropsychological aspects of orthographic representation', in: Wales and Walker, eds. (1976).

Mascaró, Joan (1976). 'Catalan Phonology'. Doctoral dissertation, MIT. Cambridge MA.

Matthei, Edward and Thomas Roeper (1983). *Understanding and producing speech.* London: Fontana.

Matthews, Peter H. (1991). *Morphology.* 2nd edn. Cambridge: Cambridge University Press.

McCarthy, John (1984). 'Prosodic organization in morphology', in: Aronoff and Oehrle, eds. (1984).

(1986). 'OCP effects: gemination and antigemination', *Linguistic Inquiry* 17: 207–263.

(1991). 'Synchronic rule inversion', *Proceedings of the Boston Linguistics Society* 17: 17–33.

(1993). 'A case of surface constraint violation', *Canadian Journal of Linguistics* 38: 169–195.

McCarthy, John and Alan Prince (1986). 'Prosodic morphology'. Unpublished manuscripts University of Massachusetts. Amherst, MA.

(1990). 'Foot and word in prosodic morphology: the Arabic broken plural', *Natural Language and Linguistic Theory* 8: 209–283.

McCawley, James D. (1986). 'Today the world, tomorrow phonology', *Phonology Yearbook* 3: 27–44.

McMahon, April M. S. (1989). 'Constraining lexical phonology: evidence from English vowels'. Doctoral dissertation, University of Edinburgh. Edinburgh.

(1990). 'Vowel shift, free rides and strict cyclicity', *Lingua* 80: 197–225.

(1991). 'Lexical phonology and sound change: the case of the Scottish vowel length rule', *Journal of Linguistics* 27: 29–53.

(1992). 'Underspecification and the analysis of dialect differences in lexical phonology', *Transactions of the Philological Society* 90: 81–119.

(1993). Review of Borowsky (1990). *Lingua* 90: 357–384.

(1996). 'On the use of the past to explain the present: the history of /r/ in English and Scots', in: Britton, ed. (1996).

(forthcoming). *Lexical phonology and the history of English.* Cambridge: Cambridge University Press.

McMahon, April, Paul Foulkes and Laura Tollfree (1994). 'Gestural representation and lexical phonology', *Phonology* 11: 277–316.

Michaels, David (1980). 'Spelling and the phonology of tense vowels', *Language and Speech* 23: 197–225.

Minkova, Donka (1991). *The history of final vowels in English: the sound of muting* (Topics in English Linguistics; 4). Berlin and New York: Mouton de Gruyter.

Mohanan, K. P. (1984). 'The phonology of /r/ in RP'. Unpublished manuscript, National University of Singapore, Singapore.

—— (1985). 'Syllable structure and lexical strata in English', *Phonology Yearbook* 2: 139–156.

—— (1986). *The theory of lexical phonology*. Dordrecht: D. Reidel.

—— (1991). 'On the bases of radical underspecification', *Natural Language and Linguistic Theory* 9: 285–325,

Mohanan, K. P. and Tara Mohanan (1982). 'Lexical phonology and the consonant system in Malayalam', *Linguistic Inquiry* 15: 575–602.

Moore, Timothy E., ed. (1973). *Cognitive development and the acquisition of language*. New York: Academic Press.

Moskovitz, Breyne A. (1973). 'On the status of vowel shift in English', in: Moore, ed. (1973).

Murray, James A. H., ed. (1888–). *A new English dictionary on historical principles.* 10 vols. Oxford: Clarendon Press.

Myers, Scott (1987). 'Vowel shortening in English', *Natural Language and Linguistic Theory* 5: 485–534.

Nathan, G. (1979). 'Towards a literate level of language', in: Clyne, Hanks and Hofbauer, eds. (1979).

NED = Murray, ed. (1888–).

Nespor, Marina and Irene Vogel (1986). *Prosodic phonology*. Dordrecht: Foris Publications.

Odden, David (1993), 'Interaction between modules in lexical phonology', in: Hargus and Kaisse, eds. (1993).

Oswalt, R. L. (1973). 'English orthography as a morphophonemic system', *Linguistics* 102: 5–40.

Paradis, Carole and Jean-Francois Prunet, eds. (1991). *The special status of coronals: internal and external evidence* (Phonetics and Phonology; 2). San Diego, CA: Academic Press.

Paul, Hermann (1887). 'Ueber die Aufgaben der Wortbildungslehre', *Sitzungsberichte der Philosophisch-Philologischen und der Historischen Klasse der Königlichen Bairischen Akademie der Wissenschaften zu München*: 692–713.

Plag, Ingo (1996). 'Selectional restrictions in English suffixation revisited: a reply to Fabb (1988)', *Linguistics* 34: 769–798.

Plank, Frans (1981). *Morphologische (Ir-)Regularitäten: Aspekte der Wortstrukturtheorie* (Studien zur deutschen Grammatik; 13). Tübingen: Gunter Narr.

Pope, Mildred K. (1934). *From Latin to Modern French with especial reference to Anglo-Norman: phonology and morphology*. Manchester: Manchester University Press.

Prinz, Michael and Richard Wiese (1990). 'Ein nicht-lineares Modell der Graphem-Phonem-Korrespondenz', *Folia Linguistica* 24: 73–103.

Prokosch, Eduard (1939). *A comparative Germanic grammar.* Philadelphia: Linguistic Society of America.

Raffelsiefen, Renate (1993). 'Relating words: a model of base-recognition. Part 1', *Linguistic Analysis* 23: 3–159.

Rainer, Franz (1988). 'Towards a theory of blocking: the case of Italian and German quality nouns', in: Booij and van Marle, eds. (1988).

Ramers, Karl-Heinz (1992). 'Ambisilbische Konsonanten im Deutschen', in: Eisenberg, Ramers and Vater, eds. (1992).

Ramsaran, Susan, ed. (1990). *Studies in the pronunciation of English: a commemorative volume in honour of A. C. Gimson.* London: Routledge.

Rapp, Karl Moritz (1836). *Versuch einer Physiologie der Sprache nebst historischer Entwicklung der abendländischen Idiome nach physiologischen Grundsätzen. 1. Band.* Stuttgart: Cotta'sche Verlagsbuchhandlung.

Rice, Keren D. (1989). 'On eliminating resyllabification into onsets', *Proceedings of the West Coast Conference on Formal Linguistics* 8: 331–346.

(1992). 'On deriving sonority: a structural account of sonority relationships', *Phonology* 9: 61–99.

Ritt, Nikolaus (1996). *Quantity adjustment: vowel lengthening and shortening in early Middle English* (Cambridge Studies in Linguistics; supplementary volume). Cambridge: Cambridge University Press.

Ross, John R. (1972). 'A re-analysis of English word stress', in: Brame, ed. (1972).

Rubach, Jerzy (1990). 'Final devoicing and cyclic syllabification in German', *Linguistic Inquiry* 21: 79–94.

Saciuk, Bernard (1969). 'The stratal division of the lexicon', *Papers in Linguistics* 1: 464–532.

Sapir, Edward (1921). *Language: an introduction to the study of speech.* New York: Harcourt, Brace.

Saussure, Ferdinand de (1916). *Cours de linguistique générale.* Publié par C. Bally et A. Sèchehaye. Paris: Payot. [Engl. transl. New York: Philosophical Library, 1959.]

Scalise, Sergio (1984). *Generative morphology.* Dordrecht: Foris Publications.

Scobbie, James (1992). 'Against rule inversion: the development of English [r] sandhi', Poster paper presented at the 7th International Phonology Meeting, Krems.

Selkirk, Elisabeth O. (1980). 'The role of prosodic categories in English word stress', *Linguistic Inquiry* 11: 563–605.

(1982a). 'The syllable', in: van der Hulst and Smith, eds. (1982).

(1982b). *The syntax of words* (Linguistic Inquiry Monographs; 7). Cambridge, MA: MIT Press.

(1984). 'On the major class features and syllable theory', in: Aronoff and Oehrle, eds. (1984).

Siegel, Dorothy (1974). 'Topics in English morphology'. Doctoral dissertation, MIT. Cambridge MA.

Sievers, Eduard (1901). *Grundzüge der Phonetik zur Einführung in das Studium der Lautlehre der indogermanischen Sprachen.* 5. Aufl. Leipzig: Breitkopf und Härtel.

Sivertsen, Eva (1960). *Cockney phonology*. Oslo: Oslo University Press.

SPE = Chomsky and Halle (1968).

Spencer, Andrew (1991). *Morphological theory: an introduction to word structure in generative grammar*. Oxford: Basil Blackwell.

Sproat, Richard (1985). 'On deriving the lexicon'. Doctoral dissertation, MIT, Cambridge, MA.

Stamirowska, K., Z. Mazur and A. Walczuk, eds. (1994). *Literature and language in the cultural context: proceedings of the inaugural conference of Polish Association for the Study of English*. Kraków: Universitas.

Stene, Aasta (1954). *Hiatus in English: problems of catenation and juncture* (Anglistica; 3). Copehagen: Rosenkilde and Bagger.

Steriade, Donca (1982). 'Greek prosodies and the nature of syllabification'. Doctoral dissertation, MIT. Cambridge, MA.

———(1995). 'Underspecification and markedness', in: Goldsmith, ed. (1995).

Strang, Barbara M. H. (1970). *A history of English*. London: Methuen.

Strauss, Steven L. (1979). 'Some principles of word structure in English and German'. Doctoral dissertation, City University. New York.

———(1982). *Lexicalist phonology of English and German*. Dordrecht: Foris Publications.

———(1983). 'Stress assignment as morphological adjustment in English', *Linguistic Analysis* 11: 419–427.

———(1985). 'A root formation component for English', in: Gussmann, ed. (1985).

Sweet, Henry (1877). *A handbook of phonetics*. Oxford: Clarendon Press.

———(1888). *A history of English sounds from the earliest period*. Oxford: Clarendon Press.

———(1904). *Elementarbuch des gesprochenen Englisch (Grammatik, Texte und Glossar)*. Oxford: Clarendon Press; Leipzig: Tauchnitz.

———(1908). *The sounds of English: an introduction to phonetics*. Oxford: Clarendon Press.

Szpyra, Jolanta (1989). *The morphology–phonology interface: cycles, levels and words*. London and New York: Routledge.

Szymanek, Bogdan (1989). *Introduction to morphological analysis*. Warszawa: Państwowe Wydawnictwo Naukowe.

Thomas, Alan R. (1967). 'Generative linguistics in dialectology', *Transactions of the Philological Society*: 179–203.

Trager, George L. and Henry L. Smith (1951). *An outline of English structure* (Studies in Linguistics. Occasional Papers; 3). Norman: Battenburg Press.

Treiman, Rebecca and C. Danis (1988). 'Syllabification of intervocalic consonants', *Journal of Memory and Language* 27: 87–104.

Trudgill, Peter and Jean Hannah (1985). *International English: a guide to varieties of Standard English*. London: Edward Arnold.

Ulbrich, Horst (1972). *Instrumentalphonetisch-auditive R-Untersuchungen im Deutschen*. Berlin: Akademie-Verlag.

van der Hulst, Harry and Norval Smith, eds. (1982). *The structure of phonological representations (Part II)*. Dordrecht: Foris Publications.

Van Marle, Jaap (1986). 'The domain hypothesis: the study of rival morphological processes', *Linguistics* 24: 601–627.

Venezky, Richard (1970). *The structure of English orthography* (Janua Linguarum: Series Minor; 82). The Hague: Mouton.

Vennemann, Theo (1972a). 'On the theory of syllabic phonology', *Linguistische Berichte* 18: 1–18.

(1972b). 'Rule inversion', *Lingua* 29: 209–242.

(1982a). 'Zur Silbenstruktur der deutschen Standardsprache', in: Vennemann, ed. (1982b).

Vennemann, Theo, ed. (1982b). *Silben, Segmente, Akzente: Referate zur Wort-, Satz- und Versphonologie anläßlich der vierten Jahrestagung der Deutschen Gesellschaft für Sprachwissenschaft* (Linguistische Arbeiten; 126). Tübingen: Max Niemeyer.

(1988). *Preference laws for syllable structure and the explanation of sound change: with special reference to German, Germanic, Italian and Latin.* Berlin and New York: Mouton de Gruyter.

Wales, Roger J. and Edward Walker, eds. (1976). *New approaches to language mechanisms: a collection of psycholinguistic studies.* Amsterdam: North-Holland.

Wang, H. Samuel and Bruce L. Derwing (1986). 'More on English vowel shift: the back vowel question', *Phonology Yearbook* 3: 99–116.

Ward, Ida C. (1939). *The phonetics of English.* 3rd revised edn. Cambridge: Heffer.

Wells, John C. (1982). *Accents of English.* 3 vols. Cambridge: Cambridge University Press.

(1990). *Longman pronunciation dictionary.* Harlow: Addison Wesley Longman.

Wiese, Richard (1986). 'Schwa and the structure of words in German', *Linguistics* 24: 695–742.

(1988). *Silbische und lexikalische Phonologie: Studien zum Chinesischen und Deutschen* (Linguistische Arbeiten; 211). Tübingen: Max Niemeyer.

(1989). 'Schrift und die Modularität der Grammatik', in: Eisenberg and Günther, eds. (1989).

Wiese, Richard, ed. (1994). *Recent developments in lexical phonology* (Theorie des Lexikons. Arbeiten des Sonderforschungsbereichs 282; 56). Düsseldorf: Heinrich Heine Universität.

(1996). *The phonology of German.* Oxford: Clarendon Press.

Williams, Theodore (1965). 'On the *-ness* peril', *American Speech* 40: 279–286.

Wójcicki, Adam (1995). *Constraints on suffixation: a study in generative morphology of English and Polish* (Linguistische Arbeiten; 340). Tübingen: Max Niemeyer.

Wood, S. (1975). 'Tense and lax vowels: degree of constriction or pharyngeal volume?' *Lund Working Papers in Phonetics* 11: 55–107.

Wurzel, Wolfgang Ullrich (1970). *Studien zur deutschen Lautstruktur* (Studia Grammatica; 8). Berlin: Akademie-Verlag.

(1984). *Flexionsmorphologie und Natürlichkeit: ein Beitrag zur morphologischen Theoriebildung* (Studia Grammatica; 21). Berlin: Akademie-Verlag.

Wyld, Henry C. (1920). *A history of modern colloquial English.* London: T. Fisher Unwin.

Yip, Moira (1987). 'English vowel epenthesis', *Natural Language and Linguistic Theory* 5: 463–484.

Zec, Draga (1995). 'Sonority constraints on syllable structure', *Phonology* 12: 85–129.

Zwicky, Arnold (1970). 'The free-ride principle and two rules of complete assimilation in English', *Papers from the sixth regional meeting of the Chicago Linguistics Society*: 579–588.

Subject index

abstractness: of the final stratum 120–30; of phonological derivations 3–4
Adjectives 75, 76, 77
Adverbs 75
Affix Ordering Generalisation (AOG) 3, 10, 11–13, 24; origin of 8, 10
affix-driven stratification: competing models of 2–3; diacritic marking in 26, 51, 53, 57, 58–9, 79; dual membership problem 21–6; failings of 53–72; and the non-productivity and non-compositionality problem 69–72; one-affix-one-stratum hypothesis 17, 19; origins of 7–11; problems with 7–52
affixation processes: format of 69–72; two types in English 7–8
affixation rules: in Stratum 2 96, 97–8; subcategorisation frame 69, 84, 96
affixes: listing of 143; stratal affiliation of 95–9; which attach on both strata 4, 22–3
Afrikaans 186
allomorphy: and cyclic phonological rules 21; prosodically conditioned in German –erei and –ei 267; in Stratum 1 21, 52
allophony, a-historic of /ɔː/ 205–6, 207–8
alphabetic writing systems, and the 'phonemic principle' 151
Alternation Condition (AC) 5, 102, 126, 132, 133–4, 145; and Strict Cyclicity Effect 126–30
ambisyllabicity 237, 271–3, 277, 289–90
American English 149, 168, 174, 284, 286
American structuralism 7, 20, 188
Australian English 249
autosegmental representations 244, 277

back-formations 33, 92, 98, 165
base categories 88; as a natural class 98; and the number of strata 87–90
base-category distinction, Selkirk's 11
base-driven stratification 4–5, 79, 106; and the Latinate constraint 59–60; morphology of 4–5, 53, 72–87; phonology

in 5–6, 97–9; principles of 53–99; and stratal affiliation of affixes 95–9; on Stratum 1 72–87; Strict Cyclicity Effect in 5, 105–20; syllabification in 6, 236–880
bases: affixes assigned by rule to their 8; categorial status of 13–14; crucial role of morphological category of 55–6, 73; lexical-category potential of 83–4; Siegel on 11
blank-filling, delinking vs. 141–5
Blank-Filling rule: on Stratum 1 160–1; triggered by syllabification 150
blocking: defined (Aronoff) 61; defined (Kiparsky) 61; failures 93–5; phonotactic 92–3; semantic 92; in word formation 2, 7, 90–5
Blocking Effect 12, 14, 15, 24, 60, 87, 282: and productivity of Stratum 2 processes 91; in German 86; on morphological side of lexical derivations 102–3
bound forms: and affixes 98; derived 83
bound roots 74, 75, 88; attachments to 13, 24, 51, 55–6; defined 72; example 80–1; fail to constitute phonological rule domains 111; in German 84–5; have no lexical categories 64, 67–8, 71–2; Latinate origin (generally) in English 13, 15; and non-productivity on Stratum 1 63–4; non-recurrent see 'cranberry morphs'; occur only on Stratum 1 64–5; in Stratum 1 bases 59; Stratum 1 morphological processes on 108; Stratum 1 affixes attach to 73; use of term 13
boundary symbols ('#' and '+') 7–8, 9, 10
boundary/consonant disjunction 148
Bracket Erasure Convention 9, 129
bracketing conventions: Kiparsky's 9–10, 238–9; Mohanan's 9
Breaking rule, postlexical 232, 233–5

'Celtic fringe' words 177
'citation form' pronunciation 239, 240, 259
CiV Tensing 121, 123, 143, 144, 162, 234

305

Index of words, roots and affixes